T5-AFK-939

The Lorette Wilmot Library
Nazareth College of Rochester

"Who Lived at Alfoxton?"

"Who Lived at Alfoxton?"

Virginia Woolf and English Romanticism

Ellen Tremper

Lewisburg
Bucknell University Press
London: Associated University Presses

LORETTE WILMOT LIBRARY
NAZARETH COLLEGE

© 1998 by Associated University Presses, Inc.

All rights reserved. Authorization to photocopy items for internal or personal use, or the internal or personal use of specific clients, is granted by the copyright owner, provided that a base fee of $10.00, plus eight cents per page, per copy is paid directly to the Copyright Clearance Center, 222 Rosewood Drive, Danvers, Massachusetts 01923. [0-8387-5365-5/98 $10.00 + 8¢ pp, pc.]

Associated University Presses
440 Forsgate Drive
Cranbury, NJ 08512

Associated University Presses
16 Barter Street
London WC1A 2AH, England

Associated University Presses
P.O. Box 338, Port Credit
Mississauga, Ontario
Canada L5G 4L8

The paper used in this publication meets the requirements
of the American National Standard for Permanence of Paper
for Printed Library Materials Z39.48–1984.

Library of Congress Cataloging-in-Publication Data

Tremper, Ellen, 1942–
    Who lived at Alfoxton? : Virginia Woolf and English romanticism / Ellen Tremper.
        p.   cm.
    Includes bibliographical references (p.   ) and index.
    ISBN 0-8387-5365-5 (alk. paper)
        1. Woolf, Virginia, 1882–1941—Criticism and interpretation.
    2. Romanticism—Great Britain—History—20th century.   3. Modernism
    (Literature)—Great Britain.   4. Influence (Literary, artistic,
    etc.)   5. Self in literature.   I. Title.
    PR6045.072Z885   1998
    823'.912—dc21   97-16907
                                                                         CIP

PRINTED IN THE UNITED STATES OF AMERICA

823.912
Woo
TCu

To Bess and Carl

But for those first affections,
Those shadowy recollections,
Which, be they what they may,
Are yet the fountain light of all our day. . . .

Contents

Acknowledgments

Wɪᴛʜᴏᴜᴛ the interest and stimulation of my students in my under-graduate and graduate classes on British modernism and seminars on Woolf at Brooklyn College, this work would never have been conceived. I am especially indebted to my graduate students (1991–95), Carmine Esposito, Susan Salz, and Georgette Fleischer, who read and commented on the complete manuscript or portions of it. Without the tireless aid of Sally Bowdoin, librarian at Brooklyn College, in helping me to locate books not part of the college collection, and often personally retrieving for me those in it, my work would have been very much more difficult and delayed. I am grateful to Elizabeth Inglis of the Manuscripts Section of the University of Sussex Library for her help in guiding me to establish contacts for copyright permissions in the United Kingdom. Without the timely intervention of Roma Woodnutt and Jeremy Crow of The Society of Authors, this book could not have gone into production. I want to thank Karen V. Kukil, Curator of the Mortimer Rare Book Room, Smith College, who arranged for the photographing of Virginia Woolf's postcard to Lytton Strachey and granted permission for its use in the cover design. I must also thank the Research Foundation of the City University of New York for a PSC-Cuny Research Grant.

To my colleagues who read sections of the manuscript and made suggestions for its improvement, Geraldine De Luca, Wendy Fairey, and Lillian Schlissel of Brooklyn College, and Patricia Laurence of City College (who was also helpful in navigating extratextual questions), I am very grateful. Two of my colleagues are due special heartfelt recognition: Roni Natov and Herbert Perluck, each for unique and equally inestimable help in all areas of my life—intellectual, emotional, and practical. The ferment of their conversation, their encouragement, and support were crucial to me and to my work.

I want to thank my wonderful children: my son Geoffrey O'Brien, an extraordinary poet and critic and, finally, my helpful gadfly; my daughter Elizabeth, a student of criticism herself; and my two younger writing sons, Teddy and Gregory. To them all, great love and appreciation for allowing me "the free use of my understanding . . . and of my room." Finally, the life-altering galvanic inspiration and vast computer literacy of my husband Peter were incomparable gifts. Without him, the courage to undertake this project and the technical acumen necessary, at so many stages, to bring it to completion would not have been mine.

* * *

I am grateful to the copyright holders and publishers for permission to quote from the following materials:

Excerpts from *Lord Jim* by Joseph Conrad, copyright © 1920 by Doubleday & Company, Inc., reprinted by permission of the publisher; excerpts from *The Letters of Virginia Woolf* II, no. 852 and from "Anon" and "The Reader" by Virginia Woolf by permission of Professor Quentin Bell; excerpts from *The Letters of Virginia Woolf* II, nos. 853, 1149, 1150; IV, no. 1990; VI, nos. 3173, 3659, 3685, 3695 by permission of the Henry W. and Albert A. Berg Collection, The New York Public Library, Astor, Lenox and Tilden Foundations; excerpts from *The Cambridge Companion to British Romanticism* edited by Stuart Curran, copyright © 1993 by Cambridge University Press. Reprinted with the permission of Cambridge University Press; excerpts from *Collected Essays,* Volume Two by Virginia Woolf, copyright © 1967 by Leonard Woolf and renewed 1995 by M.T. Parsons, reprinted by permission of Harcourt Brace & Company; excerpts from *The Common Reader* by Virginia Woolf, copyright 1925 © by Harcourt Brace & Company and renewed 1953 by Leonard Woolf, reprinted by permission of the publisher; excerpts from *The Complete Shorter Fiction of Virginia Woolf,* copyright © 1985 by Quentin Bell and Angelica Garnett, reprinted by permission of Harcourt Brace & Company; excerpts from *The Diary of Virginia Woolf:* Volume III 1925–1930, copyright © by Quentin Bell and Angelica Garnett, reprinted by permission of Harcourt Brace & Company; excerpts from *The Diary of Virginia Woolf:* Volume V 1936–1941, copyright © 1984 by Quentin Bell and Angelica Garnett, reprinted by permission of Harcourt Brace & Company; excerpts from *Moments of Being* by Virginia Woolf, copyright © 1976 by Quentin Bell and Angelica Garnett, reprinted by permission of Harcourt Brace & Company; excerpts from *Mrs. Dalloway* by Virginia Woolf, copyright © 1925 by Harcourt Brace & Company and renewed 1953 by Leonard Woolf, reprinted by permission of the publisher; excerpts from *A Room of One's Own* by Virginia Woolf, copyright © 1929 by Harcourt Brace & Company and renewed 1957 by Leonard Woolf, reprinted by permission of the publisher; excerpts from *Night and Day* by Virginia Woolf, copyright © 1920 by George H. Doran and Company and renewed 1948 by Leonard Woolf, reprinted by permission of Harcourt Brace & Company; excerpts from *The Second Common Reader* by Virginia Woolf, copyright © 1932 by Harcourt Brace & Company and renewed 1960 by Leonard Woolf, reprinted by permission of the publisher; excerpts from *To the Lighthouse* by Virginia Woolf, copyright © 1927 by Harcourt Brace & Company and renewed 1954 by Leonard Woolf, reprinted by permission of the publisher; excerpts from *The Waves* by Virginia Woolf, copyright © 1931 by Harcourt Brace & Company and renewed 1959 by Leonard Woolf, reprinted by permission of the publisher; excerpts from *The Subterfuge of Art: Language and the Romantic Tradition* by Michael Ragussis, copyright © 1978 by The Johns Hopkins University Press, reprinted by permission of the publisher; excerpts from *Romanticism and Contemporary Criticism: The Gauss Seminar and Other Papers* by Paul de Man, edited by E. S. Burt, Kevin Newmark, Andrzej Warminski, copyright © 1993 by The Johns Hopkins University Press, reprinted by permission of the publisher; excerpts from *Virginia Woolf: A Critical Study* by Avrom Fleishman, copyright © 1975 by The Johns Hopkins University Press, reprinted by permission of the publisher; *The Letters of Virginia Woolf* II, no. 641, reprinted by permission of the Mortimer Rare Book Room, Smith College; excerpts from "How Master Lost His Concubine" (17 November 1991) and "Interview with Emmanuel Ax" (11 September 1994), copyright ©1991, 1994 by The New York Times Co. Reprinted by permission; permission for all of the above materials by Virginia Woolf published in the U.S. by Harcourt Brace & Company, and for excerpts from *Between the Acts* by Virginia Woolf, *Collected Essays* IV, *Contemporary Writers* by Virginia Woolf edited by Jean Guiguet, *The Diary of Virginia Woolf* edited by Andrew McNeillie vols. I, II, IV, V, *The Essays of Virginia Woolf* vols. I, II, III edited by Andrew McNeillie, *The Letters of Virginia Woolf* vols. I, IV, VI edited by Andrew McNeillie, *Orlando* by Virginia Woolf, *A Passionate Apprentice: The Early Journals 1897–1909 Virginia Woolf* edited by Mitchell A. Leaska, *A Room of One's Own* by Virginia Woolf, *Women and Writing* by Virginia Woolf edited by Michèle Barrett, *The Years* by Virginia Woolf, and for excerpts from *Virginia Woolf: A Biography* by Quentin Bell from The Society of Authors as the literary representative of the Estate of Virginia Woolf; a revision of "In Her Father's House: *To the Lighthouse* as a Record of Virginia Woolf's Literary Patrimony" by Ellen Tremper from *Texas Studies in Literature and Language* 34, no. 1, pp. 1–40, by permission of the University of Texas Press; excerpts from *A Portrait of the Artist as a Young Man* by James Joyce. Copyright 1916 by B. W. Huebsch, copyright © 1947 by Nora Joyce, copyright © 1964 by the Estate of James Joyce. Used by permission of Viking Penguin, a division of Penguin Books USA Inc.; excerpts from *After the Deluge* I by Leonard Woolf and *The Letters of Virginia Woolf* I, no. 565, by permission of Manuscripts Section, The University of Sussex Library; excerpts from *Group Psychology and the Analysis of the Ego* by Sigmund Freud, translated by James Strachey, translation copyright © 1959, 1922 by the Institute of Psycho-Analysis and Angela Richards. Copyright © 1959 by Sigmund Freud Copyrights Ltd. Copyright © 1959 by James Strachey. Reprinted by permission of W. W. Norton & Company; excerpts from *Natural Supernaturalism: Tradition and Revolution in Romantic Literature* by M. H. Abrams. Copyright © 1971 by W. W. Norton & Company, Inc. Reprinted by permission of W. W. Norton & Company, Inc.

"Who Lived at Alfoxton?"

Introduction

Listen now to Wordsworth:

> Lover had he known in huts where poor men dwell,
> His daily teachers had been woods and rills,
> The silence that is in the starry sky,
> The sleep that is among the lonely hills.

We listen to that when we are alone. We remember that in solitude.

—"The Leaning Tower," Collected Essays 2

A study that asserts Virginia Woolf's affinity for the English Romantic writers must begin with a brief discussion of Romanticism, in fact, with Woolf's own very practical word of caution.

Evidently it is a good thing to avoid, 'except for pastime, the discussion of tendencies and movements', and stick as far as we can to the men and the books.[1]

Thus Woolf, reviewing *Romance. Two Lectures* by Walter Raleigh in 1917, anticipated one of the positions in the academic debate about Romanticism that has survived to the present. Following A. O. Lovejoy and René Wellek, two opposing camps of critics have attempted to define the historical and cultural "movement" of Romanticism: those who now predominate[2] and believe, with Lovejoy, that there is no Romanticism, indeed, no "movement," but a plurality of Romanticisms, and those who, with René Wellek, concur with what Jerome McGann calls a "unified field theory."[3] The problem with the latter is that such a definition is bound to be challenged by many exceptions, by poems and poets themselves who fall outside the limits of its purview.

Our allegiance to either of these positions is partially a matter of the era in which we reached our own critical majority and partly a reflection of which poets we love best. Although M. H. Abrams asserts that "Romanticism is no one thing," he adds of the individ-

15

ual poets and their various poems that "some prominent qualities a number of these poems share," forming "a distinctive complex"[4] related to the political revolution and reaction of the period in which they were written. One feels that his quasi-syncretic view of Romanticism (borrowing from Hazlitt, he calls it "the spirit of the age") is the product of the covert premise that Wordsworth's aesthetic theory and poetry are most characteristic and dominant in the period roughly taken to coincide with the years 1790–1830.

McGann, on the other hand, with his historical-critical bias, favors the plural Romanticisms, and does so, as well, out of his prior interest in and study of Byron, whose temperament and poetic acts so clearly are the exception, proving not the rule but, in fact, that no rule exists. However, even McGann, who, I believe, correctly distinguishes among three periods of Romanticism,[5] states that Wordsworth's "works—like his position in the Romantic Movement—are normative and, in every sense, exemplary."[6]

Fortunately, in our effort to formulate a definition of Romanticism that usefully illuminates Woolf's habits of mind, techniques, and aspirations, we need not find "'the true story, the one story to which all these phrases refer,'" as Bernard in *The Waves* would say.[7] Although Woolf was especially enthusiastic at different times about one or another of the poets of the period (Blake excepted), it was Wordsworth with whom she began her creative life and Wordsworth on whom she depended down through its home stretch. Following her advice, we will "stick as far as we can to the men and the books."

Abrams's redaction of Wordsworth's poetic program, described by the poet himself in the Prospectus, reveals Wordsworth's displacement of the Christian myth by a secularized story of the human imagination.

> Here, in short, is Wordsworth's conception of his poetic role and his great design. The author, through a "transitory Being," is the latest in the line of poets inspired by the "prophetic Spirit," and as such has been granted a "Vision" . . . which sanctions his claim to outdo Milton's Christian story in the scope and audacious novelty of his subject. The vision is that of the awesome depths and height of the human mind, and of the power of that mind as in itself adequate, by consummating a holy marriage with the external universe, to create out of the world of all of us, in a quotidian and recurrent miracle, a new world which is the equivalent of paradise.[8]

This description, drawing on Wordsworth's own biblical and apocalyptic language, may seem an inappropriately exaltative expression of Virginia Woolf's creative agenda. Yet if we substitute a more secular vocabulary for Wordsworth's, say, "conflation" or "coextension" for the "holy marriage" of imagination and external universe and Woolf's own "rapture" for "paradise," we may see the aptness of Wordsworth's self-definition to Woolf's beliefs and methods.

Although some critics object to a thinning into insignificance of the term Romanticism if it is lifted from its historical context to define the characteristics of literatures of other periods, support for doing so comes from recent readings of Romanticism that emphasize continuities between other literary "ages" and the one that concluded with the political revolutions of the 1820s. In fact, it is now a critical commonplace to reject self-avowals of discrete breaks with past practitioners and to see not merely vestiges of a prior age but its attitudes and methods, alive and well, in a succeeding one.[9] Such, I believe, is the case with the Moderns whose battle cry may have been "Make it new!" but who inevitably looked back to writers whose characteristic self-reflection and intensity of gaze were, for comparable historical reasons, congenial to themselves.[10]

For the high priests of modernism in fiction—Conrad, Forster, Lawrence, Joyce, Woolf, even the less-revered Dorothy Richardson[11]—reveal a way of looking at the world and into their own minds that to a greater or lesser extent shares the gaze of the Romantic poets.[12] Again, we may begin with Woolf: "We mean a great many things when we say that a poem is romantic. We refer to an atmosphere of vagueness, mystery, distance; but perhaps we most constantly feel that the writer is thinking more of the effect of the thing upon his mind than of the thing itself" (Essays II, 75). Of the "Romantic Moment," Abrams says:

> The illuminated phenomenological object, if transparent to a significance beyond itself, reappears as the symbol of the Symbolists, but if opaque, as the image of the Imagists; in both cases, however, the Romantic object is usually cut off from its context in the ordinary world and in common experience and assigned an isolated existence in the self-limited and self-sufficing work of art. And the Moment of consciousness, the abrupt illumination in an arrest of time, has become a familiar component in modern fiction, where it sometimes functions, like Wordsworth's spots of time, as a principle of literary organization, by signalizing the essential discoveries or precipitating the narrative resolution.[13]

Conrad's Marlow actually names these experiences "moment[s] of vision."[14] Joyce termed them "epiphanies," restoring with this name a sense of their "religious" quality. Virginia Woolf called them "moments of being." Thus, Abrams finds a continuity between the Romantics and the moderns in the significance of the arrested moment. To be sure, this is an important issue, especially since the chief quality of the moment is its luminosity, the sense that, in some mysterious way, the visible world has been stripped of its veil and now appears to the gazer, as if for the first time, in a radically new and "true" light.

Yet Forster, Conrad, and Lawrence write in the naturalistic tradition. Forster does not even privilege such moments. His narrators are, as well, too prominently recognizable as distinct and intelligently commenting voices in the novelistic polyphony for the reader to experience the merging of gazer and world. However, one might argue that his insistence on unity of all sorts—"Only connect . . ."[15]—shares the prominence of organicity in Coleridge's aesthetic theory and Wordsworth's poetry.

Lack of merging is equally true of Conrad's narrator Marlow. He has his moments of vision, but because he comments on them in his own voice, he remains recognizably separate from the world he perceives. Thus, the reader reads of, but does not participate in, Marlow's private illuminations.

Lawrence, on the other hand, despite his Romantic intensity, is a novelist of "mergers" but not of gazers. In *The Rainbow,* for example, his characters and narrators so privilege feeling over intellection that we experience a world of fused bodies and emotions but not one of conscious transformations.

However, Joyce, not only because of the phenomenon of epiphanies, but because he clearly focuses on intellectual apprehension as well as emotion, is more like Woolf, emphasizing the self-consciousness of his characters.[16] Yet our sense that Stephen Dedalus, say, is separate not only from the world on which he looks but from the narrative voice that is in, but not of, his mind prevents us from recognizing in Joyce's writing the continuously fluid union between imaginations and world that characterizes Woolf's fiction, not just in recognizable, discrete "moments of being," but throughout her seamless narratives.

The critical phrase, then, in our distinguishing the methods of the other writers of this period from Woolf's is "arrested moment." This moment for the Romantics was the experience of the "sublime," "a threefold episode of consciousness, in which a state of radical disequilibrium intervenes between a prior state of ordinary awareness and a final state of transcendent exaltation."[17] When, at the end of chapter IV of *A Portrait of the Artist as a Young Man,* Stephen sees a young girl, a beautiful seabird in the water, we identify a luminous transparency that connects gazer and world. We feel that Stephen's experience is something like Bernard's when the latter reports that he and his friends are transported by the "poetic" sublime of language.

> "I am wrapped round with phrases, like damp straw; I glow, phosphorescent. And each of you feels when I speak, 'I am lit up. I am glowing.'" (TW, 326)

For Stephen, exaltation, "the strange light of some new world" into which "[h]is soul was swooning," is a moment that passes. When he wakens from his bed of "tufted sandknolls," "the sand and arid grasses of his bed glowed no longer."[18] Immediately after, chapter V opens, quite intentionally, with a naturalistic and bathetic drop into the Dedalus family's kitchen:

> He drained his third cup of watery tea to the dregs and set to chewing the crusts of fried bread that were scattered near him, staring into the dark pool of the jar. . . . The box of pawn tickets at his elbow had just been rifled and he took up idly one after another in his greasy fingers the blue and white dockets. . . .[19]

Because of Woolf's idiosyncratic narrative voice, which uninterruptedly flows into and out of the consciousnesses of her characters without our registering its precise location, we feel the transparency of minds and their conflation with the world unique to her among the moderns. Moreover, the reader is implicated in this fluid luminosity, experiencing—instead of merely learning of an arrested moment—an extended "textual" or "readerly" sublime. With Woolf not just the "illuminated phenomenological object" but the "illuminated gazers" are "transparent to a significance beyond [themselves]," an aspect of her fiction ignored by Abrams in his global account of the modernist Moment. Indeed, the transparency of the mind and its continuity with the world are also a trope and phenomenon that Woolf names and explores in *The Waves* and elsewhere, as when Bernard says: "'I throw my mind out in the air as a man throws seeds in great fan-flights, falling through the purple sunset, falling on the pressed and shining ploughland which is bare'" (TW, 326). Woolf's self-conscious conflation of the mind and landscape is akin to Wordsworth's coextension of the imagination and the physical attributes of Mount

Snowdon and the Atlantic, seen by him in an arresting "flash" of
moonlight. He, too, throws or projects his mind out onto the landscape so that he recognizes in the latter

> . . . the emblem of a mind
> That feeds upon infinity, that broods
> Over the dark abyss, intent to hear
> Its voices issuing forth to silent light
> In one continuous stream. . . .[20]

Such characteristic Romantic perceptions of the sublime, linking
external nature and the mind, are, as well, especially obvious in
"A Sketch of the Past."[21]

One of the most often cited passages from this memoir is of an
"exceptional moment" in Woolf's childhood at St. Ives:

> I was looking at the flower bed by the front door; "That is the whole,"
> I said. I was looking at a plant with a spread of leaves; and it seemed
> suddenly plain that the flower itself was a part of the earth; that a ring
> enclosed what was the flower and that was the real flower; part earth;
> part flower.
> . . . When I said about the flower "That is the whole," I felt that I
> had made a discovery. I felt that I had put away in my mind something
> that I should go back [to], to turn over and explore. (MoB, 71)

Viewing this experience through the lens of memory, Woolf described a sort of aporia, a moment of sudden "unreadable" density
in life, but one, perhaps because of its opacity, that was significant
and memorable. Many things might be said about this statement:
for example, learning may not happen without these jolts to the
mind. But their value for Woolf lay in her ability to use them to
create order.[22] The dominant impression made by this "story" for
Virginia Stephen, the child, Virginia Woolf, the reflecting adult, and
for the reader is of the connection, wholeness, and "organicity"
with which she was left—and their importance. Her description is
a quintessential example of the way in which a new or unexpected
experience became part of an already established "whole," of a
familiar and helpful repertoire[23] that, as an adult, she generalized
into a larger pattern or "philosophy," namely, that "behind the
cotton wool is hidden a pattern; that we—I mean all human beings—are connected with this; that the whole world is a work of
art; that we are parts of the work of art" (MoB, 72). We may be
struck by how, in this private revelation of a very private experi-

ence, Woolf, moving to its broader, "philosophical" implications, emphasizes organic connection. Like the flower and the earth, she and everyone else are part of, indeed, *are* the world.

We see this conflation of self and world, the defining characteristic of Wordsworthian Romanticism, over and over again in her fiction, essays, and stories, indeed, in everything that she wrote, whether for publication or, as in this case, for more private pleasure. Bernard, the storyteller and Woolf's avatar in *The Waves*, tells the same story of relationship and wholeness:

> "And striking off these observations spontaneously I elaborate myself; differentiate myself and listening to the voice that says as I stroll past, 'Look! Take note of that!' I conceive myself called upon to provide, some winter's night, a meaning for all my observations—a line that runs from one to another, a summing up that completes." (TW, 255)

In Bernard's "elaboration" of self, there is the buried and mythic metaphor of Arachne, the spider-artist, and the similar folk metaphor of "spinning a yarn." Through it we get a sense of the artist's need to tell a story, making a pattern that explains not only the self but the world as well. Bernard's writerly sense of obligation, the issue of his self-conscious dialogue of self and soul—"to provide . . . a line . . . that completes"—is one of many metaphors in Woolf's imaginative "lumber room" which, like threads, balls of string, spider threads, and filaments, suggest sequence, connecting the "differentiated" individual both to others in the present and to the past through consciousness and its productions.

Even in the case of a nonwriter, Woolf has fun with a similar trope. In *Mrs. Dalloway*,[24] Lady Bruton, fatigued after lunching with her friends, cannot continue to produce her "spider's thread" (MD, 170)—sustained consciousness of her departed guests— which comically snaps as she falls asleep. Thus, Woolf suggests, through the imaginations of many Bernards and the consciousnesses of more ordinary and multiple Lady Brutons, a network or pattern—our culture—is formed.

The relationship between individual consciousness and culture in Woolf's work is nowhere more present than in her essays on, and fictional representations of, reading. This activity, in which she was always deeply engaged, was for her a powerful cultural nexus, through which we recognize that "we are the words; we are the music" (MoB, 72) of the world.

Woolf appreciated the many subspecies of reading, some of them "linear" and progressive and others apparently directionless and haphazard in the choice of materials and in the attention paid them. Her own vast and valued experience as a reader, described in her many critical essays on reading and rereading, points to her belief that our discovery and revelation of pattern through reading are a complicit accomplishment, the active responsibility of the reader as well as the writer. Indeed, she appreciates the political and cultural, in addition to personal, implications of reading, arguing that one cannot be a writer without, as well, being a good reader. In "The Leaning Tower," for example, she closes with an exhortation concerning these twinned and interdependent activities, advising that we must "Write daily; write freely; but let us always compare what we have written with what the great writers have written."[25]

> If we are going to preserve and to create, that is the only way. . . .
> We can begin . . . by reading omnivorously, simultaneously, poems, plays, novels, histories, biographies, the old and the new. . . . But let us bear in mind a piece of advice that an eminent Victorian who was also an eminent pedestrian gave to walkers: 'Whenever you see a board up with "Trespassers will be prosecuted", trespass at once'.
> Let us trespass at once. Literature is no one's private ground. . . . thus . . . English literature will survive this war and cross the gulf—if commoners and outsiders like ourselves make that country our own country, if we teach ourselves how to read and write, how to preserve, and how to create. (CE 2, 180–81)

Reading, a private enterprise, located in the "theatre of the brain,"[26] is, thus paradoxically, a site of cultural contestation and connection between human beings, catching us in the web of civilization and simultaneously enlarging it through our own efforts to comprehend and assimilate. Woolf would have us examine Arnoldian touchstones of excellence, not only to determine and "preserve" their qualities but also to aid us in the creation and continuation of culture.

Sometimes our reading is valuable only "to refresh and exercise our own creative powers" (CE 2, 5). As we stop and look out the window, our delight in the scene is wonderfully increased by the book we have just closed. Conversely, as in the metaphor from *To the Lighthouse,* "as one raises one's eyes from a page in an express train and sees a farm, a tree, a cluster of cottages as an illustration, a confirmation of something on the printed page to which one returns, fortified, and satisfied,"[27] our immediate lives give the aesthetic or intellectual experience of a book new and valuable meaning. As we continue reading, bringing scenes past and present into play with the words before us, the more we remember of the text and of our other experiences—of "life, itself," or, simply, "it," as Woolf's young couple calls it in "Kew Gardens,"[28]—the better we are able to create pattern. Indeed there is great value in reading as Mrs. Ramsay does, "at random . . . climbing backwards, upwards" (TTL, 178)[29] and as Virginia Woolf did at the end of her life when she was working on "Reading at Random"—her Elizabethan plays, as she wrote to Ethel Smyth, scattered on the floor of her room.[30]

Behind and beneath this project, then, is my appreciation of these compelling ideas, suggesting another Romantic conflation of consciousness and world, and formulated by Woolf with her own and others' reading strategies in mind. One could say that reading, especially for a "professional" reader, with its wonderful meanderings, repetitions, accommodations, and assimilations, leads to the exciting moment of insight, the formulation of a hypothesis or pattern, situating us and our subject in the world and its history. Of course, it is always our hope that if, also like Mrs. Ramsay, we "did not know at first what the words meant at all" (TTL, 179), we will come to appreciate the pattern they make as they resonate with the stores of our already stocked imaginations and memories. Thus, as I read Woolf, honoring her view of reading, I came to my own moment of being, my recognition of where she is poised, in the complex and rich web of western civilization.

When we come across new information, we attempt to formulate a hypothesis that accommodates it to what we already know and believe so that we can recover an equilibrium through the creation of our new explanation or pattern. My reading of Woolf's seventh novel, *The Waves,* displaced some of my former views. Often accused of being a very difficult, "writerly" text, it literally became for me, from the point of view of its subject and method, a very "readerly" one. It must be read forwards and backwards and over many times before we can assimilate it, appreciating the relation of its parts to each other and of them to the world. An interesting experiment in the doubling of its subject by the activity that conveys its subject to us, *The Waves* is a metatext on reading and its importance in the creation and definition of the individual and culture. It is about the way we read, whether our own lives, history, or a book is the object of our decoding efforts, to experience a pattern or gain psychic and cultural wholeness. Michael Ragussis expresses this idea in *The Subterfuge of Art* when he says that art, the object of our scrutiny, is, for the writer, an archaeological reconstruction of our past: "Art preserves the archaic for the artist's eye to judge and evaluate. The writers in this tradition see in our archaic past not simply an individual's childhood, but mankind's."[31]

Whether one approaches Woolf's novel from this psychoanalytic point of view, focusing on the artist and the making of art or, as I have, through pattern-creation amplified by the "curious props" of "memory and thought" (Wordsworth, 282), emphasizing the reader, as well, *The Waves* is a heady experience. The novel has been central to my understanding of the activity of reading in general, and, specifically, of my particular effort to see a pattern in Woolf's work. Before I considered it, I had the sense, as I read through her novels, essays, and diaries, that I was in some dimly remembered but clearly familiar territory, appreciating Woolf's configuration of imagination as similar to the Romantics' conception. However, only when I reread *The Waves* for the sixth chapter of this critical study, having read it before with less attention, did I recognize a pattern into which I needed to incorporate Woolf's easily documented interest in, and affection for, the writers of the English Romantic movement. Here is a record of her own significant "trespasses" onto the "common ground" of literature, a reading of reading that demonstrates her belief in a common mind connecting the individual not only to his or her contemporaries but to civilizations past. This epistemological novel is, then, a fulcrum for Woolf's career and my investigation of it, the point of balance that explains, both for her previous work and for that of her last decade, her fascination with consciousness and memory and her Romantic filiation which, are, indeed, inseparable.

Perhaps most obviously her extraordinary delineations of consciousness are a continuation and refinement of an ambiguous Romantic binarism that simultaneously recognizes and seeks to obliterate the duality of self and world.[32] Her tropes and other strategies of craft and substance, expressing the conflation of imagination and created world, are her modernist translation of an interest she did not suppress or deny.

This insight was, for me, the crystallizing moment that reestablished the equilibrium in my efforts to make sense of the "world"— in this case of the relationship between the body of Woolf's work and my own past. For a reader, such moments are an incomparably pleasurable experience, one Woolf frequently traces for her luckier and happier characters, and for herself, as well, when, in "A Sketch of the Past," she described "the rapture I get when in writing I seem to be discovering what belongs to what" (MoB, 72). Here, then, is the narrative of my reading: my recognition of the personal, cultural, and political importance to Virginia Woolf of her reading and through it, the revelation of the Romantic figure in her own carpet.

Corroborative evidence concerning consciousness and self-consciousness can be found in Leonard Woolf's analysis of the appearance in western culture of the concept of the individual. He associates its development with a perceptible change in the misery quotient of ordinary people. As economic conditions favorably altered the health and well-being of individuals in western Europe, with the result that they began to feel more pleasure in living and less that misery and want were their God-given portion, they began to conceptualize themselves as the "experiencers" of the pleasure—in short, as entitled individuals. He argues in *After the Deluge: A Study of Communal Psychology*[33] that the appearance of this concept represents a tremendous shift in the history of the organization of European society, the political climate that expresses it, and its cultural representation in art and literature. Thus, Sophocles, Thucydides, and Virgil have the same "mental attitude" as Dante, Milton, and Racine, despite the two thousand years that separate them, while Keats, Flaubert, and Ibsen, writing merely two hundred years after Racine, are of a radically different "species of animal":

> The species to which Racine belonged took everything at its face value; "the ancients" did not look round the corner or beneath the surface; they never turned their eyes from the hard, bright world immediately in front of them to peer into the dim regions of their own mind and personality. The difference is largely due to a difference in self-consciousness; the consciousness of one's own individuality, which is a common characteristic of ordinary, plain men and women to-day, is rare even in the subtlest and rarest minds of antiquity, and when it does exist, it is comparatively weak and fitful. Montaigne is a remarkable exception, and it is precisely this consciousness of himself as an individual which makes Montaigne seem so unlike his contemporaries, so much nearer to ourselves than anyone else born before 1700; he was the first modern.[34]

While Leonard Woolf examines the complex communal psychology that privileged the individual and that produced the concept of democracy, his assessment of Montaigne, echoing Virginia's *Common Reader* essay, and his contention that the ancients looked directly at the "hard, bright world immediately in front of them" and never peered into their own minds and personalities are an echo of her remarks in "The Pastons and Chaucer":

[Chaucer] turned instinctively . . . to the bright May day and the jocund landscape. . . .

Nature, uncompromising, untamed, was no looking-glass for happy faces, or confessor of unhappy souls.[35]

Leonard Woolf analyzes one of the most important shifts in the history of human psychology, one that Mr. Ramsay in *To the Lighthouse* seems to be equally interested in when he self-deprecatingly declares that he will "talk 'some nonsense' to the young men of Cardiff about Locke, Hume, Berkeley, and the causes of the French Revolution" (TTL, 70).

The dim regions of minds and personalities—the self-consciousness underlying individualism—are the object of interest in Romantic poetry and prose. The idiosyncracies of the ordinary person and the imagination of the poet himself are the subjects that Virginia Woolf, too, found congenial and described in "The Leaning Tower" as the basis of "poet's poetry." Clearly, there was a fruitful dialogue between husband and wife.

Virginia Woolf has been the subject of a great many literary comparisons. A number of readers, like Perry Meisel in *The Absent Father: Virginia Woolf and Walter Pater*,[36] and Alice Fox in *Virginia Woolf and the Literature of the English Renaissance*,[37] have ably demonstrated the influence of other than Romantic writers on her substance and style. And I am certainly not the first to see a connection between Woolf and Romanticism. As early as 1926, Edwin Muir commented that Woolf's method of characterization was "less akin to anything else attempted in the novel than to certain kinds of poetry, to poetry such as Wordsworth's, which records not so much a general judgment on life as a moment of serene illumination."[38] Since then Woolf's relation to the Romantic poets, Wordsworth and Shelley in particular, has been explored in various essays but never in a full-length study and, I believe, only with respect to her novels.[39] Such investigations have considered Woolf's Romantic debts as visible in her feminism, allusions, metaphors, lyric-narrative structures, creativity, and remembrance of childhood. However, they do not suggest that Woolf's "philosophy" of life and art, her way of looking at the world and expressing the relations of human beings to it—*her* romanticism, in short—was a mixture of temperament and exposures so early and so thoroughly determining the cast of her mind that all her writing was necessarily shaped by it.

Although the current important emphasis on context rather than text in critical theory is partly responsible for the persistent interest in Woolf's feminism, the Romantic roots of Woolf's imagination and politics—in the largest sense of that word—informing both her life and her work, also need more attention if we wish to understand her modernism.

To be sure, Woolf's writing and political action were increasingly colored throughout her career by her concern with and for women—their creativity; their political contributions, both actual and potential; and their relations with each other and with men. But her ideas evolved from the intellectual and emotional relations with (and, sometimes, opposition to) her father and, later, the members of Old Bloomsbury. Omitting some history of Virginia Woolf's relations with her father Leslie Stephen would distort her intellectual biography because they were the most complicated, but also most formative intellectually, of any in her life. Her feelings, both positive and negative, about this lovable but tyrannical man were not denied by her and were, in fact, a subject of her early short stories; her autobiographical novel, *To the Lighthouse;* and her memoirs, diaries, letters, and essays. He may even have been the "eminent Victorian" pedestrian (her salute to Lytton Strachey) whose advice to trespass she cites in "The Leaning Tower." Everywhere, in short, there is a conscious trace of his powerful influence. The quality and persistence of his presence in her writing lead me to question the adequacy of Harold Bloom's influence myth as it might apply to the family romance, both real and metaphorical, of a writer-father and girl-child, when the child, herself, grows up to become a strong writer.[40] An early instance of Woolf's acknowledgment is her short story, "The Journal of Mistress Joan Martyn," a fictional autobiographical account of the encouragement an admiring father gives his writing daughter. The first chapter, in which I examine this story, as well as the second and fifth, centers on Stephen's felt presence in Woolf's choice of careers, her subject matter, and the humanistic morality of her art and political positions.

Equally important is Woolf's apparent freedom in acknowledging a sense of kinship with the Romantics, quite literally, for example, owning Leigh Hunt as her spiritual, and far more congenial, "grandfather" than her own Victorian forebear. Crucially, these writers were first introduced to her by her father, a fact that further enriches her attachment to them. Emphasizing her own metaphor of grandpaternity, I argue that both Woolf's political positions and literary methods were grounded on those of the English Romantics. Their intellectual presence in her life was pervasive, and proof of it may be found in all of her writing, from her novels to the private communication of letters and diaries. One might start anywhere to corroborate this truth.

For example, in a 1923 review of Romer Wilson's *The Grand Tour*, Woolf says, virtually restating Wordsworth's announced intention in *Lyrical Ballads*—"to throw over [incidents and situations from common life] a certain colouring of imagination, whereby ordinary things should be presented to the mind in an unusual aspect" (Wordsworth, 485–86):

> Why is it, then, that she fails to convince us of the reality of her romance? It is because her sense of it is more conventional than original. . . . She has not, like Meredith, used her freedom from the ties of realism to reveal something new in the emotions of human beings when they are most roused to excitement. Nor has she gone the other way to work. She has not taken the usual and made it blossom into the extraordinary.[41]

Another case in point: *The Prelude* is mentioned four times in her letters, notebooks, and diaries during different periods of her life. In a letter to Saxon Sydney-Turner of 1911, she writes that her week alone in Sussex is "the ideal life—one reads so much." "I am reading the Prelude [Wordsworth]. Dont you think it one of the greatest works ever written?" Perhaps as her confidence in her judgment wanes, she adds, "Some of it, anyhow, is sublime; it may get worse" (Letters I, 460).

And then in a letter to Ethel Smyth of 18 September 1936, a reference to *The Prelude* sparks a general encomium:

> What else? O The Prelude. Have you read it lately? Do you know, its so good, so succulent, so suggestive, that I have to hoard it, as a child keeps a crumb of cake? And then people say he's dull! Why have we no great poet? You know thats what would keep us straight [a sentiment expressed by Wordsworth, as well, in "London, 1802"]: but for our sins we only have a few pipers on hedges like Yeats and Tom Eliot, de la Mare—exquisite frail twittering voices one has to hollow one's hand to hear, whereas old Wth [Wordsworth] fills the room. (Letters VI, 73)[42]

Yet beyond overt expression of admiration, affinity may prove subtle and difficult to demonstrate. And there are those who will argue that Woolf's repudiation of Wordsworth's mind in *A Room of One's Own* as having "a dash too much of the male"[43] in it saves us from any necessity of tracing connections. However, a number of important correspondences between Woolf's work and his reveal the Romantic stamp of her ideas. The first is her interest in memory and time, especially the renovating recollection of "moments of being," her version, previously noted, of "spots of time" or the sublime. For Woolf, as for Wordsworth and Hazlitt, memory fills up, in "horizontal" or historical time, "vertical" time or mind excurses, first described by Erich Auerbach in his essay, "The Brown Stocking."[44] Further, such moments in her fiction have their parallel in her critical essays. Through her recollection of texts of the past—that is, of "moments of *[historical]* being"—she meant to replicate for her contemporaries the vitalizing perceptions such literature had given her throughout her life. She believed that these moments, "threaded" together, formed a "narrative" of European culture.

The second is creativity as itself the focus of the creative work. Although we may easily find evidence of self-consciousness in such novels as *To the Lighthouse, The Waves,* and *Between the Acts,* we can also see Romantic consciousness of the creative act in her criticism and diaries. Wordsworth's discourse on the pleasure of creation from the "Preface of 1815" reads like the precursor of Woolf's remarks on her extraordinarily conscious pleasure in writing in "A Sketch of the Past":

> . . . but the Imagination also shapes and *creates;* and how? By innumerable processes; and in none does it more delight than in that of consolidating numbers into unity, and dissolving and separating unity into number,—alternations proceeding from, and governed by, a sublime consciousness of the soul in her own mighty and almost divine powers. (Wordsworth, 485–86)

Like the Romantic writers, Woolf wore the multiple hats of creative writer and critic, sharing her views on the imagination and its relation to life with her readers in the venues of the novel and essay. Thus we can find her Wordsworthian sense of the inseparable moral and aesthetic responsibilities of the poet equally present in, for example, the novel *To the Lighthouse* and in the essay "The Russian Point of View."

Despite the Romantic fascination with the fantastic that Woolf occasionally shared, as in her charming tale "The Widow and the Parrot: A True Story" (CSF, 156–63), the textures of common life as experienced from different angles of vision, or her preoccupation with ordinary people who have ordinary thoughts, is a third, compelling basis of comparison. The short stories of 1917 to 1921 and *To the Lighthouse* serve as examples.

Finally, all these subjects and issues of craft evolve from Virginia

Woolf's political values, a turn of the wheel on the veneration of the individual and consequent democratic impulse underlying the Romantic aesthetic. When, as in her last ten years, she expressed more directly the connections between aesthetic and political issues in her published writings, the private communications of letters, and the still more private ones of her diaries, Woolf defined a humanism that reflected early Romantic political aspirations far more than it did the positions of the British Left in the 1930s.

In her review of Raleigh's *Romance,* Woolf wrote:

> . . . up to a point there is nothing more real than the effect of things upon one's mind. The difficulty is to resist the temptation of conjuring up sensations for the pleasure of feeling them; and when he does that the writer is lost. For such a one,
> > . . . lives alone,
> Housed in a dream, at distance from the Kind.[45]
>
> > (Essays II, 75)

Writing "A Letter to a Young Poet" fifteen years later, Virginia Woolf continued in this strain, criticizing modern poetry for being "about nothing, if not about the poet himself."

> But what does one mean by 'oneself'? Not the self that Wordsworth, Keats, and Shelley have described—not the self that loves a woman, or that hates a tyrant, or that broods over the mystery of the world. No, the self that you are engaged in describing is shut out from all that. It is a self that sits alone in the room at night with the blinds drawn. In other words the poet is much less interested in what we have in common than in what he has apart. (CE 2, 189)

Although there are other moments in Woolf's critical writing that are equally significant for different reasons, this reflection on the nature and temper of modern poetry has exceptional meaning in relation to every aspect of Woolf's own life and writing. It is, as well, an important operative definition of some species of modernism, significant for its complaint against the contemporary poetic impulse and Woolf's differences from it, as well as for its enumeration of other subjects and method. Here is Woolf, less than a year after publishing *The Waves,* giving counterevidence to those of her readers who see her as a mystic, as she claims the importance of the concrete and the real. Her own impulse first to discover the "self" and then to reveal it to her readers through her writing is a continuation of the great English Romantic tradition that causes her to condemn here, good-naturedly but seriously, the solipsistic, detached, and often, it seems, purposely inscrutable nature of contemporary poetry.

Significantly, Wordsworth, Keats, and Shelley are the counterpoise to the clay-footed and wrong-headed poetic impulse of her day. The sense of the world behind the text, the life of the people behind the prose or poetry, captured her interest both as critic and as storyteller. She had unmistakably put her finger on the binary nature of Romantic poetry—"the mirror and the lamp"[46]—the receiving and perceiving eye or imagination and the two categories of subject found in this poetry: the reflection of the poetic mind and of the life of ordinary people.

Woolf's reading of the Romantic poet who "broods over the mystery of the world" and her own treatment of time and nature in *Jacob's Room, Mrs. Dalloway,* and *To the Lighthouse* prefigure Paul de Man's assertion of the character of Romantic poetry in "Allegory and Irony in Baudelaire."[47] There he describes it as bringing the poet (and, thus, we can assume, the reader), "into contact with his authentic temporal destiny."[48] The "Winander" boy of *The Prelude,* from de Man's perspective, is likewise Wordsworth's "precursor" whose recognition by the poet allows him to understand the illusion of the correspondence between man and nature. De Man says:

> The distinctive character of such moments of temporal recognition is always determined by the nature of the obstacle that has to be removed to make the recognition possible, by the error which hid the true predicament from sight. In the case of romanticism the error is that of a self that tries to forget its own temporal fate by patterning itself on the eternal aspects of nature; hence, a conception of the self as the pole of a subject/object relationship becomes the illusion that has to be renounced. The somber light, the harsh serenity that prevails in authentic romantic literature, expresses the difficulty of this renunciation.[49]

Woolf's conflation of self and world with which I began, is, then, for her as for the Romantics, only part of the story. The double impulse—to examine the mind in the act of discovering itself and to look at the self reflected in, and related to, the concrete and "diurnal round" (Wordsworth, 203) but there to find that "in the middle of [the] party, here's death" (MD, 279)—illuminates Woolf's work as well.

Further, we can see Woolf's lifelong preoccupation with the diurnal reflected in her short stories in which she experiments with strategies for re-creating the texture of the mind and the mind's grasp of the world. The short stories, read in the single volume edited by Susan Dick, *The Complete Shorter Fiction of Virginia Woolf,* give us a privileged view of Woolf's techniques, unfolding as if through time-lapse photography. Through the helpful juxtaposition of these texts, dated and arranged chronologically, and through their relationship to the novels Woolf was working on simultaneously, we are in an excellent position to understand her triumphs over technical difficulties. Given the wonderful unity and economy of her mind, we also see this interest reflected in her criticism, for example, in *The Second Common Reader* essay, "The Strange Elizabethans," in which she reveals her struggle, by imaginatively filling in the silences, to comprehend the texture of life behind the vaulting and opaque prose of the writers of the age of Shakespeare.

Although it may be argued whether Woolf's novels or her essays rank first, except for the student or scholar, it is undoubtedly her novels that have been and will be read more by the "common readers" of posterity. It is these books that I, too, consider the pinnacle of her many achievements, offering us a beautiful haven in the stressful busyness of our lives. Thus I read her short stories as biographical proof of her relation to Romanticism and as the literary laboratories in which she made her self-enlightening comments and experiments on interiority or self-consciousness perfected in her longer fictions. Her criticism, examined in chapters 2 and 4, is both a working through and reflection of the approaches and values of her fiction, as well as an important reading and summing up of the culture to which she was, herself, contributing. Because I am interested less in a complete reading of her fiction than I am in establishing the relation of Romanticism to Woolf's work, I consider only four of her novels: *Night and Day, Mrs. Dalloway, To the Lighthouse,* and *The Waves.*

The pianist Emanuel Ax, in a *New York Times* interview, said of the modernist composer Arnold Schoenberg that he "'was a German Romantic composer. You can hear it right away. You just have to get used to the pitches.'"

... Mr. Ax ... begins humming a familiar Viennese waltz. "Now listen again," he says, and this time he hums an unfamiliar series of pitches, preserving enough of the rhythm and dynamic structure of the original waltz to make it still recognizable.

"The difference between what I just did and Schoenberg does ... is that I chose those pitches at random. If I had gone on humming, it would have gotten boring fast, because let's face it, chaos is boring.

But Schoenberg chose his pitches deliberately, and in time your ear notices the pattern."[50]

The case of Virginia Woolf is much easier than that of Arnold Schoenberg. Her chosen pitches, although sometimes unfamiliar, are not difficult to hear. She is an English Romantic, and in time your ear notices the pattern.

There are those who support their privileging of the moments of interruption and chaos, the stuff of modernist experiment, in their readings of Virginia Woolf's works by taking her at her own words in "Modern Fiction": "Let us record the atoms as they fall upon the mind." But in the same sentence she continues: ". . . in the order in which they fall, let us trace the pattern, however disconnected and incoherent in appearance, which each sight or incident scores upon the consciousness" (CR, 150). These atoms may seem disconnected and incoherent in appearance, but they have an order, and the writer's tracing and recording of it represent both a finding and creating of pattern. And there are also her statements in "A Sketch of the Past" about her need to create pattern in order to experience pleasure in life. Indeed, her desire to create pattern reveals her participation in one herself: the long tradition of the apparent human necessity to make story and thus explain the mysterious relationship between the individual and the world the stories describe.

However, it is true that this project—to make story and explain—is a difficult one. Something resists the effort of putting into words the ineluctable modality of the visible, the audible, the tactile. The "unseizable force . . . that the novelists never catch . . . goes hurtling through their nets and leaves them torn to ribbons" (JR, 156). Whether by "them" Woolf means the nets or the novelists must remain unsettled, and perhaps the referential ambiguity suggests that the answer is both. The Romantics realized this truth and so described *Sehnsucht,* the creative energy that flows from incompleteness and disequilibrium. In this sense, as well, Virginia Woolf followed in the wake of her Romantic forebears, her desire to find a way to approximate the richness of life driving her on.

But finally her will and energy flagged. Of the artist's profound wish to close through words the gap between self and world, Ragussis says: "Even Wordsworth pictures, in the Boy of Winander episode, the infantile wish to be part of the natural world whence man came—to be an indistinct thing, the way Lucy becomes one with rocks and stones and trees, rather than the exiled human consciousness filled with pain and suffering."[51] By walking into the

River Ouse, Woolf succeeded in fully obliterating the chasm between language and the world. Yet if Woolf's overwhelming pain was related to this division, her solution, like all suicides, was a spurious one because it depended for its success on the destruction of one of the two terms—the "Word." My last chapter is a reading of Woolf's profound connection with the politics and the poetry of the "unconscious," the Romantic poetry that, for her, came closest to ending the rupture between self and world through its attempt to terminate the pain and suffering of the exiled human consciousness.

Virginia wrote a postcard to Lytton Strachey in August 1912, while she and her new husband were on their wedding trip. "Here we are," she said, "in the middle of divine country, literary associations, cream for every meal, but cold as Christmas and steady rain" (Letters II, 2). She ended with a postscript question: "Who lived at Alfoxton?" Alfoxden House, which the Woolfs visited, was the home in 1797 and 1798 of William and Dorothy Wordsworth. I will show that Virginia Woolf, herself, lived in this house.

1

Prologue: "The Journal of Mistress Joan Martyn" and Wordsworth's *Guide to the Lakes*

"Here are the poets from whom we descend by way
of the mind."
> —*Between the Acts*

Virginia Woolf's relations with her father, Leslie Stephen, were exceptional. Beyond overseeing her education at home, he felt for her an "elective affinity," unique among his children. She was the one with the literary promise, visible when she was only five or six. She was the one to whom he opened his large library, granting her liberty to roam there at will—an unusual privilege during the Victorian age for a daughter.[1] And later, when he was dying, she was the one whose help he sought in editing his last book.

She repaid his love and intellectual admiration by becoming a writer whose work visibly bore the imprint of her father's interest in history, his aesthetic values, and his ideas. But Leslie Stephen's influence did not mark his daughter's writing directly. Rather it was mediated by the poet he loved best among the "moderns"— William Wordsworth. English Romanticism and Wordsworth's poetry, in particular, made possible Virginia Woolf's transformation into a writer whose imaginative merging of history and fiction colors all her work.

To be sure, Leslie Stephen would not have objected to his daughter's becoming a novelist. Katherine C. Hill quotes several letters in which Stephen asserts that his very young daughter's verbal skills might mean a career as a novelist. However, six years later, when writing to his wife, he said that writing articles would "'be 'Ginia's line unless she marries somebody at 17' (27 July 1893)."[2]

She did not marry at seventeen, and he was correct in forecasting that she would be a writer of articles. But at twenty-four, she was attempting a very different sort of expression and, sometime within a year of writing her earliest stories, beginning "Melymbrosia," her working title for *The Voyage Out,* published in 1913.

The internal and external pressures that drove her to become a novelist are as difficult to name as is an answer to her own later question about the forces that caused the extraordinary creativity of the Brontës (CE 2, 162). An approximation, however, is found in Leslie Stephen's profound effects on his daughter. He communicated his love and admiration for literature directly and forcefully to his children through his nightly ritual of reading to them during their childhood and, to his daughters, beyond their early years.

Virginia's own words best express what this experience meant to her. In "Impressions of Sir Leslie Stephen," written by February 1905 and published in Frederic Maitland's *The Life and Letters of Leslie Stephen* in November 1906, Virginia wrote that after finishing the thirty-two volumes of the Waverley Novels, Carlyle's *French Revolution,* Jane Austen, Hawthorne, some Shakespeare, "and many other classics," "He began too to read poetry instead of prose on Sunday nights, and the Sunday poetry went on till the very end after the nightly readings had been given up" (Essays I, 128). She continues:

> His memory for poetry was wonderful; he could absorb a poem that he liked almost unconsciously from a single reading. . . . He had long ago acquired all the most famous poems of Wordsworth, Tennyson, Keats, and Matthew Arnold, among the moderns. Milton of old writers was the one he knew best. . . . His recitation . . . gained immensely from this fact [that he spoke from memory], for as he lay back in his chair and spoke the beautiful words with closed-eyes, we felt that he was speaking not merely the words of Tennyson or Wordsworth but what he himself felt and knew. Thus many of the great English poems now seem to me inseparable from my father; I hear in them not only his voice, but in some sort his teaching and belief. (Essays I, 128–29)

In her later essay, "Leslie Stephen," she added to the picture:

> And often as he mounted the stairs to his study with his firm, regular tread he would burst, not into song, for he was entirely unmusical, but into a strange rhythmical chant, for verse of all kinds, both 'utter trash', as he called it, and the most sublime words of Milton and Wordsworth, stuck in his memory, and the act of walking or climbing seemed to inspire him to recite whichever it was that came uppermost or suited his mood. (CE 4, 76–77)

Woolf's was an unusual introduction to English poetry, both affective and intellectual, particularly of Wordsworth, who heads the list of Stephen's favorites. He remained a vital voice for her until the end of her life as the dated Victorians did not.

We have seen that Woolf, when praising Wordsworth to Ethel Smyth in 1936, said: "we only have a few pipers on hedges like Yeats and Tom Eliot, de la Mare—exquisite frail twittering voices one has to hollow one's hand to hear, whereas old Wth [Wordsworth] fills the room" (Letters VI, 73). There is reason to believe that it was her father's voice that, like an auditory palimpsest, gave added depth and meaning to the printed words of the poetry. Her admiration of Wordsworth, furthermore, is reminiscent of her father's essay on the poet in *Hours in a Library:*

> I gladly take for granted—what is generally acknowledged—that Wordsworth in his best moods reaches a greater height than any other modern Englishman. . . . Other poetry becomes trifling when we are making our inevitable passages through the Valley of the Shadow of Death. Wordsworth's alone retains its power. We love him the more as we grow older and become more deeply impressed with the sadness and seriousness of life. . . . And I take the explanation to be that he is not merely a melodious writer, or a powerful utterer of a deep emotion, but a true philosopher. His poetry wears well because it has solid substance. He is a prophet and a moralist as well as a mere singer.[3]

The poetic revolution begun by Blake and enunciated by Wordsworth in the Preface to the second edition of *Lyrical Ballads* published in 1800 explains the "psycho-political" and social dimension of Virginia Woolf's writing, her insistence on the quotidian and on the ordinary experiences and emotions of ordinary people, and a metaphorical style that makes consciousness translucent and continuous with the world it perceives and reflects.

Hazlitt in 1825, in his essay on Wordsworth, was first to assess the deeply radical political nature of Wordsworth's approach and its shift away from both the aesthetic and implied political position of the poets of the preceding generation. Of Wordsworth, Hazlitt wrote:

> He takes the simplest elements of nature and of the human mind, the mere abstract conditions inseparable from our being, and tries to compound a new system of poetry from them; and has perhaps succeeded as well as anyone could. '*Nihil humani a me alienum puto*'—is the motto of his works. . . . his poetry is founded on setting up an opposition (and pushing it to the utmost length) between the natural and the artificial. . . .

It is one of the innovations of our time. It partakes of, and is carried along with, the revolutionary movement of our age: the political changes of the day were the model on which he formed and conducted his poetical experiments. His Muse . . . is a levelling one. . . . It takes the commonest events and objects . . . to prove that nature is always interesting from its inherent truth and beauty. . . . Hence the unaccountable mixture of seeming simplicity and real abstruseness in the *Lyrical Ballads.*

. . . He takes a subject or story merely as pegs or loops to hang thought and feeling on; the incidents are trifling in proportion to his contempt for imposing appearances; the reflections are profound, according to the gravity and aspiring pretensions of his mind.[4]

As with Wordsworth's Prospectus, if we translate Hazlitt's claims for Wordsworth's poetry into more contemporary language, we may see in Virginia Stephen's earliest stories the crucial presence of Leslie Stephen and the nascence of Wordsworthian Romanticism that was to color all of her mature work.

Her father's death marked the end of an era in Virginia's life. It precipitated the break-up of the establishment at 22 Hyde Park Gate, her home in London since childhood, and the move to Bloomsbury with her sister Vanessa and brothers Thoby and Adrian. Many young writers spin their first fictions out of the material they know best: themselves and their own experience. Virginia Woolf was no exception. Her early short stories reveal the autobiographical conflicts of this difficult but adventurous time. They commemorate her father's influence on her decisions and qualities of mind which lasted a lifetime.

"Phyllis and Rosamond" of June 1906 (CSF, 289) limns the choice Virginia made, not merely by leaving behind Hyde Park Gate but also the Victorian upper middle-class social world of traditional and restricting expectations for young women. The two sisters, Phyllis and Rosamond, are twenty-eight and twenty-four, exactly the same ages as Vanessa and Virginia in that year.

There are a number of parallels between the situation of her characters and her own. Through a series of commercial metaphors, Virginia describes the case of these "daughters at home" (CSF, 18) who, like other girls of their social class, are forced to fulfill the economic expectations of their family, particularly of their mother, by making the drawing room "their place of business, their professional arena" (CSF, 18) where they practice their skills on marriage prospects. Like Phyllis and Rosamond, Vanessa and Virginia were made to go into society for the same purpose by their half-brother George Duckworth, their dead mother's favorite and representative. In the memoir "22 Hyde Park Gate," Virginia Woolf claimed that in this respect, "he had done what he knew my mother would have wished him to do" (MoB, 172). In the story Rosamond weakly resists her overbearing mother and reveals her intellectual proclivities by reading Walter Pater's "Greek Studies" (CSF, 20), as Virginia actually studied Greek with the Oxford don's sister, Clara Pater.

On the other hand, the father of Phyllis and Rosamond is a benignly hovering presence. He introduces them to two young men of his acquaintance, Mr. Middleton and Mr. Carew—humorously the names of two Jacobean authors from his library to whom Leslie Stephen would have "introduced" Virginia. Nor is he criticized as their mother Lady Hibbert is. Instead, the daughters actually side with their father: "The daughters were used to these insinuations against their father: on the whole they took his side, but they never said so" (CSF, 20).[5] The two sisters meet at the Bloomsbury home of the Tristrams and talk to Sylvia, the daughter of the family, who has never had a marriage proposal and who represents the social and intellectual freedom that Vanessa and Virginia chose by moving to bohemian Bloomsbury. The name "Tristram" was an apt choice for these free spirits, given the oddities of the character of Tristram Shandy, but one also with which Virginia identified her father. In "A Sketch of the Past," Woolf wrote: "Leslie Stephen apart from his books was a figure . . . and lived a very real life in the minds of men like Walter Headlam or Herbert Fisher; to whom he was a representative man; a man with a standard they often referred to. If a man like Leslie Stephen likes *Tristram Shandy,* Walter Headlam wrote to someone, then it must be all right. That gives what I mean" (MoB, 110–11).

The young Virginia thus split her own character between the doomed, intellectually undeveloped Rosamond and the bohemian Sylvia. In this unfashionable quarter of London, Phyllis thinks: "There was room, and freedom, and in the roar and the splendour of the Strand she read the live realities of the world from which her stucco and her pillars protected her so completely" (CSF, 24). But the two young sisters feel that they have been spoiled for such freedoms, that "long captivity had corrupted them both within and without" (CSF, 26).

Such, indeed, must have been the negative feelings that Virginia harbored about herself in 1904 as she stepped out of "the cage"— her name for 22 Hyde Park Gate—replete with images of imprisonment: the "iron trellis," the "square of wall-circled garden," the "creepers [that] hung down in front of the window" (MoB, 116).

However, she emerged with a rich intellectual legacy acquired through her father's direct encouragement, which enabled her to move successfully, although not without self-doubt, into the rigorous world of her brother Thoby and his intellectually sophisticated, free-thinking Cambridge friends.

Thus, "Phyllis and Rosamond" gives an extremely contemporaneous and close approximation of the two forces Virginia felt to be vying for her mind and life near the time of the actual writing of the story. A more sublimated representation of these forces, and one in which the attraction and strength of the intellectual life happily prevails, is found in "The Journal of Mistress Joan Martyn." This story, found among Woolf's Monks House Papers, was published for the first time only in 1979 in *Twentieth Century Literature*. However, it was written during August 1906, when Virginia and her sister Vanessa were on holiday in Norfolk, staying at Blo' Norton Hall (CSF, 289). Written only two months after "Phyllis and Rosamond" and exactly two and one half years after the death of Leslie Stephen, it memorializes her father's passion for history and his hopes that Virginia would follow professionally in his footsteps as an historian and biographer.

Yet Virginia Stephen, in this second short story, did something more. Like George Eliot, focusing in *Middlemarch* on the sort of woman who might have lived in 1832 at the time of the first Reform Bill, she imaginatively merged fiction and history. Indeed, we begin to feel that the possibility of such a hybrid is, in fact, the point of her story.

The singular mixing of the "historiographic" apparatus with which she frames the story and its wholly fictional content suggests her lifelong efforts to create an interdependent structure based on history and imagination in her writing. This early work is thus a metaphor for Woolf's desire to be a writer of fiction who would, nevertheless, stay close to the intellect perspectives of her father and of the writers he encouraged her to read from his large library.

We clearly feel the veiled autobiographical presence both in the framing device and in the journal proper. As in the earlier tale of the two sisters and their friend Sylvia Tristram, Virginia Stephen split the representation of herself between Rosamond Merridew, the forty-five-year-old, exuberant historian-archaeologist, and Joan Martyn, the young woman in her twenties, keeping in 1480 the journal discovered by the historian. Yet although Virginia gave Miss Merridew the Christian name of her insecure avatar in the previous story, the middle-aged historian, like Sylvia Tristram, has tremendous self-assurance. More significantly, she has a profession.

Miss Merridew's surname says all there is to say about the joy with which she embraces her life's work. She happily asserts that she has "exchanged a husband and a family and a house in which [she] may grow old for certain fragments of yellow parchment" and further admits that "a kind of maternal passion has sprung up in [her] breast for these shrivelled and colourless little gnomes . . . with the fire of genius in their eyes" (CSF, 33). A comparable profession may well have seemed probable for Virginia who had begun writing journalistic reviews to supplement her private income. Rosamond Merridew is thus a representation of Leslie Stephen's wishes for his daughter.

Katherine Hill asserts that Virginia Woolf's approach to literary criticism—its sociological underpinnings and the informing belief that the dominant class of an age creates the new genres of literature—was influenced generally by her father's positions last enunciated in *English Literature and Society in the Eighteenth Century,* which Virginia helped him edit in his final years. But Hill's essay is silent about the more difficult issues bearing on her decision to become a writer of fiction. What forces or causes in her life other than her love of literature made her pursue this path rather than follow in her father's footsteps? Virginia Hyman offers a psychological reading in "Reflections in a Looking-Glass: Leslie Stephen and Virginia Woolf."[6] She describes Virginia's double need: to see herself as duplicating her father's life but yet to distance herself from him. Certainly there are temperamental proclivities that explain her choice as well. In a letter of 1940 to Vita Sackville-West, who had encouraged her to write a book about Bess of Hardwick, Woolf explained:

> It is angelic of you to wish me to write another book. At the same time devilish. Havent I 20 books sizzling in my head at the moment? Then you tempt me with old Bess. It is tempting of course. But I doubt if old Bess is my bird. I think she's neither one thing or the other. I mean Orlando was imagination: Roger [Fry] fact. But Bess is after all, though much spangled with Elizabethan finery, an historic figure. I should have to grub. And I dont like shoddy history. (Letters VI, 445)

If we agree that her fiction, as well as her life, bears the imprint of her struggle, a different answer can be found in Rosamond Merridew's position in ". . . Joan Martyn." Introducing her methods, Miss Merridew (if not Virginia Stephen) self-consciously asserts:

> The critics . . . complain that I have no materials at my side to stiffen these words into any semblance of the truth. It is well known that the

period I have chosen is more bare than any other of private records; unless you choose to draw all your inspiration from the *Paston Letters* you must be content to imagine merely, like any other story teller. And that, I am told, is a useful art in its place; but it should be allowed to claim no relationship with the sterner art of the Historian. (CSF, 35)

Perhaps the critic is Leslie Stephen, but the charm for Rosamond Merridew and Virginia Stephen seems precisely in the bareness of private records that gives them the freedom to imagine.

Furthermore, the intellectual combat Miss Merridew most relishes is over the sort of evidence from the past most pertinent to the historian. Starting from the reasonable but often obscured assumption that "the intricacies of the land tenure were not always the most important facts in the lives of men and women and children" (CSF, 34), she claims to have come

upon . . . [prizes] that because they are so fitful and so minute in their illumination please me even better. A sudden light upon the legs of Dame Elizabeth Partridge sends its beams over the whole state of England, to the King upon his throne; she wanted stockings! and no other need impresses you in quite the same way with the reality of mediaeval legs; and therefore with the reality of mediaeval bodies, and so, proceeding upward step by step, with the reality of mediaeval brains; and there you stand at the centre of all ages: middle beginning or end. (CSF, 34).

Indeed, her insistence on the distinction between the "prizes" most interesting to other historians and those that most appeal to her determines the key to the compromise between Leslie Stephen's professional interest in history and Virginia Woolf's own preference for the transcendent role of the imagination, of mediaeval and other "brains" in her writing. To be sure, Miss Merridew's interest emphasizes the kinds of particulars that, at least theoretically, Stephen, as distinct from others, believed are responsible for creating the character of the past and, as well, should direct the historian in his quest for this character. But more importantly, Rosamond Merridew describes the sort of "evidence" that most appeals to Woolf in the creation of fictive worlds. The subject and texture of Woolf's imaginative writing are spelled out in a way that remarkably heralds her later career. The desire for stockings— the stuff of the banal quotidian world—and the mind to which, physically and figuratively "proceeding upward step by step" they lead, represent the pith and marrow of her novelistic writing. The same democratic impulse that privileges the quotidian and thought and feeling in Woolf's later work is also strikingly present in ". . . Joan Martyn." Further, her attention to the world of nature, a result, as well, of her father's interest in and love of the natural world, which would much later transform into the idiosyncratic and totally original description of "Time Passes" in *To the Lighthouse,* is equally present here.

Clearly Woolf's sympathies and approach do not amount to a mere reductive repetition of the values and techniques of English Romanticism. To make this argument would be to violate the evidence of her fiction as well as of her own notion, expressed in "Mr Bennett and Mrs Brown," that each age enters into a complicitous agreement with its authors to create new conventions through which the ideas of that age are expressed. However, the spirit of Wordsworth hovers over the pages of ". . . Joan Martyn," reminding us of the origins of Woolf's political and literary patrimony. Since Virginia had just written a review for *The Times Literary Supplement* in June 1906, "Wordsworth and the Lakes," for which she received 9.7s, the poet's felt presence is not a surprise. "'This is the largest sum I have ever made at one blow,' she announced proudly to Violet Dickinson."[7] Her financial success made an impression on her. But so, it seems, did Wordsworth's habits of carefully recording his impressions of the landscape and his reactions to it because Virginia, in the poet's manner, attempted a minute description of the countryside of Norfolk in the journal she kept during her stay at Blo' Norton. However, she seemed subtly aware of an important difference between her journal and Wordsworth's: the absence in hers of self-conscious examination of the effects of this landscape on her imagination and feelings. She wonders about her inability to respond to what she sees every day.

> It is one of the wilful habits of the brain, let me generalise for the sake of comfort, that it will only work at its own terms.
> You bring it directly opposite an object, & bid it discourse; it merely shuts its eye, & turns away. But in one month, or three or seven, suddenly without any bidding, it pours out the whole picture, gratuitously. . . . Like the light that reaches you from the stars, it will only shine when some time after it has been shed.
> So then, to come to the heart of the discourse, there is no use in presenting here a picture of Norfolk; when the place is directly beneath my eyes. I see at this moment a wall, coloured like an apricot in the sun; with touches of red upon it. The outline & angles of the roof & the tall chimney are completely filled with pure blue sky. . . . (APA, 313)

Saying there is no use in description, she yet continues to describe. We must conclude that by "presenting" she means something other than the marketplace use of the word, depending rather on its root significance of spatial and temporal immediacy. She seems to take a leaf out of Wordsworth's autobiographical poem, *The Prelude,* the famous "spots of time" episode of Book XII. There he asserts that "An ordinary sight" from the past, coupled with another and remembered in the present, or one from the past evoked by its repetition in the present, has "A renovating virtue, whence . . . our minds / Are nourished and invisibly repaired" (Wordsworth, 345). Both for Wordsworth and Woolf, the active imagination transforms these otherwise meaningless, ordinary sights from nullities into meaningful, even restorative memories. After Wordsworth describes two chance sights from the landscape of his childhood, the gibbet and the murderer's name carved into the grass and the girl with the pitcher on her head, straining against the wind, thus married through spatial and temporal propinquity, he sums up the significance of such memories for the present.

> . . . When, in the blessed hours
> Of early love, the loved one at my side,
> I roamed, in daily presence of this scene,
> Upon the naked pool and dreary crags,
> And on the melancholy beacon, fell
> A spirit of pleasure and youth's golden gleam;
> And think ye not with radiance more sublime
> For these remembrances, and for the power
> They left behind? So feeling comes in aid
> Of feeling, and diversity of strength
> Attends us, if but once we have been strong.
> Oh! mystery of man, from what a depth
> Proceed thy honours.
>
> (Wordsworth, 346)

Wordsworth does not consider the mechanics of the re-presenting of these memories to the consciousness while Woolf simply implies that it is an unwilled process. Nevertheless, they both believe that the faculty of the imagination creatively superimposes itself on remembrance. The imagination, by simultaneously insisting on the emotional importance of the memories, thus gives new meaning to the notion of "seeing" or "presenting." The organically assimilated vision in Wordsworth's prose and poetry was conspicuously absent, Virginia felt, in her own journal.

However, while Virginia hoped that her untoward brain, refusing thus far to "discourse" or speak to her, might still have a surprise in store for her several months hence, her other literary venture,

going forward at the same time, was a less direct but more successful attempt to capture the present moment and turn it from the
forgettable into a moment of being. As an experiment in the imaginative sphere, imbued with the values of Romanticism, ". . . Joan
Martyn" is a thoughtful compromise with the expectations of Leslie Stephen. Its obvious concern with the ordinary and diurnal,
the metaphorical attention to landscape and its continuity with
the perceiving imagination, and, finally, the democratic political
impulse of the young and inexperienced writer of the diary are all
reminiscent of the methods and ideas of Wordsworth, her father's
favorite. In more than one sense, then, it is the story of "fathers"
and a daughter.

Joan's story begins with an historical comparison between the
time of her own mother's girlhood and the present. She writes:
"The state of the times, which my mother tells me, is less safe and
less happy than when she was a girl, makes it necessary for us to
keep much within our own lands" (CSF, 45). However, the present
necessity of barring the Gates against fearful intruders—the historical reality of the Wars of the Roses, which ended in 1485 at
the battle of Bosworth Field[8]—is then metaphorized in a powerful
natural image:

> I am very bold and impatient sometimes, when the moon rises, over
> a land gleaming with frost; and I think I feel the pressure of all this
> free and beautiful place — all England and the sea, and the lands
> beyond — rolling like sea waves against our iron gates, breaking, and
> withdrawing — and breaking again — all through the long black night.
> (CSF, 45)

We hear the power of Wordsworth's poetic descriptions in *The
Guide to the Lakes*. His imagination is felt everywhere as he appro-
priates the landscape of the Lake District. She thus commends his
description in her review.

> But all through this minute and scrupulous catalogue there runs a pur-
> pose which solves it into one coherent and increasingly impressive
> picture. For all these details and more 'which a volume would not be
> sufficient to describe' . . . are of such interest to him [Wordsworth]
> because he sees them all as living parts of a vast and exquisitely or-
> dered system. It is this combination in him of obstinate truth and
> fervent imagination that stamps his descriptions more deeply upon the
> mind than those of almost any other writer. (Essays I, 107)

Metaphors of organicity, used by Coleridge in his description of the
imagination,[9] enter organically and become truth in Wordsworth's

writing. Virginia apprehends this phenomenon from the ability of his imagination actually to apprehend the organic connection of the parts of the ecosystem which he visually, auditorially, and tactilely perceives and records.

Similarly, Virginia, conscious of metaphor as a vehicle for the imagination's appropriation of the world before it,[10] imputes to Joan the power to register it through metaphors—here, the presence of the world become the pressure of sea waves against the gates. Virginia's "own" imagination is very much under the influence of Wordsworth's language in the "Guide" as she borrows words and phrases from it, transforming them and making them serve her particular needs. And so we find that Wordsworth's "birch with its silver stem"[11] becomes Virginia Stephen's "beech . . . with silver gems" (CSF, 56). The suggested auditory remembrance of his words is also joined by a more conscious effort to replicate Wordsworth's precise rendering of the complexity and beauty of the natural world. Attracted to Wordsworth's "general survey" of the countryside, she then extols his "very penetrating eye" and paraphrases in her review his closer description of "the rocky part of a mountain [which] is blue or 'hoary grey', with a tinge of red in it 'like the compound hues of a dove's neck'" (Wordsworth's Guide, 28; Essays I, 106). There she praises, as well, his inclusion of "sober details [that] . . . give a tone of solidity to the whole, and suggest the rough surface of the earth, which is as true a part of the country as its heights and splendours" (Essays I, 106).

Wordsworth writes:

> The general *surface* of the mountain is turf, rendered rich and green by the moisture of the climate. Sometimes the turf . . . is little broken, the whole covering being soft and downy pasturage. In other places rocks predominate; the soil is laid bare by torrents and burstings of water from the sides of the mountains in heavy rains; and not unfrequently their perpendicular sides are seamed by ravines . . . which, meeting in angular points, entrench and scar the surface with numerous figures like the letters W and Y. (Wordsworth's Guide, 27)

Virginia similarly describes the color and the texture of the *"surface"* of Norfolk when she writes:

> Walsingham, as all the world knows, is but a very small village on the top of a hill. But as you approach through a plain that is rich with green, you see this high ground rising above you for some time before you get there. The midday sun lit up all the soft greens and blues of the fen land; and made it seem as though one passed through a soft

and luxurious land, glowing like a painted book; towards a stern summit, where the light struck upon something pointing upwards that was pale as bone. (CSF, 58)

The "compound hues" of the fen land, "the soft greens and blues," followed by the "soft and luxurious land," reminiscent of Wordsworth's "soft pasturage," and then the shift to the vertical plane, to "something pointing upwards," like Wordsworth's "perpendicular sides . . . meeting in angular points," all suggest Virginia Woolf's extraordinary aural recall, exercised frequently in her many allusions to Romantic poetry. As she said of her father's, her own "memory for poetry was wonderful."

The description Joan gives of ascending to the "stern summit" of Walsingham also seems a reworking of Wordsworth's description from the *Guide* of his ascent of Scawfell Pike on which she particularly remarks in her review. Wordsworth's sense of reverence for the wonders of nature, his own variety of religious experience, is transformed by Virginia into the only sort of religious ecstasy possible for Joan in the year 1480. Wordsworth, describing the coming of a mountain storm and then his safe reaching of the summit, says:

> I know not how long we might have remained on the summit of the Pike . . . had not our Guide warned us that we must not linger; for a storm was coming. We looked in vain to espy the signs of it. Mountains, vales, and sea were touched with the clear light of the sun. 'It is there,' said he, pointing to the sea beyond Whitehaven, and there we perceived a light vapour unnoticeable but by a shepherd accustomed to watch all mountain bodings. . . . Great Gavel, Helvellyn, and Skiddaw, were wrapped in storm; yet Langdale, and the mountains in that quarter, remained all bright in sunshine. . . .
> I ought to have mentioned that round the top of Scawfell-PIKE not a blade of grass is to be seen. Cushions or tufts of moss, parched and brown, appear between the huge blocks and stones that lie in heaps on all sides to a great distance, like skeletons or bones of the earth not needed at the creation, and there left to be covered with never-dying lichens. . . .
> . . . Afterwards we had a spectacle of the grandeur of earth and heaven commingled; yet without terror. We knew that the storm would pass away, for so our prophetic Guide had assured us. (Wordsworth's Guide, 115–16)

Joan, in her account, says:

> At last I reached the top of the hill, joining with a stream of other pilgrims, and we clasped hands, to show that we came humbly as hu-

man beings and trod the last steps of the road together, singing our
Miserere. . . .

But then the pale cross with the Image struck my eyes, and drew all
my mind, in reverence towards it.

I will not pretend that I found that summons other than stern; for
the sun and storm have made the figure harsh and white; but the endeavour to adore Her as others were doing round me filled my mind
with an image that was so large and white that no other thought had
room there. For one moment I submitted myself to her as I have never
submitted to man or woman, and bruised my lips on the rough stone
of her garment. White light and heat steamed on my bare head; and
when the ecstasy passed the country beneath flew out like a sudden
banner unfurled. (CSF, 59)

The something "pale as bone" is a transformation of the skeletons
and bones of Scawfell Pike. Woolf recalls Wordsworth's contrast
of storm and sunshine in "the sun and storm" that have weathered
the figure of Mary. Wordsworth's reverential "unwilling to lose the
remembrance of what lay before us" and "the spectacle of the
grandeur of earth and heaven commingled" reappear in "when the
ecstasy passed the country beneath flew out like a sudden banner unfurled."

However, an even more remarkable borrowing is from stanzas
III through V of "Resolution and Independence." Joan, describing
her pilgrimage to the shrine of Our Lady at Walsingham, says:

And my brain that was swift and merry at first, and leapt like a child
at play, settled down in time to sober work upon the highway, though
it was glad withal. For I thought of the serious things of life—such as
age, and poverty and sickness and death, and considered that it would
certainly be my lot to meet them; and I considered also those joys and
sorrows that were for ever chasing themselves across my life. Small
things would no longer please me and tease me as of old. But although
this made me feel grave, I felt also that I had come to the time when
such feelings are true; and further, as I walked, it seemed to me that
one might enter within such feelings and study them, as, indeed, I had
walked in a wide space within the covers of Master Richard's manuscript. (CSF, 58)

Like Joan, Wordsworth is travelling in "Resolution. . . ."

III
I was a Traveller then upon the moor;
I saw the hare that raced about with joy;
I heard the woods and distant waters roar;
Or heard them not, as happy as a boy:

The pleasant season did my heart employ:
My old remembrances went from me wholly;
And all the ways of men, so vain and melancholy.

IV

But, as it sometimes chanceth, from the might
Of joy in minds that can no further go,
As high as we have mounted in delight
In our dejection do we sink as low;
To me that morning did it happen so;
And fears and fancies thick upon me came;
Dim sadness—and blind thoughts, I knew not, nor could
name.

V

I heard the sky-lark warbling in the sky;
And I bethought me of the playful hare:
Even such a happy Child of earth am I;
Even as these blissful creatures do I fare;
Far from the world I walk, and from all care;
But there may come another day to me—
Solitude, pain of heart, distress, and poverty.

(Wordsworth, 166)

Wordsworth's meeting with the Old Leech Gatherer makes more pointed the self-conscious study of his feelings, the subject of the entire poem. Joan, as well, sees that it is possible to "enter within such feelings and study them," comparing the feelings with the play of her imagination when she had, figuratively, "walked in a wide space within the covers" of a travelling minstrel's book.

The complex "Klein bottle" or self-devolving image of her imagination's entering a work of art as it does the emotions that, likewise, it engenders, is suggested through another Wordsworthian image. Because Virginia had already cited it as an example of his "obstinate truth and fervent imagination" in her review of his *Guide* and then turned it to her own and very interesting account in the story, we are convinced of its special importance to her. Wordsworth, describing trees, says: "and the leafless purple twigs were tipped with globes of shining crystal" (Wordsworth's Guide, 127). Joan says: "I saw *them* [italics mine] as solid globes of crystal; enclosing a round ball of coloured earth and air, in which tiny men and women laboured, as beneath the dome of the sky itself" (CSF, 58).

The pronoun "them" has an ambiguous antecedent. Does Joan mean to refer to her "feelings" or to the "covers" of Richard's book? The confusion instructively suggests Virginia Woolf's dependence on Romantic metaphors for mind in which the world or the work of art is enfigured as an extension of, and continuous with, the imagination. Hermione Lee has similarly developed the idea of Woolf's use of metaphors of transparency and fire as important proof of the connection between her and the writers of the Romantic Movement.[12]

Woolf relies on such images, particularly on the figure "solid globes of crystal" and on similar ones in this story like the protective glass covering of a picture mentioned by Giles Martyn. She seems aware of the sometimes "transforming" or "preserving" properties of glass, especially as she borrows the dominant metaphor, the solid globes of crystal, from Wordsworth. Such metaphors and other similarities in perspectives and values represent important proof of the privileged position that Woolf accords to Romantic self-consciousness and to the textures of ordinary life.

Thus, the wave metaphor from the natural world in the beginning of Joan's narrative, conveying the historical moment, but equally an indication of the characteristic imagination of the narrator, is succeeded by a direct discussion of the capacity of imaginative literature to reveal the truth about the lives and the emotions of historical figures. Indeed, Joan sees imaginative literature as an alternative means both of apprehending and representing historical reality. Through it Virginia Stephen worked a compromise with her father.

Joan's family's reaction to "Mr John Lydgate's" "The Palace of Glass,"[13] "a poem written about Helen and the Siege of Troy" (CSF, 46) and a gift from her father—"my father has sent me a manuscript from London" (CSF, 46)—is the compromise with Leslie Stephen dramatically rendered. Virginia made her intentions clear through Joan's comment.

> Last night I read of Helen, and her beauty and her suitors, and the fair town of Troy and they listened silently; for though we none of us know where those places are, we see very well what they must have been like; and we can weep for the suffering of the soldiers, and picture to ourselves the stately woman herself, who must have been, I think, something like my mother. My mother beats with her foot and sees the whole processions pass I know, from the way her eyes gleam, and her head tosses. 'It must have been in Cornwall,' said Sir John [the priest], 'where King Arthur lived with his knights.' (CSF, 46–47)

The beauty of this poem and the emotions it engenders are real and powerful despite the historical ignorance of those who listen to it. The poor guess by Sir John, that Troy must have been in Cornwall, does not change the "truth" of Lydgate's words. Virginia, who was very familiar with Walter Pater's work, may well have been taking ironic pleasure in the knowledge that the site of Troy was not known until thirty-five years before she wrote her story.[14] People for thousands of years have been able to appreciate "The Iliad" and "The Odyssey" despite their lack of accurate historical and archaeological knowledge.

Joan's family is equally moved by the story of Tristram and Iseult in the book of the travelling minstrel. The description of Richard suggests the singularity of the Romantic metaphors for mind that reveal the imagination and world as coextensive. In Richard's case, art is actually an extension of the mind of the individual who creates it: "He turned to me, and wound up with a flourish of one hand with the book in it" (CSF, 54). The symbolic physical extension of the arm and hand by the book he holds is then given emotional dimension as he begins to read the story of Tristram and Iseult, which, unlike that of Helen of Troy, does take place in Cornwall. Richard's extension of himself into the story is clear from his dramatic involvement. Joan writes:

> He dropped his gay manner, and looked past us all . . . as though he drew his words from some sight not far from him. And as the story grew passionate his voice rose, and his fists clenched, and he raised his foot and stretched forth his arms; and then, when the lovers part, he seemed to see the Lady sink away from him . . . and his arms were empty. And then he is wounded in Brittany; and he hears the Princess coming across the seas to him. (CSF, 56).

The same pronominal confusion that keeps us from knowing whether, in the figure of the solid crystal globes, Joan refers to her emotions or the covers of Richard's book occurs here, for it is impossible to tell whether the "he" of the last sentence refers to Richard or Tristram. The created art is the projection of the artist's imagination, an idea reinforced through the figure Joan deploys to describe looking at the manuscript "illuminations."[15]

> . . . the capital letters framed bright blue skies, and golden robes; and in the midst of the writing there came broad spaces of colour, in which you might see princes and princesses walking in procession and towns with churches . . . and the sea breaking blue beneath them. They were like little mirrors, held up to those visions which I had seen passing in the air but here they were caught and stayed forever. (CSF, 56–57)

Art is not mimetic, that is, does not hold its mirror up to the world, as in the Aristotelian or Platonic conceptions of the relation of artist, audience, product, and world.[16] Rather, it mirrors or expresses the imagination to give form to what is inside the creative individual.

Art both issues from the imagination and extends us. But even more significant is the contrast Joan draws between the art Richard makes—the art of pure fantasy and escape—and "ordinary thoughts," not the proper subject, Joan at first believes, of stories. When Richard finishes the tale of Tristram and Iseult, the spell is broken, the moment of being is over: "But then the voice stopped; and all these figures withdrew, fading and trailing across the sky to the West where they live. And when I opened my eyes, the man, and the grey wall; the people by the Gate, slowly swam up, as from some depths, and settled on the surface, and stayed there clear and cold" (CSF, 56). The end of the illusion similarly affects Richard: "Meanwhile Richard was like a man who lets something slip from his clasp; and beats thin air. He looked at us, and I had half a mind to stretch out a hand; and tell him he was safe. But then he recollected himself, and smiled as though he had reason to be pleased" (CSF, 56). The ordinary world of the "grey wall," the Gate, and the people are nothing like the intense blue skies and princesses of the illuminations. Joan says that Richard "took his manuscript from me, and tied the covers safely across it. He placed it in his breast" (CSF, 57). His actions thus invert Jasper Martyn's generous giving of the papers with their "thick cord of green silk" (CSF, 41)—the manuscript of the "ordinary" world of Joan Martyn—to Rosamond Merridew, which prefaces the diary. The kind of art that Richard creates, like Richard himself, "the strange bird" who "By dawn . . . was out of the house" (CSF, 57), is not always there to be relied on although it is pleasurably seductive. Indeed, Joan's mother, taking pleasure in Lydgate's poetry but calling "herself an old fool for listening to stories, when the accounts had still to be made up for my father in London" (CSF, 47), may be her first teacher in this regard.

"The Journal of Mistress Joan Martyn" is an imaginative rendering of the ordinary experiences of relatively comfortable but by no means extraordinarily wealthy or socially elevated people at the end of the fifteenth century. The opacity of Elizabethan and earlier prose and the paucity of extant documents of the time, hindering the reclamation of the past, are ideas Woolf would also consider nearly thirty years later in *The Second Common Reader* essay, "The Strange Elizabethans." The desire to name the past, to make it come alive for herself and her readers, suggests, then, a second plausible explanation for Woolf's choice of fiction over history and her elevation of the ordinary into art. The attraction to the freedoms of fiction in the face of a disappointingly slight historical record is represented by the historian Drew Gilpin Faust in her review of *Celia: A Slave*. Faust remarks of the difficulties that beset the author:

> But his scanty sources compel him to guess, to speculate, to improvise, in ways that frustrate a reader eager to know more of what Celia thought and said, of how her lawyers debated their course of action. . . . In a work such as Mr. McLaurin's, history forcefully displays both its compelling strengths and its debilitating weaknesses as a mode of insight into the human experience.
>
> . . . that we must be satisfied with shadows and outlines because of the irremediable incompleteness of the historical record reminds us of how every historian is compelled to create the past out of the pieces of it that survive. Celia's story almost inevitably evokes a work whose author bypassed the constraints of history for the freedoms and challenges of fiction: Toni Morrison's extraordinarily powerful novel "Beloved," the tale of an escaped slave woman who kills her infant daughter to prevent her return to bondage.[17]

Similarly, when history provided her with so few Paston families, Woolf was drawn to invention, but invention based on historical evidence and her own experience. The family of Joan Martyn is one Woolf could have known well had she been alive in 1480, being much as her own family would have been, transported back four hundred years. Joan Martyn, herself, is like Virginia Stephen, a young woman with a talent for writing and "history" recording and, for this reason, her father's particular joy.[18] Joan mentions her father's reaction to her diary:

> My father came in yesterday when I was sitting before the desk at which I write these sheets. He is not a little proud of my skill in reading and writing; which indeed I have learnt mostly at his knee.
>
> But confusion came over me when he asked me what I wrote; and stammering that it was a 'Diary' I covered the pages with my hands.
>
> 'Ah,' he cried, 'if my father had only kept a diary! But he, poor man could not write even his own name. There's John and Pierce and Stephen all lying in the church yonder, and no word left to say whether they were good men or bad.' (CSF, 60–61)

Virginia's choice of "Stephen" for the last-named ancestor of Giles Martyn, recalling her own patronymic, thus suggests the possibility

LORETTE WILMOT LIBRARY
NAZARETH COLLEGE

of her intimate knowledge of these people and, possibly, as well, the role played by her father in the acquisition of this knowledge.

The connection between the present and the past is also the note sounded positively at the beginning of the narrative when Rosamond Merridew talks with the farmer Jasper Martyn. As the owner of Martyn Hall and, more importantly, of the journal manuscript written by his ancestor Joan Martyn, whom he refers to as his grandmother, he is the representative Englishman, tied to the land and to its history, and valuing the company of his ancestors through the written records they have created down through the centuries. Their personal accounts, in both senses of that word— their stories and their stud books—are a kind of "memory" of the past, connecting Jasper to it through his reading of them. Further, the creation of these memories, first through the writing, and their re-creation through the reading, form an indissoluble imaginative link between reader and writer. Indeed, these memories explain, as well, Rosamond Merridew's more impersonal and professional interest in stockings, to legs, to bodies to mediaeval brains—her interest, that is, in a moment of being or spot of time in the cultural past of the nation. Similarly, these "memories," we shall see, informed Woolf's sense of historiography both in "Anon" and "The Reader," and in her cultural criticism in general. When Virginia Woolf wrote to Ethel Smyth that she would "thread a necklace through English life & lit,"[19] the metaphor implied by her image transforms the moments on this continuum into pearls or beads, moments of be(ad)ing or spots of time with their renovative, even generative, effect on her audience or readers in the present.

All the "readers" in ". . . Joan Martyn" agree on the importance of the written word that commemorates the present, thus transforming it for later generations into the potentially accessible past. Rosamond Merridew, from a professional point of view, Jasper Martyn with his very personal interest in his ancestors, and Joan's father, Giles, with his prescient understanding of the importance of the historical record are all firmly convinced. Only Joan is diffident, but her diffidence stems from a certain modesty about her powers as an observer and recorder, and of the unimportance, as she sees it, of what is available for her to observe and record. Indeed, the entire story records Joan's coming to terms with the very act of journal-keeping, making history "out of the ordinary," which provides the material for a new kind of art.

The story begins as very much centered on women. With the exception of Jasper Martyn, the characters first introduced are all female: Rosamond Merridew, the narrator of the frame story, the housemaid of Martyn Hall, Mrs. Martyn, the journal-keeping Joan, and Joan's own mother. One can see why Louise DeSalvo, who not only edited and named the untitled story but also wrote about it in the critical essay "Shakespeare's *Other* Sister," claims importance for this early work as a "meditation upon the relationship between the woman as historian and history and upon the need of women such as Merridew to write women into history."[20] Although there is truth in her assertions, there are other, more compelling issues that surfaced for Virginia Stephen as she wrote this narrative in 1906.

The presence of men in this story is, indeed, delayed. However, their entrance—both of Jasper Martyn, who returns from his work in the fields and satisfies Rosamond Merridew with a history of his ancestors, and of Giles Martyn, the father of Joan, absent for most of her journal-keeping—makes possible the formative relationships and turning points of the narrative. This, then, may be a story about mothers, but it is even more significantly a story about "absent" fathers.

Rosamond Merridew is what Joan Martyn may well have become if she had lived four hundred years later. The historian's insistence on the importance of the recording of the quotidian world in her sort of historiographical account of reality is doubled in Joan's registering the impressions of the diurnal round in her journal. But Jasper Martyn, even before Rosamond opens Joan's journal, sounds the recognizably Woolfian note of the importance of the texture of the ordinary in imaginative as well as historical writing. His wife Betty has shown Miss Merridew over the house while he shows her the portraits of his ancestors—history in themselves. He saves the best for last: "'Stop a moment,' he interrupted, 'we're not done yet. There are the books'" (CSF, 40). With "temperate voice" he hands her the first lot, "merely saying" "'that's no. I: 1480 to 1500'" (CSF, 41). His casualness about the great age and possible historical importance of these and the other papers is paradoxically a function of his sense of the continuity between the present and the past. It suggests his belief that this continuity is the result of the essential sameness of the human consciousnesses spanning the centuries. He simply recognizes his ancestors' consciousness as his own and his wife's. Miss Merridew asserts:

> No words of mine . . . can give the curious impression which he produced as he spoke, that all these 'relations' Grandfathers of the time of Elizabeth, nay Grandmothers of the time of Edward the Fourth, were just, so to speak, brooding round the corner; there was none of

the pride of 'ancestry' in his voice but merely the personal affection of a son for his parents. All generations seemed bathed in his mind in the same clear and equable light: it was not precisely the light of the present day, but it certainly was not what we commonly call the light of the past. And it was not romantic . . . and the figures stood out in it, solid and capable, with a great resemblance, I suspect, to what they were in the flesh. (CSF, 43–44)

The apparent paradox of Wordsworthian Romanticism, as Miss Merridew also asserts here about Jasper Martyn's view of the historical past, is that its "friendly" acquisition of the personal past through memory is *not* romantic. On the contrary, Wordsworth mythologizes the restorative *value* of the past for the present rather than its specific attributes. Rosamond Merridew and Virginia Stephen are attracted to Martyn's *de*mythologized view of his ancestors because it makes them more real. That sense of continuity with one's "grandfathers" and "grandmothers," of whom Martyn speaks, and his way of talking about them are both explicit in Virginia Woolf's commendation of Leigh Hunt, written fifteen years later. Woolf transcribed into her diary a long passage about Coleridge from Hunt's autobiography,[21] following it with these more general remarks on the Romantics:

> L.H. was our spiritual grandfather, a free man. One could have spoken to him as to Desmond. A light man, I daresay, but civilised, much more so than my grandfather in the flesh. . . . These free, vigorous spirits advance the world, & when one lights on them in the strange waste of the past one says Ah you're my sort—a great compliment . . . Shelley died with H.'s copy of Lamia in his hand. H. wd. receive it back from no other, & so burnt it on the pyre. Going home from the funeral? H. & Byron laughed till they split. This is human nature, & H. doesn't mind owning to it. Then I like his inquisitive human sympathies: history so dull because of its battles & laws; & sea voyages in books so dull because the traveller will describe beauties instead of going into the cabins & saying what sailors looked liked, wore, eat, said: how they behaved. . . . (Diary II, 130)

She applauds the recognizable emotions of Hunt, his natural reaction to death—the release of pain through laughter that Woolf realized she herself would have expressed, if allowed, at her own mother's death[22]—and the cataloguing of the commonplace items that constitute his "inquisitive human sympathies." These items are the basis of another kind of history, appreciated by Woolf in 1921 as Rosamond Merridew appreciates Jasper Martyn's idiosyncratic "ancestor worship." She says of it: "They are, he would have told me, all flesh and blood like I am; and the fact that they have been dead for four or five centuries makes no more diffence [*sic*] to them, than the glass you place over a canvas changes the picture beneath it" (CSF, 44).

Similarly, Jasper Martyn adds of his "grandmother" Joan that she was "not remarkable" (CSF, 45). His simplicity, which keeps him from seeing the antiquarian value of his family treasures, actually masks a profound grasp of the nature of human consciousness, central to this story, and to all of Woolf's later fiction and criticism. Indirectly, he thus restates a tenet of Wordsworthian Romanticism—the importance of the ordinary and of the "not remarkable" mind that engages it.

Joan contrasts, throughout her journal, the ordinary and solid world of accounts, impending marriage contracts, and the sometimes sordid one of poor peasants, highway robbers, and "Sanctuary" men, "prowling out of bounds in search of food" (CSF, 52), with Lydgate's fictive world. The cottage of the peasant woman Beatrice Somers, "more like the burrow of some rabbit on the heath than the house of a man" (CSF, 52), is "a nightmare" (CSF, 53) to Joan from which she is happy to awake upon entering her own clean and prosperous home. However, a sympathy for the poor, unlike the chief steward Anthony's disdain when he speaks to Beatrice "as he would have spoken to some animal who had strong claws and a wicked eye" (CSF, 53), begins to glimmer in Joan as she recognizes that the lines in her mother's face "and some of the sternness of her voice, had come there . . . because she always saw not far from her such sights as [Joan] had seen today" (CSF, 53). Perhaps Julia Stephen's untiring concern for the poor served as the model for this description. However, Wordsworth's lines from "Tintern Abbey," in which the joys of unexamined childhood are contrasted with the deeper pleasure, because mixed with pain, of maturity's achieved ability to examine, suggest the basis for the entire episode of the visit to the cottages.

> . . . For nature then
> (The coarser pleasures of my boyish days,
> And their glad animal movements all gone by)
> To me was all in all. . . .
> . . . That time is past,
> And all its aching joys are now no more,
> And all its dizzy raptures. Not for this
> Faint I, nor mourn nor murmur; other gifts
> Have followed; for such loss, I would believe,
> Abundant recompense. For I have learned

> To look on nature, not as in the hour
> Of thoughtless youth; but hearing oftentimes
> The still, sad music of humanity,
> Nor harsh, nor grating, though of ample power
> To chasten and subdue. . . .
>
> (Wordsworth, 109–10)

Joan establishes one term of the Wordsworthian comparison between youth and age when she describes her walk with her brother Jeremy and the steward Anthony to the cottages.

> He [Anthony] is for ever trampling our fields, and knows them better and loves them more, so I tell him, than any human creature. . . . And, as we have trotted by his side since we could walk alone, some of his affection has become ours too; Norfolk and the parish of Long Winton in Norfolk is to me what my own grandmother is; a tender parent, dear and familiar, and silent to whom I shall return in time. O how blessed it would be never to marry, or grow old; but to spend one's life innocently and indifferently among the trees and rivers which alone can keep one cool and childlike in the midst of the troubles of the world! Marriage or any other great joy would confuse the clear vision which is still mine. And at the thought of losing that, I cried in my heart, 'No, I will never leave you — for a husband or a lover,' and straightway I started chasing rabbits across the heath with Jeremy and the dogs. (CSF, 52)

Wordsworth's ruminations terminate fruitfully, not in chasing rabbits (Wordsworth's "glad animal movements" are foregone by the time of the writing of the poem) but in his embracing of maturity and philosophic wisdom. For Joan the process of moving from the pleasures of childhood's joyful spontaneity and its rejection of the responsibilities of maturity to an acceptance of them is delayed until she returns from bearing witness to the suffering of humanity through the visit to Beatrice Somers. The sense of community she begins to feel enters into her description and metaphor-making as well.

Possibly the summer of 1480 was a hiatus in the ducal wars that had plagued England for the previous twenty-five years. Certainly, Joan's appreciation of ordinary life seems to have returned with the arrival home of her father and brothers from London. Whatever the cause, the minstrel Richard's inspiration or her father's presence, her susceptibility to "figures," the heightened sensitivity, that is, of her imagination, is apparent.

Figures are particularly important in Joan's description of the pilgrimage to Walsingham that she now makes to express her thankfulness. The Wordsworthian trope, the "solid globes of crystal," now becomes thematically significant. For as Joan walks to Walsingham, her examination of her feelings, which she has compared with her metaphorically walking "in a wide space within the covers of Master Richard's manuscript," is, indeed, one of the sights mysteriously promised by Richard to those who but look. Her feelings, the globes of crystal containing the "round ball of coloured earth and air, in which tiny men and women laboured," *are* her imagination enriched by the contemplation of ordinary men and women working on the earth. The landscape, through which she literally walks, is "a soft and luxurious land, glowing like a painted book" (CSF, 58). Her life, now that she is ecstatically alive to the miracle of the ordinary, has become an illuminated manuscript.[23]

Joan's sense that real writing is about romantic princes and princesses begins to founder as she describes the preparations for her unromantic marriage to the elderly Sir Amyas. She thinks at first that her life is nothing but the uncompelling workaday world "at the time of the Civil Wars" (CSF, 59). Joan describes her mother's "theory of ownership" (CSF, 59), attention to which must take the place of Joan's "reading of Princesses" when she is a busy and responsible married woman. However, from the romantic point of view, Joan is uncompelled by it. Her mother uses wave metaphors, "turbulent waters" and "tides," which must be kept from the land and that "one day . . . will abate" (CSF, 59). Her figures remind us of Joan's own "crashing waves" at the beginning of the journal, meant to convey the danger of the times. But her mother draws on such images for her account of a millennial reality of peace and democracy in a future prepared for by women like her. Of her mother's theory, Joan reports:

> . . . deeply though I honour my mother and respect her words, I cannot accept their wisdom without a sigh. She seems to look forward to nothing better than an earth rising solid out of the mists that now enwreathe it. . . . Then she would dream of certain great houses . . . and there would be cheer for guest or serving man at the same table with the Lord.
> And you would ride through fields brimming with corn, and there would be . . . cottages of stone for the poor. As I write this down, I see that it is good; and we should do right to wish it. (CSF, 60)

Besides reinforcing Joan's sense of the inalienable rights of men, first developed when she visited the cottages with Anthony, the surprising element of Joan's description is her declaration that her own writing makes her *see* the truth and goodness of her mother's vision. Thus, while the seductiveness of fantasy still lingers, the ordinary as subject begins to prevail for Joan who adds: "Yet what it is that I want, I cannot tell, although I crave for it, and in some secret way, expect it" (CSF, 60).

Joan's developing self-conscious sense of authorship is made even more important in "Last Pages" through the record of her conversation with her father concerning the importance of using her writing skill to record history. But the two do more than discuss Giles Martyn's desire to add a description of himself to the historical record. He ends by saying: "My fathers were much as I am. . . . Why they might walk in at the door this moment, and I should know 'em, and should think it nothing strange" (CSF, 61).

This conversation impresses upon Joan and equally upon us the sense of the repetitiveness of ordinary life, of the similarity between the present generation and her ancestors, the idea of history first expressed by Jasper Martyn to Rosamond Merridew. And so the story, in its insistence on the value of recording such "immemorable" existence and consciousness of it, has come full circle. That it should be her father who strengthens Joan's conviction of this truth is significant as is his injunction, "'Well then Joan, you must keep your writing, . . . or rather, I must keep it for you. . . . our descendants shall have cause to respect one of us at least'" (CSF, 61).

Giles then asks Joan to accompany him to the church, where, he says, "'I must see to the carving on my father's tomb'" (CSF, 61),[24] a request that is reminiscent of Jasper Martyn's guided tour for Miss Merridew of his ancestral portraits. Joan's thoughts, as she walks, are turned to her pride in her writing: "there were few women in Norfolk who could do the like" (CSF, 61). Only her pride has kept her at her labors "For, truly, there is nothing in the pale of my days that needs telling; and the record grows wearisome" (CSF, 61). The pull of the fantastic, the desire to write about "Knights and Ladies and of adventures in strange lands" (CSF, 62) is still strong despite her father's commendation of her writing about the diurnal round. However, this is her last expression of such a desire. Fittingly, her final embrace of the wonder of ordinary life and the fiction that depends on it is effected through a transition that may well be based on Wordsworth's *Guide*. For Joan's "Captains" and "soldiery" (CSF, 62) seen in the clouds seem a reworking of one of Wordsworth's stories of a similar exercise of the imagination in the *Guide*.

While we were gazing around, 'Look,' I exclaimed, 'at yon ship upon the glittering sea!' 'Is it a ship?' replied our shepherd-guide. 'It can be nothing else,' interposed my companion. . . . The Guide dropped the argument; but before a minute was gone he quietly said, 'Now look at your ship; it is changed into a horse.'. . . . We laughed heartily; and, I hope, when again inclined to be positive, I may remember the ship and the horse upon the glittering sea; and the calm confidence, yet submissiveness, of our wise Man of the Mountains. (Wordsworth's Guide, 114–15)

The movement from the fantastic to reliance on the wisdom of his guide, the down-to-earth "Man of the Mountains," is mirrored in Joan's story, which also ends in reliance on her realistic mother's opinion. Describing the clouds as shapers of the fantastic, she adds: "But as my mother would say, the best stories are those that are told over the fire side. . . . I have always thought that such stories came partly out of the clouds, or why should they stir us more than any thing we can see for ourselves? It is certain that no written book can stand beside them" (CSF, 62). Reality is more interesting than fantasy. Joan allies herself with the tradition of writing about the ordinary of which she is the fictional ancestress. Wordsworth's self-imposed task was to give this assertion concrete form in *Lyrical Ballads*. When she says "No book can stand beside" the tales of true life, she is thinking of books that have already been written, for none, in her experience, takes the ordinary as subject. However, her assertion "that such stories come partly out of the clouds" suggests Virginia's attraction to writing, which takes the real and historical for its subject but orders it according to the greater freedoms of fiction.

She renders her final reconciliation of history and imagination through Joan's desire, in the church, to "do some small act that would give [the ancestors in their sarcophagi] pleasure. It must be something secret, and unthought of—a kiss or a stroke, such as you give a living person" (CSF, 62). For Joan and her father, as for Jasper Martyn after them, these dead ancestors are "living," familiarized and loved through an act of imagination. For Virginia the imaginative act of writing was equally one of love, dedicated to her father, her own ancestor, who had empowered her.

2
Epilogue: "Anon" and "The Reader"

"How am I burdened with what they drew from the earth; memories; possessions. This is the burden that the past laid on me, last little donkey in the long caravanserai crossing the desert."

—Between the Acts

"THE Journal of Mistress Joan Martyn" records the growth of Virginia Stephen's imaginative mind. With its fictive autobiographical elements, it is a prelude to her full-scale although still fictive "Prelude," *To the Lighthouse*. On 1 February 1941, more than thirty-four years after finishing that story, she wrote to Ethel Smyth of a project in which she was currently engaged—one that she saw unfolding, but not, perhaps, finishing, in the midst of the cataclysmic events of World War II.

> Did I tell you I'm reading the whole of English literature through? By the time I've reached Shakespeare the bombs will be falling. . . . Thank God, as you would say, one's fathers left one a taste for reading! Instead of thinking, by May we shall be—whatever it may be: I think, only three months left to read Ben Jonson, Milton, Donne, and all the rest! (Letters VI, 466)

That project was not casual, having a more formal purpose: the writing of a history of English literature, the book that would thread "a necklace through English life and lit." She had gotten as far as a number of incomplete drafts of two essays, "Anon" and "The Reader," before her death in March 1941. With a certain poetic justice, these two essays were not published until 1979, in the same issue of *Twentieth Century Literature* as "The Journal of Mistress Joan Martyn."

This short story and the essays in literary history bracket Woolf's lifelong interest in the relationship between the pressures of social forces and the imaginative production of writers, famous and obscure, and in her successful merging of history and imaginative writing. They also reveal Woolf's belief that a study of the lives of the relatively poor and unknown has always yielded the richest understanding of historical processes and their evolution toward the present moment.

The two essay fragments are the beginnings, according to Woolf's notes, for a summing up and explanation of the growth of the collective imagination of the culture. If in ". . . Joan Martyn" Wordsworthian tropes and values color her fiction, then the mature writer, more than ever mindful of them, took a leap beyond the Romantics in her last critical essays into the operations of consciousness responsible both for the individual creative act and the historical development of culture.

Four assumptions of Woolf's cultural theory rest and build on the tenets of Romantic critical theory and praxis: the nature of the impulse that gives rise to aesthetic production, the development of the vernacular, the movement from "conviction" to self-consciousness in artists and readers, and the correlated development of temporal nonlinearity, both in the structuring and "reading" of the aesthetic product. All these issues are related, as Woolf reveals in her narrative of aesthetic-historical development, from its beginnings in the anonymous oral tradition to its later flourishing in printed, "authored" work.

Woolf began this project with essays on the writer and the reader.[1] Even in the oral tradition of "Anon," like Master Richard in ". . . Joan Martyn," "singing his song at the back door" (A & R, 383), the anonymous songmaker and storyteller in the broadest sense is a reader, and every listener, literally adding to, and inscribing him or herself in the song or text, is a writer. Woolf had written in "The Novels of Thomas Hardy" of the historical continuation of this collaboration: "It is for the reader, steeped in the impressions, to supply the comment" (SCR, 254). These two collusive activities—reading and writing—are indissolubly linked and form that intricate web of ideas and attitudes that define a culture. Thus, as Woolf says in "The Reader": "So many private people are pressing their weight of unexpressed emotion upon the writers consciousness" (A & R, 398). Although emphasizing the interdependence of these occupations, as she did in many other essays, Woolf also suggests the dialectical relationship between cultural production and all the values of a society. Indeed, by privileging language and imaginative production and engagement in her analysis of historical development, and by arguing that they are of "a piece with the instinct that sets us preserving our bodies, with clothes, food, roofs, from destruction" (A & R, 403), Woolf made her unique contribution to cultural theory. Her notes for "Reading at Random," her provisional name for this project, make her intention clear:

> It would begin from the writers angle .. That is: we all feel the desire to create. The curiosity to know about others in the same condition. This wd. lead to an introduction: about the germ of creation: its thwartings: our society: interruption: conditions. . . . I shd. therefore take a poem & build up round it the society wh. [c] helps it. (A & R, 375–76)

Although Romantic criticism deals with the question of the origins of art and the aesthetic impulse, the Romantic "expressive theory" of aesthetic production is primarily concerned with the contemporary poet and the nature of the "private" and individual experience of creation.

> . . . the central tendency of the expressive theory may be summarized in this way: A work of art is essentially the internal made external, resulting from a creative process operating under the impulse of feeling, and embodying the combined product of the poet's perceptions, thoughts, and feelings. The primary source and subject matter of a poem, therefore, are the attributes and actions of the poet's own mind; or if aspects of the external world, then these only as they are converted from fact to poetry by the feelings and operations of the poet's mind. ('Thus the Poetry . . .' Wordsworth wrote, 'proceeds whence it ought to do, from the soul of Man, communicating its creative energies to the images of the external world.'). . . . The paramount cause of poetry is not, as in Aristotle, a formal cause, determined primarily by the human actions and qualities imitated; nor, as in neoclassical criticism, a final cause, the effect intended upon the audience; but instead an efficient cause—the impulse within the poet of feelings and desires seeking expression, or the compulsion of the creative imagination which, like God the creator, has its internal source of motion.[2]

Wordsworth's contemporaries translated the experience of the living poet back into prehistory to argue that the spontaneous overflow of powerful feeling, the Wordsworthian wellspring of poetic production, was similarly the basis of all poetry. Thus, they believed the origin of poetry to be "in the passionate, and therefore, naturally rhythmic and figurative, outcries of primitive men."[3] Virginia Woolf similarly built on the expressive element, the impulse to make song, but supported by the vast amount of reading she was doing for her project, she shifted the emphasis in her essays from the personal and the private need for utterance to the "social" experience of aesthetic production that rests in "the common belief" (A & R, 384). This shift establishes a new efficient cause for creation in the social relationship between "author" and "reader" and is not to be confused with a final cause—the effect intended upon the audience—of neoclassical theory. Her insight depends on the sociologically and historically driven literary criticism of Leslie Stephen and, as well, on her understanding of the notion of "communal psychology,"[4] a concept undefined and unexplored until the end of the nineteenth century.

Wordsworth vaguely suggests the idea of communal psychology when he terms the site of the origin of poetic utterance "the soul of Man." The poet is elevated, through this locution, into representative man and, by extension, becomes synonymous with "men." Wordsworth thus moves effortlessly from the individual to the group. His conflation is reasonable because he believed the place of the poet in relation to other men to be that of first among equals. What is true for the poet is, therefore, only a little less true for ordinary men. However, since in his judgment the poet and other men are alike in kind and differ only in degree, ordinary men cannot logically be the motive force behind a radical alteration in the poetic voice. Similarly, although in 1800 Wordsworth believed that the poet was capable of morally challenging the political, social, and cultural deconstruction of present-day civilization, he did not fully recognize that these latter forces, as in a reversible chemical reaction, might be equally responsible for the creation of his own and others' newly emerging poetic voices. Although personally moved by the possibilities for humanity promised by the French Revolution, in delineating his new poetic credo he did not suggest that his methods and goals were a product of the social and political forces that propelled the French bourgeoisie into action—that is, the emerging communal psychology of democracy. Rather he explained his own fervent belief in the principles of democracy, outlined in "A Letter to the Bishop of Llandaff,"[5] as the result of growing up among simple country people, where "Distinction lay open to all that came / And wealth and titles were in less esteem / Than talents, worth, and prosperous industry" (Wordsworth, 309: *The Prelude,* Book IX, 11. 230–32). Further, he was free of the class prejudices that might have formed his views had he been reared among aristocrats in the city (Wordsworth, 309: 11. 215–22). The "auxiliar light" that "Came from [his] mind" was "for the most, / Subservient strictly to external things / With which it communed" (Wordsworth, 215). From his perspective his poetic revolution and the political upheaval in France were coeval but not causally connected.

However, forty years later, political events in Europe—the Chartist Movement in England, the Risorgimento in Italy, and the unification of the German principalities, for example—created a clearer intellectual recognition that communal psychology had a real existence of its own, capable of affecting the individual. In the case of Teutonic identity, the myth-based, emotionally driving music of Richard Wagner was an element in a dialectic, both creating and created by the cultural and political psychology.[6]

The idea of "group consciousness" was later explored in a literary context by Jules Romains whose work Virginia Woolf knew and had reviewed.[7] Allen McLaurin reminds us of the moments, particularly in novels like *Mrs. Dalloway* and *The Waves*, in which Woolf breaks away from the commonsense theory that lies behind William James's notion of "stream of consciousness"—that consciousness is private and unique to a given individual—and moves in the direction of Romains's *Unanimisme*—an exploration of the rise of feelings in individuals that unite members of a group. The sense that at her dinner in *To the Lighthouse* Mrs. Ramsay has created unity or a sort of group consciousness among her guests is an example of the phenomenon, as is the audience's reaction to the pageant in *Between the Acts*. However, the more politically complex concept of a diffusive communal belief surfaces as a substantive issue in Woolf's literary criticism.

Although the efforts of Romains, and Woolf after him, cast such group feeling in a positive light, McLaurin also points out that Leonard Woolf, Virginia, and other members of Old Bloomsbury had been influenced, as well, by a book on group consciousness by Wilfred Trotter, *Instincts of the Herd in Peace and War*,[8] which takes a dimmer view of the collective behavior of humans. McLaurin quotes Woolf's diary entry for November 1917, both to prove her familiarity with the book and to suggest her growing belief in its ideas.

Old Roger [Fry] takes a gloomy view, not of our life, but of the world's future; but I think I detected the influence of Trotter & the herd, & so I distrusted him. Still, stepping out into Charlotte Street, where the Bloomsbury murder took place a week or two ago, & seeing a crowd swarming in the road & hearing women abuse each other & at the noise others come running with delight—all this sordidity made me think him rather likely to be right. (Diary I, 80)

The base aspects of group behavior are dwelt on in her description of the crowd. However, Leslie Stephen and her husband's idea that forces in society generate the nature, even the genres, of art was a countervailing influence for Woolf who needed, in the dark days of 1940 and 1941, to believe in the possibility of social creation rather than destruction. We can imagine that she was anxious to memorialize such achievements to prove that English culture had a future as well as a past.

Mrs. Dalloway holds the apparently mystic belief that "the unseen part of us . . . might survive, be recovered somehow attached to this person or that, or even haunting certain places after death" (MD, 232). In fact her notion is not otherworldly if, as Woolf herself did, one regards consciousness and its contents as aspects of the world of matter. Woolf's beliefs that social forces inform the nature of aesthetic production and that, conversely, the memory of such production has an influence on those who have been touched by it rest on the assumption that an imaginative impulse is part of the material world. The writing of a group of essays that would explain the creation of a national literature from the point of view of developing consciousness—not merely of individual writers, but of an entire society of auditors and readers—is simultaneously her explanation of the past culture and gage that one will exist in the future. Such a project is Wordsworthian in its effort to make aesthetic and political sense for a threatened society and Shelleyan in its belief that cultural production *is* the salvation of the body politic.

Wordsworth could have viewed the new kind of poetry he was writing—extolling the virtues of the common man and of nature—as a parallel to the flowering in the French Revolution of the political values of eighteenth-century social theorists. He believed in the sanative powers of his poetry, its ability to correct the moral failings of a society facing the pressures created by the growing industrial revolution. In this way his poetry was political. Woolf, however, went further than the Romantics in comprehending the dialectic between art and social forces. She explains the relationship between them more consciously, relying on her father's position, last enunciated in *English Literature and Society in the Eighteenth Century.*[9] Although Leslie Stephen was never a Marxist, he was, perhaps, the first English critic to appreciate the role played by social and political forces in determining the nature of culture and its productions.[10] John Bicknell, in his essay on Stephen's *English Thought in the Eighteenth Century,* notes of Stephen's theory of the history of ideas: "the immediate causes of change are to be sought rather in social development than in the activity of a few speculative minds. A complete history of thought would have to take into account the social influences . . . of the varying phases of opinion."[11] For example, Stephen believed that we learn most fully how "ordinary people believed in devils and in a material hell lying just beneath our feet"[12] from Dante's vision in the *Divina Commedia* rather than from Aquinas because

> The great poet unconsciously reveals something more than the metaphysician. . . . the imagery which he creates may still be a symbol of thoughts and emotions which are as interesting now as they were six hundred years ago. This man of first-rate powers shows us . . . the real charm of the accepted beliefs for him, and less consciously for others. . . . they really laid so powerful a grasp upon him because they . . . express[ed] the hopes and fears, the loves and hatreds, the moral and political convictions which were dearest to him.[13]

Dante lives on, unlike the philosophers of his day, because his language embodies the emotions of common men and women and directs us back to our cultural past through the experiences we share with them. Literature does more than take the common man as subject or transform, by its example, his moral being. Stephen, and Woolf after him, regarded it as political in the broadest sense in that it expresses the aspirations, the system of belief of the dominant class, which inheres in a culture at a particular period. If Leslie Stephen tried to demonstrate the vitality of the connection between literary expression and contextual social forces, then Woolf's project, "to thread a necklace through English life and lit," was equally an attempt to make sense of these cultural aspirations, to "tell" them, in both senses of the word, like rosary beads and like a story. As her letter to Ethel Smyth suggests, the business of telling, which requires the antecedent and very difficult effort to make sense of history, was synonymous for her with securing personal salvation through the busy and absorbing work of reading through masses of material. However, more spiritual salvation was inextricably connected with arguing for the vitality and durability of this culture, now beset by the destructive enemy across the English Channel. Although the final form of this group of essays remains unclear,[14] she began with "Anon," commemorating early English literature with its roots in the common consciousness of the culture.

Considering the uncertainty of Woolf's plans for "Reading at Random," or "Turning the Page," as she later called it, or even for the one essay "Anon," we must treat all the material as valid expressions of her ideas which, with successive revisions, would naturally be condensed in places and expanded in others, as she read and thought more. In constructing a text for "Anon" from the manuscripts and typescripts, Brenda Silver has drawn primarily from Woolf's third, or "C" version, as she has named it, but where sense requires it, has included passages from the prior versions. However, her notes to the essay include extensive passages from the earlier drafts, which often correspond to the plan Woolf created in "Notes for Reading at Random," the record of an outline for an entire book of which "Anon" and "The Reader" would have been two essays.

Material from the second typescript of "Anon," which Silver omits from her "definitive" text but includes in the notes, brings together the Romantic expressive theory of creation, the Shelleyan political or messianic function of art, the materialist theories of aesthetic production of Leslie Stephen, and the notion of group consciousness that determines the shape of a particular "song." After beginning with a description of the primeval forest of Britain, Woolf continued:

. . . .2. . . .

The heart of this vast proliferation of printed pages remains the song. The song has the same power over the reader in the 20th century as over the hearer in the 11th. To enjoy singing, to enjoy hearing the song, must be the most deep-rooted, the toughest of human instincts comparable for persistency with the instinct of self preservation. It is indeed the instinct of self preservation. Only when we put two and two together—two pencil strokes, two written words, two bricks {notes}[15] do we overcome dissolution and set up some stake against oblivion. The passion with which we seek out these creations and attempt endlessly, perpetually, to make them is of a piece with the instinct that sets us preserving our bodies, with clothes, food, roofs, from destruction.

But the printing press brought into existence forces that cover over the original song—books themselves, and the readers of books. If science were so advanced that we could at this moment X ray the singers mind we should find a nimbus surrounding the song; a stream of influences. Some we can name—education; class; the pressure of society. But they are so many, and so . . . interwoven and so obscure that it is simpler to invent for them nonsense names—say Nin Crot and Pully. Nin Crot and Pully are always at their work, tugging, obscuring, distorting. Some are visible only to the writer. Others only to the reader. . . . The song beneath is only to be discovered in a flash of recognition . . . when their beards bristle; [or when] . . . a thrill runs down the nerves of the thigh. . . .

. . . .3. . . .

> That babbling, child like, story telling singer, that gossip at the farm
> yard door, that innocent eyed, naked, alternately lustful, obscene and
> devout singer, who was now and again a great artist died in 147[8]{7},
> And with him died the part of his song that the audience sang—the
> voice that filled in pauses, and added sometimes a nonsensical chorus.
> (A & R, 403–4)

Anon, the singer at the back door of the "great house" and the
only door of the hovel, symbolizes the universal impulse to express
oneself through song or art. The instinct to give form to and convey
outward the emotions—the heart of expressive theory—is, however, quickly transformed by Woolf into another instinct: self-
preservation. This second instinct has, furthermore, political dimension and ramifies for Woolf, writing not just about personal,
but about group or cultural, survival.

Woolf gives prominence to the Wordsworthian assumption—that
the poet is a man speaking to other men—through her depiction
of the audience's response to the song of Anon and, later in the
essay, to the discussion of the development of the vernacular as
the medium of aesthetic expression. In the present the beard bris-
tles, the thrill runs down the thigh as we hear the song. But the
audience of Anon contributed its own chorus, "bearing the burden" of the song along with the singer. This choral addition was
the expression of group consciousness that equally accounts for
the forces of "Nin Crot and Pulley" (A & R, 404), those "invisible
influences" in society which both inform art and create a context
for it. Thus the Romantic individual expressive impulse becomes
the common belief, aesthetic production occurring only in the context of, and revealing, those social relations.

Woolf avoided a conventional approach to history yet wrote a
history of English literature by setting out to extrapolate the social
and political realities of the quotidian and transforming them,
imaginatively, into poetry. To this end she began the C draft by
quoting from G. M. Trevelyan's *History of England* (1926). "'For
many centuries after Britain became an island' the historian says
'the untamed forest was king. Its moist and mossy floor was hidden
from Heavens eye by a close drawn curtain woven of innumerable
tree tops'" (A & R, 382). What appealed to her about this passage,
we can imagine, is the historian's word painting. Through it she
could concretize the prehistorical reality with which she chose to
begin her account. "On those matted boughs innumerable birds
sang," she continues, "but their song was only heard by a few skin

clad hunters in the clearings. . . . But the tree had to be felled; and a hut made from its branches before the human voice sang too" (A & R, 382). The imitation of bird song, perhaps the inspiration for the voice of the human singer, as in a Romantic etiology, could not be a motive force until some degree of social organization or community had come to exist. Thus, for Woolf, art was always the product of a community of men with their common belief.

The metaphor that expresses this common belief is another variant of the Romantic metaphor for mind that makes the objective world continuous with the mind's projection of itself.

> It was Anon who gave voice to the old stories, who incited the peasants when he came to the back door. . . . He led them to the haunted tree; to the well. . . . If we could see the village as it was before Chaucers time . . . we should see tracks across the fields joining manor house to hovel, and hovel to church. . . . But there was also the other less visible connection—the common belief. That track between the houses in the village has been grown over,—like the track along which the pilgrims road to Canterbury,—no one rides that way now. But before Chaucers time it was trod daily. . . . (A & R, 383–84)

The paths worn on the ground are a physical extension of the common belief—the "paths" of the mind. When Woolf says "no one rides that way now," we feel the words slide in meaning between the literal and figurative. Virginia Stephen had superficially examined those literal, physical connections in ". . . Joan Martyn" through Joan and the steward Anthony's visit across the fields to the primitive hovel of the peasants. The "A" draft of "Anon," even more clearly than the "C," expresses the connection between the track on the ground and the track through the mind. There Woolf says of the Elizabethan manor house like Penshurst:

> Could we see it as it is said that the airman sees a village <field> from the air with the scars of other villages <old roads> and other houses on it. we should see the great house connected with the village. . . . But there was also the other connection—the common belief. That bond between the great house and the small has faded. . . . So the scholars tell us of the roads now faded in the mind. (A & R, 406)

Woolf's metaphor for mind and its products—emotional ideas or ideated feelings, the common belief—suggests the nerves and synapses of brain circuitry. But cerebral connections issue in material ritual. Joan, on her way along the road, that scar on the ground, to worship Our Lady at Walsingham, transforms the collective or common belief into physical reality. She translates the experience through a metaphor for art, the Wordsworthian crystal globes that, like the pages of Master Richard's manuscript, contain imaginative worlds—tiny men and women laboring to make a life, a community, for each other. We see that what had been an element in a story of 1906 became a consciously examined cultural phenomenon in 1940.

Although Woolf mentions neither "burden" nor "ground," terms for the chorus of the song, both imply social purpose and community. Similarly, they suggest the very unmetaphorical common paths (scars on the ground) described by Woolf that, in their turn, through purposeful travel on them, made possible an expression of "the other less visible connection," the common belief. Woolf traces through the centuries the effort to make song, shared by Anon and his/her audience, as the English language begins to serve both the peasants and the people living in the great house, who historically had derived their art from across the channel in France or from ancient Greece and Rome.

Woolf argues that the growing use of the vulgar tongue as the medium of exchange between the common and aristocratic elements of society and the innovation in the technology of production determined the history of the culture. For without the elevation of English into the language of artistic expression, there could have been no developing self-consciousness of the creative act.

She proves her point by transforming historical source-texts into imaginative narrative, intuiting the displacement of Latin by English from the priest Hugh Latimer's sermons. Thus she tells his personal tale and the history of the culture, shaping a story "of flesh and blood" (A & R, 387).

Despite the existence of printed books for more than half a century, Latimer, making his rounds of the country parishes found, in 1549, "the door [of the Church] fast locked against him" and the people "gone abroad to gather for Robin Hood," "a Traitor, and a Thief," in his estimation (A & R, 386). He therefore "shut his book and went out among the poor; into the prisons, into the fields. 'The cry of the workmen is come up into my eares' he said. . . . He found the poor without a goose or a pig for the great were enclosing the fields" (A & R, 386). Although Woolf is writing about attitudes that brought about vast historical change, she makes her language richly concrete with the words Latimer used to influence his auditors. In telling his story, she deconstructs the Romantic metaphor of the illumination of mind and external world, revealing its real physical basis in the particular case of Latimer's life and death.

There is only a short pace left him before he too will stand outside the Bocardo at Oxford and feel the flames on his own flesh. So he pours out his anger; so he lights up the state of England . . . in a voice that stumbles, that uses the plain language of the farm. . . . And yet for all his urgency, his severity, he is a man of flesh and blood. He cracks his joke. He tells his story. . . . But he sees . . . what superstition and ignorance are rife in the land. It is for light and learning that he cries. (A & R, 387)

The ultimate illumination or extension of himself is not merely of the mind but of his entire body, consumed by the flames of his martyrdom. The poor were deeply enmeshed in their superstitions. He therefore "went about England preaching in English, no matter if he preached on horseback or stood under a tree . . . or preaching to the King in person" though he might be brought "to the faggot" (A & R, 387). Woolf's transformation of Latimer's sermons into historical narrative represents the Romantic engagement with the events of the quotidian world and the metamorphosis of the merely ordinary into the extraordinary. Her attraction to Latimer, who decried the condition of England, equally adumbrates the Romantic democratic tradition: "while the peasants are starving, and continuing their gross superstitions, he sees everywhere the great houses rising" (A & R, 388) with their "luxury, [their] immorality" (A & R, 388).

Wordsworth's insistence on the importance of describing "incidents and situations from common life . . . in a selection of language really used by men" (Wordsworth, 446) is the main thread in Woolf's argument here and after when she writes of the Elizabethans. She principally directs her attention to their language, remarking, as in "The Strange Elizabethans," that these people "were silent. There is no little language nothing brief, intimate, colloquial. When they write the rhythm of the Bible is in their ears. It makes their speech unfamiliar" (A & R, 388).

Wordsworth, with a very specific agenda for language, complained of the distancing effect of the poetic diction of the Augustan age. Woolf argues that Elizabethan written language obscured not only the expression of the "common belief" but also the doings in the great house.

They [wrap themselves] about in a cumbrous garment when they [try] to talk. . . . we cannot hear the rough English voice that they heard at the back door. the voice of . . . the minstrel. Nor can we see the paths that led to the well and the tree. . . . The gay and sumptuous house full of oaths and coarseness and also of learning, of courtesy, is silent; a house full of furniture and finery but without inhabitants. (A & R, 389)

Thus, although Woolf is able to make a story of Latimer's sermons because his voice reveals his "curious sympathy for the human" and "tells his story," she cannot turn other Elizabethan source-texts into narrative, precisely because they do not equally tell theirs. The quotidian world is not seen through the stiffness and formality of Elizabethan prose. Lady Ann Bacon "admonishes; she exhorts. The actual object—it is a basket of . . . strawberries is approached circuitously ceremoniously" (A & R, 388–89). The written words are still of the oral tradition: "they could not . . . follow the pace of the speaking voice. They could not enter into the private world" (A & R, 389).

Yet in another way the formal, written, and printed language of the Elizabethan Edmund Spenser struck a blow against the unconscious Anon. Spenser, the first poet to whom Woolf attributes self-consciousness about the English poetic tradition, "was separate . . . from his audience. They no longer joined in the song and added their own verses to the poem" (A & R, 388).[16]

Thus Woolf, deploying Wordsworth's spots of time on the "macro" scale, opens up a corridor of memory, connecting the present with the infancy of the culture. Among animals only humans have the imagination necessary to envision inwardly the continuity of consciousness. Woolf has employed this gift of imagination, aware of Wordsworth's sense of this spiritual resource. As she wrote "Anon," she reverted in letters and diaries to the idea that for her and for her whole society there was no future beyond this dark night of its soul when facing the threat of a German invasion. In a letter to Ethel Smyth of 1 March 1941, she wrote that she was

at the moment trying, without the least success, to write an article or two for a new Common Reader. I am stuck in Elizabethan plays. I cant move back or forwards. . . . Thats why I cant break into politics. . . .
If you want to picture me at the moment then you must strew the floor with mouldy dramatists. . . . Do you feel, as I do, when my head's not on this impossible grindstone, that this is the worst stage of the war? . . . I was saying to Leonard, we have no future. . . . What I feel is the suspense when nothing actually happens. (Letters VI, 475)

Yet from Woolf's letters and diaries and from "Anon" itself, we can also extrapolate: a culture that can remember from where it comes has a chance of surviving. Such memory is inextricably bound to self-consciousness—the greatest of the Romantic legacies.

Consciousness of consciousness is at the heart of Woolf's investigation in "Anon" and all her other critical writing and fiction. We see its importance here when she ends by saying, "we must turn to one of these commentators who tell us so much about the invisible influences" (A & R, 404, "A" draft). To write history is necessarily to be conscious of the relation of the past to one's present. But to write history is not necessarily to be equally conscious of the activity of writing. Woolf's effort to write about writing about history represents a further degree of consciousness, the self-consciousness of the poet or artist who, in the manner of the Romantics, uses words centered on the creative act itself. Thus Woolf, like contemporary historiographers, has advanced beyond "these commentators," for example, William Harrison, one of the contributors to Holinshed's *Chronicles* (A & R, 408).

[H]e does not hear the voice of Anon; he scarcely listens even to the song of Chaucers Canterbury pilgrims. For the English past as Harrison saw it, served only to show up the material change—the change that had come over houses, furniture clothing. There was no English literature to show up the change in the mind. (A & R, 385)

Harrison cannot see the intellectual growth of the culture. But through the operations of her Romantically tutored consciousness Woolf does. Her history of the early artist or Anon, "sometimes man; sometimes woman" (A & R, 382), is both the history of the "poet[s'] mind[s]" and of the songs, the culture, they have made.

Thus Woolf creates a continuum, beginning with Anon, who does not distinguish himself from his audience and who is relatively unconsciousness of his art, and ending with the present-day writer's overt consciousness of her own. This, in brief, is the history that Woolf attempts to trace in her essay: the movement from the unself-conscious singer to the beginning of his death with the invention of the printing press that attached his name to the work of art and "brought the past into existence. . . . brought into existence the man who is conscious of the past the man who sees his time, against a background of the past; the man who first sees himself and shows himself to us" (A & R, 385). Her revising of the essay is interesting not merely for the reorganization we see from draft to draft but for her transformation of historical material which allowed her, as in ". . . Joan Martyn," to fly by the nets of hard fact and create a picture rounded by an imaginative narrative that fills up the blank interstices of historical time, making a seamless story. She was, as she said in her diary, trying to find the end of a ball of string and winding out.

In the "C" version of "Anon," Woolf describes the death of Anon by "printing press" by the third page but also registers the paradoxical fact of his preservation through the very instrument that ended the long reign of the oral tradition. Woolf's sensitivity to the texture of language and her own strong sense of story make an imaginative narrative of their own. For she hears in Caxton's printed version of *Morte Darthur* "the voice of Anon murmuring still" (A & R, 384), that is, "the reservoir of common belief that lay deep sunk in the minds of peasants and nobles" (A & R, 384).

Two important ideas dominate her discussion and suggest the continuity of her thought from ". . . Joan Martyn" to the end of her creative life. The first is implied in her assertion: "Everything is stated. The beauty is in the statement, not in the suggestion" (A & R, 384). She demonstrates it with a description from Malory: "under a laurel tree he saw her lie upon a quilt of green samite and a knight with her, and under their heads grass and herbs" (A & R, 384). She continues: "The world is seen without comment; did the writer know what beauty he makes us see?" (A & R, 384). The inverse of this position—that everything is stated—is that "self consciousness had not yet raised its mirror" (A & R, 384), for Malory is a writer of "conviction" who unself-consciously accepts the status quo.[17] The Romantic self-conscious appreciation of the doubleness of the creative act—the mind functioning as both mirror and lamp—was absent from Anon's productions and cannot be found in Malory's oral-tradition writing despite its reproduction in print. Spenser, on the other hand, was self-conscious. He looked back to Chaucer, his opposite in conviction.

> Those depths, those long years of anonymous minstrelsy, folk song, legend and words that had no name attached to them, lay behind him. Their confusion pressed upon him. He was conscious of them. 'For why a Gods name' he exclaimed 'may not we, as else the Greeks, have the kingdom of our own language. . . .'? He was word conscious; an artist; aware of his medium; that words are not paint, nor music; but have their possibilities; their limitations. To be thus aware the writer must have a past behind him. To Spenser the golden age was Chaucers. . . . (A & R, 390)

To look back to Chaucer was also to be more distanced from the common belief than Malory. Spenser saw in *The Faerie Queene*

"Knights and ladies with regret, desire, but not with belief" (A & R, 391).

Woolf argues that Spenser was self-conscious about the creative act as well. She extends the Romantic metaphor for creativity as an outflow of light from its source, the imagination, through her description of his "irradiated" (A & R, 391) poetry and also of Spenser's achievement and failure as she places him "standing on the threshold of the 'gay and sumptuous house' at Penshurst" (A & R, 389), "half in shadow, half in light" (A & R, 391). Unable to "speak through the mouths of individuals," he is the unrealized artist in shadow. But as the first self-conscious writer, "bitterly conscious of his relation [to] the world, of the worlds scorn" (A & R, 391), he is in the light. She thus brings together, through the metaphor of light or its absence, both creation and self-consciousness of the creative act. Spenser's self-consciousness began a tradition leading to her own experiments in exteriorizing character, which would not have been possible without a self-conscious building upon the achievements of others.

Yet the movement from the pictorial epic and, alternately, lyric outcry of Spenser to the exteriorized drama of personal emotion in Woolf's novels depends on the inclusion of the voice of Anon, on the expression of the common belief in "the old play that the peasants acted when spring came and to placate the earth, the mummer hung himself with green leaves" (A & R, 392). Latimer had made "it possible for the gentry and the commons to sit together in one house listening to a play" (A & R, 392). Thus, poetry was rescued "from the leisured listening in the great room" and "from the back door" (A & R, 392) of the great house by the democratic spirit of Anon, by the voice of the poet speaking to men in a selection of their own language.

Woolf, by this point, has arrived at the Elizabethan dramatists, the place where, as she wrote to Ethel Smyth, she was stuck and where, perhaps not coincidentally, she ended her essay. The great pageant of the theater, for her, is the individuation of the speaking voice: "Then the King spoke. . . . At last one man speaks in his own person. The wandering voices are collected, embodied. . . . The world takes shape behind him" (A & R, 393). Yet these words, despite their loveliness, fail, for they are not the words of Tamburlaine. They are, rather, the words of the poet, prompted by the demands of "Nin Crot and Pulley." "The play is still in part the work of the undifferentiated audience, demanding great names, great deeds, simple outlines, and not the single subtlety of one soul" (A & R, 394). Thus, despite the printing press, anonymity and its twin orality remain the dominant force in the theater. The audience, its faculty of criticism unexpressed, and the play itself are all still profoundly part of this tradition. "The lack of Marlowes name, or of Kyds, shows how largely the play was a common product, written by one hand, but so moulded in transition that the author had no sense of property in it. It was in part the work of the audience" (A & R, 395). The presence of the "common people," the "apprentices, citizens, soldiers" (A & R, 395), "draw[s] up the extravagance the hyperbole as a sheet of paper draws up the fire. . . . they . . . made the playwright capable of his great strides, of vast audacities beyond the reach of the solitary . . . writer with his mind fixed upon the reader in the great room" (A & R, 395). Woolf's fire metaphor, expressing the Romantic extension of the poet's mind into the world that it ignites and transforms with its illuminating and heat-producing energy, suggests her belief in the social nature of aesthetic production.

Her argument bears on the characteristic Wordsworthian belief in the importance of the common people to the development of art. But we can also hear the voice of Leslie Stephen as he had sounded it on the Elizabethan theater at the beginning of *English Literature and Society in the Eighteenth Century*. He argues that the theater flourished at this time because it expressed the social and political aspirations of the dominant class, happily in synchrony with the aspirations of the common people. Stephen's macrocosmic view of the genre explains why it is the dominant art form of the period. Woolf's more microcosmic analysis of language, like her father's view, is based on the political dialectic of the two social classes that attended the plays: the common people in the penny, and the aristocracy in the sheltered, seats.

Although the anonymous common belief, the democratic force in the development of the theater, created the hyperbole, the violence, and coarseness of the play, the aristocracy's contempt for the play's subjects, for the playwrights' lives, and for the hyperbolical ranting caused an equally important expansion of language serviceable to the emerging art form. Bacon's self-consciousness about language, revealed in his contemptuous description of plays in "Of Masques and Triumphs"—"'These things be but Toyes'"— created an expanding medium of expression for the theater through the model of his own prose. Woolf says: "Bacons contempt was for hyperbole; not for the art of speech. He was teaching the ranting players to speak slowly, closely, subtly. He was proving that there is another kind of poetry, the poetry of prose. He was bringing the poetry of the mind into being. And thus by increasing the range of the poet, by making it possible for him to express more, he was making an end of anonymity" (A & R, 397).

The union, then, of the "nameless vitality, something drawn from the crowd in the penny seats and not yet dead in ourselves" (A & R, 398), and an increasingly serviceable poetic prose caused the demise of Anon. With it the playwright could produce "individualised . . . single and separate figures" (A & R, 398) recognized by the audience as "our selves," her effort in her own fiction. Woolf has constructed the critically conscious and, therefore, humanizing bridge of memory that spans the centuries of cultural development between Anon and herself.

We owe to Shakespeare this final development of "differentiated" characters, of Henry the Sixth, Hamlet, and Macbeth. Yet Woolf does not regard the dialectical progression as ending with "The Tempest," the most complete flowering of his art. The last words of the essay are "But the play has outgrown the uncovered theatre where the sun beats and the rain pours. That theatre must be replaced by the theatre of the brain. The playwright is replaced by the man who writes a book. The audience is replaced by the reader. Anon is dead" (A & R, 398).

As in ". . . Joan Martyn," Woolf ends this essay with Leslie Stephen in mind. His macrocosmic analysis of the development of the genres in response to the economic and social forces at work in an age is the underlying presence in her assertion that the next age had outgrown the theater, turning for its entertainment to the limitless "theatre of the brain." This gesture of her intellectual respect also creates another bridge—between this and her last essay fragment, "The Reader."

The connection between the two essays suggests Woolf's intention to proceed with the historically seamless movement of "Anon" in the essays that were to follow in "Reading at Random." A unified structure would double her sense of self and cultural continuity from the present to an uncharted and feared future.

Although we recognize Leslie Stephen's presence in Woolf's discussion of the change from the anonymous literature of the early Elizabethan theater to printed and authored books, Hugh Latimer again makes concrete the formal and historical transition from the first to the second essay. Her opening sentence draws on her narrative in "Anon": "The great house that Latimer deplored becomes solid and entire in the pages of Lady Anne Cliffords diary" (A & R, 427). Woolf's fascination with the lesser genres of "literature," biographies and diaries, a passion she shared with Rosamond Merridew of ". . . Joan Martyn," is behind her knowledge of Lady

Anne's life and an important expression of the Romantic attachment to the texture of the diurnal round. As Rosamond Merridew explains her interest in Dame Elizabeth Partridge's desire for stockings as leading to "the reality of mediaeval brains," and from thence to "the centre of all ages: middle beginning or end," Woolf, generalizing on her own interest in such material, wrote of its importance in "How Should One Read a Book?"

> Biographies and memoirs . . . light up innumerable such houses; they show us people going about their daily affairs, toiling, failing, succeeding, eating, hating, loving, until they die. . . .
> But also we can read such books with another aim, not to throw light on literature, not to become familiar with famous people, but to refresh and exercise our own creative powers. (SCR, 261, 263)

This passage illuminates the Romantic desire for articulating the elements of the solid world and for revealing both our own and the writer's creative encounters with it, sparked either by life itself or a specialized instance of it, memoir reading. It also reminds us that Woolf purposely blurs the distinction between writing and reading because she considered them complementary or collusive activities of consciousness. The illumination of the world, the result of the light of the individual mind trained on it—the nature of the mediaeval, or any other, brains of which Miss Merridew speaks—is also joined here by another Romantic issue, equally a feature of "The Reader," namely, the relationship between time and human consciousness.

Woolf was attracted to Lady Anne Clifford of *The Second Common Reader* essays "Donne After Three Centuries" and "How Should One Read a Book?" because Lady Anne is a "common reader," that particular instance of "Nin Crot and Pulley," who, by exerting tugs on a writer, is responsible for cultural production. The story that Woolf makes in "The Reader" of Lady Anne's attachment both to the physical—"as if to solidify her possessions she wrote out inventories of them" (A & R, 427)—and to the spiritual, "excellent Chaucer's book" (SCR, 34), establishes the importance of reading in the lives of the literate aristocracy. Further, Lady Anne's critical spirit was elicited by the act of reading as it was not by going to the theater: "But it is only when she reads that she comments. When she goes to the play she says only 'Supped with my Lord and Lady Arundel and after supper I saw the play of the Mad Lover'" (A & R, 427–28). The subtext of Woolf's discussion of the critical spirit suggests the relationship of consciousness and time. The forwards and backwards play of the mind is now possible as the reader contemplates the text, outmoding the strict chronological progression from the present to the future required by the spectacle of a theatrical event.

Indeed, Woolf asserts that "when the playhouses were shut . . . the reader was born" (A & R, 428). The auditory and visual senses required by the playhouse are replaced by the free play of the imagination that can "deepen and revise the impression" (A & R, 428) of printed words which, in turn, leads to the development of the "metaliterature" of criticism. However, the lack of a large reading public, she says, explains the paucity of literary criticism. This same undeveloped reading public accounts, where such criticism does exist, for its general nature and lack of interest in "particular books and persons" (A & R, 428). "Nin Crot and Pulley" are very much in evidence in this essay.

Of the reader who has become "distinct from the spectator," she says: "His sense of words and their associations develops. A word spelt in the old spelling brings in associations" (A & R, 428). In other places, as in the villagers' historical pageant in *Between the Acts* or in *The Waves*, Woolf argues that the viability of a culture is, in fact, dependent on our "memory" of these associations, causing us to feel one with the group. This cultural phenomenon, on the macroscale, is equivalent to Wordsworth's sense of self as dependent on the corridor created by memory from childhood to maturity.

Yet although these associations may be historical and cultural in character, they are also significantly "nonlinear," taking up, as we muse, the sort of "vertical time" that distracts the reader from real or chronologically progressive events. The reader, in other words, as he becomes more specialized, "attach[ing] himself to certain aspects of the printed words" (A & R, 428), parallels Woolf's own fictive characters who retreat from awareness of the present as they consider certain aspects of their own and others' lives through associative consciousness.

In keeping with her father's dialectical sense of the relation of social forces and cultural production, Woolf makes concrete her idea of the "common belief" by crossing over from a description of the reader to the reader's effect on the writer. The reader's attachment to "certain aspects" of the words exerts a pull on the writer whose way of representing the world through words is, in part, thus determined for him. "And the curious faculty—the power to make places and houses, men and women and their thoughts and emotions visible on the printed page is always changing" (A & R, 428). The assumption of her 1924 essay, "Mr Bennett and Mrs Brown," has paramount political reality in 1940–41 as Woolf, training her eye on the present, says: "His [the reader's] importance can be gauged by the fact that when his attention is distracted, in times of public crisis, the writer exclaims: I can write no more" (A & R, 428).

The faltering of Woolf's project is explained by her belief that in this time of national crisis she was writing for an audience that could attend to nothing but the newspaper. Thus, Isa, in *Between the Acts,* written around the same time: "What remedy was there for her at her age—the age of the century, thirty nine—in books? . . . For her generation the newspaper was a book."[18]

But Woolf's choice of Robert Burton and *The Anatomy of Melancholy,* her example for the development of the book and the presence of the reader "while the play was still on the stage" (A & R, 428), is even more autobiographically revealing. She implies the identity of the self-conscious reader and writer. Not only is Burton "the writer completely conscious of his relation with the reader" (A & R, 429), but the reader is reciprocally conscious of the self-revealing writer. The readers capable of such consciousness are not of that "very large class of perfectly literate people who strip many miles of print yearly from paper yet never read a word" (A & R, 428). Rather, they are like Lady Anne, reading Chaucer's book when in need of solace and finding that "'a little part of his beauteous spirit infuses itself'" (SCR, 34) in them. These readers of active imagination convert the black marks of the text into a voice that says: "I am a bachelor. I am neither rich nor poor. I am a tumbler over of other mens books. I live in college rooms. I am a spectator not an actor" (A & R, 429). When we read in this imaginative way, we also make leaps not possible in the playhouse. We travel over the world with Burton "In pursuit of melancholy . . . though he has never left his college room" (A & R, 429), yet "We are at a remove from the thing treated. We are enjoying the spectacle of melancholy, not sharing its anguish" (A & R, 429).

Such intercourse between writer and reader is possible because of the new sense of time that has replaced the tyrannically chronological progression of the play. Woolf's last paragraph, her last words on art, remarkably conflate her most potent ideas about character, consciousness, and time.

It is here that we develop faculties that the play left dormant. . . . Now the reader is completely in being. He can pause; he can ponder;

he can compare; he can draw back from the page and see behind it a man sitting alone in the centre of the labyrinth of words in a college room thinking of suicide. . . . He can read directly what is on the page, or, drawing aside, can read what is not written. There is a long drawn continuity in the book that the play has not. It gives a different pace to the mind. We are in a world where nothing is concluded. (A & R, 429)

Is it Burton or Woolf or both sitting in a room thinking about suicide? Beyond the answer to this teasing question provoked by Woolf's dramatic decision to end her own life merely weeks after she had written these words, this paragraph is a Rosetta Stone. Through it we can decode the most important aesthetic principles of her work. Burton's book stimulates her to consider ideas absolutely central to the bases of her art which, with remarkable persistency, endured from her early short stories and essays to the end of her life. The sense that consciousness works through time and that the schemata of consciousness are not linear, that memory is central to one's definition of self, that creativity is a self-conscious and self-reflexive act, are Woolf's ideas, founded on the Romantic aesthetic. Perhaps they remain attractive to us today because we have not ceased to be Romantic. The last sentence of this essay fragment, doubly reminding us of the self-referential and indeterminate nature of any text, also suggests important aspects of modernism dependent on Romantic self-consciousness. The following chapters demonstrate the expression of these ideas in the variety of genres that compelled Virginia Woolf's creative attention: the short story, the essay, and the novel.

3

Romantic Transformations: *Night and Day* and the Stories of *Monday or Tuesday*

> Tempted by the sight to continue her imaginative reconstruction of the past, Mrs. Swithin paused; she was given to increasing the bounds of the moment by flights into past or future; or sidelong down corridors and alleys. . . .
>
> —*Between the Acts*

"LIFE," says Woolf in Modern Fiction, "is not a series of gig lamps symmetrically arranged" (CR, 150). Thus, Woolf begins to assess the possibilities for the representation of life, enunciated more positively as she continues: "life is a luminous halo, a semi-transparent envelope surrounding us from the beginning of consciousness to the end" (CR, 150). The experience of living *is* perception, for it is a luminous halo, a source of light, surrounding us but having its origins in consciousness. Woolf thus conflates the imagination and the external world, making them coextensive, as in Romantic metaphors for mind. The trope suggests one of her strategies for representing perception or consciousness, the business of the writer as she has defined it.

Consciousness holds the unique position of being both a part of life and a perceiver of it. Additionally, consciousness, illuminated by its own "halo," sometimes catches itself in the act of perception. A particular variety of such moments Woolf would later call "moments of being." And insofar as they are part of the creative process, they seem to have functioned for her as did Wordsworth's "spots of time" with their "renovating virtue."

The above is a fuller account of creativity than Woolf gives in "Modern Fiction." However, in the context of discussing the creation of a fictional representation of life in this essay, she begins to take the Romantic metaphor for mind and deploy it, not merely as subject, but also as method.

Virginia Woolf's effort to create new possibilities of representation through connecting narrative voice and perceived world marked a period of experimentation prompted by the Woolfs' purchase in 1917 of their first printing press and establishment of their business venture, The Hogarth Press. Her letters reveal that she felt liberated from the expectations of commercial publishers and consequently from the conventions of fiction because she could now publish her own work. "Modern Novels," the original of "Modern Fiction," was written at this time, appearing in *TLS* on 10 April 1919 (CR, 256), just before the publication of her second novel, *Night and Day*.[1]

Yet although Woolf was successful in transforming Romantic metaphors, attitudes, and interests into narrative strategies in the short stories written between 1917 and 1921, limitations of craft rather than any imposed by the world at large hampered her in the longer venue of the novel. Thus, in *Night and Day,* the characteristic Woolfian balancing or fusion of narrating consciousness and world is not much in evidence.

However, there is an exception. Woolf, in *Night and Day,* despite the conventional form of the novel, is actually revolutionary in her representation of gender relations, relying on an interesting conflation of consciousnesses and outer world to prove her point. She inventively makes the case against a Victorian opposition to women's emancipation of all sorts through Romantic metaphors revealing the similarity of women's and men's intellectual capacities and qualities of mind. Her demonstration thus overturns a rigid code of social conventions and distinctions based on gender and destructive of human potential.

The first scenes of *Night and Day* hint at the importance of Romanticism to the entire novel. Ralph Denham, an intellectually promising young man invited to Sunday tea, is shown the literary remains of the great poet Richard Allardyce, Mrs. Hilbery's father. Thus, Woolf opens her novel with a situation reminiscent of Henry James's "The Aspern Papers" in which a literary sleuth attempts to steal the letters and memorabilia of a dead Romantic poet. Readers have assumed that Shelley was the model for James's fictional poet. In Woolf's plot the importance of the literary past and its influence on the present is established as in James's story.

Based on our sense of the representation of present time in the novel—just before World War I—Allardyce would be an early Victorian, and not a Romantic, poet. Yet it seems likely that Woolf wanted to suggest characteristics of the earlier period. The name of Allardyce's poem, "Ode to Winter," and the allusions to his irregular domestic affairs and liaisons, recall the poetic form, subject, and freedom from convention of certain Romantic poets, particularly of Shelley, whose name is mentioned frequently in the novel.[2] Shelley was very probably in Woolf's mind since, as she reports in her diary for 27 January 1917, she had had a discussion about him with Janet Case. She wrote: "We talked about my novel . . . & about Shelley, & Poets & their immorality. She said that in her young days she would have disapproved of Shelley's relations with women—But the old sister dodged in & out, which made conversation about morality uneasy" (Diary I, 29).

Another indication that Woolf modeled Richard Allardyce on the Romantics is that Katharine sees her grandfather as Virginia Woolf, after reading his autobiography, imagined Leigh Hunt to stand in metaphorical relation to herself. Woolf, who called Hunt her "spiritual grandfather," revealing her sense of kinship with Romantic writers, expressed her feelings through Katharine's.

> From hearing constant talk of great men and their works, her earliest conceptions of the world included an august circle of beings to whom she gave the names of Shakespeare, Milton, Wordsworth, Shelley . . . who were . . . much more nearly akin to the Hilberys than to other people. They made a kind of boundary to her vision of life, and played a considerable part in determining her scale of good and bad in her own small affairs. Her descent from one of these gods was no surprise to her. . . .[3]

Of the "moderns" Woolf mentioned no one more than Shelley and Wordsworth in her diaries and letters. The line of descent in Woolf's own life was not, however, as in Katharine's, through her mother, but spiritually through her father, who had introduced Virginia to these poets through his Sunday readings and his incantatory repetition of their verses.

Mrs. Hilbery's passionate veneration of the great poets of the past is part of the general atmosphere of heightened emotion as, from early on, the novel is defined through its romantic interests. Ralph Denham, leaving the Hilberys', walks down the street talking to himself: "'She'll do. . . . Yes, Katharine Hilbery'll do. . . . I'll take Katharine Hilbery'" (NaD, 24). Thus, the novel is charged with romanticism in both senses of the word.

The novel is, in fact, a latter-day version of *A Midsummer Night's Dream* in which the characters romantically sort and resort themselves until they emerge from the woods, or Kew Gardens, in the right couplings. Intensity in certain states of consciousness—for romantics and Romantics—is evident as the romance between Ralph and Katharine "heats" up, their energies metaphorically transformed into light. Woolf makes use of Romantic tropes for mind, seen in as early a work as "The Journal of Mistress Joan Martyn." The imaginations of Katharine, Ralph, and Mary Datchet, as they encounter and name the real world, are coextensive with it through a Romantic irradiation both of life and of the perceiving eye. However, Woolf goes beyond a mere demonstration of the characteristics of the human imagination through her interior portraits of the three main figures.

The romantic action of the novel occurs against a background chorus of Katharine's aunts, chanting the received wisdom of the Victorian patriarchy with regard to relations between the sexes. From two of the aunts we hear:

> "In our young days, Mr. Denham, we used to say that we knew which of our friends would become judges, by looking at the girls they married. And so it was, and so, I fancy, it will always be. . . ."
>
> Mrs. Cosham approved of this sentiment with more ponderous sagacity from her side of the tea-table, in the first place by swaying her head, and in the second by remarking:
>
> "No, men are not the same as women. I fancy Alfred Tennyson spoke the truth about that. . . ." (NaD, 151–52)

Katharine's third aunt, Lady Otway, concurs and goes further. Asserting that "'It doesn't follow that if a man can do a thing a woman may too'" (NaD, 210), she continues, "'that it's no good being married unless you submit to your husband'" (NaD, 211).

By contrast, Woolf's "mindscapes" demonstrate the similarity of the sexes and suggest that the infrastructure of social relations, based on invalid assumptions of difference, should be dismantled. Thus, the mind portraits of the three main characters, revealing the dialectical relation of imagination and world—that is, the imagination's intense reaction to emotional stimuli and transformation of the observed world, and its own subsequent modification—become thematically significant. Such images of transformation are in evidence from the earliest stages of the story as when the narrator says of Mary:

> Mary felt a lightness of spirit come to her, as if she had put off the stout stuff of her working hours and slipped over her entire being some vesture of thin, bright silk. . . . She knelt before the fire and looked out into the room. The light fell softly, but with clear radiance . . . and the room, which was set with one or two sofas resembling grassy

mounds in their lack of shape, looked unusually large and quiet. Mary
was led to think of the heights of a Sussex down, and the swelling green
circle of some camp of ancient warriors.
. . . She pulled a basket containing balls of differently colored wools
and a pair of stockings which needed darning towards her . . . while
her mind, reflecting the lassitude of her body, went on perversely, con-
juring up visions of solitude and quiet, and she pictured herself laying
aside her knitting and walking out on to the down, and hearing nothing
but the sheep cropping the grass close to the roots. . . . (NaD, 48)

This "moment of being," the lightness of spirit of which she is
aware—biologically, as we now know, triggered by the release of
endorphins—is responsible for her perception of the transforming
quality of the firelight and of her freshly perceived sense of the
familiar surroundings. It leads to the further imaginative leap—
away from present space and time and into a wholly fictional scene
of her own creation—centered in the mind's eye but set on the
Sussex downs.

Through Mary's mental "translation" onto the downs, she hears
the sheep cropping the grass "close to the roots." Ralph's critical
glance at his family's house issues in a similar metaphor: "It was
a threadbare, well-worn house that he thus examined, as if the
inmates had grazed down all luxuriance and plenty to the verge of
decency . . ." (NaD, 35). And shortly after, Mary, describing the
animated guests sitting on the floor of her room, says: "'They're
exactly like a flock of sheep, aren't they?' . . . referring to the
noise that rose from the scattered bodies beneath her" (NaD, 57).
Thus, through the controlling metaphor of the sheep, we get a
privileged and compelling view, not only of Mary's and Ralph's,
but of Woolf's imagination, impelled in moments of creative rapture by the same impulses that govern the minds of her characters.

Woolf's metaphorical transformation of the ordinary, significant
considering Mary's prospective romantic pleasure in seeing Ralph
among her guests, is, then, an example of her reliance on the eye
that half perceives and half creates. Most frequently, it is an eye
that sees best in solitude.

Her translation into contemporary and useful currency of the
Romantic metaphor that merges mind with perceived world is apparent from Woolf's understanding of the importance of solitude
to the individual's sense of self. For her, the ability to remain sane
in a world that constantly erodes the ego, threatening its unitary
nature, is dependent on solitude in time and space.[4]

Wordsworth makes a characteristic and similar claim for solitude
in "Tintern Abbey."

> Knowing that Nature never did betray
> The heart that loved her; 'tis her privilege,
> Through all the years of this our life, to lead
> From joy to joy: for she can so inform
> The mind that is within us, so impress
> With quietness and beauty, and so feed
> With lofty thoughts, that neither evil tongues,
> Rash judgments, nor the sneers of selfish men,
> Nor greetings where no kindness is, nor all
> The dreary intercourse of daily life,
> Shall e'er prevail against us, or disturb
> Our cheerful faith, that all which we behold
> Is full of blessings.
>
> (Wordsworth, 110–11)

The paramount connection of the poet with nature, expressed in "Tintern Abbey" and continued in "Intimations of Immortality"— that communion, leading to creation, gives "relief" that once more makes the poet "strong," is equally apparent in the "spots of time" episode of Book XII of *The Prelude*. There Wordsworth attributes to solitary scenes of childhood the ability to affect "our minds / [So that they] Are nourished and invisibly repaired" (Wordsworth, 345, ll. 214–15). In an intellectual climate that had begun to honor Freud's explanations of the dynamics of personality and feel comfortable with his metaphors for the mind, Woolf passed them by for the Romantic conception of the relationship between the individual and the world and Wordsworth's characteristic imagery to express it. Such preference in *Night and Day* and *Jacob's Room* is particularly surprising when we consider that The Hogarth Press published translations of Freud's writings from 1921 on.[5]

Woolf's recourse to explanations for the mind and creativity that embrace the Romantics' unifying view of man and nature rather than to one that insists on divisions within the individual and a chaotic world into which one cannot easily integrate—essential assumptions of other modernist writers—shows the persistence and usefulness to her of this perspective. Her reliance on it is convincingly evident in her description of Katharine and Ralph's intensely experienced need to find one another, the prelude to the verbal consummation of their love, and in Mary Datchet's equally stunning discovery that a new love has come to take the place of her old one for Ralph. In this context, Theseus's words in *A Midsummer Night's Dream* take on special significance.

Theseus. . . . Lovers and madmen have such seething brains,
Such shaping fantasies, that apprehend

More than cool reason ever comprehends.
The lunatic, the lover, and the poet
Are of imagination all compact.[6]

In the case of Woolf's lovers, the imagery of their romantic anag-
norises is borrowed from the Romantic poets: glass, light, and fire.
Ralph first looks for Katharine, his imagination stirred and energized by the thought of approaching her house.

> . . . an odd image came to his mind of a lighthouse besieged by the
> flying bodies of lost birds, who were dashed senseless, by the gale,
> against the glass. He had a strange sensation that he was both light-
> house and bird; he was steadfast and brilliant. . . . In his state of physi-
> cal fatigue, details merged themselves in the vaster prospect, of which
> the flying gloom and the intermittent lights of lamp-posts and private
> houses were the outward token. . . .
> Lights burnt in the three long windows of the drawing-room. . . . in
> Ralph's vision, the center of the dark, flying wilderness of the world;
> the justification for the welter of confusion surrounding it; the steady
> light which cast its beams, like those of a lighthouse, with searching
> composure over the trackless waste. In this little sanctuary were gath-
> ered together several different people. . . . Physically, he saw them
> bathed in that steady flow of yellow light which filled the long oblongs
> of the windows. . . . At length . . . he allowed himself to approach the
> figure of Katharine herself; and instantly the scene was flooded with
> excitement. He did not see her in the body; he seemed curiously to
> see her as a shape of light, the light itself; he seemed, simplified and
> exhausted as he was, to be like one of those lost birds fascinated by
> the lighthouse and held to the glass by the splendour of the blaze.
> (NaD, 394–95)

Ralph is lighthouse, glass, and bird. The interior of Katharine's
house, flooded with light, is also a lighthouse with its "steady light"
searching the trackless waste of the world. As he imagines the
figure of Katharine, distinguished from those of the other inhabitants of the room, the scene becomes "flooded" with excitement,
and she "a shape of light, the light itself." Thus through conflated
images of light, Woolf translates the intensity of Ralph's love-
heightened imagination, equivalent to the Romantic coextension of
the imagination with the world it perceives and transforms.

For the Romantic poet, the heightened imagination was the agent
permitting his fusion with the external world and his forging,
through words, the art that describes both his emotions and the
objects of his contemplation. Although in later novels Woolf questions the Romantic correspondence between man and nature, here

she takes the metaphors of correspondence as an appropriate depiction of passion because they accurately reveal the lovers' overpowering sensation of union with the objects of their love.

Katharine's intensity parallels Ralph's fusing of subject and object. Attempting to meet Ralph at his office, she is similarly drawn to the three tall lighted windows behind which she believes him to be working.

> The great gas chandeliers were alight in the office windows. She conceived that he sat . . . in the front room with the three tall windows. . . . The square itself . . . its atmosphere of industry and power . . . as if the sky itself, with its gray and scarlet clouds, reflected the serious intention of the city beneath it, spoke of him. . . . The deep roar filled her ears; the changing tumult had the inexpressible fascination of varied life pouring ceaselessly with a purpose . . . its complete indifference to the individuals, whom it swallowed up and rolled onwards, filled her with at least a temporary exaltation. The blend of daylight and of lamplight . . . gave the people who passed her a semi-transparent quality. . . . She stood unobserved and absorbed, glorying openly in the rapture that had run subterraneously all day. Suddenly she was clutched, unwilling, from the outside, by the recollection of her purpose in coming there. . . . She . . . looked for her landmark—the light in the three tall windows. . . . Ralph's three windows gave back on their ghostly glass panels only a reflection of the gray and greenish sky. (NaD, 438–39)

The office workers have left for the day—the meaning of "the ghostly glass panels" of the windows, no longer luminous and full of promise. Katharine's romantic moment of being, the agent of her exaltation and apprehension of the glory of the life of the city, deserts her as she registers Ralph's physical absence.

Woolf similarly records the transformation of Mary Datchet's unrequited love for Ralph. Here, too, the fire and light imagery suggests the intensity of the young woman's feelings. The narrator and Mary collude in the young woman's self-conscious awareness of this imagery, thus making it possible for Mary to convert her feeling for Ralph into another emotion that enables her to survive her anguish over his loss. Shortly after Katharine unsuccessfully seeks Ralph, she visits Mary, who begins to speaks to Katharine of her own love for him:

> She could not remember it any more. She pressed her eyeballs until they struck stars and suns into her darkness. She convinced herself that she was stirring among ashes. . . . She was astonished at her discovery. She did not love Ralph any more. She looked back dazed into

the room, and her eyes rested upon the table with its lamp-lit papers. The steady radiance seemed for a second to have its counterpart within her; she shut her eyes; she opened them and looked at the lamp again; another love burnt in the place of the old one, or so, in a momentary glance of amazement, she guessed before the revelation was over and the old surroundings asserted themselves. . . .

"There are different ways of loving," she murmured, half to herself, at length. (NaD, 447)

Woolf unites Mary's imagination and the objective world through the uniquely Romantic metaphor of mirror and lamp. But Mary sees more than the lamp; her eyes rest, that is, not only come to light upon, but also to find, in the other sense of that word, ease in making contact with the papers. They are the papers of her new political project which reanimate and energize her towards the close of the novel. In effect, they are a "different way[. . .] of loving" that "burn[s] in the place of the old one" for Ralph. These papers help Mary decide, much as the salt cellar does Lily Briscoe in *To the Lighthouse,* to commit herself to a career instead of to marriage.[7] Further, as in that early instance in which Mary's intensity transforms the familiar objects of her room, now, too, we see that her intensity has transformed her things, made them absent to her consciousness, before the moment of being "was over and the old surroundings asserted themselves" once again.

However, the most interesting fusion and transformation in this series of mental events is the first mentioned: Mary's pressing of "her eyeballs until they struck stars and suns into her darkness." Woolf's description of this action brings to a curious pitch the Romantic fusing of subjective imagination and external world. Are the stars and suns—both a metaphor for imaginative intensity and an actual, somatically induced occurrence—in Mary's imagination or in the physical world, albeit of her own body? And is there even a point in making the distinction between the two in this case? Woolf hyperbolically represents the transforming powers of mind. The imagination induces a transformation of the world in the presence of romantic passion and also when under the opposite necessity of ardently falling out of love.

Woolf breaks with convention in describing Mary's action, a "presocial," indecorous manipulation of a part of the body. Her use of the word "eyeballs," far more precise than "eyes," reminds us of a somatic reality that was never approached in mainstream fiction until the twentieth century. Woolf is modernist in taking such freedom and in her thematic approach to her subject in *Night and Day,* depending on the Romantic construct of the relationship between subject and object—the mind's encounter with the world. She suggests, as well, that the imagination of both men and women, in a heightened state of passion, shares a quality with the creative mind. In the conclusion of *A Room of One's Own,* she speculates:

> But the sight of the two people getting into the taxi and the satisfaction it gave me made me also ask whether there are two sexes in the mind corresponding to the two sexes in the body, and whether they also require to be united in order to get complete satisfaction and happiness. And I went on amateurishly to sketch a plan of the soul so that in each of us two powers preside, one male, one female; and in the man's brain, the man predominates over the woman, and in the woman's brain, the woman predominates over the man. The normal and comfortable state of being is that when the two live in harmony together, spiritually cooperating. If one is a man, still the woman part of the brain must have effect; and a woman also must have intercourse with the man in her. Coleridge perhaps meant this when he said a great mind is androgynous. It is when this fusion takes place that the mind is fully fertilised and uses all its faculties. Perhaps a mind that is purely masculine cannot create, any more than a mind that is purely feminine, I thought. (ROO, 102)

Katharine's secret love for the traditionally male studies of mathematics and astronomy and Mary's strong organizational skills employed in the women's suffrage campaign demonstrate, in a conventionally thematic way, Woolf's contention that there is a "woman-manly" aspect to their minds. Conversely, Ralph's interest in poetry suggests a "man-womanly" principle (ROO, 102). However, Woolf's recording of their perceptual and metaphor-making activity, under the pressure of their passion, reveals the congruence of their imaginations and, in this regard, Woolf's belief in the possibility of the equality of the sexes.[8] Such delineations are the first signs of Woolf's new narrative strategies.

That she was searching for a new way to represent reality is clear from her comments to friends. Her remarks written just two days apart, on 24 and 26 July 1917, in letters to Clive Bell and David Garnett, indicate her thoughts about the shape of fiction. To Bell, answering his letter praising "The Mark on the Wall," one of the two pieces printed as the first publication of The Hogarth Press, Woolf wrote: "Its an absorbing thing (I mean writing is) and its high time we found some new shapes, don't you think so?" (Letters II, 167). To Garnett, in the same vein:

I'm very glad you liked the story. In a way its easier to do a short thing, all in one flight than a novel. Novels are frightfully clumsy and overpowering . . . still if one could only get hold of them it would be superb. . . . one ought to invent a completely new form. Anyhow its very amusing to try with these short things, and the greatest mercy to be able to do what one likes—no editors, or publishers, and only people to read who more or less like that sort of thing. (Letters II, 167)

Obviously she did not believe that the comparative ease with which she could master new techniques in the short story extended to *Night and Day* on which she was working at this time. Her metamorphosis into a modernist writer depended on her creative application of the Romantic understanding and recording of mental activity, not only to subject matter but to narrative form. The short stories of 1917 to 1921 were the literary laboratories for her longer works. The difference between the "shape" of the short stories and of *Night and Day* lies primarily in her Romantic narrative strategies.

Woolf saw the Romantic poets as her "relations," as fathers, grandfathers, or even, in the case of Byron, as a candidate for lover. Aside from the diary references to Shelley, on 7 and 8 August 1918, she remarks on her willingness to fall in love with Byron (Diary I, 180), "the badness of B.'s poetry" (180), *Don Juan* as "the most readable poem of its length ever written" (180–81), and she compares Byron with Wordsworth and Keats: "But he never as a young man, believed in his poetry; a proof, in such a confident dogmatic person, that he hadn't the gift. The Wordsworths and Keats' believe in that as much as they believe in anything" (180).

Wordsworth and Keats are for her the high water mark, the truly gifted of any century, as the present tense of the verb "believe"— which transforms them into representative poets—suggests. More directly of Wordsworth, she wrote in 1918: "We had the bee and the blossom in no metaphorical sense at Asheham. Once more my memory is most centred upon an afternoon reading in the garden. I happened to read Wordsworth; the poem which ends 'what man has made of man'. The daffodils were out & the guns I suppose could be heard from the downs. Even to me, who have no immediate stake, & repudiate the importance of what is being done, there was an odd pallor in those particular days of sunshine" (Diary I, 131). Not merely Woolf's sense of the appositeness of Wordsworth's sentiment to these last months of the war—the contrast between the harmoniousness of nature and the maltreatment of man by man—but her choice of Wordsworth as current reading material and the strength of the impression made by her reading of him (she picked this particular day out of a number of similar ones to describe), attest to the vitality of his presence in her creative life. Again, on 31 January 1921, of a conversation with Lytton Strachey: "Talk about Keats & Wordsworth & C.[arrington] and P[artridge]" (Diary II, 88). Wordsworth and Keats take their place in an immediate way beside the people in her circle of friends whose lives make the basis of good gossip. Less than a month later, Wordsworth stands as an exemplar of value for her. She writes on 1 March: "The truth is that I have an internal, automatic scale of values; which decides what I had better do with my time. It dictates 'This half hour must be spent on Russian' 'This must be given to Wordsworth.' or 'now I'd better darn my brown stockings.'" (Diary II, 94). However, the profound importance of these writers is seen most clearly in the narrative techniques she had begun to employ in her stories.

As experiments these stories are not of one piece. Her approach varies tremendously from one to another in their content and presentation of subject. In fact, it would be hard to categorize a number of them as stories at all. They are more nearly essays or sketches, slices not of "life," in the conventional sense of life's "exteriority," but of a consciousness operating imaginatively in various ways in relation to interior rather than exterior events. However, if there is one attribute that binds them together, it is "intensity." Through them Woolf was learning how to make the luminous halo of life glow more brightly than it does either in *The Voyage Out* or in *Night and Day*. Intensity, both in narrative strategy and choice of subject—the nature of imagination—connects Woolf's experiments in fiction to the poetic experiments of the Romantics.

Shelley, among other authors, is the subject of a conversation in one of these stories, "The Evening Party" (CSF, 91). However, "The Mark on the Wall," Woolf's first attempt at a break with traditional storytelling, is a substantial exploration of Romantic themes. Woolf's story, as Janet Lumpkin has noted,[9] is a rejection of the old Victorian "public" order with its rules for everything, represented by the stiff conventions of Sunday dinners with tapestry table cloths, Whitaker's Table of Precedency, and "the habit of sitting all together in one room until a certain hour, although nobody liked it" (CSF, 80). These seemingly eternal verities, especially for the children who suffered them, had come crashing with the advent of the Great War. Implicitly and in contrast to these "stabilities," the primacy of the private life, of consciousness as the center of this life and as a subject to be explored by the creative artist—the revolutionary theme and basis of technique for the Romantics—is Woolf's subject here. Thus, briefly stated, for the Romantics and for Woolf, choice of subject and change in technique have relation to the alteration in the social order created by political events of cataclysmic proportion. War, particularly, breaking the comfort and orderliness of the quotidian, creates the need in human beings, especially the most sensitive and articulate, to reassess the way they have more or less unconsciously lived and worked. Frequently, the result of this reassessment is a rejection of the old values, based in part on the reasonable assumption that these ideas may have contributed to the present state of violence and disruption. Woolf's attitudes and aesthetic revaluations have their antecedent in the case of the Romantics who viewed the French Revolution as the obvious outgrowth of the stagnancy of the *ancien régime* and who included, in this category, the rigid and worn aesthetic criteria of the Augustans.

Woolf's subject in "The Mark on the Wall" is the private life of the mind, its flight from thought to thought, often describing a circular journey from the present moment into the depths of memory and back. The nature of a mark on the wall, six or seven inches above the mantelpiece in the room in which the narrator sits, is merely the apparent focus of investigation. It chiefly serves as a reference point for the mind's voyages from, and returns to, the near-past-become-present moment of the "story-essay." The narrator begins: "Yes, it must have been the winter time, and we had just finished our tea, for I remember . . ." (CSF, 77).

The words "I remember" represent both the fulfillment of possibility and the problem for the human being and that special case of the human being, the writer. We must be able to remember in order to make sense of the world and tell our stories to ourselves and others. However, Woolf's metaphor, "How readily our thoughts swarm upon a new object, lifting it a little way, as ants carry a blade of straw so feverishly, and then leave it" (CSF, 77), suggests the difficulty of ordering our thoughts and, more difficult still, especially for the writer, conveying the feelings attached to them. Woolf expresses the writer's perplexity in "How Should One Read a Book?" when she says:

> Perhaps the quickest way to understand the elements of what a novelist is doing is not to read, but to write; to make your own experiment with the dangers and difficulties of words. Recall, then, some event that has left a distinct impression on you—how at the corner of the street,

perhaps, you passed two people talking. A tree shook; an electric light danced; the tone of the talk was comic, but also tragic; a whole vision, an entire conception, seemed contained in that moment.

But when you attempt to reconstruct it in words, you will find that it breaks into a thousand conflicting impressions. Some must be subdued; others emphasised; in the process you will lose, probably, all grasp upon the emotion itself. (SCR, 259–60)

The difficult effort to maintain a grasp upon the emotion when writing down the words that convey the actual events generating it is parallel to her task in "The Mark on the Wall" of grasping the imaginative embrace of life revealed in the quirky and subtle shifts from thought to thought and image to image. Woolf metaphorically asserts the writer's dilemma—the very one she is trying to solve in "the Mark on the Wall" by allowing the mind's movements to govern sequence and subject—when she describes an interrupted conversation with the former owner of her house:

he was . . . saying that . . . art should have ideas behind it when we were torn asunder, as one is torn from the old lady about to pour out tea and the young man about to hit the tennis ball in the back garden of the suburban villa as one rushes past in the train. (CSF, 77)

She unravels a string of thought to its end, only to reveal the ultimate impossibility of knowing more about the former owner than one does about the young man glimpsed from the receding train, because she is building the case for her subject—the nature of the difficulties encountered by the imagination, not only in "life" but in the re-creation of life, the creation of narrative sequence. She is describing loss—loss of sequence or the suspension of the flow of words, of pouring tea, of hitting a tennis ball—for the observing and recording consciousness. Such loss of knowledge about others is registered as irritation or, worse, pain.

We can understand the "Romantic" solution to her problem when we consider "A Sketch of the Past," written twenty-two years after "The Mark on the Wall." In this memoir Woolf similarly and self-consciously writes of narrative sequence and conveying emotion. Beginning with the difficulties of the memoir writer, she girds her loins and says of one of her *two* "first" memories:

So without stopping to choose my way, in the sure and certain knowledge that it will find itself—or if not it will not matter—I begin: the first memory.

This was of red and purple flowers on a black ground—my mother's dress; and she was sitting either in a train or in an omnibus, and I was on her lap. I therefore saw the flowers she was wearing very close; and can still see purple and red and blue, I think, against the black; they must have been anemones, I suppose. Perhaps we were going to St Ives. . . . (MoB, 64–65)

The flowers on the "Giant" (CSF, 78) mother's dress were seen "very close" by the little girl, who, with the hyperopic eyes of small children, was "unable to focus [her] eyesight" (CSF, 78). Her description of an intensity or sense of ecstasy, of rapture, as she calls it in the same memoir, "of lying in a grape and seeing through a film of semi-transparent yellow" (MoB, 65), is amplified, several pages later, by her other early memory of flowers to which she self-consciously attaches the name "moment of being": she was "looking at a plant with a spread of leaves" (MoB, 71). Such moments, equivalent to Wordsworth's "spots of time," become a source of enabling satisfaction for her when, as an adult, she writes them down.

> It is or will become a revelation of some order; it is a token of some real thing behind appearances; and I make it real by putting it into words. It is only by putting it into words that I make it whole; this wholeness means that it has lost its power to hurt me; it gives me, perhaps because by doing so I take away the pain, a great delight to put the severed parts together. Perhaps this is the strongest pleasure known to me. It is the rapture I get when in writing I seem to be discovering what belongs to what; making a scene come right; making a character come together. From this I reach what I might call a philosophy . . . that behind the cotton wool is hidden a pattern; that we— I mean all human beings—are connected with this; that the whole world is a work of art; that we are parts of the work of art. . . . we are the words; we are the music; we are the thing itself. (MoB, 72)

Woolf's creative impulses and the quality of the actual experience of creation are comparable to Coleridge's notion of the "esemplastic" imagination[10] and Wordsworth's explanation of the conditions of composition in the Preface to *Lyrical Ballads*. They are the basis of her modernism. In "The Mark on the Wall," we can see the potency for Woolf in retrieving something from her personal past that has issue in satisfying two kinds of writerly "imaginative desire." The first is the creation of a specific image, for example, "thick stalks, and rather higher up perhaps, rose-shaped blots of an indistinct colour — dim pinks and blues" (CSF, 78). The other is the "esemplastic" or shaping activity of the imagination that puts the real thing behind appearances into words to make a character, here, the character of mentation or imagination, come together in a sequence that conveys emotion.

In the Preface to *Lyrical Ballads,* Wordsworth describes the creation of poetry as a kind of rapture: the transformation of the imagination in its recollection of an experience from the tranquil vantage of the present. In "The Mark on the Wall," as in "Kew Gardens" and the other stories of this period, Woolf tries to reach "some real thing behind appearances," the *ding an sich* of her father's rationalist philosophy, but through what is distinctly her own invention: a narrative voice whose apprehension of the wholeness of reality, the intensity of life's halo, is made luminous through a highly metaphorical language that connects her with her past. Her choice of words and of word patterns makes us believe that, indeed, when she wrote, Woolf saw the world through a womblike "film of semi-transparent yellow."

Two or three moments in "The Mark on the Wall" reveal how Woolf, creating her operative definition of mind, depended on her own spots of time, specifically described in "A Sketch. . . ." As for Wordsworth, these moments were the wellspring of her creativity.

The beginning of the story reveals the imagination's power to transform the external world through metaphor-making, enriched by memory of the distant past of childhood. The recollection of the past and the circular return to the present affirm the Romantic tradition of the excitation of the imagination through the artifacts recovered from the corridors of memory.

> I looked up through the smoke of my cigarette and my eye lodged for a moment upon the burning coals, and that old fancy of the crimson flag flapping from the castle tower came into my mind, and I thought of the cavalcade of red knights riding up the side of the black rock. Rather to my relief the sight of the mark interrupted the fancy, for it is an old fancy, an automatic fancy, made as a child perhaps. (CSF, 77)

As readers we sense a contradiction. The narrator expresses annoyance with the involuntary transformation of the flaming coals into flapping flag and castle tower, which images, she implies, have originated in fire-gazing in childhood. Her irritation comes from recognizing the worn groove of this memory trace. And yet the freshness of the opening of this essay—beyond the charm of the extraordinarily casual and intimate conversational tone of the discourse—depends on the vividness of the metaphors that are, if not for the writer, at least for the reader, powerful and new. The writer fully knows, we imagine, that the metaphors make for interest (why else would she have left them in their prominent position?). Our readerly confusion, then, draws our attention to Woolf's subtext: the organic relationship of imagination and memory.

That the operations of the mind are the real subject of the essay is underscored by the metaphoric description of thoughts in the second paragraph: "How readily our thoughts swarm upon a new object" (CSF, 77). The actual mark on the wall, as it excites specu- lation that makes the mind first wander and then recall attention to itself in the present moment, inspires a circular journey of thought from the surface to the depths and back. But getting up to examine the mark to determine its nature may not stop such circular mind travels

> because once a thing's done, no one ever knows how it happened. Oh! dear me, the mystery of life! The inaccuracy of thought! . . . what an accidental affair this living is . . . let me just count over a few of the things lost in our lifetime, beginning, for that seems always the most mysterious of losses—what cat would gnaw, what rat would nibble — three pale blue canisters of book binding tools! Then there were the bird cages, the iron hoops, the steel skates. . . . (CSF, 78)

The canisters of bookbinding tools may reflect Woolf's memory of her plans to learn bookbinding in 1901 with her cousin Emma Vaughan, mentioned in a note for 9 October 1917, in her diary (Diary I, 57).[11] However, the real importance of this list of lost objects is that it is an inventory of loss, not only of a child's belong- ings but of childhood itself, and so leads the narrator to recall one of her earliest and most significant memories. She attempts "to express the rapidity of life, the perpetual waste and repair; all so casual, all so haphazard" (CSF, 78) through the images "Shot out at the feet of God entirely naked! Tumbling head over heels in the asphodel meadows like brown paper parcels pitched down a shoot in the post office!" (CSF, 78). The narrator then deploys a moment of being from her childhood in her description of "after life":

> The slow pulling down of thick green stalks so that the cup of the flower, as it turns over, deluges one with purple and red light. Why, after all, should one not be born there as one is born here, helpless, speechless, unable to focus one's eyesight, groping at the roots of the grass, at the toes of the Giants? (CSF, 78)

Her question is a reasonable one because it refers to two moments in one's personal history that are identical insofar as birth cannot be remembered nor unconsciousness after death imagined. The mythical images the narrator supplies are, then, necessary psychologically to her and to all of us, a kind of "racial memory" of events of the profoundest importance which, in the absence of such figuration, cannot be considered. The source of this image is Woolf's own early experiences, sitting on her giant mother's lap unable to focus on the flowers of Julia Stephen's dress, and looking at the flower next to the front door at St. Ives. The circular flights of the mind constitutive of the "plot" of this story lead the narrator back metaphorically into that period of preverbal existence in which the child is most completely merged with the mother and world.

Woolf most considerately and clearly described this merging when she wrote in "A Sketch . . .": "we are the words; we are the music; we are the thing itself." Even the ambiguous form of "The Mark on the Wall," suggesting an imperceptible sliding between an imaginative short story and a factual essay, serves as a metaphor for the fusing of the imagination and the world beyond the individual mind.

The remainder of "The Mark on the Wall" is the continuation of the cyclic and associative flow of ideas and images, connecting the "hard separate facts" (CSF, 79) of the surface or present moment— the unknown nature of the mark on the wall—with the mind voyages of other spaces and times, apparently connected, as well, to the preoedipal world of the opening of "A Sketch. . . ." She describes a

> very pleasant world. A quiet spacious world, with the flowers so red and blue in the open fields. A world without professors or specialists or housekeepers with the profiles of policemen, a world which one could slice with one's thought as a fish slices the water with his fin, grazing the stems of the water-lilies, hanging suspended over white sea eggs. . . . How peaceful it is down here, rooted in the centre of the world and gazing up through the grey waters, with their sudden gleams of light . . . if it were not for Whitaker's Almanack — if it were not for the Table of Precedency! (CSF, 81–82)

Imagination is thus once more incited by the preoedipal past. However, the landscape of the past is extensive. Once we begin to wander in it, we may bump up against an unedenic moment. The narrator's attention seems to have hit against one of these dangerous shoals. *Whitaker's Almanack,* a book of hard facts, and the Table of Precedency, with its reminder of rigid hierarchies, recall the narrator's mind to the present and another and more serious instance of patriarchal horror—the war and its harsh and difficult realities. In the only instance of dialogue in the piece, the voice reports:

> Someone is standing over me and saying —
>   'I'm going out to buy a newspaper.'
>   'Yes?'
>   'Though it's no good buying newspapers. . . . Nothing ever happens. Curse this war; God damn this war! . . . All the same, I don't see why we should have a snail on our wall.'
>   Ah, the mark on the wall! It was a snail. (CSF, 83)

Convention suggests that the presence of dialogue in fiction serves as incontrovertible evidence of a reality beyond the solipsism of the narrative voice. Dialogue functions as a device that emblematizes the world—the "other"—which must be embraced by the individual imagination. The answer about the nature of the mark on the wall is, then, not surprisingly, "supplied" by the other voice of the story. However, the final "joke" is, of course, that this other voice is just as, and no more, real than the narrative voice, both finally being creations of the imagination of the author.

Such assertions about the representation of the world and of mind in fiction might be made about any piece of writing. However, Woolf self-consciously invites these particular ruminations on the part of her reader not merely through a casual drawing of attention throughout "The Mark on the Wall" to the complex relationship between the imagination and the world it receives and perceives but by actually making the mind the central subject of the piece. "The Mark on the Wall" is too slight to be subtitled "The Growth of a Poet's Mind" because it is not a macrocosmic history of the imagination's development. However, in a way that parallels, indeed, in its sophistication goes beyond Wordsworth's endeavors in *The Prelude,* it attempts to understand, through a "synchronic," microcosmic portrait, the mechanisms of memory and imagination.

Intensity permits the beauty and accuracy of her description. She has found a method for creating it through what Edward L. Bishop, writing about "Kew Gardens," calls her

> flexible narrative style which allows her to move without obvious transition from an external point of view to one within the mind of a character, and back again, thus fusing the physical setting with the perceiving consciousness. . . . Further, it is a mode which invites the reader's participation in the process, so that the reality Woolf conveys is appre-

hended through the process of reading. . . . the reader becomes conscious of moving *among* words, just as the characters do.[12]

Aside from her subject—the nature of mind—with its parallel to Wordsworth's in *The Prelude,* we can recognize the Romantic basis of Woolf's narrative approach. For Bishop's remarking on the fusion of the perceiving consciousness with the setting is another way of naming the Romantic metaphor for mind that describes imagination as coextensive with the world it perceives. In "The Mark on the Wall" and "Kew Gardens," Woolf has made the leap from metaphor as subject to metaphor as method. Indeed, she goes beyond the Romantics in extending the fusion of consciousness and setting with a further one, created for the reader through a compelling invitation to move among the words that luminously convey the halo of life.

The reader's sense of immediacy and excitement in sharing the movements of the narrator's mind in "The Mark on the Wall" continues in "Kew Gardens." In this third person narrative, Woolf's technique is both more complex and demanding of the writer's ingenuity and sympathies. Her desire, to reproduce her sense of the luminosity of life, is perhaps even more obvious here as Woolf carefully chooses her words to create in her readers the sense of beauty we get from the apparent effortlessness of her prose. Through this medium she makes us see the particular embrace of reality of which her imagination is capable.

Woolf organizes the sketch through an alternate training of the narrative gaze on a flower bed in Kew Gardens, in which a snail progresses over and under the vegetable obstructions in its path, and on four different groups of people who walk by the bed, unaware of the snail's existence. The equal intensity of the imaginative embrace of the snail's being, of the flowers', and of the human characters' gives this story its unique and gorgeous quality.

However, another interesting and complex issue emerges in this story. Woolf keeps two orders of "writerly being" before her. The first is the capturing of the preverbal world in words that, because of their beauty, make us see through them to the various life forms they register. The second is her attention to the text itself, to words as having a life of their own. These two aesthetic experiences may at first seem to be in conflict with one another. But as Woolf shows through the four vignettes of "Kew Gardens," they re-create different levels of absorption into the moment, essentially the experience Woolf describes as a moment of being and return to consciousness of one's present surroundings. That is, as we read, we dive into the emotion created by the text and resurface to look at the very words that have made it.

The luminosity shared both by the imagination and life itself is evident from the first paragraph in which the narrator describes the quality of the light falling on the flower bed and into the eyes of the people passing along a path in Kew Gardens.

> From the oval-shaped flower-bed there rose perhaps a hundred stalks spreading into heart-shaped or tongue-shaped leaves half way up and unfurling at the tip red or blue or yellow petals. . . . The petals were voluminous enough to be stirred by the summer breeze, and when they moved, the red, blue and yellow lights passed one over the other, staining an inch of the brown earth beneath with a spot of the most intricate colour. The light . . . expanded with such intensity of red, blue and yellow the thin walls of water that one expected them to burst and disappear. . . . Then the breeze stirred . . . and the colour was flashed into the air above, into the eyes of the men and women who walked in Kew Gardens in July. (CSF, 84)

The flower image recorded in "A Sketch . . ." resurfaces in modified form as it does in "The Mark on the Wall." The light a priori enters and "colours" the narrator's eyes, illuminates the flowers, a drop of water, the earth, a pebble, and a snail, and ultimately enters into the receiving eyes of the men and women, equally coloring their imaginations. Woolf's sense of the Romantic coextension of mind and world and the power of the past are underscored by the dramatic interlude that follows: Simon and Eleanor's recapturing of past moments as they walk by the flower bed, energized by their recollections of passionate intensity.

Simon's memory of the day when he came to Kew with Lily and begged her to marry him is concentrated in two remembered images: a square silver shoe buckle and a dragonfly. When Simon asks his wife Eleanor if she minds his thinking of the past, she responds:

> 'Why should I mind, Simon? Doesn't one always think of the past, in a garden with men and women lying under the trees? Aren't they one's past, all that remains of it, those men and women, those ghosts lying under the trees. . . . one's happiness, one's reality?' (CSF, 85)

We think of Wordsworth's "hour / Of splendour in the grass, of glory in the flower" that "nothing can bring back" (Wordsworth, 190), but we also recall Woolf's own version of Wordsworth's spots of time, her moments of being with their distinctly preoedipal quality, since Eleanor sums up her comparable memory:

'For me, a kiss. Imagine six little girls sitting before their easels twenty years ago, down by the side of a lake, painting the water-lilies, the first red water-lilies I'd ever seen. And suddenly a kiss, there on the back of my neck. And my hand shook all the afternoon so that I couldn't paint. I took out my watch and marked the hour when I would allow myself to think of the kiss for five minutes only — it was so precious — the kiss of an old grey-haired woman with a wart on her nose, the mother of all my kisses all my life.' (CSF, 85)

Eleanor describes an ordinary moment (perhaps made more intense by the gratuitous expression of mother-love), transformed into one of *rapture,* of preoedipal bliss, and merged with fresh perception and creativity. Here, as in Woolf's memories of early childhood in St. Ives, the moment is associated with a flower and literally flowers into an extraordinarily intense and satisfying experience—the mother of all Eleanor's later kisses.

The evocative and delicate images Woolf creates make us respond strongly or "fuse" with the remembered experience of Eleanor, enticing us into our own emotion through their beauty. Not only the narrative voice, then, but the dramatic dialogues as well, create the intensity that allows us to see and feel this moment, a moment that is remarkable for its unique merging of ordinary experience and extraordinary elements of feeling.

The window onto this emotion closes as the family passes the flower bed, and the narrative eye is retrained on a different kind of life, that is, the animal and vegetable world of the patch of earth. But before she is done with Simon and Eleanor, the narrator says that as they walked on, they "soon diminished in size among the trees and looked half transparent as the sunlight and shade swam over their backs in large trembling irregular patches" (CSF, 85). For the narrator they are absorbed into the world they have been engaged by, a kind of emblematic depiction of the coextension of the imagination and life. The images of transparency, trembling sunlight and shadow, make manifest Romanticism's naming of the relationship between the world and the mirroring and creating mind.

The description of the snail's shell "stained red, blue and yellow for the space of two minutes or so" (CSF, 85) is a similar metaphorical depiction of the blending of subject and world. The narrative voice then reconfirms the apparent metaphorical fusion by using language that reflects its own imaginative effort to enter into the life of the snail. Twice the voice uses the word "appear" to describe the snail's activity: "the snail . . . now appeared to be moving very slightly," and "It appeared to have a definite goal in front of it" (CSF, 85). The first use merely suggests the narrator's effort at observational accuracy. The second, however, moves into the realm of a subjective and, therefore, imaginative, categorization of the snail's activity. To ascribe a goal to the snail and to the "high-stepping angular green insect" (CSF, 85) in the snail's path is to attempt to merge with the insects and to see the world from their anthropomorphized perspective. The narrator's use of the relative pronoun "who" instead of "which" indicates the intensity of the anthropomorphic gaze.[13]

The verbal effort to fuse with the intentions of the insects gives way to another object. From this point on in the sketch, language, as a level of being sometimes distinct from and sometimes merging with the preverbal, interests us as we double the mind movements of Woolf's characters. The deranged man, who next walks by the flower bed, does not interest us as he does the "two elderly women of the lower middle class. . . . [who] [l]ike most people of their station . . . were frankly fascinated by any signs of eccentricity betokening a disordered brain, especially in the well-to-do" (CSF, 86). Rather, we pay notice because in this tableau Woolf first makes conscious the issue of language, of words as a medium not only of exchange between individuals but as the creators of our personal biospheres, since they are an expression of the perceiving imagination that, in turn, colors the world for the individual who uses them. The elderly man, explaining the way in which the spirit world may be contacted, says:

'You have a small electric battery and a piece of rubber to insulate the wire — isolate? — insulate? — well, we'll skip the details. . . . All arrangements being properly fixed by workmen under my direction, the widow applies her ear and summons the spirit by sign as agreed. Women! Widows! Women in black — '
Here he seemed to have caught sight of a woman's dress in the distance, which in the shade looked a purple black. . . . But William caught him by the sleeve and touched a flower with the tip of his walking-stick in order to divert the old man's attention. . . . the old man bent his ear to it and seemed to answer a voice speaking from it. . . . (CSF, 86)

The old man's confusion over "isolate" and "insulate" reminds us of the existence of words *qua* words. Woolf suggests their dynamic interaction with the quiddities of the world through the appearance of a woman in a black dress as the man utters words that seem to create a corresponding reality within his field of vision. The symbolic or imaginative order fuses with the observable world. Further, his bending to hear the voice of the flower, followed by the rich imagery excited by this pressure, reminds us of the potency of Woolf's preoedipal flower associations that also lie beneath the fusing of subject and object in "The Mark on the Wall" and the beginning of "Kew Gardens."

The next two vignettes concerning the lower middle-class women and the young lovers are even more pointedly about words—the products of the imagination—as the imagination's mediators of reality. Romanticism's self-consciousness of the act of creativity is thus brought down to the morphemic unit. The "piecing together [of] their very complicated dialogue" (CSF, 87)—the narrator's naming of the women's activity—is represented in stylized form:

'Nell, Bert, Lot, Cess, Phil, Pa, he says, I says, she says, I says, I says, I says —'
'My Bert, Sis, Bill, Grandad, the old man, sugar,
Sugar, flour, kippers, greens
Sugar, sugar, sugar.' (CSF, 87)[14]

Although the women have "energetically" engaged in this conversation, the heavier of them now "looked through the pattern of falling words at the flowers standing cool, firm and upright in the earth, with a curious expression" (CSF, 87). The words that have consumed her attention no longer interest her as, like the old man before her, she is drawn into the world of the flowers. She "ceased even to pretend to listen to what the other woman was saying. She stood there letting the words fall over her . . . looking at the flowers" (CSF, 87). The uncanny ability of the mind to move in and out of present reality, commemorated in the mind travels of "The Mark on the Wall," is dramatically demonstrated in this little "story." Words are themselves doubly real, being both a thing in themselves and, as code, a representation of another order of reality. They vie for mind-space on both these levels with the preverbal order of being represented by the flowers.

This story having ended, the narrator once more and for the last time concentrates her gaze upon the snail who anthropomorphically "considered every possible method of reaching his goal" and "was doubtful whether the thin texture [of a leaf] . . . would bear his weight" (CSF, 87). This judgment, in turn, "determined him . . . to creep beneath it" where he "was taking stock of the high brown roof and was getting used to the cool brown light when two other people came past outside on the turf" (CSF, 87–88). As a strategy for creating, quite literally, a focal point for the reader, the snail and the flower bed passages are quite effective. But beyond reminding us of the geographical center of "Kew Gardens"— the only thing the passersby share—these sections assert the primacy of the preverbal reality with which art, Woolf felt, must engage.[15] This reality is finally reduced and, at the same time, paradoxically enlarged through the apparently aimless conversation of the pair of young lovers which leads the young woman to call the experience of Kew—itself Woolf's shorthand for life— by the one amorphous pronoun "it." Commenting on the cheap admission to Kew, the young woman says:

> 'What's sixpence anyway? Isn't it worth sixpence?'
> 'What's "it" — what do you mean by "it"?'
> 'O anything — I mean —you know what I mean.' (CSF, 88)

Beneath the insignificance of their words—words uttered by lovers whose intensity of being is in their passionate love that words can never adequately match—lies Woolf's profound assertion about the limits of meaning and language.

> Long pauses came between each of these remarks: they were uttered in toneless and monotonous voices. The couple . . . together pressed the end of her parasol deep down into the soft earth. The action and the fact that his hand rested on the top of hers expressed their feelings in a strange way, as these short insignificant words also expressed something, words with short wings for their heavy body of meaning, inadequate to carry them far and thus alighting awkwardly upon the very common objects that surrounded them and were to their inexperienced touch so massive: but who knows (so they thought as they pressed the parasol into the earth) what precipices aren't concealed in them, or what slopes of ice don't shine in the sun on the other side? (CSF, 88)

The physical pressing of the parasol and touching of hands, expressing the intensity of emotion, have their parallel in the insignificant words that alight or press upon the common objects. As for Ralph Denham and Katharine Hilbery in Kew Gardens, intensity transforms the world these lovers inhabit. But here, as well, Woolf makes a second claim for language, which can powerfully transform the ordinary objects of life. The equality of these two transformations is made clear through the paradoxical obscurity of the ambiguous pronominal references in "inadequate to carry *them* far and thus alighting awkwardly upon the very common objects that surrounded *them* and were to *their* inexperienced touch so massive" (my emphasis). We cannot tell whether these pronouns refer to the words with short wings or to the lovers themselves. Thus, Woolf suggests the imaginative fusion with the world that seems to occur both with romantic passion and, for the writer, in the process of creation.

The attribution of the adjective "massive" creates similar ambiguity. Does it modify the words or the common objects to which they refer? Here, then, is a second fusing of the imaginative and the real. A cascade of questions follows: "but who knows . . . what precipices aren't concealed in them, or what slopes of ice don't shine in the sun on the other side? Who knows? Who has ever seen this before?" (CSF, 88). Does Woolf desire to clear up or further complicate meaning for the reader? Apparently these questions refer to the words with their "heavy body of meaning," but because there is a fusion between the metaphorical and the real, the questions might equally refer to the common objects.[16] The correctness of this conjecture is supported by the sentence that follows, reporting on "events" not transcribed through direct discourse, that is, the girl's words and her lover's unspoken response:

> Even when she wondered what sort of tea they gave you at Kew, he felt that something loomed up behind her words, and stood vast and solid behind them; and the mist very slowly rose and uncovered — O Heavens, — what were those shapes? — little white tables, and waitresses who looked first at her and then at him; and there was a bill that he would pay with a real two shilling piece, and it was real, all real, he assured himself, fingering the coin in his pocket, real to everyone except to him and to her; even to him it began to seem real. . . . (CSF, 88)

Just as the old man's words, "Women in black," seem to have produced, in the distance, a woman wearing a black dress, so here Trissie's wonder seems to reveal, even produce, "loom[ing] up behind" them, "vast and solid," the real world of Kew with its white tables, waitresses, and bills. The mist that dissipates may be equally an atmospheric event or a metaphoric clearing of the young man's mind through the agency of Trissie's words that make him see and tether him, once again, to the perceivable world.

The return to the preverbal world, heralded by his words to himself, "it was real, all real," is comparable to the narrator's associational return to the mark on the wall. Trissie's lingering on in the preoedipal imaginative order—"forgetting her tea, wishing to go down there and then down there, remembering orchids and cranes among wild flowers, a Chinese pagoda and a crimson-crested bird" (CSF, 89)—despite the peremptory command of her young man, is a tribute to the strength of the imagination which, for a time, even in the presence of the powerful world of solid objects, can captivate and hold the mind in thrall.

However, the young man's will to break her spell and have her join him in the real world of teatime is overpowering: "but he bore her on" (CSF, 89). And so ends the fourth tableau of "Kew Gardens." Now the narrator, in the final and wonderfully crowded last paragraph, creates a succession of images and metaphors that reveals the richness of the narrator's own imagination. She piles image on top of image, of sight, sound, and texture, thus transforming the world and the engaged imagination. First the narrator describes the absorption of the couples into the circumambient air: "[they] were enveloped in layer after layer of green-blue vapour, in which at first their bodies had substance and a dash of colour, but later both substance and colour dissolved in the green-blue atmosphere" (CSF, 89). The perceived union of bodies and air functions, as in the description of the disappearing Eleanor and Simon, as an emblem of the imaginative conjunction of mind and world.

The hopping thrush is transformed into a mechanical bird and the white dancing butterflies into "the outline of a shattered marble column" (CSF, 89). The glass roofs of the greenhouse merge with the palms within, so that the trees are perceived as "shiny green umbrellas" (CSF, 89). There is an auditory merging noted, as well: "in the drone of the aeroplane the voice of the summer sky murmured its fierce soul" (CSF, 89).

Color becomes shape, becomes people, becomes color once again, as atmospheric heat is transformed into color. "Yellow and black, pink and snow white, shapes of all these colours, men, women and children, were spotted for a second upon the horizon, and then, seeing the breadth of yellow that lay upon the grass, they wavered and sought shade beneath the trees, dissolving like drops of water in the yellow and green atmosphere, staining it faintly with red and blue" (CSF, 89). Woolf has returned to the motif of merging in the first paragraph of the story: the flower petals become "red, blue and yellow lights . . . staining an inch of the brown earth beneath with a spot of the most intricate colour" (CSF, 84).

The voices of these people, like the drone of the aeroplane that becomes the voice of the soul of the sky, are metamorphosed into "flames lolling from the thick waxen bodies of candles" (CSF, 89). The narrator, in a brilliant operational definition of the imagination's ability both to impose order on the world and to receive impressions, makes an assertion and then contradicts it as reality makes its own assertion, overcoming reverie:

> Voices . . . wordless voices, breaking the silence suddenly with such depth of contentment, such passion of desire, or, in the voices of children, such freshness of surprise; breaking the silence? But there was no silence; all the time the motor omnibuses were turning their wheels and changing their gear; like a vast nest of Chinese boxes all of wrought steel turning ceaselessly one within another the city murmured; on the top of which the voices cried aloud and the petals of myriads of flowers flashed their colours into the air. (CSF, 89)

We find the psychological explanation for the momentary transcendence of reality over imagination—the apprehension of the noise of the city when first the narrator apprehends only silence—in the imagination's own attempt to find correspondingly accurate images for the things of this world. The effort to hear clearly and thus describe the character of the voices of the men, women, and children, particularly of the children, characterized as having "such freshness of surprise," enables the narrator to hear accurately the circumambient sounds. She now hears the noise of the buses. Yet the creative imagination reasserts its primacy as transmission gears become the ceaseless turning of a nest of Chinese steel boxes that become the murmuring of the entire city.

Finally, the power of the imagination is subliminally acknowledged with the closing words of the sketch—"the petals of myriads of flowers flashed their colours into the air" (CSF, 89). The imagination does not merely transform the apprehended world. It is also able to shape the total product of its unique invention, the work of art. By repeating the words of the first paragraph, the narrator draws conclusion and beginning together. This restatement is a self-conscious authorial reminder to the reader that these words are the products of the creative imagination, the plastic substance of the writer's craft. The image of the flowers, then, serves as the last, perhaps most powerful, example in its pointing beyond itself to the "fact" of creation, of fusion of creator and audience, suggesting Woolf's leap beyond Romanticism's self-consciousness. We are in the presence of something new: self-consciousness of self-consciousness.

A similar examination might be made of each of the stories of this period. Although Woolf deploys different narrative strategies in each, they share with "The Mark on the Wall" and "Kew Gardens" a privileged view of the imagination's heightened apprehension and appropriation of reality, the nature of the creative act being the real subject of each sketch. The power of the imagination to transform and create a fiction about the real world is the center both of "Sympathy" and "An Unwritten Novel." In "The String Quartet," Woolf fuses with the heard music to suggest a new way of recording reality and honoring the movements of the mind with which she had been experimenting in all her shorter fictions. From an historical perspective, Woolf suggests that the assumptions underlying the imagination's new embrace of reality have been made possible by the extraordinary interruption of business-as-usual during the war: "'Still, the war made a break —'" (CSF, 132). That there is a need for, and possibility of, the integration of art and the diurnal is clear from "Monday or Tuesday," the story preceding "The String Quartet" in *The Complete Shorter Fiction.*

"Monday or Tuesday" suggests the direction of Woolf's subject and methods in her novels, beginning with *Jacob's Room.* It is a short but elegant example of the possibility of portraying the ordinary as captivating. Woolf fully appreciated the difficulty of the task. She wrote of this problem in a letter to Janet Case, four days after the one to Vanessa in which she mentions the question of her having time to write "Monday or Tuesday."

> Well, last night Lady Robert Cecil stayed here; on Sunday I take tea with Countess [Katharine] Cromer; on Monday I dine with Roger Fry, and on Friday—a very shady party in Chelsea. Doesn't it look grand? The truth is nothing is like what its written like. I mean, Lady Robert is the most modest and humble of women. I penetrated to her bedroom, and examined her night clothes—pink muslin with a pink lace cap, and a prayer book by the bed. (Letters II, 445)

Although the remark about the difficulty of capturing the truth with the written word is a parenthetical prelude to the faintly comic description of Nelly Cecil that follows, it is not, for that reason, any less accurate. It is especially telling when preceded by the letter to Vanessa that mentions a conceived story, the subject of which would be just this problem.[17] Such difficulty is a theme to which Woolf would recur again and again, particularly in some of the essays in *The Common Reader* series.

That the "truth" is easier to reach when one is not attempting to make out a special case or looking for the representative of a broad class is conveyed in Woolf's title for her story which, as she wrote to Vanessa, she meant to use as the title for the whole collection of stories. Monday and Tuesday are merely two successive days of the week, neither its beginning nor end. Woolf's title creates the impression that these days are randomly chosen. Through the conjunction "or," they are granted equivalence, reducing any special status even further. They confirm Woolf's determination to focus on the ordinary. Her choice has both political and aesthetic ramifications, resurrecting the paradox of Wordsworthian Romanticism: its contemplation and beatification of the humble and ordinary in life.[18]

The brief sketch indicates a number of strategies for recording truth in a representation of life as, by contrast, the speaker in Keats's "Ode to a Nightingale" attempts different strategies to evade it. Imaginative identification with nature through the heron, the more specific writerly attempts to convey reality directly through the recording of multitudinous stimuli—"(a cry starts to the left, another to the right. Wheels strike divergently . . .) — for ever desiring — (the clock asseverates with twelve distinct strokes that it is midday; light sheds gold scales, children swarm) — for ever desiring truth" (CSF, 131)—or through metaphor—"laboriously distilling a few words" (CSF, 131).

But the strategies give way to a question that overrides the assurance of the assertions. The narrator asks " — and truth?" (CSF, 131). She does not take unquestioning comfort in a belief that the "truth" of existence can be conveyed by the asseverations of a symbolic code, whether through realism: "while outside a van discharges, Miss Thingummy drinks tea at her desk, a plate-glass preserves fur coats — " (CSF, 131); or through abstract poetic description: "Flaunted, leaf-light, drifting at corners, blown across the wheels, silver-splashed . . ." (CSF, 131).

Having attempted direct and metaphorical representations of reality, the narrator-writer focuses on her own imagination, the perceiver and interpreter of truth, as it is stirred by literature: "From ivory depths words shed their blackness, blossom and penetrate" (CSF, 131). The narrator describes the imagination's excitation by the symbolic code of ink-black letters in a book that raise specters in the mind. "Fallen the book; in the flame, in the smoke, in the momentary sparks — or now voyaging, the marble square pendant, minarets beneath and the Indian seas, while space rushes blue and stars glint — truth? or now, content with closeness?" (CSF, 131). Are these mind-pictures truth? Are they of an equality with the pictures of the "real" world? Is there, in fact, such a thing called truth at all? Or has the narrator given up the very difficult effort of deciding any of these questions and of conveying truth, subsiding into a lower animal state, and being merely "content with closeness" (CSF, 131)?

Yet the narrator ultimately reverts to the belief that there is something incontrovertibly out there, beyond the imagination of the individual, that can and must be communicated to the reader. "Lazy and indifferent the heron returns; the sky veils her stars; then bares them" (CSF, 131). Time, as well as space, conveys to the narrator the separate reality of the world. The narrator is not physically with the heron at this point, but somewhere else, appreciating its "return," both temporally and spatially. The narrator similarly concedes that the veiling and unveiling of the stars is not of the imagination's agency but is a real event, happening through time because of the movement of the clouds.

We are left, then, throughout this collection of stories, with the impression that Woolf has appreciated the value and the difficulty of her new narrative concern: both to find a way of conveying the evanescence of conscious thought, of the impressions of the world lodged briefly or more permanently in the mind, and of the firmness of the world beyond the individual that yet can be known only through the agency of the imagination.

Her apprehension of, and effort to communicate, the quiddity of things—in her own terms, the wholeness of the moment of being—are, psychologically, aspects of the preoedipal impulse towards connection and satisfaction in unity, in the fusing of subject and object, mind and matter, individual and world. That she experienced the creative urge as an avatar of the preoedipal state of blissful wholeness is evident from her description of it in "A Sketch of the Past." But from the perspective of literary history, we can recognize the shapes of her creation in relation to the Romantics' characteristic merging of the individual and the universe. Woolf transformed their efforts by extending the process of fusion; the reader is welcomed and granted access to the privileged moment through her narrative experiments. As we read, our internalization of the rich texture of Woolf's expression generates in us, not too hyperbolically, something akin to preoedipal bliss that paradoxically gives us a sense of wonderful psychic enablement, moving us beyond ourselves.

Woolf applied the results of her experiments to the most engrossing aspect of her work, the writing of novels. *Jacob's Room,* begun when these stories had not all been finished, is her first attempt in the new direction. Yet most readers see flaws in that novel and feel that she did not completely succeed in the extended form as she had in the more limited short sketches. It would take this failed effort at conveying the luminous halo of life and her numerous inquiries into the nature of fiction in her critical essays, later collected in *The Common Reader,* for her to succeed with *Mrs. Dalloway* and the novels written after.

4

"Self-consciousness" and "Conviction" in
The Common Reader

> . . . and so to some reflections apparently written casually but full of profundity (profound criticism is often written casually) about some book I have been reading, some out-of-the-way book.
>
> —*The Waves*

VIRGINIA Woolf's abiding purpose in *The Common Reader* essays was to examine the idiosyncratic efforts made by writers in different ages to capture reality. Her organization of these essays reveals another, collateral interest: to account for the development of modernism, the contemporary manifestation of a writer's particular engagement with the world, and, ultimately, to recommend the strategies of the present day, despite their shortcomings. Her choice of name for the two volumes suggests, as usual, Woolf's sense of the reciprocity of the acts of writing and reading. As she states in her foreword, this name comes from Dr. Johnson who, in his "Life of Gray," describes "the pursuit of reading [as] carried on by private people" (CR, 1) or "the common reader," "'for by the common sense of readers . . . must be finally decided all claim to poetical honours'" (CR, 1).

Woolf's further explanation of Johnson's phrase "poetical honours" implicates Leslie Stephen in the grounding of his daughter's critical approach because she uses the phrase to suggest the repository of the values of a culture. "[T]he common sense of readers," she says, "defines," "dignifies," and "bestows upon a pursuit which devours a great deal of time, and is yet apt to leave behind it nothing very substantial, the sanction of the great man's approval" (CR, 1). The response of the private reader—that sense of excitement that boils up within us as we acknowledge that this is what we "have always felt and known and desired" (ROO, 75)—when multiplied ten thousand times so that it becomes a judgment of the public, reflects that intricate web of values, the common belief, or "Nin Crot and Pulley," as she called it in "Anon," that dialectically meshes with literature and art and defines an age.[1] The "nothing very substantial" constitutes the invisible shifts in attitudes and values in any one reader, "the ideas and opinions which, insignificant in themselves, yet contribute to so mighty a result" (CR, 2). The mighty result is the distribution of "poetical honours" (CR, 1) or, as Stephen would have translated, the powerful though vaporous forces that shape the character of a particular period and make us prefer and memorialize one artist instead of another. Further, taking a historical perspective and so adumbrating aesthetic reception theory, Woolf contextualizes the works she considers, recognizing that the reader of one age inscribes himself in the text and reads it differently from a reader in another. Defoe, as she points out, was not read by his contemporaries as she reads him in 1919.[2]

We may, however, doubt the authenticity of Woolf's notion of the common reader when she describes the aims of his reading. "Above all," she says, "he is guided by an instinct to create for himself, out of whatever odds and ends he can come by, some kind of whole — a portrait of a man, a sketch of an age, a theory of the art of writing" (CR, 1). Our first problem of interpretation arises from the apparent contradiction of the words "guided" and "instinct." "Guided" suggests conscious, volitional decision making; "instinct," unconscious, unmediated behavior. Also Woolf's emphasis on the desire for seeing a pattern, for creating "some kind of whole," says more, perhaps, about the defining quality of her modernism and her sense of the nature of the artist than it does about her mythical model for a private, pleasure-seeking reader. For although she argues that "the first process" of reading is "to receive impressions with the utmost understanding" and the second, to "make of these fleeting shapes one that is hard and lasting" (SCR, 266), she would later cynically describe many readers as merely stripping with their eyes miles of ink from paper annually. Such readers, for the most part, are not impelled to bring the writer's or their own impressions together, to "put two and two together," whereby both as readers and artists, "we overcome dissolution and set up some stake against oblivion" (A & R, 403). We suspect, with good cause, that Woolf is writing about her own reading practices in both *Common Reader* volumes.

Her desire to impose an order, to create some kind of whole, is expressed in each of these two books through a theme common to the essays and traced by her mainly through a chronologically sequential approach to literary artifacts. But although Woolf may choose in both collections to discuss literature or subjects of the same period, the story in each volume is told from a different perspective or, more precisely, focal point or level. The figure of a microscope with different powers of magnification, the eyepiece of which can be focused down through successive layers of cells, enabling the viewer to appreciate at one time the larger, and at another the finer, details of the various structures of the specimen, suggests both the unique character of each of these critical volumes and of Woolf's historical view in both. This figure, too, foregrounds the critical reader's participation, through perception, in the identification of the important structures that describe an author's style or approach and, beyond that limited objective, the qualities that define an age.

The two *Common Reader* volumes hold a position of special importance in the canon of her criticism because these were the only collections of critical writing Woolf published during her lifetime. Although the individual essays may be matched or even overshadowed in worth by others she did not anthologize, Woolf's principles in the choosing and grouping of these subjects give the shape of these books special interest. She did not attempt to find the end of a ball of string and unwind it as she would do in "Anon." Yet although she did not suggest historical continuity, by bringing these essays together (and often mentioning the next subject at the end of an essay or the previous one at the beginning of another), she arranged a series of landmarks through which she could examine the mutual relations of life and art through the centuries. Her diary speculations about the shape of a book she might write for The Hogarth Press on "perspective" in fiction might equally apply to *The Second Common Reader:*

> This book for the H.P.: I think I will find some theory about fiction. . . . The one I have in view, is about *perspective.* . . .
> I don't think it is a matter of 'development' but something to do with prose & poetry, in novels. For instance Defoe at one end: E. Brontë at the other. Reality something they put at different distances. One would have to go into conventions; real life; & so on. (Diary III, 50)

Woolf in *The Second Common Reader* studies prose style from the Elizabethan age to the modern as a function of "different distances" from reality with its vertical and horizontal time, its moments of being and non-being—which "theory—[she] should have to support . . . with other things" (Diary III, 51). Her very specific point of view amounts to the high level of microscopic magnification. On the other hand, the low level, through which we appreciate the broad structures—the "archiplot" of the first *Common Reader*— is the history of self-consciousness or its absence in the writers and in the common readers, themselves, who people the historical pageant. Both for Virginia and Leonard Woolf, this quality of mind defines the moderns and first appears as an important historical phenomenon in the late eighteenth century, the age of revolution and Romanticism.[3] Through examining each writer's unique engagement with the world in the first *Common Reader,* she establishes the intricate and dependent relations of self-consciousness, tropic language, and the ordinary, both as subject and method. As we consider these essays for her definitions of the writer's activity, we shall see that Romantic critical theory and practice, Wordsworth's in particular, shape her ideas.

We begin the discussion of Woolf's critiques of the writers on whom the common readers of the centuries have bestowed the poetical honors with Wordsworth's definition of the poet's activity and of human nature.

> What then does the Poet? He considers man and the objects that surround him as acting and re-acting upon each other, so as to produce an infinite complexity of pain and pleasure; he considers man in his own nature and in his ordinary life as contemplating this with a certain quantity of immediate knowledge, with certain convictions, intuitions, and deductions, which from habit acquire the quality of intuitions; he considers him as looking upon this complex scene of ideas and sensations, and finding everywhere objects that immediately excite in him sympathies which, from the necessities of his nature, are accompanied by an overbalance of enjoyment.
>
> . . . He considers man and nature as essentially adapted to each other, and the mind of man as naturally the mirror of the fairest and most interesting properties of nature. (Wordsworth, 455)

The sense of interpenetration, the resonance between the mind and external nature and the delight that self-conscious recognition of this relationship produces—according to Wordsworth, the principal subjects of the poet's art—are reflected in Woolf's words from *A Room of One's Own.*

> Nature, in her most irrational mood, has traced in invisible ink on the walls of the mind a premonition which these great artists confirm; a sketch which only needs to be held to the fire of genius to become

visible. When one so exposes it [the premonition] and sees it come to life one exclaims in rapture, But this is what I have always felt and known and desired! And one boils over with excitement, and, shutting the book even with a kind of reverence as if it were something very precious, a stand-by to return to as long as one lives, one puts it back on the shelf. . . . (*ROO*, 75)

The verbs "exposes," "sees," and "exclaims" and the participles "felt," "known," and "desired" reveal the active engagement of self and world both in the reading and the writing process. "One boils over with excitement" equally suggests that aesthetic responsiveness originates within.[4] Wordsworth's sense of the pleasure of intuition and Woolf's exposure of the premonition come to the same thing: *active recognition* that the mind mirrors, as Wordsworth says, the external world.

In 1928, the same year as the lectures at Girton and Newnham Colleges that together became the essay *A Room of One's Own,* Woolf wrote in *Orlando:*

For the shadow of faintness . . . deepened now, at the back of [Orlando's] brain (which is the part furthest from sight) into a pool where things dwell in darkness so deep that what they are we scarcely know. She now looked down into this pool or sea in which everything is reflected—and, indeed, some say that all our most violent passions, and art and religion are the reflections which we see in the dark hollow at the back of the head when the visible world is obscured for the time. She looked there now, long, deeply, profoundly, and immediately the ferny path up the hill along which she was walking became not entirely a path, but partly the Serpentine; the hawthorn bushes were partly ladies and partly gentlemen sitting with card cases and gold-mounted canes; the sheep were partly tall Mayfair houses; everything was partly something else, and each gained an odd moving power from this union of itself and something not itself so that with this mixture of truth and falsehood her mind became like a forest in which things moved; lights and shadows changed, and one thing became another.[5]

The metaphor of the dark hollow at the back of the brain from which emotion, art, and religion issue as reflections suggests that these feelings, both the unshaped violent passions and the shaped and shaping experiences of art and religion, are not the result of any external agency. Her intuition, revealed in these metaphors, of the structural origins of these profoundest expressions of certain human needs—that they are part of the architecture of the brain itself—parallels Noam Chomsky's theory of a generative grammar, the expression of the universal need for a structured language as inhering in the genetic code of human beings. Gerald Edelman's position that particular neuronal clusters in the brain, through a process equivalent to Darwinian selection, are "chosen" to respond to certain external stimuli also resonates with Woolf's metaphor.[6] The need to make art, to form systems of expression and of belief—the artist, linguist, and neurobiologist suggest—is a matter of matter.

But for Woolf the brain does more. As Orlando looks into this darkest recess of the mind, the sights of the external world mix with what they are not. The ferny path becomes the Serpentine. Sheep become partly Mayfair houses. As for the Romantics, imagination and, through it, the most concentrated form of imaginative seeing, art, actively transform the observable world as well as mirror it.

The locus of critical activity or, strictly speaking, the desire for such activity, is implicitly in this same metaphorical dark pool. "I feel too," she wrote in November 1931, "at the back of my brain, that I can devise a new critical method; something far less still & formal than these Times articles. . . . There must be some simpler, subtler, closer means of writing about books, as about people, could I hit upon it" (Diary IV, 53–54). Her method was based on the Romantic expression of the relation between mind and world. Like Wordsworth, defining a new poetics in the Preface, she wanted to "mitigate the pomposity & sweep in all sorts of trifles" and "envelop each essay in its own atmosphere" (Diary II, 261). Beginning *The Common Reader* with "The Pastons and Chaucer" seems equally a means of grounding her collection in the ordinary world of Monday or Tuesday.

Woolf suggests in the first *Common Reader* that the phenomenon of self-consciousness constitutive of modernism is traceable in Western Europe to Thomas Browne and Montaigne. However, she creates a baseline view of the question in her first and second essays, "The Pastons and Chaucer" and "On Not Knowing Greek." The first essay is a paradigmatic discussion of the relation between the unself-conscious, common-reading Pastons and the equally unself-conscious writing Chaucer, on whom the Pastons and others like them have bestowed poetical honors. Although "On Not Knowing Greek" is an examination of metaphor-making, usually a by-product of self-consciousness, she introduces her subject with the observation that we cannot make assumptions about Athenian common readers and the nature of their minds as we do with the knowable Pastons, and, therefore, we cannot extrapolate from them the texture of the culture. Thus, we stumble on a historical paradox common to all her essays on common readers or the lives of the obscure: all these common readers are themselves writers, since without their additions to the written record, she would have no knowledge of them. In the case of the Athenians, Woolf is unable to locate a comparable writing audience.

Thus, the relations of the Pastons and Chaucer is a happy subject as through it she can, with justice, establish the blurred distinction between readers and writers. The similarities of the letters and of the poetry serve as an index to Woolf's and our contemporary supposition that reading and writing are interdependent, collusive activities. Because both the Pastons and Chaucer contributed to the historical record, they enable Woolf to speculate about the shared view of reality held by the writers and common reader-writers of this particular period. Margaret Paston strikes the note of the age:

> Indeed, had Mrs. Paston chosen, she could have told her children how when she was a young woman a thousand men with bows and arrows and pans of burning fire had marched upon Gresham and broken the gates and mined the walls of the room where she sat alone. But much worse things than that had happened to women. She neither bewailed her lot nor thought herself a heroine. The long, long letters which she wrote so labouriously in her clear cramped hand to her husband . . . make no mention of herself. The sheep had wasted the hay. Heyden's and Tuddenham's men were out. . . . They needed treacle badly, and really she must have stuff for a dress.
> But Mrs. Paston did not talk about herself. (CR, 6)

Woolf, through the repetition of the assertion "But Mrs. Paston did not talk about herself," defines the sense of self of Mrs. Paston, in particular, and of the whole age, in general. To be sure, Mrs. Paston thought of herself in a material way—"really she must have stuff for a dress"—which certainly implies a body that fits into one.[7] But Woolf's finer discrimination is that these people were not in the habit of considering their minds as organs in distinction from, and capable of comprehending, the material world they inhabited. Whether or not historically accurate, her notion of the opacity-of-the-mediaeval-mind-to-itself guides her discussion of both the utilitarian prose and the poetry of this period.

She argues that this was a period of capital accumulation with emphasis almost exclusively on the exterior life of the material world: "To buy land, to build great houses, to stuff these houses full of gold and silver plate (though the privy might well be in the bedroom), was the proper aim of mankind" CR, 6). Thus, equally for these people, "The soul was no wisp of air, but a solid body capable of eternal suffering, and the fire that destroyed it was as fierce as any that burnt on mortal grates" (CR, 7).

Similarly, in characterizing Chaucer's poetry, Woolf indirectly claims that it takes its character from his notion of his own soul, which, according to the mediaeval view, is no wisp of air but a solid body. And so he projects a world that is solid, transcribing it in unadorned, unmetaphorical language.

> Without possessing a tithe of the virtuosity in word-painting which is the modern inheritance, he could give, in a few words, or even, when we come to look, without a single word of direct description, a sense of the open air.
> And se the fresshe floures how they sprynge — that is enough.
> Nature, uncompromising, untamed, was no looking-glass for happy faces, or confessor of unhappy souls. She was herself; sometimes, therefore, disagreeable enough and plain, but always in Chaucer's pages with the hardness and the freshness of an actual presence. Soon, however, we notice . . . the solidity which plumps it out, the conviction which animates the characters. (CR, 13)

And yet Chaucer's world, although it resembles life in its solidity and conviction, "is not in fact our daily world. It is the world of poetry" (CR, 18) although paradoxically the intensity of our perception of this world cannot be proved by quoting any verse in particular.

> From most poets quotation is easy and obvious; some metaphor suddenly flowers; some passage breaks off from the rest. But Chaucer is very equal, very even-paced, very unmetaphorical. . . .
> . . . there is a special stimulus in seeing all these common things so arranged that they affect us as poetry affects us, and are yet bright, sober, precise as we see them out of doors. There is a pungency in this unfigurative language; a stately and memorable beauty in the undraped sentences which follow each other like women so slightly veiled that you see the lines of their bodies as they go. . . . (CR, 19)

Chaucer's world is illuminated by intense sunlight. The hidden metaphor in her one word "bright" suggests Woolf's assumption about the coextension of the imagination of the artist and the world created, in the writer's case, through the medium of language. Yet she implies that Chaucer is himself not aware of this illumination as proceeding from his own imagination. She bases her proof on other assumptions about metaphor central to her ideas concerning the representation of the world by the modern artist and suggested by her own practice in this description. What sets Chaucer apart from the moderns, she says, is his unmetaphorical language. Metaphor indicates a self-consciousness about language that has yet to come into being and must wait, as we learn from "The Elizabethan Lumber Room," for the advent of the Elizabethan stage. The quality we define as Romantic, that nature *is* a "looking-glass for happy faces, or confessor of unhappy souls," is not to be found in Chaucer's poetry. Woolf operatively suggests the distinction between the two kinds of language, translating the unmetaphorical, direct quality of Chaucer's words through her own metaphoric comparison of the beauty of undraped sentences and women slightly veiled.

The etiology of the modern case, her own, is thus established through her discussion of Chaucer's unself-consciousness or conviction. Chaucer's omission of self from his poetry, much like Margaret Paston's in her letters, is also owing to the unspoiled condition of the natural world and the preference, both in readers and writers, for fact and event-driven narratives of a traditional sort, no longer produced because no longer desired by her contemporaries.

> Nothing happens to us as it did to our ancestors; events are seldom important; if we recount them, we do not really believe in them; we have perhaps things of greater interest to say, and for these reasons natural story-tellers like Mr Garnett, whom we must distinguish from self-conscious story-tellers like Mr Masefield . . . have become rare. (CR, 11–12)

Margaret Paston had written to her husband that "The sheep had wasted the hay." Her son, Sir John, turned from the world to seek solace in Chaucer. Yet he similarly desired fact and event-driven narrative—"To learn the end of the story" (CR, 11). Woolf also explains the mediaeval reader's desire, like the poet's, to see the "unspoilt" "virgin land, all unbroken grass and wood" (CR, 12), the world he knew.

The moderns' self-consciousness has its material basis as equally and oppositely John Paston and Chaucer's unself-consciousness had theirs. The moderns cannot capture the wondrous natural world because nature is no longer in the same unspoiled condition. "The state of the country, considering how poets go to Nature, how they use her for their images and their contrasts even when they do not describe her directly, is a matter of some importance" (CR, 12). Woolf describes a descent from a golden to an iron age. She compares Chaucer with his unspoiled world to Wordsworth and Tennyson who, in their relatively more fallen times, because of the necessity of their taking the country as opposed to the city as "the sanctuary of moral excellence," indulge in a "morbid . . . nature worship" (CR, 12). However, she concedes that these latter "were great poets. In their hands, the country was no mere jeweller's shop, or museum of curious objects to be described, even more curiously, in words" (CR, 12). But Woolf's contemporaries, because they are "Poets of smaller gift" and nature is even more spoiled in the twentieth century, are "confined to little landscapes, to birds' nests, to acorns with every wrinkle drawn to the life. The wider landscape is lost" (CR, 12). The poetic project of imaging nature has become one of conscious priestly virtue with its nature worship and, in its most debased state, of self-conscious commodity fetishism in the confines of a jeweler's shop.

However, Woolf's assumption about the unself-consciousness of the mediaeval mind, that it did not regard itself as a reflector of the world, moderates as she describes the unique collusion of the reader and the writer. She applies the same figures to Sir John Paston, her first-named common-reader, as she does to Joan Martyn when Woolf describes Paston's reaction to Chaucer's words. Living near the Chapel of Our Lady in the town of Norwich (CR,7), as does Joan in ". . . Joan Martyn," Sir John "would sit reading Chaucer, wasting his time, dreaming — or what strange intoxication was it that he drew from books?" (CR, 11). His energized imagination permitted him to see "Lydgate's poems or Chaucer's, like a mirror in which figures move brightly, silently, and compactly, showed him the very skies, fields, and people whom he knew, but rounded and complete" (CR, 11). Virginia Stephen, borrowing a figure from Wordsworth, has Joan compare the experience of the expansion of her imagination, excited by Master Richard's book. The "feelings" she "might enter within" are "solid globes of crystal; enclosing a round ball of coloured earth and air, in which tiny men and women laboured, as beneath the dome of the sky itself" (CSF, 58). John Paston's sense of the poetry is also like Joan's description of the words of Richard's book. The words metaphorically open up "broad spaces of colour. . . . They were like little mirrors, held up to those visions which I had seen passing in the air but here they were caught and stayed forever" (CSF, 56–57).

Woolf implies, in general, that the desire to read, to get into the frame of mind (an expression that, itself, suggests that the activity has an artful purpose and outcome) in which there is pleasure in the use of the imagination is a luxury based on prior capital accumulation. Sir John with "the instincts of enjoyment rather than of acquisition" (CR, 9) and whose particular "luxurious tempera-ment" led him to this unmaterially productive occupation is her case in point. Describing the transformation of this family in his person but implying a broad historical shift based on the accumula-tion of wealth in the entire upper class of a society, Woolf says: "But inwardly there was a change. It seems at last as if the hard outer shell had served its purpose and something sensitive, appre-ciative, and pleasure-loving had formed within" (CR, 9). This change parallels Woolf's description of Joan, distinguished from her more utilitarian mother at the end of ". . . Joan Martyn."

Woolf begins and ends her essay with the story of John Paston's failure to build a tomb for his father—a matter of respect and decorum, we remember, not neglected by Joan Martyn's father. The "method" of the Paston letters is "to heap up in mounds of insignificant and often dismal dust the innumerable trivialities of daily life, as it grinds itself out, year after year. And then suddenly they blaze up; the day shines out, complete, alive, before our eyes. . . . There is the ancient day, spread out before us, hour by hour" (CR, 21). Woolf ties letters and poetry together once more.

> But when Chaucer lived he must have heard this very language, matter of fact, unmetaphorical, far better fitted for narrative than analysis, capable of religious solemnity or broad humour, but very stiff material to put on the lips of men and women accosting each other face to face. In short, it is easy to see, from the Paston letters, why Chaucer wrote not *Lear* or *Romeo and Juliet,* but the *Canterbury Tales.* (CR, 22)

The central issue for Woolf in this paradigmatic essay is, then, aesthetic self-consciousness of one's medium, with tropic language functioning as the barometer. Woolf, in praising Chaucer, tries to be evenhanded, to argue that Chaucer's and the moderns' ap-proaches are merely two different strategies for conveying the real-ity behind the text. However, one sort of reality—the existence of minds in the act of thinking, and more particularly, as in the case of the Romantics, thinking about the making of art—cannot be captured through Chaucer's language. Woolf implies that the his-torical movement in literature from Chaucer to the present is a progression, in the root sense of that word, ending with the modern writer who, as she says, has "perhaps things of greater interest to say."

It may then seem either that we have misunderstood Woolf's intentions or that Woolf herself has misjudged her design when we consider that the second essay on the Greeks is out of chronological sequence. However, its very placement serves as a metaphor for this "unplaceable" classical literature along a continuum that begins with Chaucer and the Pastons and ends with her contemporaries. Yet in another sense there is a direct line of descent from the Greeks to the moderns, which accounts for Woolf's intense interest. Writing of the "reality" of character, of the mere "shell of a person that is seen by other people" as compared with substantial figures enlarged "with the green of forest depths," and built upon the composite reflections of these characters, Woolf says in "The Mark on the Wall":

> And the novelists in future will realise more and more the importance of these reflections, for of course there is not one reflection but an almost infinite number; those are the depths they will explore, those the phantoms they will pursue, leaving the description of reality more and more out of their stories, taking a knowledge of it for granted, as the Greeks did and Shakespeare perhaps. . . . (CSF, 79–80)

The Greeks in their transcription of character and of reality, are then unique.[8] They have created the great archetypes of western culture. They "remain in a fastness of their own" (CR, 23) because we do not have a connection to them, provided, as Woolf says, by "our ancestors' lives" and enriched, "later, as records increase and memories lengthen" by the "nimbus of association" that surrounds each historical figure (CR, 23). In the Greeks "the stable, the permanent, the original human being is to be found" whereas the characters of Chaucer are "the varieties of the human species" (CR, 27).

Considering language, Woolf finds herself perplexed "with the insoluble question of poetry and its nature, and why, as she [Electra] speaks thus, her words put on the assurance of immortality" (CR, 28). When Woolf reads the plays of Aeschylus, she feels she is in the presence of pure poetry, concentrated, as in the work of the moderns, in tropes so that these dramas are made

> tremendous by stretching every phrase to the utmost, by sending them floating forth in metaphors, by bidding them rise up and stalk eyeless and majestic through the scene. . . . It is necessary to take that dangerous leap through the air without the support of words which Shakespeare also asks of us. For words, when opposed to such a blast of meaning, must give out . . . and only by collecting in companies convey the meaning which each one separately is too weak to express. Connecting them in a rapid flight of the mind we know instantly and instinctively what they mean, but could not decant that meaning afresh

into any other words. There is an ambiguity which is a mark of the
highest poetry; we cannot know exactly what it means. (CR, 30)

Woolf's paradox that words, or concatenations of words, produce
images that come as close as possible to striking the imagination
instantly, instinctively, and wordlessly is paralleled by her claim
that the Greek dramatists "attain that unconsciousness which
means that the consciousness is stimulated to the highest extent"
(CR, 37). She is describing an experience of the sublime that depends on the substitution of the text for elements of the natural
world. Both her statements eerily invoke the meaning and very
words of a contemporary of William Blake's, the mythographer
Richard Payne Knight. Of Greek poetry, Knight wrote:

> The obscurity of the lyric style of Pindar and the Greek tragedians
> does not arise from any confusion or indistinctness in the imagery; but
> from its conciseness and abruptness; and from its being shown to the
> mind in sudden flashes and corruscations [*sic*], the connection between
> which is often scarcely perceptible.[9]

Such image-producing language is, then, not solely an attribute of
self-conscious contemporary writers but has a history that goes
back in the West, beyond Shakespeare and the Renaissance, to the
very beginnings of recorded literature.

Thus, Woolf argues that the figurative language of these plays
is not ornamental but radically central to aesthetic pleasure and
intuition. Correlatively, she is most interested by literature in
which the power of language is bound to its ability to excite the
image-making potential of the receiving and modifying imagination
of the reader. Her assertion is, likewise, a reprise of Edmund
Burke's description of the nature of the sublime poetic text:

> . . . I think there are reasons in nature why the obscure idea, when
> properly conveyed, should be more affecting than the clear. It is our
> ignorance of things that causes all our admiration, and chiefly excites
> our passions. Knowledge and acquaintance make the most striking
> causes affect but little. . . .
>
> But let it be considered that hardly any thing can strike the mind
> with its greatness, which does not make some sort of approach towards
> infinity; which nothing can do whilst we are able to perceive its bounds;
> but to see an object distinctly, and to perceive its bounds, is one and
> the same thing. A clear idea is therefore another name for a little idea.[10]

If we substitute her "unconsciousness" for Burke's "infinity" and
Woolf's "the consciousness is stimulated to the highest extent"

for his "strike the mind with its greatness," we see that Woolf's sense of the pleasure of the text, the poetic sublime, is an avatar of the Burkean, and, as well, of a number of instances of the Romantic, sublime, which were predicated on indeterminacy and illimitableness. "On Not Knowing Greek" is, then, a natural step to her third essay on the metaphoric language of the first truly great period in the national literature, the Elizabethan age.

The first three essays of *The Common Reader,* despite their disparate subject matter, thus constitute a discussion of self-consciousness and the related production of metaphorical language. As in the mediaeval world of the Pastons, capital accumulation explains the production of literature in the age of Elizabeth.

"The Elizabethan Lumber Room," beginning with the title itself, proceeds with its operative proof that tropes reflect a high degree of literary consciousness. The movement of the essay, unlike the structure of the first two, is completely controlled by the extended metaphor of the lumber room—a physical storeroom of exotic treasures retrieved from voyages of exploration. The wonder of this metaphor is that Woolf transforms its meaning as her argument progresses, not by changing it but by sliding the signified under the signifier: she modifies the tenor, leaving the vehicle in place. Woolf, however, does not impute self-consciousness to the Elizabethans, despite their production of metaphors. Self-conscious, tropic language merely functions reflexively, governing the argument of Woolf's essay. For as she states, metaphor is decorative rather than structural in the poetry and prose of this era. Metaphor was not for the Elizabethans what it was for the Greek dramatists in whose plays it was essential to structure and meaning, creating for the reader the poetic sublime.

However, this essay is pivotal in *The Common Reader,* not because it shows Woolf to be the highly self-conscious crafter of language and shaper of meaning we already know her to be, but rather because of its concluding assertion concerning the importance of Thomas Browne to the historical development of self-conscious intellectual thought in Europe. She suggests, in the manner of her father, a significant dialectical relationship between material change in society, in art forms, and, in what she discovers in Browne, his mold-breaking habits of mind and their expression.

Yet because this essay is so obvious an example of Woolf's metaphoric criticism, a defense against the clichéd charge that it is "impressionistic" is in order. Imagery, of course, is at the heart of her so-named impressionism. Thomas McLaughlin says that her essays "are impressionistic, non-systematic, belle-lettristic. They are intuitive rather than methodical." Yet he agrees that this view "held by her detractors and many of her defenders" is "simplified if not inaccurate."[11] In the same vein of faint praise for her method, René Wellek asserts: "The standard of judgment implied in these essays is the preference for the universally human, for the power of generalizing, of creating situations and characters which (like Hardy's characters) persuade us that there is 'something symbolical about them which is common to us all.' 'Imagination is at its freest when it is most generalized.'"[12] The most comprehensive comment on Woolf's impressionism is Barbara Currier Bell and Carol Ohmann's.

> Woolf, of course, uses a great deal of imagery in her criticism; the fact has been often observed but by no means (or seldom) connected with the common reader. First of all, we like imagery. In an effort to please us, Woolf uses it as liberally as cooks use seasoning. Second, we need imagery. Many of the ideas Woolf puts forth, particularly in the aesthetic essays, are essentially abstruse, and images are the fastest, most concrete, and effective means of explanation—that is, if they are of a certain kind: either simple, or striking, or both.[13]

Yet Woolf does not "sprinkle" her criticism with "image" seasoning. Such a "decorated" prose style is what she derogates in the Elizabethans whose rich imagery ultimately cloys. It is true that imagery is an "effective means of explanation" of "abstruse" ideas as Bell and Ohmann say, but to reduce in this way the defining quality of Woolf's writing is to miss its power and its essential, Romantic-modernist implication.

When we turn to the essay on "The Sentimental Journey" in *The Second Common Reader,* we are struck by her citation from Sterne's book and her comment:

> For my own part, by long habitude, I do it so mechanically that when I walk the streets of London, I go translating all the way; and have more than once stood behind in the circle, where not three words have been said, and have brought off twenty different dialogues with me, which I could have fairly wrote down and swore to. . . .

> It is thus that Sterne transfers our interest from the outer to the inner. . . . In this preference for the windings of his own mind to the guide-book and its hammered high road, Sterne is singularly of our own age. In this interest in silence rather than in speech Sterne is the forerunner of the moderns. (SCR, 81)

The use of metaphors is equally borne out of an "interest in silence," out of a desire to bypass the chattering intellect and, through the "rapid flight of the mind" to produce an instant and "somatic" understanding in the reader that causes us to sense the sublime, or, like Bernard in *The Waves,* to "glow, phosphorescent" (TW, 326). Metaphors excite a potent memory. They recall one's own experiences of the body—of sight, touch, smell—so that we sense a "fit" between our own "knowledge" and the writer's words. Sometimes, as she said in "On Not Knowing Greek," we cannot "decant . . . meaning afresh into any other words." The indeterminacy of Woolf's images transforms her criticism into the highest kind of art, creating a "readerly" sublime for her readers.

Thus, we appreciate her metaphor of the lumber room as she describes the real catalogue of commodities—the "ancient sacks, obsolete nautical instruments, huge bales of wool, and little bags of rubies and emeralds" (CR, 39)—with which Hakluyt stuffs the sentences of his *Voyages,* indeed, which are, themselves, the sections of it. His descriptions entered into the imaginations of the Elizabethans so that they yearned for the exotic experiences of the explorers. Some of them were actually induced to make their own voyages, to accumulate their own capital. But for those who stayed at home, the appetite for extravagant adventure was satisfied vicariously through art. "Thus," Woolf says, "we find the whole of Elizabethan literature strewn with gold and silver; with talk of Guiana's rarities, and references to that America — 'O my America! my new-found-land' . . . — which was not merely a land on the map, but symbolised the unknown territories of the soul" (CR, 43).

The new cultural influence of the voyages of exploration entered into the language of the plays. "All this, the new words, the new ideas, the waves, the savages, the adventures, found their way naturally into the plays which were being acted on the banks of the Thames" (CR, 42). But beyond the new vocabulary and a new subject matter, Woolf argues that the language of poetry was stylistically affected by this influence. Exaggeration, repetition, abundance of imagery, all of which characterize the public language of poetry and the prose that has not yet broken away from poetic utterance, make the Elizabethan style very different from the undraped sentences of Chaucer.

However, the demands of dramatic form in which "people had to meet, to quip and crank, to suffer interruptions, to talk of ordinary things" (CR, 45) eventually created a need for, and made possible, the transformation of the "lumber room" style. We remember that in "Anon" Woolf complains of the difficulty of finding examples of "small-talk" amongst the Elizabethans. However, here she asserts that it appears in the comedies, thus taming and making earth-bound a prose style that "could speak magnificently, of course, about the great themes — how life is short, and death certain; how spring is lovely, and winter horrid" but that was "almost incapable of fulfilling one of the offices of prose which is to make people talk, simply and naturally, about ordinary things" (SCR, 9).

The other element needful for bringing prose to perfection was "the growth of self-consciousness" (CR, 45) which, in "Notes on an Elizabethan Play," Woolf describes as the antidote to the lack of "solitude" and "privacy" of the always public world of the stage—"full of tedium and delight, pleasure and curiosity, of extravagant laughter, poetry, and splendour" (CR, 57). The desire for ordinary things and the luxury of retreat into self-consciousness, at the heart of Wordsworthian Romanticism, thus also help explain the eventual cultural fatigue brought on by the theater and the turning towards a solitary engagement of reader and book that Leslie Stephen delineated in *English Thought in the Eighteenth Century.* Woolf's description of this shift heralds the third and closing subject of her essay: the man Thomas Browne and his examination and revelation of self.

Thus, the metaphor of the lumber room, already used by Woolf to make real both the subject matter and extravagant style of Elizabethan poetry and prose, is now pressed into service to communicate the richness of the solitary and self-conscious musings of Thomas Browne, the Norwich physician and author of *Religio Medici* and *Urn Burial,* the first autobiographer and "the first to make us feel that the most sublime speculations of the human imagination are issued from a particular man, whom we can love" (CR, 47). This metaphor explodes with intensity in the last sentences of the essay as its meaning drops into the dark pool at the back of our minds. We intuitively recognize that feeling of rightness or fit between Woolf's words and the memory of our experience.

Whatever he writes is stamped with his own idiosyncrasy, and we first become conscious of impurities which hereafter stain literature with so many freakish colours that, however hard we try, it is difficult to be certain whether we are looking at a man or his writing. Now we are in the presence of sublime imagination; now rambling through one of the finest lumber rooms in the world — a chamber stuffed from floor to ceiling with ivory, old iron, broken pots, urns, unicorns' horns, and magic glasses full of emerald lights and blue mystery. (CR, 47)

The man and his writing, his imagination and the printed page are, in this final tribute, actually coextensive. Here Woolf makes clearer the force of the original metaphor as applied to the chapters and sentences of Hakluyt. Is it possible to say, and, if so, is there a point in saying, whether the words on the page are a thing disembodied or separated from the writer and presented to the world in the form of paper, glue, ink, and symbols, or are they a revelation of the maker, the man who collected herbs and wrote of the marvels of his own mind? Is writing a product of the imagination or the imagination itself made substantial? The Romantic metaphor for mind that would blur the distinction between the two—the impression mind makes on the world as it stains the white radiance of eternity—is implicit in the trope "impurities which hereafter stain literature with so many freakish colours." Woolf created a similar metaphor of transparency for the men, women, and children at the end of "Kew Gardens"—"they wavered and sought shade beneath the trees, dissolving like drops of water in the yellow and green atmosphere, staining it faintly with red and blue" (CSF, 89). Here it becomes a metaphor for historic influence, a way of making us feel that the relationship between a writer, his sense of self, and his words was permanently altered by Thomas Browne's self-conscious revelation of his own mind.

Woolf's Romantic sense that the imagination is continuous with the world it perceives is reinforced by Browne's own sense of the wonders of his mind as he writes in *Religio Medici:* "'We carry with us the wonders we seek without us; there is all Africa and her prodigies in us'" (CR, 46). And so, the aptness of Woolf's lumber room image. Thomas Browne, her own predecessor in self-consciousness, has supplied it, thereby substantiating her argument concerning the historic development of prose.

Sir Thomas Browne is again mentioned at the end of "Notes on an Elizabethan Play" with Donne and Montaigne, as "the keepers of the keys of solitude" (CR, 57). Browne and Montaigne get special poetical honors from Woolf, being the first two self-conscious autobiographers in the history of western literature. Thus, striking the note of self-consciousness a second time, she introduces Montaigne, the subject of the fifth essay.

No subject could be closer to Woolf's heart than Montaigne, a thinker and writer who was her "semblable," her "frère." As with all her other essays on the life of a subject, Woolf intuits Montaigne's life, "reads" his story, from his essays. Because Montaigne's life was so much a matter of the examination of his own thoughts, the life she gives us here is actually a compilation of his attitudes. They read like a compendium of Romantic social and aesthetic values.

To begin, Woolf writes of self-consciousness, appreciating the challenge of making the pen accurately convey the elusive quality of thought. She quotes Montaigne:

> 'Tis a rugged road, more so than it seems, to follow a pace so rambling and uncertain, as that of the soul; to penetrate the dark profundities of its intricate internal windings; to choose and lay hold of so many little nimble motions; 'tis a new and extraordinary undertaking, and that withdraws us from the common and most recommended employments of the world. (CR, 59)

Woolf eagerly endorses his assertion; the process of capturing the flow of our thoughts with a rigid pen, of translating into writing "the strange, pleasant process called thinking" (CR, 59) is the rub. She deploys the Romantic metaphor of illumination: "The phantom [the difficulty of expressing our thought to someone else] is through the mind and out of the window before we can lay salt on its tail, or slowly sinking and returning to the profound darkness which it has lit up momentarily with a wandering light" (CR, 59). Yet Woolf argues that this original thinker, almost singly the author of the western tradition of self-consciousness in art, was equally one of the originators of the "Romantic" veneration of the quotidian.

Woolf's discussion in "The Paston's and Chaucer" of the traits of solidity and conviction and of their corollary, the unselfconsciousness "of the parts and functions of the body" (CR, 15) on which much of Chaucer's humor depends, leads her to describe the character of Chaucer's poetry that is also a desideratum for Wordsworth in *Lyrical Ballads:* his ability to convey the texture of ordinary life. "[Chaucer] will tell you what his characters wore, how they looked, what they ate and drank, as if poetry could handle the common facts of this very moment of Tuesday, the sixteenth day of April, 1387 . . . without dirtying her hands" (CR, 16). Montaigne's belief in the importance of remaining close to ordinary people because "He could never see that his own green peas were so much better than other people's" (CR, 61) and his interest in their thoughts and language place him even closer to Wordsworth. Woolf transcribes:

> It appears, then, that we are to aim at a democratic simplicity. We may enjoy our room in the tower, with the painted walls and the commodious bookcases, but down in the garden there is a man digging who

buried his father this morning, and it is he and his like who live the
real life and speak the real language. (CR, 62)

On the other hand, she appreciates Montaigne's inconsistency, his
simultaneously held belief in the meanness of men. His expression
reminds us of Wordsworth, that lover of Man, as he condemns men
in the aggregate in *The Prelude* in "Book Seventh: Residence in
London." Woolf, transcribing Montaigne, writes: "But again, what
a vile thing the rabble is! 'the mother of ignorance, injustice, and
inconstancy . . .'" (CR, 62). But "We must dread any eccentricity
or refinement which cuts us off from our fellow-beings. Blessed
are those who chat easily with their neighbours about their sport
or their buildings or their quarrels, and honestly enjoy the talk of
carpenters and gardeners. To communicate is our chief business
. . ." (CR, 64). Montaigne sounds even more like Wordsworth as
Woolf transcribes: "For ourselves, who are ordinary men and
women, let us return thanks to Nature for her bounty by using
every one of the senses she has given us" (CR, 65). Woolf's deep
appreciation for Montaigne's delight in the examination of self is
a still better decoding of the Wordsworthian credo that life is remarkable, the ordinary extraordinary, and that the imagination itself creates the miracles it registers. She translates Montaigne's
ideas, which resonate so profoundly with Romantic theory.

> Let us simmer over our incalculable cauldron, our enthralling confu-
> sion, our hotch-potch of impulses, our perpetual miracle — for the soul
> throws up wonders every second. Movement and change are the es-
> sence of our being; rigidity is death . . . let us say what comes into
> our heads, repeat ourselves, contradict ourselves, fling out the wildest
> nonsense, and follow the most fantastic fancies without caring what
> the world does or thinks or says. For nothing matters except life; and,
> of course, order. (CR, 63)

Chaos and indeterminacy and, on the other hand, our need for
order, are privileged in this passage and in Woolf's modernism. It
reads like the urtext of Lily Briscoe's discoveries about self, world,
and art in *To the Lighthouse* as well as the collusive musings of
the beach walkers and the narrator about chaos and the desire for
order in "Time Passes."[14]

Montaigne's appreciation for the transforming abilities of the
imagination, for the continuity between mind and world, is appreciated by Woolf who suggested a similar relationship between the
rational and the imaginative in *To the Lighthouse*. Montaigne, she
notes, was entranced by every fact of existence:

. . . [one] must have curtains to one's bed; and, what is rather curious, began by liking radishes, then disliked them, and now likes them again. No fact is too little to let it slip through one's fingers, and besides the interest of facts themselves there is the strange power we have of changing facts by the force of the imagination. Observe how the soul is always casting her own lights and shadows; makes the substantial hollow and the frail substantial; . . . is as much excited by phantoms as by reality; and in the moment of death sports with a trifle. (CR, 66)

Woolf's Romantic confirmation in her own novels of the existence of a dually receptive and perceptive faculty, making possible her moments of being, is theoretically articulated by Montaigne. She finds it remarkable that he should have lived when he did and have expressed these ideas, so indistinguishable from those of the moderns.[15] But her conclusion most extraordinarily defines Montaigne as Woolf's alter ego.

He laid hold of the beauty of the world with all his fingers. He achieved happiness. If he had had to live again, he said, he would have lived the same life over. But, as we watch with absorbed interest the enthralling spectacle of a soul living openly beneath our eyes, the question frames itself, Is pleasure the end of all? Whence this overwhelming interest in the nature of the soul? Why this overmastering desire to communicate with others? Is the beauty of the world enough, or is there, elsewhere, some explanation of the mystery? To this what answer can there be? There is none. There is only one more question: 'Que scais-je?' (CR, 67–68)

These are the very questions that Woolf asked herself as she wandered through Russell Square in 1926: "Yet I have some restless searcher in me. Why is there not a discovery in life? Something one can lay hands on and say 'This is it?' . . . A sense of my own strangeness, walking on the earth is there too: of the infinite oddity of the human position; trotting along Russell Squre [*sic*] with the moon up there . . ." (Diary III, 62). Here is Woolf's willingness to rest finally with ambiguity, to face the indeterminacy of the world and the soul and, on the other hand, to recognize the need for order but not to impose it as a simple solution. . . . That Woolf recognized the straight line of descent from Montaigne to herself and the moderns is no wonder. But he was unique. The line of descent was broken, as the essays on the duchess of Newcastle, Evelyn, Defoe, Addison, "The Lives of the Obscure," and the subjects of "Outlines" prove.

Yet Montaigne, with his curiosity about the common man, is also a fit introduction to these essays of the middle third of *The Common Reader*. A glance at the table of contents, including the essays above and "Taylors and Edgeworths," "Laetitia Pilkington," and "Miss Ormerod," suggests that Woolf has strayed far from her principle of selection because many of the essays are on men and women whose writing never received wide acclaim during their lives and certainly would not be remembered by history were it not for the *uncommon* tastes and values of Virginia Woolf. These subjects, actually common readers themselves and not great writers, have been chosen by Woolf who, influenced by her father's view of history, saw them as defining through their own life-plots the qualities and values of the ages in which they lived. This category of human beings was always to interest her. She says in *Orlando:*

> And indeed . . . the most successful practitioners of the art of life, often unknown people by the way, somehow contrive to synchronise the sixty or seventy different times which beat simultaneously in every normal human system so that when eleven strikes, all the rest chime in unison. . . . Of them we can justly say that they live precisely the sixty-eight or seventy-two years allotted them on the tombstone. (O, 305)

Woolf's interest in writing about them expresses the democratic impulse, characteristic of Chaucer's poetry and Montaigne's essays, but brought to its fullest expression in Wordsworth as he pays homage to the lives of ordinary men and women.

A distinction must be made between Addison and Defoe and the other subjects of these essays because the former are writers who have left their mark on two important genres, the essay and the novel. But with the other subjects, we feel that Woolf's interest in them was actuated, as was her character Clarissa Dalloway's, by her love for life and her appreciation of the biographies that explore it.

We feel Woolf's interest in the sharpness and particularity with which some of these "common reader"–writers were able to convey their lives. As she says of Richard Lovell Edgeworth, memoirist and father of the minor novelist Maria:

> To muse, to repent, to contemplate were foreign to his nature. His wife and friends and children are silhouetted with extreme vividness upon a broad disk of interminable chatter. . . . But his power is not limited to people; landscapes, groups, societies seem, even as he describes them, to split off from him. . . . they live with a peculiar beauty, fantas-

tic, solemn, mysterious, in contrast with Edgeworth, who is none of these things. (CR, 115)

And thus, as well, Clarissa (conceived in 1922, two years before this essay was published) responds to the beauty of the morning: "What a lark! What a plunge! . . . How fresh, how calm . . . chill and sharp and yet . . . solemn" (MD, 3).

The secrets of these ordinary people's lives satisfied the gossip in her. She says in "Jane Austen": "As for the gossip, gossip which has survived its day is never despicable; and with a little re-arrangement it suits our purpose admirably" (CR, 134). But part of the pleasure for her in writing these essays was that "making up" these lives was almost like writing fiction: "It is so difficult to refrain from making up scenes which, if the past could be recalled, might perhaps be found lacking in accuracy. . . . Certain scenes have the fascination which belongs rather to the abundance of fiction than to the sobriety of fact" (CR, 113). These "characters," we feel, served her in the same way that Wordsworth's idiosyncratic figures in *Lyrical Ballads* did him. They are not memorable for their contributions to the progress of mankind nor even for their part in a historically compelling intrigue, but in their private lives they had interesting and complex relations with others; they had deep feelings. In short, they are life itself, the very people who have given the poetical honors to the other subjects of this same volume and, in so doing, have opened for us a window onto the past. They are, themselves, cultural spots of time or moments of being through which we feel the texture of the age in which they lived. In the aggregate they are our collective memory, our cultural history.

Although John Evelyn has been consigned to the minor league of literary history, he is part of a group occupying a place between the truly obscure and the writers with the highest poetical honors in *The Common Reader*. But like the obscure, he is lacking in the attribute of self-consciousness that defines Montaigne's essays and the poetry and prose of the Romantics. To desire fame—the currency that buys immortality—as did the duchess of Newcastle, is not necessarily to be conscious of the workings of the mind or of writing as a reflection of these mind movements. The same can be said of Evelyn. Woolf asserts that "His writing is opaque rather than transparent; we see no depths through it, nor any very secret movements of mind or heart" (CR, 84). Nevertheless, despite an artlessness of style, she sees in his diary an "artistic method," "of going on with the day's story circumstantially, bringing in people who will never be mentioned again, leading up to crises which never take place" (CR, 85). The "rambling" nonmethod of Evelyn's diary suggests the ordinariness of life, of fleeting thoughts with their loose associations, hares started but not brought to ground— the sort of artlessness that Woolf converted into a method that would accurately mime wandering movements of mind in response to the unextraordinary stimuli of ordinary existence. Evelyn's diary, in this sense, is a model for her new way of telling a story.

The suggestiveness of "a vanishing coat-tail" (CR, 85), evoking in the reader an imaginative response so that we participate in or actually make up the story of a never-to-be-mentioned-again figure, accounts as well for Woolf's interest for another reason. We read such books, Woolf says in "How Should One Read a Book?" in order "to refresh and exercise our own creative powers" (SCR, 263). The experience of our encounter with Evelyn's diary, as with so many of the writings of these minor figures, is that it is as close to the nonreading of nonwriting as she can envision. Our engagement with the book becomes an enacting of "life itself," made possible by an unconscious pairing of the contents of the book, "its record of vanished moments and forgotten lives told in faltering and feeble accents that have perished" (SCR, 263), with the scene viewed through "an open window on the right hand of the bookcase. . . . its unconsciousness, its irrelevance, its perpetual movement — the colts galloping round the field, the woman filling her pail at the well, the donkey throwing back his head . . ." (SCR, 263). When Woolf says that "The greater part of any library is nothing but the record of such fleeting moments in the lives of men, women, and donkeys" (SCR, 263), she creates an ambiguity that argues for the power of such nonliterature. Are these fleeting moments in the books of the library, in the scene outside the window, or mixed together in the mind of the reader conscious of both? They enter into our life, complicating and enriching its texture by drawing on our creative powers. One aim, in fact, of Woolf's book of critical essays is to help the reader to see the benefits of becoming a "common reader," of discovering the vast pleasure in this collusive exercise of the mind. Casually conversational in tone, these assertions nevertheless suggest Wordsworth's august, almost religious description of "a new world" of high consciousness, at the end of "Book Thirteenth" of *The Prelude.*

> . . . as ruled by those fixed laws
> Whence spiritual dignity originates,
> Which do both give it being and maintain

> A balance, an ennobling interchange
> Of action from without and from within;
> The excellence, pure function, and best power
> Both of the object seen and eye that sees.
>
> (Wordsworth, 356)

Thus, Woolf arrives at the antecedents of the novelistic tradition. Although she argues in "Defoe" that he is not merely one "of the great plain writers" but the originator of the school "whose work is founded upon a knowledge of what is most persistent, though not most seductive, in human nature" (CR, 93), her essay lacks the interest of the others. Perhaps the fault lies in Woolf's acknowledgment that Defoe is mixed with the root of her earliest life, with her childhood "impressions . . . that last longest and cut deepest" (CR, 86). Having had *Robinson Crusoe* read to her as a child, Woolf speculates, accounts for her belief that "The book resembles one of the anonymous productions of the race rather than the effort of a single mind" (CR, 86). With this assertion we are able to see the connection between the unifying theme of *The Common Reader* and that of the later "Anon." The writers who exhibit what Woolf calls "conviction," that is, tacit belief in, and synchrony with, the values of their age, are those who are least self-conscious in the sense that she has applied that term to Browne and Montaigne. By comparison, Chaucer, Evelyn, and Defoe are a repository of the social and cultural history of England. We presume that through writers like them she had hoped to unwind the ball of string to its end in "Turning the Page."

Perhaps Woolf agreed that her essay on Defoe had not been a complete success because he is the only writer represented in both *Common Reader* volumes. In her second essay, she explains his idiosyncratic perspective in fiction, with its basis in the "facts" of the world expressed through her wonderful metaphor of the solidity and irrefutability of an artifact.

> There are no sunsets and no sunrises; there is no solitude and no soul. There is, on the contrary, staring us full in the face nothing but a large earthenware pot. We are told . . . that it was the 1st of September 1651; that the hero's name is Robinson Crusoe; and that his father has the gout. . . . Reality, fact, substance is going to dominate all that follows. (SCR, 54)

Woolf sees Defoe's perspective, as she did the Pastons', as a function of the aspirations of a particular social class. With some humor, Woolf parodies Defoe's middle-class, matter-of-factual substance: "the cats were not the same cats that had come in the ship. Both of those were dead; these cats were new cats, and as a matter of fact cats became very troublesome before long from their fecundity, whereas dogs, oddly enough, did not breed at all" (SCR, 58). Nature and God shrink in importance as rationality and reality gain preeminence. "And so by means of telling the truth undeviatingly as it appears to him . . . he comes in the end to make common actions dignified and common objects beautiful" (SCR, 57).

Fact, then, without attendant analysis, reigns. Through the foregrounded earthenware pot, Defoe has "roped the whole universe into harmony" and made us see "the solitudes of the human soul" (SCR, 58). Thus, the difference between Defoe's and Woolf's perspectives is the complete submergence of self in phenomena in Defoe's writing and the balance of the two in Woolf's.

Although Daniel Defoe is the only writer Virginia Woolf considered in both volumes of *The Common Reader,* she may have casually mentioned or written about Jane Austen more frequently and in more essays than she did any other novelist. The Brontës, particularly Charlotte, are close seconds.

In 1917 Woolf had written a review of Edith Birkhead's *The Tale of Terror. A Study of the Gothic Romance* (Essays III, 307). There she wished that Birkhead had "enlarged her scope to include some critical discussion of the aesthetic value of shock and terror, and had ventured some analysis of the taste which demands this particular stimulus" (Essays III, 305). Three years before, Woolf had written a review of *Trivia* by Logan Pearsall Smith (23 May 1918) in which she said:

> If we are not mistaken, it is his purpose to catch and enclose certain moments which break off from the mass, in which without bidding things come together in a combination of inexplicable significance, to arrest those thoughts which suddenly, to the thinker at least, are almost menacing with meaning. Such moments of vision are of an unaccountable nature; leave them alone and they persist for years; try to explain them and they disappear; write them down and they die beneath the pen. (Essays II, 250–51)

Of interest here is that she attaches the name "moments of vision" to intellectual events and argues that Smith's literary purpose is to re-create these intellectual events for the reader: "to arrest those thoughts . . . almost menacing with meaning." Clearly there is a relationship between these thoughts—"of an unaccountable nature"—and "the aesthetic value of shock and terror" that Woolf later believed was capable of explanation and would have liked

Edith Birkhead to explore. She was beginning to isolate and define the psychological phenomenon that in "A Sketch of the Past" she would call "moments of being." These moments, first experienced by her in childhood, were distinguished by "a sudden violent shock" (MoB, 71). They were of two kinds: those, like the feelings that resulted from the fight with her brother Thoby or from hearing about Mr. Valpy's suicide, which "ended in a state of despair" (MoB, 71) and those, like her recognition that the flower and earth were one, which ended "in a state of satisfaction" (MoB, 71) and wholeness. Although the former sort produced in her "a peculiar horror and a physical collapse" (MoB, 72), she was, later in life, to feel:

> . . . as one gets older one has a greater power through reason to provide an explanation; and that this explanation blunts the sledge-hammer force of the blow. . . . though I still have the peculiarity that I receive these sudden shocks, they are now always welcome; after the first surprise, I always feel instantly that they are particularly valuable. And so I go on to suppose that the shock-receiving capacity is what makes me a writer. (MoB, 72)

Woolf operatively defines the phenomenon of the Romantic sublime, the "threefold episode of consciousness, in which a state of radical disequilibrium intervenes between a prior state of ordinary awareness and a final state of transcendent exaltation."[16] She is also exploring "the taste which demands this particular stimulus." The fight with Thoby and hearing of the suicide caused her to feel horror and ended in despair. Yet, as with the flower, Woolf's ability later in life to transcend the shock by writing it down, helped her to recognize that the shock or blow would "become a revelation of some order" made "real by putting it into words" (MoB, 72). She describes the writer who experiences a "rapture" through "discovering what belongs to what; making a scene come right; making a character come together" (MoB, 72)—the writer who "arrest[s] those thoughts . . . almost menacing with meaning." Woolf does what she would have wished Edith Birkhead to do: articulate the aesthetic value of shock and terror.

Thus, Woolf recognizes that the "natural" sublime—the fight, the suicide, the flower—part flower/part earth—is translatable into a "textual" sublime, a re-creation of emotion on the page that works similarly for both writer and reader, making us feel that "we are the words; we are the music; we are the thing itself" (MoB, 72). The "arrest" by the writer—his putting the "menacing" idea into words—is a recapitulation of the instant terror or horror and then the distancing of that emotion which ends in a state of glowing exaltation, the result of our recognition of safety.[17] She explored this idea in her essays on Austen and the Brontës. It is, of course, an idea at the heart of Romantic critical theory and practice.

Even the comparatively standard reading of Jane Austen, with which she concludes her 1913 review of two books on Austen, hints at this "profound general statement" (CR, 234).

> . . . she possessed in a greater degree perhaps than any other English woman the sense of the significance of life apart from any personal liking or disliking; of the beauty and continuity which underlies its trivial stream. A little aloof, a little inscrutable and mysterious, she will always remain, but serene and beautiful also because of her greatness as an artist. (Essays II, 14)

Woolf tentatively suggests that Austen is conscious of moments of being that separate themselves from the cotton wool—of "the beauty and continuity which underlies [life's] trivial stream"—and which, in turn, make her "a little aloof" and "mysterious." These are adjectives with which one describes the individual in isolation from his or her fellows, in moments when one's consciousness may be concentrated on the beauty and "purest ecstasy" (MoB, 65) of life. That Woolf should so describe Jane Austen, the doyenne of the drawing room, the creator of dialogue so perfect that all the screen writers of the cinematic versions of her novels, beginning with the 1940 Aldous Huxley-Jane Murfin *Pride and Prejudice,* have had only to lift speeches from her pages, suggests that Woolf is enraptured by a unique idea. We see it flower in *The Common Reader,* and it causes us to read Austen in a new way.

She begins the essay as we might expect. All we know about Austen "is derived from a little gossip, a few letters, and her books" (CR, 134). Her sister Cassandra burnt almost all of her letters. Her brothers were very fond and proud of her. She wrote *Love and Freindship* "to amuse the schoolroom" (CR, 135), but there is in it "a note which never merges in the rest, which sounds distinctly and penetratingly all through the volume" (CR, 136). This is the note of laughter but not the indiscriminate laughter of a girl of fifteen. Rather, "at fifteen she had few illusions about other people and none about herself. Whatever she writes is finished and set in its relation, not to the parsonage, but to the universe. She is impersonal; she is inscrutable" (CR, 136).

These adjectives, however, move the essay in another direction. They look back to the words "aloof" and "mysterious" of Woolf's

1913 review and prepare for the statement "Her genius is freed and active. At once our senses quicken; we are possessed with the peculiar intensity which she alone can impart" (CR, 138). Woolf's deliberate focus in *The Common Reader* on Austen's juvenilia and her unfinished novel *The Watsons,* rather than on her acknowledged masterpieces, allows her to concentrate on the "peculiar intensity" that stands out in relief in these comparative failures. The genius Woolf divines is a romantic genius, a reading of Austen that runs counter to received opinion.

Woolf avers: "It is against the disk of an unerring heart, an unfailing good taste, an almost stern morality, that she shows up those deviations from kindness, truth, and sincerity which are among the most delightful things in English literature" (CR, 141). Certainly this statement is no surprise and might well be the basis of a classical view of Austen's qualities and strengths. However, she continues:

> In *The Watsons* she gives us a foretaste of her power. . . . Here is nothing out of the way; it is midday in Northamptonshire; a dull young man is talking to a rather weakly young woman on the stairs as they go up to dress for dinner, with housemaids passing. But, from triviality, from commonplace, their words become suddenly full of meaning, and the moment for both one of the most memorable in their lives. It fills itself; it shines; it glows; it hangs before us, deep, trembling, serene for a second; next, the housemaid passes, and this drop, in which all the happiness of life has collected, gently subsides again to become part of the ebb and flow of ordinary existence. (CR, 142)

Woolf describes an instance of the sublime, an arrested moment for her characters that "glows" and "hangs" "deep" and "trembling" before us. Her adjectives suggest the danger/rapture of these unexpected rips in the cotton wool. Woolf implies that Austen's peculiar gift to excite the imagination, in the manner of the Romantics', implicates the reader in a "textual" or poetic sublime that elevates us emotionally before we descend to a lower level of "narrative experience." Her method thus doubles her characters' subsidence into "the ebb and flow of ordinary existence." Woolf's sense that Austen's peculiar gift is to excite the reader's imagination, to make us collaborate and supply what the writer has left out, transforms her novels into works of romantic indeterminacy.

This reading of Austen is surely idiosyncratic. It prepares us for Woolf's speculations regarding Austen's last completed novel, *Persuasion,* which is not quite like the others. "The boundaries," Woolf asserts, "were marked; moons, mountains, and castles lay on the other side. But was she not sometimes tempted to trespass for a minute? Was she not beginning, in her own gay and brilliant manner, to contemplate a little voyage of discovery?" (CR, 143). Woolf writes about a change that might have occurred in Austen's style had she lived to tell another tale. For Woolf sees in *Persuasion,* as well as a peculiar beauty, "a peculiar dullness" (CR, 143) that marks a transition to another creative period. She asserts that Austen is a little bored with the world she had until this time observed so minutely. Her comedy is cruder and the satire harsher than in her other novels. In short, "She is no longer freshly aware of the amusements of daily life" (CR, 143), but that is because "she is trying to do something which she has never yet attempted" (CR, 143–44).

> She is beginning to discover that the world is larger, more mysterious, and more romantic than she had supposed. . . . She dwells frequently upon the beauty and the melancholy of nature, upon the autumn where she had been wont to dwell upon the spring. . . . But it is not only in a new sensibility to nature that we detect the change. Her attitude to life itself is altered. She is seeing it, for the greater part of the book, through the eyes of a woman who, unhappy herself, has a special sympathy for the happiness and unhappiness of others, which, until the very end, she is forced to comment upon in silence. Therefore the observation is less of facts and more of feeling than is usual. (CR, 144)

Extrapolating from *Persuasion* and guessing as well that had she lived longer Austen would have been influenced by the wider experience her success would have brought her, Woolf imagines the effects on the six other novels Austen would have written.

Woolf retrospectively anticipates that Austen's "new" method would have emphasized moments of being. She would have centered the "action" less in the drawing room and focused less on "man and men"—that is, on the relations between people—and more, we can imagine, in a private space like a study or boudoir or out of doors and on the relations of people to "life itself." Woolf thus imagines a "romanticized" Austen, revealing in these unwritten, darker novels the mind's "marriage" to the natural world through self-conscious reflection on its own relation to it. As is already true of *Persuasion,* her novels would have "trusted less . . . to dialogue" (CR, 145) and more to "reflection to give us a knowledge of her characters" (CR, 145). Thus, Austen's own narrative method would have privileged the very processes of mind that she would explore in her characters.

Woolf's is an unusual critique of Austen, focusing, to alter the words of Wallace Stevens's "Snow Man," on the "something that is not there" as well as "the something that is." The intensity of Woolf's mature gaze on this imagined development, that is, her rereading of Austen, is a gage of her own transformation into a great essayist and writer of romantic novels of the future.[18]

Woolf's revaluation of the Brontës is similar. Her "*Jane Eyre* and *Wuthering Heights*" is a finely discriminated appreciation of Charlotte and Emily, the origins of which are traceable, as with the essay on Austen, to her earlier reviews.

Charlotte Brontë's passion was certainly the subject of her previous essays. The felt life of *Jane Eyre* is, to a certain extent, according to Woolf, vitiated by Charlotte's grinding of the gender ax. Woolf compares Brontë with Jane Austen and Shakespeare who, she asserts, taking a leaf from Coleridge's book, because they are never *partis pris*, are both invisible in the text and, as a result, more flawless writers. Yet despite her criticism, there is praise, as well, for all of Charlotte Brontë's "force, and it is the more tremendous for being constricted, [which] goes into the assertion, 'I love', 'I hate', 'I suffer'" (CR, 157). These powerful forces are validated by Woolf herself when she reduces suffering Susan's emotions in *The Waves* to "I hate, I love" (TW, 348) and makes the unhappy Isa recognize that the plot of Miss La Trobe's pageant in *Between the Acts* is a vehicle "to beget emotion. There were only two emotions: love; and hate" (BtA, 90). The plots of the Brontës' novels, thus reduced, cause Woolf to see Charlotte and Emily Brontë as poets, and Romantic poets, in particular.

> It is here that she takes her seat; it is the red and fitful glow of the heart's fire which illumines her page. In other words, we read Charlotte Brontë . . . for her poetry. . . . Hence it is that both Emily and Charlotte are always invoking the help of nature. They both feel the need of some more powerful symbols of the vast and slumbering passions in human nature than words or actions can convey. (CR, 158–59)

They found these symbols, as did the Romantics, in nature. In this essay, written originally in 1916, Woolf, recognizing an objective correlative before Eliot invented the term in his 1919 essay on "Hamlet," describes Charlotte's use of nature: "So she calls in nature to describe a state of mind which could not otherwise be expressed" (CR, 159).

However, there is a difference between the sisters. Charlotte was poetic, but Emily was "a greater poet than Charlotte" (CR, 159).

> There is no 'I' in *Wuthering Heights*. There are no governesses. There are no employers. There is love, but it is not the love of men and women. Emily was inspired by some more general conception. The impulse which urged her to create was not her own suffering or her own injuries. She looked back upon a world cleft into gigantic disorder and felt within her the power to unite it in a book. That gigantic ambition is to be felt throughout the novel — a struggle, half thwarted but of superb conviction, to say something through the mouths of her characters which is not merely 'I love' or 'I hate', but 'we, the whole human race' and 'you, the eternal powers . . .' the sentence remains unfinished. (CR, 159–60)

Woolf suggests that high art must in some way transmute or rise above personal pain. The process by which such a cleansing is achieved may well be akin to Wordsworth's recollection of emotion in tranquility.

With her statement "the sentence remains unfinished," Woolf actually adumbrates contemporary Romantic critical discourse, which explores the "unreadability" of the literature as itself productive of the poetic sublime.[19] Her description of Emily Brontë's indeterminacy is, as well, comparable to her acknowledgment of the aporia or unreadable density of, for example, her own moment of being with the flower, which "thought" she had "put away in [her] mind . . . to turn over and explore" (MoB, 71). We also recognize that this description of Emily Brontë's only novel reads like an earlier version of Woolf's own experience while writing and of her "philosophy" of art. It is precisely because such moments in life and literature cannot be fully decoded that they resonate with "glowing" indeterminacy. As in the case of Woolf's description of Austen's moving beyond the drawing room and dialogue to the fluidity of consciousness and the dialectical relationship of self and nature, this is another instance of Woolf's aesthetic exploration of shock and terror—the arrested moment of the text—in which we feel the illumination of the "readerly" sublime.

In specifically outlining the characteristics of a new kind of novel, one that would redefine the distance between the writer and reality, Woolf writes in "The Narrow Bridge of Art":

> In the first place, one may guess that it will differ from the novel as we know it now chiefly in that it will stand further back from life. It will give, as poetry does, the outline rather than the detail. . . . It will tell us very little about the houses, incomes, occupations of its characters. . . . With these limitations it will express the feeling and ideas of the characters closely and vividly, but from a different angle.

It will resemble poetry in this that it will give not only or mainly people's relations to each other and their activities together, as the novel has hitherto done, but it will give the relation of the mind to general ideas and its soliloquy in solitude. For under the dominion of the novel we have . . . come to forget that a large and important part of life consists in our emotions towards such things as roses and nightingales, the dawn, the sunset, life, death, and fate; we forget that we spend much time sleeping, dreaming, thinking, reading, alone. . . . The psychological novelist has been too prone to limit psychology to the psychology of personal intercourse; we long sometimes to escape from the incessant, the remorseless analysis of falling into love and falling out of love, of what Tom feels for Judith. . . . We long for some more impersonal relationship. We long for ideas, for dreams, for imaginations, for poetry. (CE 2, 224–25)

In her 1917 review of Edward Thomas's *A Literary Pilgrim in England,* Woolf had written of Thomas Hardy's and Emily Brontë's evocations of landscape:

The sense of country which both Mr Hardy and Emily Brontë possess is so remarkable that a volume might be spent in discussion of it. We should scarcely exaggerate our own belief if we said that both seem to forecast a time when character will take on a different aspect under the novelist's hand, when he will be less fearful of the charge of unreality, less careful of the twitterings and chatterings which now make our puppets so animated and for the most part so ephemeral. (Essays II, 163)

As her review of Thomas's book pointedly reveals, Woolf's conception of the poetic novel of the future, which gives "the relation of the mind to general ideas and its soliloquy in solitude," rather than the ephemeral specifics "of what Tom feels for Judith," was alive in the nineteenth century. We easily recognize that her essay of 1927 describes not the future of the novel but its near past in the hands of the writer of *Mrs. Dalloway* and *To the Lighthouse.* Even more apparently, it is her blueprint for the not-so-distant *The Waves.* Although Woolf's aesthetic desiderata were her outline for how to "Make it new!" she unearthed them in her Romantic rereading of her historical "sisters." In them she discovered the "novel" interests and techniques of the novel of the future, central to her conception of the modernist project.

The essays on Austen and the Brontës, with their Romantic reading of the relation of the mind of the novelist to the world, lead towards a better definition of the tasks of modern literature and a final privileging of the present moment with its particular approaches to fiction, flawed though they may be. Woolf's chief target in "Modern Fiction" is the materialism of the Edwardian writers, Bennett, Galsworthy, and Wells, whom she faults for their attention to trivialities, to the shell rather than the pith of existence, that is, the human consciousness that confronts the world. She proposes a different path for the novel—one that reads like a revision of the Preface to *Lyrical Ballads* and *The Prelude,* with their insistence both on the primacy of ordinary experience as the stuff of poetry and the mind's recording of and responding to such experience.

> Let us record the atoms as they fall upon the mind in the order in which they fall, let us trace the pattern, however disconnected and incoherent in appearance, which each sight or incident scores upon the consciousness. Let us not take it for granted that life exists more fully in what is commonly thought big than in what is commonly thought small. (CR, 150)

Woolf praises James Joyce's different direction, his avoidance of "whatever seems to him adventitious, whether it be probability, or coherence, or any other of these signposts which for generations have served to support the imagination of a reader when called upon to imagine what he can neither touch nor see" (CR, 151). Yet she criticizes his method and mind for being "centred in a self which, in spite of its tremor of susceptibility, never embraces nor creates what is outside itself and beyond" (CR, 151).

Her criticism of Joyce is the same she makes of modern poetry when in "A Letter to a Young Poet" she faults the moderns for remaining in the cramped and uninteresting quarters of their own minds rather than embracing the world as did Keats and Shelley. And so, having exonerated herself from charges of priggishness by ultimately criticizing Joyce not for what he includes but for "how much of life is excluded or ignored" (CR, 152), Woolf turns to the Russians, whom she praises for their open-ended fiction that mirrors the inconclusiveness of much of life. But again there is a reservation. The truth-to life of this method paradoxically accounts for our dissatisfaction.

> . . . we might speak of the inconclusiveness of the Russian mind. It is the sense that there is no answer, that if honestly examined life presents question after question which must be left to sound on and on after the story is over in hopeless interrogation that fills us with a deep, and finally it may be with a resentful, despair. (CR, 153)

For there is something the Russians leave out and that is "the instinct to enjoy and fight rather than to suffer and understand" (CR, 154). In praising the tradition of English fiction, an alternative to the Russian point of view, she lauds it for its *inclusiveness* as it "bears witness to our natural delight in humour and comedy, in the beauty of the earth, in the activities of the intellect, and in the splendour of the body" (CR, 154)—in short, for addressing the richness and variety of life she values in "A Letter to a Young Poet."

That there is worth in two traditions so dissimilar is Woolf's ultimate proof of the "infinite possibilities of the art" of fiction and also that "'The proper stuff of fiction' does not exist; everything is the proper stuff of fiction" (CR, 154). Nevertheless, Woolf has made it clear in this seminal essay in which she defines the raw stuff of fiction as "an ordinary mind on an ordinary day" with its "myriad impressions — trivial, fantastic, evanescent, or engraved with the sharpness of steel" (CR, 150) that whatever else might be incorporated into fiction, the Romantic balance or continuity between the mind and the external world must be at its center. Her assertion concerning the response of the mind to external stimuli and the character of the written record of that response, briefly cited in chapter III, is one of Woolf's best descriptions of modern fiction.

> From all sides they come, an incessant shower of innumerable atoms; and as they fall, as they shape themselves into the life of Monday or Tuesday, the accent falls differently from of old; the moment of importance came not here but there; so that, if a writer were a free man and not a slave, if he could write what he chose, not what he must, if he could base his work upon his own feeling and not upon convention, there would be no plot, no comedy, no tragedy, no love interest or catastrophe in the accepted style, and perhaps not a single button sewn on as the Bond Street tailors would have it. Life is not a series of gig lamps symmetrically arranged; life is a luminous halo, a semi-transparent envelope surrounding us from the beginning of consciousness to the end. (CR, 150)

Her statement is obviously a forerunner of her description of the novel of the future in "The Narrow Bridge of Art." Communication of that complex being, a character, connected by so many and such intricate tethers to the world and to others, Woolf offers, is the stuff of the most interesting modern fiction. Woolf's wonder about the contemporary audience in "The Patron and the Crocus" and her commitment in "The Modern Essay" to the overarching

and shaping Romantic imagination—"the back of an idea, something believed in with conviction or seen with precision and thus
compelling words to its shape" (CR, 221)—are also antecedent to
her question, "How to write well?" (CR, 210). She approaches an
answer to this query in "Joseph Conrad" and the last essay in the
collection, "How It Strikes a Contemporary."

As in "The Modern Essay," "conviction" guides her discussion
of Joseph Conrad, written originally for *TLS* as a literary obitu-
ary.[20] She is intrigued by the rational analyst Marlow's description
of "'a moment of vision'" (CR, 227). But as much as Woolf valued
Marlow's insight into those idiosyncratic moments that she believed conferred a secular blessing, she recognized that he was
giving "bad advice" to his creator in the later novels because
"Above all, perhaps, he did not take into account how, if Conrad
was to create, it was essential first that he should believe" (CR,
229).

In "The Pastons and Chaucer," Woolf, speaking of the character
Griselda, had said:

> There is no blur about her, no hesitation . . . she is content to be
> herself. Upon her . . . the mind can rest with that unconscious ease
> which allows it . . . to endow her with many more qualities than are
> actually referred to. Such is the power of conviction, a rare gift, shared
> in our day by Joseph Conrad in his earlier novels, and a gift of supreme
> importance, for upon it the whole weight of the building depends.
> (CR, 14)

Thus Woolf, writing of Conrad, has come full circle. But we feel
that her restatement has the force of incremental repetition. Now
we have read through all the essays of *The Common Reader* and
feel, more fully and concretely, what Woolf means when she says
that the shaping imagination which determines "the whole weight
of the building" is itself formed by its commitment to a set of
values. "The art of writing has for backbone some fierce attachment to an idea. It is on the back of an idea, something believed
in with conviction" (CR, 221) that writing succeeds. Conviction is
not merely a matter of a naive, uncritical, or unconscious acceptance by a writer of the values of an age. Although such acceptance
is also associated with a second class of writers like Addison, conviction, in fact, may be personal and idiosyncratic and not necessarily divorced from self-consciousness. Thus, if Woolf had written
an essay on Wordsworth, she could have placed him in the company of Chaucer and Conrad.

Woolf's attachment to the idea of the shaping imagination and its convergence with her notion of conviction define her modernism and suggest a traditionalism belied by many contemporary readings of her work. As Mark Goldman says of Woolf's critical survey of the novel:

> Mrs. Woolf's approach to the modern novel and to her own fiction is more traditional or conservative than has generally been recognized. Even her crucial interest in a possible balancing of prose and poetry in fiction is incorporated into a more conservative theory of a new synthesis for the modern novel; and her own fiction may be seen as a more comprehensive and even realistic progress toward this synthesis rather than, as critics have described her creative history, an increasingly subjective evolution that reached its zenith in *The Waves* and declined steadily thereafter in vain attempts to repeat her earlier performances.[21]

Thus, with the supporting weight of all the essays in *The Common Reader* and Goldman's independent assessment of Woolf's critical position and of her creative evolution, we come to the last essay in the book, "How It Strikes a Contemporary," Woolf's words on the state of the art of modern literature in comparison with the writing of the past.

With its double focus on contemporary criticism and literature, Woolf relies in this essay, as Matthew Arnold did, on touchstones to determine excellence in the present. She thus creates a kind of post hoc rationale for having attempted a survey of landmarks—*The Common Reader* we have been reading.

Suggesting her own critical method, she distinguishes between judgments for the nonce and those for the ages.

> Reviewers we have but no critic; a million competent and incorruptible policemen but no judge. . . . Nowhere shall we find the downright vigor of a Dryden, or Keats with . . . his profound insight and sanity . . . or Coleridge, above all, brewing in his head the whole of poetry and letting issue now and then one of those profound general statements which are caught up by the mind when hot with the friction of reading as if they were of the soul of the book itself. (CR, 233–34)

Two of her three "judges" are Romantic; Coleridge, in particular, with his "esemplastic imagination," is capable of an organic wholeness, her index to the highest kind of art.

Clearly, Woolf believed that the function of criticism is to cause a wonderful intellectual reverberation in common readers, such that they will recognize their own thoughts "when hot with the

friction of reading as if they were of the soul of the book itself."
"That's it!" we say. "That's the truth, the point." Here is the sense
of excitement that comes from the recognition, the feeling that we
have been profoundly touched. The excitement of this moment
is itself partly created by our sense of a shared insight. Woolf's
description of our response is based on the underlying assumption
of the Romantic continuity between the individual mind and the
world, as the rest of the essay proves.

And so, not impressions, but profound general statements are
the soul of Woolf's critical method. Although she was a reviewer,
she strove to be, and succeeded as, a critic. She attempts to define
modern literature about which, she argues, there is never agreement and to explain its charm for us even when it measures up
poorly against the touchstones of the past.

The present is "a lean age" as far as masterpieces go, but Woolf
is optimistic. The basis of her feeling is her sense of the attrac-
tiveness of life, its differences from the past, and the ability of
modern literature to capture life-as-it-is.

> We are sharply cut off from our predecessors. A shift in the scale —
> the sudden slip of masses held in position for ages — has shaken the
> fabric from top to bottom, alienated us from the past and made us
> perhaps too vividly conscious of the present. . . . New books lure us
> . . . partly in the hope that they will reflect this re-arrangement of
> attitude — these scenes, thoughts, and apparently fortuitous groupings
> of incongruous things which impinge upon us with so keen a sense of
> novelty — and, as literature does, give it back into our keeping, whole
> and comprehended. (CR, 236–37)

The balancing act of art, to record the chaos but to make something whole of it, is once more foregrounded. But on the other
hand, contemporary literature causes "a profound dissatisfaction"
as Woolf, in a cinematic metaphor, remarks on its "appearance of
being noted under pressure, taken down in a bleak shorthand which
preserves with astonishing brilliance the movements and expressions of the figures as they pass across the screen" (CR, 237). She
thus registers her own unhappiness with modernist literature which
privileges the fragmentary and the chaotic without molding them
into that state of wholeness that it is literature's responsibility to
create. She turns in her dissatisfaction once more to the masterpieces of the past, "impelled not by calm judgement but by some
imperious need to anchor our instability upon their security" (CR,
237). What she finds is "an unabashed tranquility in page after page
of Wordsworth and Scott and Miss Austen which is a sedative to

the verge of somnolence" (CR, 237–38). "They seem deliberately to refuse to gratify those senses which are stimulated so briskly by the moderns . . . above all, the sense of the human being, his depth and the variety of his perceptions, his complexity, his confusion, his self, in short" (CR, 238).

However, in the intentionally indeterminate manner of this essay, Woolf again undercuts her apparent denial of the greatness of these writers. For she asserts that the security and tranquility we feel in the presence of this older literature is based on the authors' "power of their belief — their conviction, that imposes itself upon us. In Wordsworth, the philosophic poet, this is obvious enough" (CR, 238), but she notes that it is equally true of Scott and Austen. "In both there is the same natural conviction that life is of a certain quality. . . . For certainty of that kind is the condition which makes it possible to write. To believe that your impressions hold good for others is to be released from the cramp and confinement of personality" (CR, 238). She has already remarked on Emily Brontë's "superb conviction."

Conviction, which equals shaping imagination, is once more, and for the last time, at the center of Woolf's own critical commitment. And so this collection of essays, itself molded into wholeness by Woolf's imagination and conviction, ends with a prescription both for contemporary critics and writers. As for the critics, she bids them "take a wider, a less personal view of modern literature" and "say something interesting about literature itself," seeing "the past in relation to the future; and so prepare the way for masterpieces to come" (CR, 240–41). This injunction, at the heart of her method in *The Common Reader,* would no doubt have equally determined her direction in the collection "Turning the Page." Despite recognizing the rupture between the present and the past, marked by the cataclysm of World War I, Woolf also believed that it was foolish to examine apparent trends over the short distance. The patient and instructive historical approach, relying on the big picture to sort out the masterpieces from the also-rans, has its parallel in Woolf's advice to creative writers. In a conclusion that purposely cancels itself, Woolf recommends that writers work by whatever lamp they have and not worry about posterity.

To sum up, then — if indeed any conclusion is possible when everybody is talking at once and it is time to be going — it seems that it would be wise for the writers of the present to renounce the hope of creating masterpieces. Their poems, plays, biographies, novels are not books but notebooks, and Time, like a good schoolmaster, will take

them in his hands, point to their blots and scrawls and erasions . . .
but he will not throw them into the waste-paper basket. . . . It is from
the notebooks of the present that the masterpieces of the future are
made. (CR, 240)

Even here Woolf's images reflect her allegiance both to a rationalist privileging of chaos and Romantic desire for shaping and order.
Reality, she believed, is both, and the translation of reality onto
the page, the obligation and goal of the writer. Her most daring
experiment in this direction is *To the Lighthouse*. But there her
blithe personification of "Time" as the "good schoolmaster" is replaced by a ruthless examination of the medium in which we live,
in the manner of the writers of authentic Romantic literature.

5

"Death and the Maiden": Romanticism in *Mrs. Dalloway* and *To the Lighthouse*

"Fade far away and quite forget what thou amongst the leaves hast never known. . . ." Isa supplied the first words that came into her head by way of helping her husband out of his difficulty.

"The weariness, the torture, and the fret . . ." William Dodge added, burying the end of his cigarette in a grave between two stones.

—*Between the Acts*

As she was working on her revisions of *To the Lighthouse*, Woolf wrote a note in her diary for 23 November 1926:

Life is as I've said since I was 10, awfully interesting—if anything, quicker, keener at 44 than at 24—more desperate I suppose, as the river shoots to Niagara—my new vision of death; active, positive, like all the rest, exciting; & of great importance—as an experience. 'The one experience I shall never describe' I said to Vita yesterday. (Diary III, 117)

Paul de Man's assertion in "Time and History in Wordsworth" is strikingly similar in the importance he places on the poet's confrontation of his end: "what Wordsworth strives to conquer, on the relentless fall into death, is the time, the surmise that would allow one to reflect upon the event that, of all events, is most worth reflecting on but hardest to face. . . ."[1] If we agree with de Man's judgment, Woolf's claim that her own death would be the one event she would never describe is a misrepresentation. For like Wordsworth in *The Prelude*, she had already created, both in *Mrs. Dalloway* and in her "Prelude," *To the Lighthouse*, a novel (in both senses of the word) means of describing her own mortality. Her distinction in "A Sketch of the Past" between the "cotton wool" of "non-being" and the extraordinary self-consciousness and pleasure of "being," which latter was responsible, she said, for "the rapture I get when in writing I seem to be discovering what belongs to what" (MoB, 72), is another way of expressing "the relationship between empirical and poetic self" that defines romanticism.[2] De Man argues that the "entire effort [of the poet] has been directed toward freeing himself, by reflection, from the burden of his own empirical contingency. In his attempt, he has indeed transcended his actual self into a language, a work that now exists outside himself."[3] This description of the transcendence of the poetic over the empirical self also explains Woolf's Romantic and illusion-free account of time and mortality in both novels.

In *Mrs. Dalloway* two causes of death are named—one natural and one inflicted by humans—by the third page. Clarissa thinks of her own brush with death in the influenza epidemic of 1918—"(but that might be her heart, affected, they said, by influenza)" (MD, 4) and also of the Great War—"the War was over, except for someone like Mrs. Foxcroft at the Embassy last night eating her heart out because that nice boy was killed . . . but it was over; thank Heaven—over" (MD, 5). Yet Woolf's dramatization of the beliefs—that our "relationships toward time have a priority over relationships toward nature" and that "the relationship between the self and time is necessarily mediated by death"[4]—inheres most truthfully in her language: in her figures, grammar, and syntax.

Clarissa Dalloway takes an extraordinary pleasure in living. She comments on her love directly: "Such fools we are, she thought, crossing Victoria Street. For Heaven only knows why one loves it so, how one sees it so . . . creating it every moment afresh" (MD, 5). As she is about to leave her house in Westminster to buy flowers for her evening party, she thinks:

> what a morning—fresh as if issued to children on a beach. What a lark! What a plunge! For so it had always seemed to her, when with a little squeak of the hinges, which she could hear now, she had burst open the French windows and plunged at Bourton into the open air. How fresh, how calm, stiller than this of course, the air was in the early morning; like the flap of a wave; chill and sharp and yet (for a girl of eighteen as she then was) solemn, feeling as she did, standing there at the open window, that something awful was about to happen; looking at the flowers, at the trees with the smoke winding off them and the rooks rising, falling. . . . (MD, 3)

Woolf thus suggests, through linked metaphors, the wonderful economy of the mind: Clarissa's own image of the beach drives her choice of the noun and verb pair "plunge" and "plunged" and her particular image for the country air, "like the flap of a wave; chill and sharp." But Woolf's language does more. Through it an English woman foresees her death. "What a lark! What a plunge!" from its suggestion of soaring heights to depths, translates the sheer sweep and magnitude of life into a vertical "fall," repeated in "the rooks rising, falling," from its great pleasures to its end. Here, then, on this first page, is the first of many prefigural representations of death—the "something awful" that "was about to happen," not just to Clarissa but to all of us. "Such fools we are" (MD, 5), Mrs. Dalloway's translation of Puck's words—"Lord, what fools these mortals be!"—at the beginning of her paean to life, thus recalls, by a literary "exclusion," our mortality. Images of falling as in "so on a summer's day waves collect, overbalance, and fall; collect and fall . . ." (MD, 58) or Septimus's "Miracles, revelations, agonies, loneliness, falling through the sea, down, down into the flames. . . ." (MD, 216) specifically prefigure Septimus's literal fall to his death but, more generally, the ineluctable mortality that ends our conscious time on earth. Jactitation, the sense that one is falling in one's sleep—"Richard, Richard! she cried, as a sleeper in the night starts and stretches a hand in the dark for help" (MD, 70), a simile that makes palpable Clarissa's sense of her end—and "It was all over for her. The sheet was stretched and the bed narrow. . . . He has left me; I am alone forever, she thought. . . ." (MD, 70) are two other proleptic representations of death.

Even more compelling than these repetitions are Woolf's syntactical and grammatical conflations of past, present, and future through which we register our mortality. De Man has pointed out that Wordsworth, in the Winander Boy section of *The Prelude,* manages to reflect on his own death in the future by focusing on a retrospective event, the death of someone else—that of the boy whose grave lies in the churchyard. He argues: "But the strategy that allows for this conquest is temporally complex: it demands the description of a future experience by means of the fiction of a past experience which is itself anticipatory or prefigurative. . . . This temporal perspective is characteristic for all Wordsworth's poetry. . . ."[5] The dizzying sense that one feels when one confronts one's own end and, consequently, must imagine "a world seen without a self" (TW, 376) is created syntactically by Woolf through the "hanging" participial phrase in the middle of the sentence on the first page—"feeling as she did." We cannot determine whether the phrase represents Clarissa in past time at eighteen, standing at the open window at Bourton, or Mrs. Dalloway just moments before she leaves her house in London in the present. If we read the phrase as a description of her feeling in the past at Bourton, we are disappointed by the lack of any subsequent confirmation of Clarissa's premonition. Clarissa's next memory, that is, Peter's meeting her in the garden and saying "'Musing among the vegetables?'" (MD, 4), could hardly be such an event. We might then be justified in assuming that her feeling suggests a moment of being, perhaps triggered by the mind's response to the distant view seen from the window in which she glimpses her own mortality.[6] If, on the other hand, one reads it as an occurrence in present time, one would have to say that Mrs. Dalloway is self-consciously reflecting on her present choice of words to describe her memory of the air of Bourton—"chill and sharp and yet . . . solemn." In other words, she understands that these adjectives are mediated by her sense that "something awful" is about to happen in the future which, for us, as readers of the aesthetic "event" of the novel, might be, as we think of its shape retrospectively, its movement towards the death of Septimus Warren Smith, or, more globally, its suggestion, through the incremental repetition of many images, that something awful—the inevitability of the loss of consciousness through death—is "about to happen" to all of us, albeit at some unspecifiable time in the future. Thus, our interpretive difficulty over the "site" of present time does not prevent us from arriving at the same place. But as readers who see the story "feelingly," through the pressures of images and syntax, we are forced to honor the indeterminacy that doubles Clarissa's aural image of the squeaking "hinges" of the past heard now. Our dizzying predicament of syntactic "nonsolution" becomes itself a prefigurement of our own "fall" into death.

Such a conflation of past, present, and future also occurs in the song of the vagrant, singing, across from Regent's Park Tube station, with "the voice of no age or sex, the voice of an ancient spring spouting from the earth" (MD, 122).

> Through all ages—when the pavement was grass, when it was swamp, through the age of tusk and mammoth, through the age of silent sunrise, the battered woman—for she wore a skirt—with her right hand exposed, her left clutching at her side, stood singing of love—love which had lasted a million years, she sang, love which prevails, and millions of years ago, her lover, who had been dead these centuries, had walked, she crooned, with her in May; but in the course of ages, long as summer days, and flaming, she remembered, with nothing but red asters, he had gone; death's enormous sickle had swept those tremendous hills, and when at last she laid her hoary and immensely aged head on the

earth, now become a mere cinder of ice, she implored the Gods to lay by her side a bunch of purple heather, there on her high burial place which the last rays of the last sun caressed; for then the pageant of the universe would be over. (MD, 122–23)

The description begins with a series of "regressive" images suggesting a movement away from present and into past time: pavement, to grass, to swamp, from the present to the prehistoric age of tusk and mammoth, to a world of silent sunrise without life. But then the song moves back from the past through a curious grammatical ellipsis. Between the story of her lover's disappearance—"he had gone"—and "when at last she laid her hoary and immensely aged head on the earth, now become a mere cinder of ice," the narrative slips from the real past into the future of a completed action viewed retrospectively. This, indeed, would be the only perspective possible, were there an observing consciousness, when "the pageant of the universe would be over." "Death's enormous sickle," we must imagine, accounts for the shift from the true past into a "retrospectively" envisioned future. From silent sunrise to dying star, the vagrant's seamless song of the natural universe is the "truth" about time and mortality that the clocks of Harley Street, in their "Shredding and slicing, dividing and subdividing" (MD, 154–55), do not reveal. They "tell time," but these clocks, representing human evasion through encouraging the belief that we are in control, do not "tell" the real story of time.

Woolf also dramatizes the truth about time by conflating images of future, present, and past. Although such a superimposition must be accomplished sequentially or linearly by a writer, our "after image" of the superimposition suggests the montage technique of *nouvelle vague* cinema, a "Last Year at Marienbad" of dream-consciousness. Clarissa, talking to Peter Walsh in the present, says merely five words.

"Do you remember the lake?" she said, in an abrupt voice, under the pressure of an emotion which caught her heart, made the muscles of her throat stiff, and contracted her lips in a spasm as she said "lake." For she was a child, throwing bread to the ducks, between her parents, and at the same time a grown woman coming to her parents who stood by the lake, holding her life in her arms which, as she neared them, grew larger and larger in her arms, until it became a whole life, a complete life, which she put down by them and said, "This is what I've made of it! This! . . ." She looked at Peter Walsh; her look, passing through all that time and that emotion, reached him doubtfully; settled on him tearfully. . . .

"Yes," said Peter. "Yes, yes, yes," he said, as if she drew up to the surface something which positively hurt him as it rose. Stop! Stop! he wanted to cry. For he was not old; his life was not over; not by any means. He was only just past fifty. (MD, 63–64)

The conflated images of the child playing and the adult carrying a completed life are Clarissa's visceral acknowledgment of the lapse of time from past to present, leading, instantaneously and inescapably, to an anticipated future; the spasm at lip, throat, and heart are a parallel registration of the proleptic "fall" into death. That Peter recognizes Clarissa's "mortal" meaning is clear from his own contradictory acknowledgment and denial—"'Yes, yes, yes'" and "Stop! Stop!" Almost wordlessly, for Peter does not see the images we see, Clarissa conveys the wordless truth—her translation of the "rusty pump" / female vagrant, issuing its song: "ee um fah um so / foo swee too eem oo—" (MD, 122). Her spasm is another instance of her "indescribable" sensation of a pause, which Clarissa attributes to her damaged heart, just before Big Ben strikes the hour. This pause, another prefigural fall into death, is perhaps a more truthful record of time than Big Ben's timekeeping. "The leaden circles dissolved in the air" (MD, 5), a sentence repeated at intervals throughout the narrative, is the reality of our paltry efforts to "keep" time; the sound waves are part of the fluid movement of the natural world, of space and time, that cannot be kept or halted by any human endeavor.

There is finally no evasion of the truth for the three main characters in *Mrs. Dalloway*. Peter Walsh understands it when he hears the wail of the ambulance carrying Septimus's lifeless body to the hospital (a useless evasion of reality by the Bradshaws of the world). For him it is "a moment, in which things came together; this ambulance; and life and death" (MD, 230). Clarissa painfully acknowledges the announcement of Septimus's death—"in the middle of my party, here's death, she thought" (MD, 279)—with death syntactically sandwiched in the middle of life, both its external manifestation—her party—and its internal, her consciousness, "she thought." Septimus's death leap is not an evasion but an act of defiance against the Harley Street doctors who would "shred" and "slice" his life until they were convinced that he was convinced that he had control of it—the very illusion Woolf dramatically and grammatically negates.

Yet as complex as the ideas and feelings are in *Mrs. Dalloway*— Clarissa's regrets over Peter and gratitude to her husband Richard, her satisfying hatred of Miss Kilman, her acknowledgment of time and death—the "family romance" at the center of *To the Light-house* infinitely complicates the story of one day on which a woman will give an evening party. And in the later novel, as well, there is also art and its relation to the family romance, human consciousness, and the natural world. The sense of the novel's complexity is almost comically denied in Woolf's first assertion of her plan: "This is going to be fairly short" (Diary III, 18). But it is certainly indicated by what follows: "to have father's character done complete in it; & mother's, & St Ives; & childhood; & all the usual things I try to put in—life, death, &c. But the center is father's character, sitting in a boat, reciting We perished, each alone, while he crushes a dying mackerel—" (Diary III, 18–19). However, the centrality of Leslie Stephen to the fullness of Woolf's plan has unconscionably been ignored in feminist readings of the novel.[7]

The honorifics "Mr." and "Mrs.," conjunctively so linked and followed by a surname, suggest union. But when, in *To the Light-house,* they are transformed into Christian names for the powerful parental figures of the novel and appear, most often, separately, they suggest a gender- and character-based polarity, which over the years has invited repeated critical attention.[8] The questions generated by this opposition are prompted, in part, by the hope that taking the measure of these fictive parents in this most obviously autobiographical book will lead us to the mysterious source of Virginia Woolf's own creative impulse and history.

In most early readings, there is a correlation between the degree to which Mrs. Ramsay's character is perceived as both attractive and the focus of the novel and an equally corroborative relation between the lack of appeal and unimportance of Mr. Ramsay. But like the old man and woman of the weather house, the two have suffered a connected reversal of fortune. For most readers are now willing to concede that Mr. Ramsay is more benign than previously thought[9] while Mrs. Ramsay, seen as the "Angel in the House," is no longer regarded as unequivocally saintly.

However, these revised judgments are only superficially signifi-cant, for the issue of centrality is now dissociated from that of appeal. Mrs. Ramsay, that is, continues to be regarded as the more important character and commands, by far, more space in the lit-erature, especially now that her effect on Lily Briscoe has become a major topic of critical discourse.

The Chodorovian and/or Lacanian view of the novel—based on a belief in the preoedipal recalling of, or fusing with, the absent mother—puts a new wrinkle into the center-stage role of Mrs.

Ramsay while relegating Mr. Ramsay to an even more minor part in the drama.[10] Of those offering this reading, only Elizabeth Abel in "'Cam the Wicked': Woolf's Portrait of the Artist as Her Father's Daughter"[11] undertakes an extensive evaluation of Mr. Ramsay to prove the ill effects, for a daughter, of falling under paternal influence. Yet she omits the real artist in the novel, Lily Briscoe, mentioning her only in the last paragraph of her essay as proof of the majority opinion concerning Woolf's apparent judgment: that Lily Briscoe, like all other females, must, for her own good, "think back through our mothers [here, Mrs. Ramsay] if we are women" (ROO, 79).[12]

With just a few exceptions,[13] it was only in the late 1970s that Lily became the focus of critical scrutiny. However, with this artist figure, we can begin to counter the claim of the preoedipal readings—that the creative impulse is freed through a reclamation of the symbolic mother—and to correct the equally erroneous impression created by Abel that Mr. Ramsay's presence has a stultifying effect on history making or artistic creation. For Mr. Ramsay is the motive force responsible for Lily's transformation into a human being and artist of consequence.

To the Lighthouse is about a woman's development and her intellectual and emotional debt to a man. As her diary suggests, Woolf saw this novel as the book in which she would record the history of her difficult yet fruitful relations with her father. Similarly, the novel also points to Woolf's literary patrimony: the presence of Wordsworth and, to a lesser degree, of Virgil in her style and, more substantively, in her sense of the relations of art, nature, and time.

Although we may not deny the importance of her mother's, she wrestles in this book with the difficult yet necessary assimilation of her father's perspective. With it she resolves her own and her character Lily Briscoe's creative difficulties. Her novel memorializes Stephen through a restating and enacting of Wordsworth's aesthetic credo: art is the language that registers the necessary and enriching moral struggle with life and death. Indeed, *To the Lighthouse* is a double paradigm of William Butler Yeats's oracular pronouncement: "All creation is the result of conflict."[14] The book itself—testament to her ability to create—and the story contained—the revelation of her struggle to do so—both express this truth.

This novel is not one that, like Topsy, "just grew." Its ultimate shape conformed to Woolf's original intentions for her project. Her diary entry written just before she drafted the final section of "The Lighthouse" underscores the impression of Mr. Ramsay's centrality created by the text. "So it will be done. . . . At this moment I'm casting about for an end. The problem is how to bring Lily & Mr R[amsay]. together & make a combination of interest at the end" (Diary III, 106).

How to bring Lily and Mr. Ramsay together determined not only Woolf's resolution of the novel but its entire course, as well. For through their relations Woolf is able operatively to define her conception of art. We may keep Woolf's goal in mind by investigating the nature and effect of one sort of tropic language in the novel—the language of heroic convention—which prefigures and so makes possible the created and "creating" communion of Lily and Mr. Ramsay, altering Lily as a human being and artist and changing Woolf's novelistic technique as well.[15]

The story of Lily's acceptance of Ramsay and of her transformation into a human being and artist of spiritual consequence—the center of *To the Lighthouse*—is (to use Lily's own language) an instance of the successful traversal of the dark passage from the conception to the work for Woolf. She recorded the fleeting impressions that would take shape as the novel in her diary for 13 June 1923 as she wrote of sitting in Mary Sheepshanks's Golders Green garden.

> The fresh breeze went brushing all the thick hedges which divide the gardens. Somehow, extraordinary emotions possessed me. . . . Often now I have to control my excitement—as if I were pushing through a screen; or as if something beat fiercely close to me. What this portends I don't know. It is a general sense of the poetry of existence that overcomes me. Often it is connected with the sea & St Ives. Going to 46 continues to excite. . . . The sight of 2 coffins in the Underground luggage office I daresay constricts [?] all my feelings. I have the sense of the flight of time; & this shores up my emotions. (Diary II, 246)

It is extraordinary that so much of this catalogue, appearing in what could have been only a chance description, actually found its way into the novel: the fresh breeze, the hedges, the sea and St. Ives, and the coffins (her dead parents?) which provoked a Clarissa-like spasm. The entry reminds us of the thematic centers of *To the Lighthouse,* namely, "the poetry of existence," "the sense of the flight of time," mortality, and the shoring up of Lily's emotions or, put another way, the creative power that becomes hers when she is able to incorporate all these other ideated emotions into her art. The rich texture of Woolf's expression develops the complex relationship of these elements. She re-creates for the reader, as for Lily, a similar "shoring up" of the emotions or sense of wonderful psychic enablement.

For always, with Woolf, the poetry of her prose moves us with painful pleasure beyond ourselves. Finishing *Mrs. Dalloway,* Woolf felt that she was heading, technically, in the right direction, and had, as it were, struck "pay dirt": "However, I'm sure I've now got to work with my pick at my seam, if only because my metaphors come free, as they do here" (Diary II, 312). Images are both a gauge of her health and the architectural basis of composition. Under the rubric "Returning Health," she wrote in 1926, when concluding *To the Lighthouse:* "This [returning health] is shown by the power to make images: the suggestive power of every sight & word is enormously increased" (Diary III, 104). Her observations suggest the aptness of a metaphorical analysis to the structure of the text.

By the time she was writing *Mrs. Dalloway,* Woolf had mastered a technique of incremental repetition and interweaving of image clusters.[16] Such patterns are the creations of the disembodied narrative voice in seamless combination with the imaginations of the characters.[17] When writing *To the Lighthouse,* she also depended on such textual elaboration to organize the stuff of ordinary experience and broaden its symbolic implications. This elaboration represents her conscious reworking and rewording of those fleeting impressions in the Golders Green garden. It becomes the medium through which she expresses her profoundest idea—the Yeatsian "All creation is the result of conflict." For through the character of Lily Briscoe, Woolf leads us to the truth that any art worth making arises out of a morally enriching conflict with life itself. The aesthetic ethic thus conceived, her own version of the Wordsworthian "see[ing] into the life of things," is rendered through these metaphorical patterns and her treatment of time.

Woolf resolves Lily Briscoe's dilemma through the creative offices of Lily's own conscious imagination. This organ, the Wordsworthian "eye, and ear,—both what they half create, / And what perceive" (Wordsworth, 110), is responsible for the transformation that ultimately enables her to create successfully a moral aesthetic. Granting Lily "authorship," Woolf so contrives Lily's metaphors— the personal music that registers her way of seeing—that they become the means through which she begins to hear "The still, sad music of humanity" (Wordsworth, 110), and thus enable her to make art in a different way. For language has a reflexive effect on its maker. Or, to resort once again to a useful Yeatsian formulation, "the mirror turns lamp."[18] Her technique thus represents a significant advance over her method in *Mrs. Dalloway.* In Woolf's 1924 novel, although we recognize the idiosyncratic emotion and mentation of the characters through their personal images, the image patterns tying characters together are a purely authorial device for establishing a dramatically ironic communication with her readers and do not, in themselves, constitute a resolution of the theme.

The "heroic" imagery in *To the Lighthouse,* effecting Lily's transformation, depends on the symbolic freight of masculine footwear in folk stories in which boots metonymically reveal activity and accomplishment.[19] Western culture has a legacy of many tales of adventurous fellows, like Puss in "Puss in Boots" and the unpromising hero of Norwegian stories, actually named Boots,[20] who seek their fortunes, performing intrepid feats along the way. "Pulling oneself up by the bootstraps"—self-actualization—is a locution based on this tradition.

"Booting up," a recent addition to our language from the argot of hackers, meaning the initial autoinstruction of a computer, despite its masculine roots in popular culture, is an apt metaphor for *To the Lighthouse,* often regarded as a woman's novel. Although Mr. Ramsay's boots function as the local symbol of the masculine principle, booting up, deriving from heroic convention, is still more deeply and generally an enfigurement of the novel's very "action." But the traditional language of masculine adventure leads Lily Briscoe to a very different kind of adventure in art and life. Woolf's metaphors mediate between the rhetoric of the heroic tradition and passage of a spiritual sort, the conflict that leads to creation. *To the Lighthouse* is the record of the adventure of Lily Briscoe, who makes a seminal stop at "the blessed island of good boots" (TTL, 230), which in turn permits the continuation of her voyage to a new place, a *terra incognita,* but immediately recognized by her as her spirit's place of rest. The arduous trek is managed only through her donning of the boots, the masculine principle, making possible an inclusive creative androgyny.[21]

The "putting on" is managed textually through the developing and complex relationship between the metaphorical patterning, on the one hand, and both the narrative voice and the character of Lily Briscoe, on the other. The conflict in Lily's mind between herself and Mr. Ramsay, a conflict that, moreover, exists as well for the narrative voice, another representative of Woolf's perspective, is resolved through acquiring such of Mr. Ramsay's values as are expressed through the rhetoric of the heroic mode. The way we name the world determines how we see it. Thus, the lexical choices made by Lily and the narrative voice transform their apprehension of it. The metaphorical patterning based on heroic convention is the record of Lily's "talking" herself into a new apprehension and acceptance of Mr. Ramsay, which ultimately alter her as a human being and as an artist. However, the course of action she follows is worked out only in the last section of the novel after the preparatory realignments and pertinent questions of the most abstract of the sections, "Time Passes."

We remember the second "chapter" of *To the Lighthouse* as unpeopled by the inhabitants of the Ramsay household. Yet the beginning of "Time Passes" is the conclusion of Mrs. Ramsay's dinner party. Significantly, as all the family and guests are retiring, Lily asks: "'Do we leave that light burning?'" (TTL, 189). Of equal moment, we learn that while all the other guests put out their lamps, Mr. Carmichael, the poet, stays awake: "Mr. Carmichael, who liked to lie awake a little reading Virgil, kept his candle burning rather longer than the rest" (TTL, 189). To underscore the importance of this information, the narrator repeats it, gnomically bracketed, at the end of section II: "[Here Mr. Carmichael, who was reading Virgil, blew out his candle. It was midnight]" (TTL, 192).

Woolf thus makes a symbolic claim for heightened consciousness in the artist, reminiscent of her description of James, who "has the power to crystallize and transfix the moment" (TTL, 9), and of Wordsworth's position in the Preface to *Lyrical Ballads*. Carmichael, a poet with a well-received book, is the only instance of a recognized artist in the novel. *And* he is male. More meaningfully, as we later learn in "The Lighthouse," Mr. Carmichael's interest in Virgil, if we credit Lily's description, may be related to the apparently Virgilian character of his own poetry.

> She had never read a line of his poetry. She thought she knew how it went though, slowly and sonorously. It was seasoned and mellow. It was about the desert and the camel. It was about the palm tree and the sunset. It was extremely impersonal; it said something about death; it said very little about love. (TTL, 289–90)

A second signal conveyed by the repetition of the candlelight reading of Virgil is that it adumbrates the Virgilian character of this section of the novel. Like Carmichael's, the poetry here is highly impersonal, suggesting both death and the inimicality of nature despite the human desire to detect correspondence and resonance between the natural world and the imagination.[22] Thus, the Virgilian worldview is not only a possible analogue for Mr. Carmichael's poetry, in general (stopping short of the conclusion of the *Aeneid* with which artistic and ethical position Carmichael will be identified by the end of the novel), but it explains the narrator's developing point of view in, and the texture of the poetic project of, "Time Passes." This section of poetic prose is, further, more than the locus of the Virgilian progression from the *Eclogues* through the *Georgics;* it is also an astute evaluation of the Wordsworthian apprehension of the imagination's relation to the natural world and time. "The obstructions nature puts in the path of man" and the relation of man to nature are first understood through an imaginative apprehension of the correspondences between the two. However, as "Time Passes" continues, a "mortal" aesthetic, expressed as time's transcendence over nature, a response, most pointedly mediated by the cataclysm of war—"something had boiled and bled" (TTL, 201)—registers the narrator's ambivalence concerning the authenticity of the initially posited romantic correspondence between man and nature, expressed in the following:

> In those mirrors, the minds of men, in those pools of uneasy water, in which clouds forever turn and shadows form, dreams persisted, and it was impossible to resist the strange intimation which every gull, flower, tree, man and woman, and the white earth itself seemed to declare (but if questioned at once to withdraw) that good triumphs, happiness prevails, order rules. . . . (TTL, 198–99)

The foregoing is merely a précis of the complex dialectical "plot" of "Time Passes." J. Hillis Miller has argued[23] that the very nature of language, replete with its tropes for making sense of the world, forces us into an anthropocentric understanding of all experience. That is, we are born into a world in which our inherited language compels us to name the world in terms that reflect the inescapable human effort to understand from our somatically experiential point of view. Thus, willy-nilly, we ascribe to inanimate objects, plants, and animals the human qualities and activities we know most intimately. So, for example, the narrator registers the erosive and destroying capacity of the air currents with "even the prying of the wind, and the soft nose of the clammy sea airs, rubbing, snuffling, iterating, and reiterating their questions—'Will you fade? Will you perish?'" (TTL, 195). The very nature of language creates the illusion that a correspondence does, indeed, exist between nature and man. Miller's assertion leads to his final question: "What is the sex of the one who says of the night airs, 'almost one might imagine them questioning, creeping, wondering, sighing'?"[24] He bases his answer on Woolf's discussion of what it means to write like a woman, or a man, or androgynously, in *A Room of One's Own*.

> writing like a woman and writing like a man tend to change places or values in the moment of being defined and enacted. The male thinks he writes constatively, but in fact his affirmations are groundless performatives. The woman writer knows there is no truth, no rhythm but the drumbeat of death, but this means that her broken, hesitant rhythms are in resonance with the truth that there is no truth. Writing like a woman is superior to male writing by being truly constative rather than unwittingly performative. Back and forth from one extreme to the other Woolf's thought alternates. . . . Woolf is no more able than any male writer to do without some form, however surreptitious, of the constative notion of authenticity in writing.[25]

However, we may approach Woolf's project in "Time Passes" without the difficulties of negotiating the undecidable question of what it means to write "like" either sex. What does Woolf do when she writes not *like* a woman but *when* she writes? The answer lies not only in the tropes but in the illocutionary "as ifs," the marvelous word juxtapositions, the typographical marks, and the curious syntactic shifts and slides in "Time Passes," indeed, in all of *To the Lighthouse,* that elaborate the story of how Lily Briscoe develops the "seeing eye" of the artist.

At the beginning of this section, Lily has no special relation to Mr. Carmichael nor will she have until, in "The Lighthouse," the two are together on the lawn during the morning of Mr. Ramsay's trip. Nevertheless, Woolf here prepares symbolically for the later synchrony of their imaginations. We retrospectively comprehend her design at the end of the chapter when, ten years after Mr. Carmichael first extinguishes his candle, Lily returns to the Ramsays' house. This time, in section X, Augustus Carmichael's nocturnal activity is bracketed along with Lily's in a parenthetical contrast.

> (Lily was tired out with travelling and slept almost at once; but Mr. Carmichael read a book by candlelight). . . . Gently the waves would break (Lily heard them in her sleep); tenderly the light fell (it seemed to come through her eyelids). And it all looked, Mr. Carmichael thought, shutting his book, falling asleep, much as it used to look. (TTL, 214)

Although she falls asleep while he remains awake, she stays conscious, through sleep, of the sound of the waves and of the light that penetrates her lids. And while Mr. Carmichael "sums up" the view, Lily first returns to consciousness with the dawn.

But Woolf only adumbrates their imaginative synchrony at this point in the narrative. Lily's consciousness must be transformed before it can mediate effectively between reality and her blank canvas. Questions about the nature of life, the importance of relationships and choices, must be posed if not answered before one becomes a "seeing" artist who can interpret the world for others. In short, one must have lived and felt and developed a body of values. Mr. Carmichael's successful poetry, although apparently purged of emotion, has behind it the depth of his feeling for Andrew, killed instantaneously by an exploding shell in the war. Lily recalls somebody's saying "that when he had heard of Andrew Ramsay's death . . . Mr. Carmichael had 'lost all interest in life'" (TTL, 289).[26]

"Time Passes" also functions as a bridge between the relatively undeveloped Lily of the first section and the artist of "The Lighthouse" in another way. Although the characters who populate "The Window" are offstage except at the very beginning and end, the section is not without its human presence, concretely in the form of the industriously laboring Mrs. McNab, Mrs. Bast, and George, and more abstractly in the nameless beach walkers who pose a series of questions about life.[27] On 27 February 1926, before she was quite finished with "The Window," Woolf recorded in her diary the impressions of her Russell Square walk, cited in chapter 4, which became the stuff of this next section: "Yet I have some restless searcher in me. Why is there not a discovery in life? . . . A sense of my own strangeness, walking on the earth is there too: of the infinite oddity of the human position . . . with the moon up there, & those mountain clouds. Who am I, what am I, & so on: these questions are always floating about in me: & then I bump against some exact fact—a letter, a person, & come to them again with a great sense of freshness" (Diary III, 62–63). She vouchsafed these subjective musings of hers to the "beach walkers" of "Time Passes," who function as a Greek chorus, presenting the cosmic view of human activity. Their philosophic interrogatives occur with some regularity throughout these pages, creating a poetic cadence that binds the section together. They ask the large, difficult questions that a sensitive human being, particularly an artist, is impelled, in the Virgilian or Wordsworthian strain, to ask and find answers to.

> should any sleeper fancying that he might find on the beach an answer
> to his doubts . . . no image with semblance of serving and divine

promptitude comes readily to hand bringing the night to order and making the world reflect the compass of the soul. . . . (TTL, 193)

The mystic, the visionary, walking the beach on a fine night, stirring a puddle, looking at a stone, asking themselves "What am I," "What is this?" had suddenly an answer vouchsafed them: (they could not say what it was) so that they were warm in the frost and had comfort in the desert. (TTL, 197–98)

As summer neared . . . there came to the wakeful, the hopeful, walking the beach . . . imaginations of the strangest kind. . . . In those mirrors, the minds of men . . . dreams persisted, and it was impossible to resist the strange intimation . . . that good triumphs, happiness prevails, order rules. . . . (TTL, 198–99)

The poetically structured questions of this section constitute a sort of metapoetry, an operative definition of the creative and interpretive powers of the mature artist. The form and substance of art are expressed in these revelatory descriptions of the human being's regard for nature and desire to see correspondence between the natural and the human, and the contrary, nature's inimical relation to us. They reveal another correlated contradiction as well: the presence in the world of good and beauty and the existence of evil. This theme is a re-presentation of Virgil's in the *Georgics*. World War I on the global level, personal loss and private grief caused by the deaths of Mrs. Ramsay, Prue, and Andrew, inform these speculations with particular poignancy, their soul-shocking revelation, within brackets, of an "exact fact" functioning as the pungent antistrophe to the choric voice. How, Woolf asks, with such gratuitous loss, do we make sense of life, considering, as well, the simultaneous existence of beauty and good? An artist, whether Virgil, Wordsworth, Woolf, Carmichael, or Lily, needs to tackle such obdurate philosophical dilemmas or fails to make us feel and "see." One of these beach walker passages will demonstrate Woolf's strategic deployment of language to show us how and what Lily (and she) do see.

At that season those who had gone down to pace the beach and ask of the sea and sky what message they reported . . . had to consider among the usual tokens of divine bounty—the sunset on the sea, the pallor of dawn, the moon rising, fishing-boats against the moon, and children making mud pies or pelting each other with handfuls of grass, something out of harmony with this jocundity and this serenity. There was the silent apparition of an ashen-coloured ship for instance, come, gone; there was a purplish stain upon the bland surface of the sea as if something had boiled and bled, invisibly, beneath.[28] This intrusion into a scene calculated to stir the most sublime reflections and lead to the most comfortable conclusions stayed their pacing. It was difficult blandly to overlook them, to abolish their significance in the landscape; to continue, as one walked by the sea, to marvel how beauty outside mirrored beauty within.

Did Nature supplement what man advanced? Did she complete what he began? With equal complacency she saw his misery, his meanness, and his torture. That dream of sharing, completing, of finding in solitude on the beach an answer, was then but a reflection in a mirror, and the mirror itself was but the surface glassiness which forms in quiescence when the nobler powers sleep beneath? Impatient, despairing yet loth to go (for beauty offers her lures, has her consolations), to pace the beach was impossible; contemplation was unendurable; the mirror was broken.

[Mr. Carmichael brought out a volume of poems that spring, which had an unexpected success. The war, people said, had revived their interest in poetry.] (TTL, 201–2)

This last of the beach walker passages until section X, in which there is a modification of the pattern, has all the elements of those that come before. There is the periodic structure of the prose, achieved through the delaying of the object of the verb by the insertion of an interrupting prepositional phrase ("had to *consider* [among the usual tokens of divine bounty—the sunset on the sea . . .] *something* out of harmony with this jocundity and this serenity"), which literally bars our immediate comprehension. Syntax thus doubles meaning: "intrusion . . . stay[s] [our] pacing." We cannot easily understand the discordance in the scene nor the disharmony between the scene and the harmonic, unitary "compass of [our] soul[s]."

There is only one instance here of "as if" and none of the similarly performing "seemed"—two locutions that occur with great frequency in the entire "Time Passes" section. These expressions, which self-consciously draw attention to the approximateness or only partial reliability of the figurative language the narrative voice is deploying, are not a matter of writing "like a woman." They are Woolf's enfigurement of the real truth of Romanticism: that the poet's language colludes in establishing a correspondence between man's imagination and the natural world but that this correspondence is merely the expression of a devout human wish, recognized as such when our "nobler powers" (our reason and the "eye" through which "We see into the life of things"[29]) are fully awake. Thus, the narrator "unsays" the prosopopoeias, deflating their power, by underscoring the inexactness of the correspondences they imply. These figures are merely "as ifs" and not "the thing itself."[30]

Conversely, however, they are also potent tools for writers. They cannot do without them if they desire to make us see the world in a way that makes sense to us, limited as we are by our anthropocentrism. Thus, we and the artist are caught in a paradox: recognition of the fallibility of such figures and active need of them. This paradox is brilliantly enacted in the syntax of the question: "That dream, of sharing, completing, of finding in solitude on the beach an answer, was then but a reflection in a mirror, and the mirror itself was but the surface glassiness which forms in quiescence when the nobler powers sleep beneath?" It is a difficult sentence, requiring that one reread it to comprehend it because its meaning is subverted by syntax and punctuation. It begins as a declarative, $a = b$, dream was but reflection, mirror was but glassiness. We confidently intone a statement, lowering the voice as we proceed. But then we are surprised into the necessity of raising the pitch of the voice, the signal for an interrogative. Again, Woolf says and unsays. Strangely, the assertion, dream is but a reflection, is the unsaying, the denying of the truth of correspondence, while the question ending the entire sentence unconfirms that assertion, paradoxically affirming that the correspondence might be true. The dizzying quality of these slides and shifts in meaning and syntax teases us out of thought, again doubling the plight of the beach walkers who, the narrative voice reports in the next sentence, are simultaneously "Impatient" and "loth to go" because they have found, as has the reader, facing this syntactical conundrum, that "contemplation was unendurable." The result of ceasing to contemplate, of turning off the flow of one's interior language—the source of correspondence—is that "the mirror was broken." Finally, we think, Woolf or the narrative voice has undeniably asserted the real truth, ending the indeterminacy of the foregoing. Yet again we are surprised into another reversal that reestablishes the strange equilibrium of indeterminacy that governs "Time Passes." For the one-sentence paragraph that follows, reintroducing the artist Mr. Carmichael and his success as a poet (the sentence itself made indeterminate through the constricting and qualifying brackets enclosing it), reasserts the human need to create art that seeks to pattern and organize the universe, suggesting precisely through the figurations of language the probability of correspondence. The "revived . . . interest in poetry" establishes equally the human need to appreciate the world in terms of such correspondence.

Woolf both recognizes the impotence of "like" when one tries to describe the thing itself[31] and the apparent illusion created through its use. And so she leads us paradoxically to two truths that cannot be gainsaid. In section VII, immediately following, the narrator says, "waves disported themselves like the amorphous bulks of leviathans whose brows are pierced by no light of reason" (TTL, 202) and "the flowers standing there, looking before them, looking up, yet beholding nothing, eyeless, and so terrible" (TTL, 203). Again there is the truth that these two figures reveal: first, the artist needs to create correspondences, no matter their reality; and second, the correspondences thus created reveal the truth that they do *not* represent the truth about the world. The whales are not *like* human beings, equipped as they are with no reasoning faculty, and even less so, then, are waves. The flowers "look up" but do not see because they are without sight. But the recognition that the inanimate world is without perception and consciousness ultimately leads back to the truth that our own conscious "tenure" is terminated when we disappear from the world as sentient bodies. The eyelessness of the flowers is "so terrible" because it reminds us of our own mortality. Poetic illusion presses through to the truth.

Not accidentally, the last of these beach walker sequences literally runs into a sentence revealing Lily's thought as she lies in bed, too exhausted to read, at the end of "Time Passes."

> Then indeed peace had come. . . . and whatever the dreamers dreamt holily, dreamt wisely, to confirm—what else was it murmuring—as Lily Briscoe laid her head on the pillow in the clean still room and heard the sea. Through the open window the voice of the beauty of the world came murmuring, too softly to hear exactly what it said—but what mattered if the meaning were plain? entreating the sleepers . . . if they would not actually come down to the beach itself at least to lift the blind and look out. They would see then night flowing down in purple; his head crowned; his sceptre jewelled; and how in his eyes a child might look. . . .
>
> Indeed the voice might resume . . . why not accept this, be content with this, acquiesce and resign? . . . until, the birds beginning and the dawn weaving their thin voices in to its whiteness . . . the sun . . . broke the veil on their eyes, and Lily Briscoe stirring in her sleep. She clutched at her blankets as a faller clutches at the turf on the edge of a cliff. Her eyes opened wide. Here she was again, she thought, sitting bolt upright in bed. Awake. (TTL, 213–14)

This return visit to the Ramsays' home occurs after the war is over. The doubts the cataclysm has raised are, once more, subdued.

Thus, when "indeed peace had come," the illusion of romantic correspondence, the triumph of emotion over reason, is reasserted as in "the voice of the beauty of the world" asking the sleepers, "why not accept this, be content with this, acquiesce and resign?" However, Lily's violent jactitation—"She clutched at her blankets as a faller clutches at the turf on the edge of a cliff," after the sun "broke the veil on their eyes"—like Mrs. Dalloway's, marks Woolf's imaginative concurrence with Wordsworth's poetics in asserting "a contact with nature" that "then grows beyond nature to become a contact with time."[32] Woolf's radical understanding of the relationship of man and nature, yielding the truth that we are first creatures of time, ultimately links together Mr. Carmichael, Mr. Ramsay, Lily, and the narrator. The artist, ever hopeful of achieving through pattern the sense of correspondence, is, if successful, paradoxically confronted by the truth of her illusion. Moreover, she is self-consciously aware of this enigmatic truth. In a neat inversion of Joyce's Molly, whose consciousness goes down the drain—an iconical dot—at the end of the "Penelope" section of *Ulysses,* Woolf puts the procreative woman to rest and announces the emergence into consciousness of the woman-artist. The last nonsentence sentence of the section—the one word "Awake"—suggests that Lily is joining the ranks of the artists who, like Carmichael, keep their candles burning "rather longer than the rest."

Symbolically the questioning chorus of beach walkers has passed the baton or brush to Lily, the newest member of the "great clan" of artists, now awake for the agon—her embracing of these issues in her own painting. "Time Passes" has served as the figural representation of the struggle to achieve such an art, which soul-searching and searing process Woolf dramatically delineates in the novel's final section, "The Lighthouse."

The first sentences of this section are, in fact, a variation of the beach walkers' questions: "What does it mean then, what can it all mean? Lily Briscoe asked herself" (TTL, 217). That Lily recognizes the phrase as a "catchword," "caught up from some book, fitting her thought loosely" (TTL, 217), is only proof that she must find an authentic, idiosyncratic "voice" through which to reformulate these questions.

Lily's development as an artist depends also on distancing herself from Mrs. Ramsay. Despite her powerful feelings for the older woman, Lily is unable to transmute these into art because Mrs. Ramsay does not offer, through her own model of feminine experience, the analytic and/or phenomenological perspective of life—

her husband's point of view. Woolf proposes this perspective as an important aspect of aesthetic intellection. Peter Knox-Shaw says that Ramsay "becomes, in effect, the custodian of the 'real thing behind appearances.'"[33] Woolf fully develops the requisite merging of imaginative intuition and an empirical grasping of phenomena—the receptive/creative Wordsworthian imagination—only in "The Lighthouse." But this other thing needful—the receiving eye—is adumbrated in "The Window" when Lily attempts an analytical explanation of her canvas for Mr. Bankes.

> She took up once more her old painting position with the dim eyes and the absent-minded manner, subduing all her impressions as a woman to something much more general . . . which she had seen clearly once and must now grope for among hedges and houses and mothers and children—her picture. It was a question, she remembered, how to connect this mass on the right hand with that on the left. (TTL, 82–83)

Lily, reimpersonating herself as the artist, unconsciously discovers that she cannot do so carrying the baggage of Victorian womanhood; she must, as it were, subdue "all her impressions as a woman." In other words, she cannot take Mrs. Ramsay as the model for her life if she is to be an artist because Mrs. Ramsay fails to put her into analytical relation with the phenomenal world of hedges and houses and mothers and children, of "this mass on the right hand with that on the left," with the hard truths of existence.

Some of these hard truths, the deaths of the Ramsay family members, have made her suffer acutely. She experiences a profound sense of alienation and failure, which, ten years before, had kept her from finishing the painting of Mrs. Ramsay and James sitting in the window. The narrative voice informs us:

> Sitting alone . . . she felt cut off from other people, and able only to go on watching, asking, wondering. The house, the place, the morning, all seemed strangers to her. . . . How aimless it was, how chaotic . . . she thought. . . . Mrs. Ramsay dead; Andrew killed; Prue dead too—repeat it as she might, it roused no feeling in her. And we all get together in a house like this on a morning like this, she said, looking out of the window. It was a beautiful still day. (TTL, 218–19)

She is attempting to express the excruciating paradox, although death and cruelty exist, life goes on amidst beauty, which the narrative voice shapes in "Time Passes." Like Wordsworth who in the Preface discusses the presentation of pain in poetry, Lily begins to consider such questions. However, she suffers from "the feel of not to feel it" and will not be able to create form out of chaos until she breaks through the sterility of emotional isolation. This moment and issue in her development as an artist are both significant. For what has marked Lily's personality and, thus, her aesthetic "disability" until this point is a withdrawal from people and life, signaled by her flinching under the scrutiny of people's eyes as she worked at her easel and by her life-shaping decision not to marry. Her sometimes painful contact with others has not been the productive pain of the artist who recognizes, through a higher consciousness than Lily's, the searing necessity of an isolation or removal from life if one is to recapture it aesthetically—Wordsworth's "long half hour . . . / Mute, looking at the grave in which he lies!" (Wordsworth, 250, ll. 396–97).

Lily was standing outside when she had painted Mrs. Ramsay. Then her position had represented mere social isolation as opposed to aesthetic distancing as she painted the mother and son framed in the window. But her viewpoint has changed, for Lily herself now looks *out* through the window.

She pretends to drink out of her empty coffee cup to avoid Mr. Ramsay, "to escape his demand on her, to put aside a moment longer that imperious need" (TTL, 219). Curiously, avoiding Mr. Ramsay by keeping her head down is a repetition of an earlier moment of ambivalence that concluded positively. Praising him to Mr. Bankes, Lily had thought ten years before:

> A bit of a hypocrite? she repeated. Oh, no—the most sincere of men, the truest (here he was), the best; but, looking down, she thought, he is absorbed in himself, he is tyrannical, he is unjust; and kept looking down, purposely, for only so could she keep steady, staying with the Ramsays. Directly one looked up and saw them, what she called "being in love" flooded them. They became part of that unreal but penetrating and exciting universe which is the world seen through the eyes of love. (TTL, 72)

Now Lily's refusal to look up suggests that she is, unawares, still in that state of "'being in love.'" Thus her recognition that there is, ultimately, no escape from this human communion and, further, her resolution, in the face of her fear, to paint the picture Mr. and Mrs. Ramsay had effectively kept her from finishing ten years earlier, are newly explicable and compelling.

> Suddenly she remembered. When she had sat there last ten years ago there had been a little sprig or leaf pattern on the tablecloth, which

she had looked at in a moment of revelation. There had been a problem about a fore-ground of a picture. Move the tree to the middle, she had said. She had never finished that picture. She would paint that picture now. (TTL, 220)

A psychic spring (sprig?) has been pressed. This, the first of her reclamations of the past—the sequence of events that had led up to her decision not to marry—is the first evidence of a kind of autopsychoanalytic therapeutics, fostered by her interaction with Mr. Ramsay, which she will be able to continue until she achieves a psychic and creative "cure."

However, the painter's "block" does not really begin to break up until she stops fighting off Mr. Ramsay's demands. "Let him be fifty feet away . . . he permeated, he prevailed, he imposed himself. He changed everything. She could not see the colour; she could not see the lines. . . . That man, she thought, her anger rising in her, never gave; that man took. She, on the other hand, would be forced to give" (TTL, 223). She is both bitter about her loss of Mrs. Ramsay, Mr. Ramsay's fault, she believes, and about the knowledge that she will be the next sacrifice on the altar of his outrageous claims. It is hard enough to suffer the friendly gaze of another. Mr. Ramsay is the preeminent enemy. He is not merely, existentially speaking, "other." He is the *other* other,[34] the Male she so signally rejected when she moved the salt cellar ten years before. Yet even then, as we have seen, her ambivalent attitude, bordering on sexual confusion, had suggested her attraction, in addition to fear.

To understand Lily's complex feelings for Mr. Ramsay in "The Lighthouse," we return to Lily's efforts to paint the picture of Mrs. Ramsay and James as she stands on the lawn, between the house and the bay. We must consider as well the narrator's perceptions also reflecting Woolf's attitudes. Lily hears Mr. Ramsay, "at once so ridiculous and so alarming" (TTL, 30), shouting Tennyson's "Charge of the Light Brigade." The poem, from Lily and the narrator's perspective, serves most to commemorate the foolishness, indeed, the stupidity of the masculine world of boots, underscored by the line "Someone had blundered" (TTL, 31). Lily, with a sexual terror, sees Mr. Ramsay "coming down upon her," almost knocking over her easel, before "he turned sharp, and rode off, to die gloriously she supposed upon the heights of Balaclava" (TTL, 29).

No wonder that, after the fear of his transgression, Lily preserves herself with this "distancing" irony and regards the careful and meditative footfall of the asexual William Bankes as safe. Yet

William believes that Lily is sympathetic to Ramsay in this embar-
rassing revelation—the poetic recitation—of a private act. And
perhaps Mr. Bankes's silent commendation of Lily's bootlike
shoes—"Her shoes were excellent, he observed. They allowed the
toes their natural expansion" (TTL, 31)—is Woolf's sign that Lily,
still unawares, is in league (seven league?) with Mr. Ramsay and
a fraternity of masculine adventurers.

Lily, thinking of how one judges people, chooses Mr. Ramsay
and Mr. Bankes as her example. This is not the first time in the
novel, nor the last, that the energy and roundedness of the former
are compared favorably with the asexuality and desiccation of the
latter. She is listening to a voice that was

> her own voice saying without prompting undeniable, everlasting, con-
> tradictory things. . . . You have greatness . . . but Mr. Ramsay has
> none of it. He is petty, selfish, vain, egotistical . . . but he has what
> you (she addressed Mr. Bankes) have not; a fiery unworldliness . . .
> he loves dogs and his children. He has eight; Mr. Bankes has none. . . .
> All of this . . . danced up and down in Lily's mind, in and about the
> branches of the pear tree, where still hung in effigy the scrubbed
> kitchen table, symbol of her profound respect for Mr. Ramsay's mind,
> until her thought which had spun quicker and quicker exploded of its
> own intensity; she felt released. . . . (TTL, 40–41)

Lily's initial indictment of Mr. Ramsay transforms into orgasmic
pleasure as she commends his sexual fertility and fertile mind. Her
avoidance of him is thus a reflex of her attraction.

Woolf reveals her own profound attraction to her father by ven-
turing through the narrative voice into the heroic world of boots,
not long after Lily's "release." Despite the obvious undertones of
irony[35] in this description, the seamless fusing of the narrative
voice and Ramsay's thought purposely obfuscates the point of view
so that we hear her love for this complex man.

> And his fame lasts how long? It is permissible even for a dying hero
> to think before he dies how men will speak of him hereafter. . . . The
> very stone one kicks with one's boot will outlast Shakespeare. . . . (He
> looked into the hedge [as Lily will do when she paints]). . . . Who
> then . . . shall blame the leader of the doomed expedition, if, having
> adventured to the uttermost . . . and fallen asleep not much caring if
> he wakes or not, he now perceives by some pricking in his toes that
> he lives, and does not on the whole object to live. . . . Who will not
> secretly rejoice when the hero puts his armour off, and halts by the
> window and gazes at his wife and son . . . though still lovely and
> unfamiliar from the intensity of his isolation . . . and finally putting his

pipe in his pocket and bending his magnificent head before her—who will blame him if he does homage to the beauty of the world? (TTL, 56–57)

We feel the ultimate humanity of this abstract intellect when the voice describes Ramsay in relation to others.

He inspired in William Bankes (intermittently) and in Charles Tansley (obsequiously) and in his wife now . . . profoundly, reverence, and pity, and gratitude too, as a stake driven into the bed of a channel upon which the gulls perch and the waves beat inspires in merry boat-loads a feeling of gratitude for the duty it is taking upon itself of marking the channel out there in the floods alone. (TTL, 69)

The point of view is solely the narrator's and unequivocally conveys sympathy for Ramsay's intellectual heroism. We remember it when Lily is confronted by the aged man in "The Lighthouse."

Thinking it "simpler then to have it over," she mechanically attempts to "imitate from recollection the glow, the rhapsody, the self-surrender she had seen on so many women's faces (on Mrs. Ramsay's, for instance)" (TTL, 224). Yet Lily's eventual surrender to more positive feelings for Mr. Ramsay is suggested by the last sentence of this section: "She would give him what she could" (TTL, 225). The unadorned expression represents a more heartfelt effort and fuller sense of his need than does her original ironic imitation of "so many women."

She stands before him, like a stone, unable to give him the sympathy he craves, and thinks that "It was immensely to her discredit, sexually, to stand there dumb" (TTL, 228). The ambiguous locution perhaps suggests consciousness of her own attraction. But the emotional logjam breaks up when Lily notices Mr. Ramsay, exasperated with her, regarding his untied bootlaces. Mrs. Ramsay had once thought herself not good enough to tie them (TTL, 51). Now Lily symbolically performs that act.

Remarkable boots they were too, Lily thought, looking down at them: sculptured; colossal; like everything that Mr. Ramsay wore. . . . She could see them walking to his room of their own accord, expressive in his absence of pathos, surliness, ill-temper, charm.
"What beautiful boots!" she exclaimed. She was ashamed of herself. To praise his boots when he asked her to solace his soul. . . . to say . . . "Ah, but what beautiful boots you wear!" deserved, she knew . . . in one of his sudden roars of ill-temper, complete annihilation.
Instead, Mr. Ramsay smiled. His pall, his draperies, his infirmities fell from him. (TTL, 229)

Her spontaneity saves the day. In a lovely inversion of King Lear's disrobing in the hovel ("Off, off, you lendings!") as he learns to sympathize with humanity, Lily metaphorically dons these extraordinary, "colossal," heroic boots and "learns" the hitherto alien sensation of giving sympathy to another.

We have seen previous instances of Lily's adoption of the language of heroic convention. In "The Window," as she paints her picture of Mrs. Ramsay and James, she does not achieve what she wishes to do with her canvas—a difficulty, we suspect, she has come up against before. Lily then renders her own sense of inadequacy as an artist in terms of the terrors of the unprotected child— figuratively, a covert criticism of Mrs. Ramsay's powerlessness to help her transmute life into art.

> She could see it all so clearly, so commandingly, when she looked: it was when she took her brush in hand that the whole thing changed. It was in that moment's flight between the picture and her canvas that the demons set on her who often brought her to the verge of tears and made this passage from conception to work as dreadful as any down a dark passage for a child. Such she often felt herself—struggling against terrific odds to maintain her courage; to say: "But this is what I see; this is what I see". . . . (TTL, 32)

Yet she also perceives herself as capable of "struggle" and "courage," suggesting the vocabulary of heroic convention already associated with Mr. Ramsay from the second page of the novel.

> What he said was true. It was always true. He was incapable of untruth; never tampered with a fact; never altered a disagreeable word to suit the pleasure or convenience of any mortal being, least of all his own children, who, sprung from his loins, should be aware from childhood that life is difficult; facts uncompromising; and the passage to that fabled land where our brightest hopes are extinguished, our frail barks founder in darkness . . . one that needs, above all, courage, truth, and the power to endure. (TTL, 10–11)

The passage or adventure of life needs for its successful completion, in addition to acts of imagination like Mrs. Ramsay's, the qualities he names that permit one to face one's end. At this early point in the novel, Lily's unconscious assimilation of a masculine strategy for success, both in language and in life, prefigures and is ultimately responsible for her successful traversal of the passage from the conception to the work, the "dark passage" "to that fabled land where our brightest hopes are extinguished." She has begun to employ that heroic rhetoric, Woolf's tropes for the analytic mind, heralded by Ramsay's negative weather forecast and the subsequent memorializing of his passion for the unadorned truth. This appropriation signals her incipient acceptance of him and its consequent transformation of herself.

But now Lily's appreciation of Mr. Ramsay's boots is a kind of symbolic explosion of the lexical "putting on" that has preceded it. Ten years earlier at Mrs. Ramsay's dinner party, she had saved Charles Tansley as a favor to Mrs. Ramsay. However, this charged moment with Mr. Ramsay, bearing so much symbolic freight for her, is different. Her praise, coming from what unknown depths, releases Mr. Ramsay from his gloom and sets him riding his hobby horse, moments before he undertakes the adventure planned ten years before—the trip to the lighthouse with his children, Cam and James.

> He would have her observe (he lifted his right foot and then his left) that she had never seen boots made quite that shape before. . . . They had reached, she felt, a sunny island where peace dwelt, sanity reigned and the sun for ever shone, the blessed island of good boots. Her heart warmed to him. . . .
>
> Why, at this completely inappropriate moment . . . should she be so tormented with sympathy for him that, as she stooped too . . . she felt her eyes swell and tingle with tears? Thus occupied he seemed to her a figure of infinite pathos. He tied knots. He bought boots. There was no helping Mr. Ramsay on the journey he was going. But now just as she wished to say something, could have said something, perhaps, here they were—Cam and James. (TTL, 229–30)

For the reader the wonder of this moment is Lily's revelation that she is both able to feel for and succor another human being. This newfound gift, which has preeminently marked Mrs. Ramsay as an artist of life, now frees Lily psychically and aesthetically. The cosmic questions of the beach walking chorus, though never without a struggle, are, henceforth, given authentic expression by her.

Now reiterating Ramsay's own view of himself and still deploying his metaphors, Lily thinks that Mr. Ramsay "had all the appearance of a leader making ready for an expedition," leading "the way with his firm military tread, in those wonderful boots" (TTL, 231). Lily, too, has embarked on her own parallel adventure, a solitary engagement of the spirit rather than one of the body but fraught with equal danger. Her adventure of creation depends on memory. Thus, we should not be surprised that Wordsworth's entire poetic project, the result of spontaneous emotion recollected in tranquility, is in Woolf's own memory as she sees Lily safely to her destination.

Never before has Lily allowed herself to experience grief over the loss of Mrs. Ramsay. She now feels the sharp sting of the untented wounds of memory, but she is also awakened to a sense of self and of her powers because of it. However, something beyond the recovery of Mrs. Ramsay leads to Lily's metamorphosis. Certainly she reclaims Mrs. Ramsay's extraordinary ability to transmute the full moment of life into a kind of artistic *tableau vivant* through a succession of memories. Yet Lily's continuing feeling of fellowship with Mr. Ramsay, her sense that he is a worthy object of her sympathy—not altogether a new sensation for her—keeps alive in her the suggestion of their parallel adventures: his on the water, hers on the shore in front of her empty canvas.

Mr. Ramsay's own sympathy for life, which has caused him "to cumber himself definitely with fluttering wings and clucking domesticities" (TTL, 37), shows him worthy of Lily's. There is, for example, that memorable moment of literary susceptibility in which he forgets himself, his ambitions and cares, and feels, as he reads Walter Scott, that it doesn't

> matter a damn who reached z (if thought ran like an alphabet from A to Z). Somebody would reach it—if not he, then another. This man's strength and sanity, his feeling for straight-forward simple things, these fishermen, the poor old crazed creature in Mucklebackit's cottage made him feel so vigorous, so relieved of something that he felt roused and triumphant and could not choke back his tears. (TTL, 179–80)[36]

Lily appreciates Mr. Ramsay's "sudden recovery of vitality and interest in ordinary human things" (TTL, 233). He is no longer as "other" as she has perceived him. Her sense of him as he is about to embark on his voyage to the lighthouse reveals the truth about Lily as well. To her "it seemed as if he had shed worries and ambitions, and the hope of sympathy and the desire for praise, had entered some other region, was drawn on, as if by curiosity, in dumb colloquy, whether with himself or another, at the head of that little procession out of one's range" (TTL, 233). Her words convey Ramsay's connection to the heroic tradition, suggesting the forces that have impelled the male in his conquest of unknown territory. But Woolf makes it clear that Lily, "curiously divided, as if one part of her were drawn out there [on the water with Ramsay]" (TTL, 233–34), is engaged in the same heroic struggle, "in dumb colloquy," her other half "fixed . . . doggedly, solidly, here on the lawn" (TTL, 234). Reminding us of Ramsay's own locution, "facts uncompromising," we learn that "her canvas," having "floated up and placed itself white and uncompromising directly before her" (TTL, 234), is Lily's own battleground, comparable to the water of the bay. Her struggle to transform it, to make it convey her sense of life, to answer through her art the question "what can it all mean?" is equally heroic. She expresses herself in the heroic mode: in "the presence of this formidable ancient enemy of hers" (TTL, 236), she is about to exchange "the fluidity of life for the concentration of painting" (TTL, 237). In front of her canvas and filled with doubt, Lily remembers the detracting voice of her enemy Charles Tansley, the masculine other, "saying she couldn't paint, saying she couldn't create" (TTL, 237). Yet by an ironic, though not unpredictable, twist, this memory catalyzes the stalwart woman into successful creation. Here the language also suggests a parallel with the activity of Mrs. Ramsay. For her "dipping among the blues and umbers" (TTL, 237) and then stroking (daubing?) them onto the canvas is like Mrs. Ramsay's "diving into the soft mass [of the Boeuf en Daube]" and "peer[ing] into the dish, with its shiny walls and its confusion of savoury brown and yellow meats" (TTL, 151). Charles's words, rhythmically repeated by Lily, cause her mind to throw "up from its depths, scenes, and names, and sayings, and memories and ideas, like *a fountain spurting over that glaring, hideously difficult white space,* while she modelled it with greens and blues" (TTL, 238; my emphasis). Faced with a comparable act of male aggression, Mrs. Ramsay, hoping to repair her husband's damaged ego, pours "*erect into the air a rain of energy, a column of spray. . . .* [I]nto this fecundity, *this fountain and spray of life,* the fatal sterility of the male plunged itself, like a beak of brass, barren and bare" (TTL, 58; my emphasis).

Through memory Lily recovers a "spot of time," a "moment of friendship and liking—which survived" and "stayed in the mind affecting one almost like a work of art" (TTL, 240). As with Wordsworth, it becomes the basis for creation in the present. Recovery of this memory fosters an answer to her reformulation of the beach walkers' question: "What is the meaning of life?" (TTL, 240).

That was all—a simple question; one that tended to close in on one with years. The great revelation had never come. . . . Instead there were little daily miracles, illuminations, matches struck unexpectedly in the dark; here was one. This, that, and the other; herself and Charles Tansley and the breaking wave; Mrs. Ramsay bringing them together;

Mrs. Ramsay saying, "Life stand still here"; Mrs. Ramsay making of the moment something permanent (as in another sphere Lily herself tried to make of the moment something permanent)—this was of the nature of a revelation. In the midst of chaos there was shape. . . . (TTL, 240–41)

In the Wordsworthian vein of "little daily miracles," Woolf valorizes the ordinary, the diurnal, which rolls us round "with rocks and stones and trees" (Wordsworth, 115). Through it Lily creates an "aesthetic ethic." It shapes her painterly course as her conscious mind returns to the present and keeps both her inner and outer eye on Mr. Ramsay's boat, taking "its way with deliberation past the other boats out to sea" (TTL, 242). As she has felt it for Mrs. Ramsay, Lily's sympathy is activated by "the man who had marched past her, with his hand raised, aloof, at the head of a procession, in his beautiful boots" (TTL, 271).

Some readers have argued that the recovery of the mother figure is of primary psychological importance for Lily. This reclamation is necessary to another outcome—the successful composition of her painting. Yet the recovery is itself the result of the spiritual dialectic whose terms are Lily and Mr. Ramsay. This latter union, established through Lily's active sympathy, has propelled her into a confrontation of the empty canvas and supports her continued aesthetic success. Because of it Lily is able to go "on tunnelling her way into her picture, into the past" (TTL, 258), a process comparable to Woolf's own: "my tunnelling process, by which I tell the past by installments, as I have need of it" (Diary II, 272).

Through a symbolic sleight-of-hand, Woolf intensifies Lily's sympathy by re-creating it in Cam, her double, sitting in the boat with her father. Reinforcing the symbolic compression of the artist and the girl through Cam's questions, which recall the beach walkers and Lily's queries, Woolf makes this shift through the repetition of the fountain imagery with which Woolf has already created an identity between Lily and Mrs. Ramsay.

What then came next? Where were they going? From her hand, ice cold, held deep in the sea, there spurted up a fountain of joy at the change, at the escape, at the adventure (that she should be alive, that she should be there).[37] And the drops fallen from this sudden and unthinking fountain of joy fell here and there on the dark, the slumbrous shapes in her mind; shapes of a world not realised but turning in their darkness, catching here and there, a spark of light. . . . (TTL, 280–81)

The fountain imagery has, as well, a source other than the self-referential instances of the text. The narrator's collusive recording of the contents of Cam's consciousness draws on the ninth stanza of Wordsworth's "Intimations of Immortality."

> O *joy!* that in our embers
> Is something that does live,
> That nature yet remembers
> What was so fugitive!
> The thought of our past years in me doth breed
> Perpetual benediction. . . .
> Not for these I raise
> The song of thanks and praise;
> But for those obstinate questionings. . . .
> Blank misgivings of a Creature
> *Moving about in worlds not realised. . . .*
> But for those first affections
> Those shadowy recollections,
> Which, be they what they may,
> Are yet the *fountain light* of all our day. . . .
>
> (Wordsworth, 189–90; my emphasis)

Cam's repetition of key words of this poem, suggesting the spiritual importance of the reclamation of childhood memories, signals her own childhood memory of pleasure in her father's study where "Just to please herself she would take a book from the shelf and stand there, watching her father write" (TTL, 281).

Through her recollection of this comforting childhood experience, she recovers sympathy for her father, which alters her previous mood of antagonism. In fact, Cam has admitted to herself: "For no one attracted her more; [her father's] hands were beautiful, and his feet, and his voice, and his words, and his haste, and his temper, and his oddity, and his passion" (TTL, 253). Her little "story of adventure about escaping from a sinking ship" (TTL, 280) now puts her, like Lily, in league with the heroic. Woolf's Wordsworthian locution, "shapes of a world not realised," suggesting, as in *The Prelude* (Wordsworth, 201, Book I, ll. 390–400) and in "Intimations," a moral conversion of sorts—and then the memory shift to the pleasure of Cam's standing in her father's study, where she had gone for information, explain Cam's attachment to and dependence on Mr. Ramsay's being heroically incapable of untruth, his never tampering with a fact, and his asking her "as gently as any one could, Was there nothing he could give her?" (TTL, 282). Woolf, as well as the reader, recognized and deeply valued the extraordinariness, given the historical moment, of her father's allowing her, at the age of fifteen, the full run of the Stephen library.

Similarly, Woolf seems to have had Wordsworth in mind when she describes Cam, resolutely resisting her father's entreaty about a new puppy. "And as sometimes happens when a cloud falls on a green hillside . . . and it seems as if the hills themselves must ponder the fate of the clouded. . . . so Cam now felt herself overcast, as she sat there among calm, resolute people and wondered how to answer her father" (TTL, 250). The Miltonic delaying of the subject, the extended simile, and the use of Wordsworth's very words "sometimes" and "seems" are all reminiscent of "Resolution and Independence" where, in the extended metaphor of the ninth and tenth stanzas, he describes the old Leech-gatherer: "As a huge stone is sometimes seen to lie. . . . Such seemed this Man, not all alive or dead" (Wordsworth, 167). Woolf's use of the adjective "resolute" seems to confirm the stylistic origin of her prose.

Woolf's echoes of Wordsworth, the chronicler of the importance of childhood and of childhood memories, are singularly striking as she dramatizes Cam's dependence on her father. Thus Woolf registers her own sense of literary sympathy and patrimony in a particular case as well as in the more pervasive themes of the novel. Cam's name, mentioned by both Elizabeth Abel and Margaret Homans as possibly deriving from the *Aeneid,* suggests another instance of Woolf's "patriliteral" descent.

There is no better proof of Cam's sympathy with her father than her repetition of his words from Cowper's "The Castaway" (comparable to Lily's adoption of heroic metaphors) as she sinks into a fructifying doze: "About here, she thought, dabbling [for which read dipping, daubing, diving] her fingers in the water, a ship had sunk, and she murmured, dreamily half asleep, how we perished, each alone" (TTL, 284). Just as Lily has come to feel sympathy for Mr. Ramsay by imitating "the glow, the rhapsody, the self-surrender" of Mrs. Ramsay, so now Cam, by "dabbling" (echoing both the name of Mrs. Ramsay's culinary creation and her "diving," as she serves it, into its "soft mass"), comes to a moment—marked by her recognition of the place where the ship has sunk and murmuring of the poetic line—which represents for the reader linguistic and psychological confirmation of her patrilineal descent as well. Because these words are reminiscent of Lily's "dipping among the blues and umbers" (TTL, 237), as she successfully paints her way into the past, they establish another thread of tropic connection between the girl and the artist.

Lily considers the effect of distance, of perspective, both literally and metaphorically, in art and in life. Such distance, a necessity for the artist, is symbolically represented through Lily's "step-daughter" status in relation to Mr. and Mrs. Ramsay. Not their daughter, although her responses to them are frequently those of a biological child, her aesthetic detachment is enfigured in her virtual remove from them. As Lily has already noted, distant views disturb since they remind "the gazer . . . of a sky which beholds an earth entirely at rest" (TTL, 34). Thus the position of Mr. Ramsay's boat, out in the middle distance, upsets "some harmony in her own mind" (TTL, 286), creating aesthetic disharmony and causing her to express a distrust of language as a signifier of experience. She "wishe[s] to get hold of . . . that very jar on the nerves, the thing itself before it has been made anything" (TTL, 287), the Ramsayan *ding an sich* behind appearances, just as Woolf was wrestling with the same idea: "This is what the book would be that was made entirely solely & with integrity of one's thoughts. Suppose one could catch them before they became 'works of art.'? Catch them hot & sudden as they rise in the mind" (Diary III, 102). Thus, Woolf dramatizes the failing illocutions, the "as ifs" of "Time Passes."

Lily achieves an aesthetic solution by diving into unsolicited Wordsworthian memories. From Mr. Carmichael, with whom she shares the "exalted station," the Parnassian world of the lawn, and who seems "to share her thoughts" (TTL, 288), she moves associatively to Mrs. Ramsay and her gift for social relations, her way of seeing people, her way of saying.

Learning from Mrs. Ramsay how to see better, Lily, the artist, can now put the marriage of her figurative parents into "perspective." Her aesthetic remove from them, like the child's from the stepmother in fairy tales, helps to sharpen her gaze. "It was no monotony of bliss—she with her impulses and quicknesses; he with his shudders and glooms. . . . And there would fall between them sometimes long rigid silences . . . which annoyed Lily" (TTL, 296). Memory of the discord stops creative activity in the present until, serendipitously, someone inside the house moves, throwing a triangular shadow over the step outside the window—the very shape with which Lily had represented Mrs. Ramsay and James, ten years before. With the return of her creative mood, she is able to formulate an answer to the question of the relationship between art and life, in the manner of Wordsworth, whose self-appointed task it was, in *Lyrical Ballads,* to ensure that "ordinary things should be presented to the mind in an unusual aspect" (Wordsworth, 446–47). Lily, both as human being and artist, now wants "to be on a level with ordinary experience, to feel simply that's a chair, that's a table, and yet at the same time, It's a miracle, it's an ecstasy" (TTL, 300). But in keeping with the alternating pulse of creation and frustration that has characterized her efforts to translate vision into paint, the shadow disappears, enfiguring the inevitable and—in the case of Woolf, the creative artist—fortunate death of one's parents. Her desire transforms the symbolically empty step into her painful loss of Mrs. Ramsay and need for Mr. Ramsay. Yet sometimes loss is gain (" . . . other gifts / Have followed; for such loss, I would believe, / Abundant recompense" [Wordsworth, 110]) because, in this case, Lily, as Woolf did when writing *To the Lighthouse,* finds inner reserves of strength to compensate for her felt abandonment.

Yet Woolf first expresses Lily's feelings of isolation through another symbolic compression. As Lily's attraction to Ramsay is suggested through Cam's, her sense of alienation from others is doubled in James, as he steers the boat, thinking of his father and "that loneliness which was for both of them the truth about things" (TTL, 301). Woolf thus dramatizes an uncompromised existence, enfigured heroically in James's "We are driving before a gale—we must sink" (TTL, 302).

Mr. Ramsay's sympathetic nobility now overwhelms both Cam and James as it has Lily. Inscrutably, he sits in the boat, waiting to reach shore, reacting with balance to Macalister's report of three men drowned. To his children he seems to think to himself, "But why make a fuss about that? Naturally men are drowned in a storm, but it is a perfectly straightforward affair, and the depths of the sea . . . are only water after all" (TTL, 306). Thus Woolf approves the intellectual heroism of her father, who recognized the illusion of correspondences and the truth of "We perished each alone." Cam and James's sense that Mr. Ramsay, about to spring to land, is thinking, "There is no God" (TTL, 308), suggests the fraternity of the modernist imagination which numbers among its members Lily and Mr. Carmichael. His position also doubles Virgil's, the narrator's view of inimical nature in "Time Passes," and Wordsworth's "uncertain heaven" (Wordsworth, 250, l. 387). The philosophers, the poets, and the artists have offered their answers to the choric questions.

Woolf privileges the sense of a spiritual fraternity through the synchrony of Ramsay's landing at the lighthouse, Lily's "He has landed. . . . It is finished," and Mr. Carmichael's "They will have landed" (TTL, 309). She offers this simultaneity—her final proof that we are embedded in time—as symbolic assurance of Lily's new ability to bond to others, paradoxically, through the creation of aesthetic distance. "With an eye made quiet by the power / Of harmony, and the deep power of joy," she is now able to "see into" the heart of life and art (Wordsworth, 109). And like Mr. Carmichael, who "stood there as if he were spreading his hands over all the weakness and suffering of mankind" (TTL, 309), she, too, is like Virgil who "by emphasizing not the courage of an idealistic triumphant Aeneas but the anguish of his beaten rival, Turnus, at the conclusion of the *Aeneid,* . . . sides, as he does from the start of *Eclogue* I, with troubled humanity."[38] The sympathy is both Mr. and Mrs. Ramsay's gift. Yet Lily's heightened state is rendered through attachment to a symbolic patriarchy.

Our parents, limited by the constraints of their own time and place, give us what they can. For Virginia Woolf, with Victorian parents, it was a culturally predictable dichotomy, along gender lines, of feeling and thought, much in the tradition of the marriage of Harriet Taylor and John Stuart Mill.[39] But as flawed as our mothers and fathers are, we are in need of the gifts of both. If we can forgive them their trespasses against us, we are blessed with a sense of freedom and enablement. Perhaps, for some women, this is more the case with their fathers than their mothers. Certainly, this was true for Woolf whose actual relationship with Leslie Stephen was both lengthier and more complex than hers with Julia who died when she was only thirteen. Had he lived, she felt certain, she would never have been able to write (Diary III, 208). However, he died in 1904, and all of her writing represented a symbolic forgiving of this domineering but sympathetic and intellectually powerful man. Cam, Mr. Ramsay's biological daughter and thus, in a way, Woolf's closest representative in the novel, hardly demonstrates "the narrative costs of paternal filiation."[40] The narrative success of *To the Lighthouse* is a "telling" tribute to his influence.

But the text must have the last word. Lily reaches a state of spiritual calm, certitude, and forgiveness in the final moments of *To the Lighthouse.* She sees Mr. Carmichael looking across the bay to the lighthouse island where Ramsay has landed and imagines the poet in an act of benediction, "surveying, tolerantly and compassionately, their [mankind's] final destiny" (TTL, 309). With Mrs. Ramsay gone and Mr. Ramsay leagues away, Lily is alone in time and space. But Lily has been, as it were, re-beneficed by them. Their sympathy reshapes her aesthetic "consideration" (in both senses of that word) as she remarkably recovers the past and freshly connects to the present and future, enabling her to paint in a novel way.[41] Likewise Woolf suggests a new art form, but one based on the past, in her diary note on the creation of *To the Lighthouse:* "(. . . I have an idea that I will invent a new name for my books to supplant 'novel'. A new — by Virginia Woolf. But what? Elegy?)" (Diary III, 34).

Elizabeth Abel points out that Woolf's interrogative has been ignored by those who choose to read the novel as elegiac.[42] Perhaps, in the case of *To the Lighthouse,* "epic" would have done better. It suggests both the past, in which a foundation for the present and future is celebrated (as in the *Aeneid*), and the heroic proportions of the spiritual adventure of Lily Briscoe, who with "extreme fatigue" has had her vision. For "with her little puckered face and little Chinese eyes" (TTL, 156), Lily, through struggle, has come to the cosmic conclusion of all creators: "All things fall and are built again, / And those that build them again are gay."[43] In that spirit, she thinks: her picture, "would be destroyed. But what did that matter?" (TTL, 310). Now as one of the "great clan" (TTL, 9), she makes her final stroke in the center of her canvas, repeating to herself the words with which she had registered Mr. Ramsay's landing—"it was finished"—and solving the compositional difficulty of her art and life. We might say of her, as Yeats did of the three "Chinamen" in "Lapis Lazuli," a poem about the important place of "renovating" art in our lives:

> Their eyes, mid many wrinkles, their eyes,
> Their ancient, glittering eyes are gay.[44]

6

The Waves and "the world of memory and thought"

And what can this sorrow be?

It is brewed by the earth itself. It comes from the houses on the coast. We start transparent, and then the cloud thickens. All history backs our pane of glass. To escape is vain.
—*Jacob's Room*

As this extraordinarily lovely description suggests, life forces us to grow into complex beings, aware of its sorrows as well as beauty. We become our own mirrors, our experience or history "backing," like silver, our early painless transparency, transforming us into self-reflective creatures. Inescapably, we learn to view our emotions and development; self-consciousness makes us recognizably human. Virginia Woolf tried to convey something of this transformation in *Jacob's Room* but was unable to make palpable Jacob's growing sense of self so that this poignant statement of the narrator's remains external to his character. The first sentence of the novel, abstracted from Betty Flanders' letter—syntactically perfect but "referentially" incomplete or semantically anomalous— "'So of course,' wrote Betty Flanders, pressing her heels rather deeper in the sand, 'there was nothing for it but to leave'" (JR, 7), is a frustration to the reader and becomes, retrospectively, an iconographic representation of the unknowability of Jacob. To be sure, Woolf consciously explores this problem of representation in fiction:

But though all this may very well be true—so Jacob thought and spoke—so he crossed his legs—filled his pipe—sipped his whiskey . . . rumpling his hair as he did so, there remains over something which can never be conveyed to a second person save by Jacob himself.

191

> Moreover, part of this is not Jacob but Richard Bonamy—the room; the market carts; the hour; the very moment of history. (JR, 72–73)

Perhaps, too, the difficulty Woolf had in creating a "knowable" Jacob in a novel that privileges consciousness over a world of fur boas, tiepins, and buttons lies in another character's opinion of him: that he is "unconscious" (JR, 117). Yet ultimately we feel that our failure to lay salt on the character's tail is the failure of Woolf's narrative strategy because she was able to solve the problem of communicating character in *Mrs. Dalloway* and *To the Lighthouse.* Thus, Jacob remains a lovely arabesque, "exquisite outlines enclosing vacancy" (JR, 155).[1] However, beginning with *Orlando,* in which Woolf's grasp of narrative invention was much stronger, she was able to explore, more satisfactorily than she did in *Jacob's Room,* the intersection of history and cultural or group consciousness, on the one hand, and, on the other, individual consciousness, in their joint formation of personality and character.

Neville, one of the six narrating voices in *The Waves,* expresses something of the sentiment of the narrator of *Jacob's Room.* He reflects, in middle age, on the development of consciousness, personality, and the history or shape of his life.

> "I took the print of life not outwardly, but inwardly upon the raw, the white, the unprotected fibre. I am clouded and bruised with the print of minds and faces and things so subtle that they have smell, colour, texture, substance, but no name." (TW, 324)

Woolf chose to read *The Prelude* while writing *The Waves.* In August 1929, when she was working on "The Moths," her first title for the novel, Woolf committed to her diary—a written form of memorializing—a comment on the poem.

> Tea at four . . . & then I come out here & write several letters . . . & then I read one book of the Prelude. . . . Here I will copy some lines I want to remember,
>
> The matter that detains us now may seem,
> To many, neither dignified enough
> Nor arduous, yet will not be scorned by them
> Who, looking inward, have observed the ties
> That bind the perishable hours of life
> Each to the other, & the curious props
> By which the world of memory & thought
> Exists & is sustained.

They are from the 7th book of the Prelude [Book VII, 458–465]. A very good quotation I think" (Diary III, 247–48).[2]

Woolf recorded these lines about memory because they captured her ideas so articulately. Indeed, at the center of *The Waves* is the question, as in Wordsworth's autobiographical poem, of the relationship between the need for personal narrative or story, and consciousness and its subspecies, memory. She was interested in Wordsworth's sense of the relations of memory, percipience, and feeling in establishing our selfhood and the qualities of our imaginations, as Neville suggests. Wordsworth's is not the "biographic style" that "tack[s] together torn bits of stuff" with its "phrases laid like Roman roads across the tumult of our lives, since they compel us to walk in step like civilised people with the slow and measured tread of policemen though one may be humming any nonsense under one's breath at the same time" (TW, 356). Rather, Wordsworth captured in his poem Bernard's sense that "Outside the undifferentiated forces roar; inside we are very private, very explicit, have a sense indeed, that it is here, in this little room, that we make whatever day of the week it may be" (TW, 353).

In "A Sketch of the Past," Woolf noted: "I feel that strong emotion must leave its trace; and it is only a question of discovering how we can get ourselves again attached to it, so that we shall be able to live our lives through from the start" (MoB, 67). In the novels that succeeded *Jacob's Room,* she was able to work out techniques of narrative and character development that depend on this process of reattachment. Woolf had relied heavily on the memory of her own childhood summers at Talland House in St. Ives, Cornwall, and of her parents in her creation of *To the Lighthouse.* In that novel she examines the importance of memory for the creative artist through Lily Briscoe's efforts to repaint a composition she had begun and abandoned ten years before, the subject of which was Mrs. Ramsay. Mrs. Ramsay as subject of the new painting can be recovered by Lily only by the artist's "tunneling into the past." But Woolf's consciousness of memory in *The Waves* goes beyond such dependency. Here there is the indirect articulation of the function of memory of the narrative devices: the past tense of the italicized chapter prologues and the conventional "metastory" communications within the chapters, the quotation marks and grammatical directives implying the past, as in "Bernard said" or "Rhoda said." More directly and self-consciously, the character-narrators note memory, particularly Louis with his developed historical awareness, Rhoda, keenly conscious of the impairment of this organ within her, and Woolf's storyteller avatar, Bernard. Memory, investigated both as to its importance and the ways in which it works, thus marks the texture of the novel as a whole so that we feel a mirroring or self-reflexive quality about the text as we read and reread. The novel, as an instance of the uniquely human activity of storytelling, and storytelling pitched to its zenith as conscious art, relying both in its production and for its subject on memory, is, like Wordsworth's poem, self-commenting.

However, Wordsworth's poem, with its subject and actual composition dependent on "the world of memory and thought," although Woolf's point of embarkation, does not go as far as her own meditation on meditation. Wordsworth considers the influence of public or historical experience, coeval with his life, and personal experience as responsible for the formation of his character and imagination. He even considers books, which are, in effect, repositories of cultural experience, in the formation of his character, but not insofar as they are such repositories. Woolf, on the other hand, in making the general case for the development of character, extends responsibility for our uniqueness, but also our similarity, to the historical forces and resulting accumulation of knowledge that have preceded our begetting and birth. These connections, particularly guided or inspired by Wordsworth, reveal again the impress of Leslie Stephen, the historian and admirer of Wordsworth, on his daughter's mind and in her work.

Samuel Johnson had James Boswell, but Rousseau, Wordsworth, Coleridge, Hazlitt, and De Quincey had themselves. Although there are exceptions, Montaigne and Browne, for example—noted, as we have seen, by Woolf herself—the autobiographical form, that written recovery of self, focusing on the mind and its creativity, was an idiosyncratic Romantic idiom. Indeed, Woolf comments explicitly on this phenomenon in *A Room of One's Own* where she writes: "Nothing indeed was ever said by the artist himself about his state of mind until the eighteenth century perhaps. Rousseau perhaps began it. At any rate, by the nineteenth century self-consciousness had developed so far that it was the habit for men of letters to describe their minds in confessions and autobiographies" (ROO, 53). The Romantics were the first to take seriously the premise that the life of the mind determines the course of events in one's "outer" life.[3]

Rousseau, as Woolf saw, understood this idea when he wrote, at the beginning of the *Confessions:*

> I am commencing an undertaking, hitherto without precedent, and which will never find an imitator. I desire to set before my fellows the

likeness of a man in all the truth of nature, and that man myself. Myself alone! I know the feelings of my heart, and I know men. . . . I have unveiled my inmost self even as Thou hast seen it, O Eternal Being.[4]

Virginia Woolf, through her characters in *The Waves,* asks a concomitant question: Does it not help, in "breasting the world" (TW, 223), to know from where I have come and understand how that has determined who I am? Thus, the six speaking characters of this novel become their own fates, spinning, through memory and self-consciousness about their minds' contemplation of past, present, and future, the trajectory and the texture of the thread—the "wandering thread" (TW, 209), as Bernard calls it—that defines their lives. Their desire to do so is evidence of universal human behavior—the need to make story, to impose order on experience by becoming conscious that there is a wandering thread in apparent incoherence.

Woolf goes so far as to imply that sequence is health and, because story is sequence, story is health. Neville says:

"Let Bernard begin. Let him burble on, telling us stories, while we lie recumbent. Let him describe what we have all seen so that it becomes a sequence. Bernard says there is always a story. I am a story. Louis is a story. There is the story of the boot-boy, the story of the man with one eye, the story of the woman who sells winkles. . . ." (TW, 200)

The desire to make sequence moves Bernard who, when his "power fails him and there is no longer any sequence . . . gap[es] as if about to burst into tears. Among the tortures and devastations of life is this then—our friends are not able to finish their stories" (TW, 201).

It is not only Bernard who needs to order experience by putting it into words. Louis, too, is aesthetically tortured by the desire "to fix the moment in one effort of supreme endeavour. . . . This I see for a second, and shall try tonight to fix in words, to forge in a ring of steel" (TW, 201).

By contrast Rhoda experiences the world as discrete moments, a sign of her pathology. Even as a child she says:

"Look, the loop of the figure is beginning to fill with time; it holds the world in it. . . . I myself am outside the loop. . . . crying, 'Oh, save me, from being blown for ever outside the loop of time!'" (TW, 189)

As an adult she adds: "'I cannot make one moment merge in the next. To me they are all violent, all separate'" (TW, 265). She recognizes that the others "'stand embedded in a substance made of repeated moments run together'" (TW, 330). Bernard, shedding one of his "life-skins" and still disoriented says: "'But observe how dots and dashes are beginning, as I walk, to run themselves into continuous lines, how things are losing the bald, the separate identity that they had as I walked up those steps'" (TW, 306). And even clearer are his words at the very end of his final soliloquy:

> "But wait. While they add up the bill. . . . I will record in words of one syllable how also under your gaze with that compulsion on me I begin to perceive this, that and the other. The clock ticks; the woman sneezes; the waiter comes—there is a gradual coming together, running into one, acceleration and unification. . . . I regain the sense of the complexity and the reality and the struggle, for which I thank you." (TW, 380–81)

Discrete impressions not only must run together but must also be "'coax[ed] into words'" (TW, 307). Story encodes and memorializes sequence and thus restores us to health. Psychic health, then, depends on memory. Susan, standing lost, "'with tears in [her] eyes remembering home,'" is more integrated than Jinny who, when she "'read[s] . . . cannot follow any word through its changes . . . cannot follow any thought from past to present'" (TW, 203). Making up a story about oneself, as Bernard self-consciously does and the others do as well without announcing their intentions, is "reading" one's character, one's life plot, and, at the same time, constructing oneself[5]—that is, making guesses, affirming intuitions that may have consequences for future action and behaviors. In reading this book, we imitate the characters' efforts. Both acts, making up stories and reading, require self-consciousness or self-reflexivity. One's personal history, both the character's and ours, and understanding of it are behind the creative act.

Related to this proposition is our understanding that the characters' personalities, based, in part, on memory of themselves, are, at the same time, idiosyncratic or differentiated one from another, and exemplary, expressing what is common to all our experience. Each of the six is unique, but each is also part of a tradition, in this case, the progression of western civilization. In her essay "On Being Ill," published in 1930 while Woolf was writing *The Waves,* she explicitly mentions the existence of a collective imagination. In a paragraph in which she recurs to the dominant image of *The Waves*—"The wave of life flings itself out indefatigably" (CE 4, 198)—she refers to "The co-operative imagination of mankind" (198). Reading *The Waves* is a complicated process that includes remembering its various parts as we proceed unimpeded, turning back the pages when our memory is fuzzy, and, when we pause in the act of decoding, thinking about or contextualizing it in our own lives. Contextualizing includes, as well as recognizing the obvious parallels to, and differences from, our personal experiences, our knowledge of Woolf's oeuvre, of other literature, and of history. Reading, an activity made possible by the collective intelligence of civilization, compels us to discover that each of us is, likewise, the product of the same forces determining the personalities of Woolf's fictive characters. Inscribing ourselves in the text becomes an example of precisely the individuating and "collectivizing" processes that are Woolf's interest in it.[6] Thus, writing and reading—enactment and reenactment—are collusive agents in "remembering" her story.

The collectivizing impulse is at work when we read this book, as any other, and find points of intersection between it and our prior experience. Further, collectivization shares something with the concept of anonymity in the production of art, Woolf's interest in 1940, when she began working on "Anon." However, there is an important glimpse of it in 1939 in the passage cited previously from "A Sketch of the Past" where she writes:

> It is a constant idea of mine; that behind the cotton wool [of existence] there is hidden a pattern; that we—I mean all human beings—are connected with this; that the whole world is a work of art; that we are parts of the work of art. *Hamlet* or a Beethoven quartet is the truth about this vast mass that we call the world. But there is no Shakespeare, there is no Beethoven; certainly and emphatically there is no God; we are the words; we are the music; we are the thing itself. (MoB, 72)

We are able to inscribe ourselves into the text and music, that is, because we are there already—being the words, the music, the thing itself. We are the anonymous "authors" who find the "hidden pattern" that is there to be found.

As infants we learned by recognizing patterns—similarities and differences. This process is an aspect of cognitive development, enabling us to learn about the space we inhabit. To make use of this space, we need to see pattern. Pattern retrieves experience from chaos. Art, which is pattern exponentially raised, elevates our level of self-consciousness about our pattern-making propensity.

This concept of anonymity, as Woolf uses it, depends on a recognition that the cultural history of civilization impinges on, or enters into, the individual mind. The artist, to look at this issue from the point of view of production, resonates with the minds of readers only because we are the words, the music, the patterned world. As Eleanor in *The Years* thinks to herself: "Does everything then come over again a little differently? she thought. If so, is there a pattern; a theme, recurring, like music; half remembered, half foreseen? . . . a gigantic pattern, momentarily perceptible? The thought gave her extreme pleasure: that there was a pattern. But who makes it? Who thinks it? Her mind slipped. She could not finish her thought."[7] This is what history—the making of our collective story through the memory of events—shows us. This is what the universal need to make story proves. We are all similar, having the same impulses, taking pleasure in the making and recognition of pattern. Like the Romantics', Woolf's vision of the mind is a democratic one. When Woolf says that there is no Shakespeare or Beethoven, she implies that we all share a propensity for narrative structure. We are, in other words, all authors; our sense of excitement, or "rapture," when we read a text or listen to music is the recognition of authorship and pattern-making in ourselves.

One might choose many examples to demonstrate Woolf's notion of the intersection of consciousness, memory, and history. One is Bernard's transcription of his particular experience of leaving the first school he has attended with his friends.

> "This is the final ceremony," said Bernard. ". . . We are overcome by strange feelings. . . . One wants to say something, to feel something, absolutely appropriate to the occasion. One's mind is primed. . . . And then a bee drifts in and hums round the flowers in the bouquet which Lady Hampton, the wife of the General, keeps smelling to show her appreciation of the compliment. If the bee were to sting her nose? We are all deeply moved; yet irreverent; yet penitent; yet anxious to get it over; yet reluctant to part. The bee distracts us. . . . Humming vaguely, skimming widely, it is settled now on the carnation. Many of us will not meet again. We shall not enjoy certain pleasures again, when we are free to go to bed, or to sit up, when I need no longer smuggle in bits of candle ends and immoral literature. The bee now hums round the head of the great Doctor. Larpent, John, Archie, Percival, Baker and Smith—I have liked them enormously. I have known one mad boy only. I have hated one mean boy only. I enjoy in retrospect my terribly awkward breakfasts at the Headmaster's table with toast and marmalade. He alone does not notice the bee. If it were to settle on his nose he would flick it off with one magnificent gesture. . . . Now we are dismissed—Louis, Neville and I for ever. . . . We rise, we disperse; the pressure is removed. The bee has become an insignificant, a disregarded insect, flown through the open window into obscurity. Tomorrow we go." (TW, 215–16)

These observations of Bernard's, the recognized "official" story-teller (although by no means the only one) among the group of friends, reveal the richness and complex interdependence of types of conscious activity: "the wreath'd trellis of the working brain."[8] There are statements of interpretation of his own feelings, asser-tions made on the basis of his thoughts about others', proleptic statements, based on remembered past experience, recollection of past events, summations and generalizations. Possibly the most interesting are the self-conscious reflections on the mind itself, suggested through Bernard's consideration of the mental tension caused by an insignificant "insect" that temporarily gains impor-tance because it might interrupt the leave-taking ceremony.

Bernard is telling the story while at the same time "reading" it, inscribing himself in the experience through interpreting the com-plex set of interactions between his thoughts and the external world. His self-conscious acts of mentation—metonymically repre-senting the central interest of the novel—are an updating of the activity of the author of *The Prelude,* the tracing of the growth of the poet's imagination. Wordsworth situates himself amidst personal and public-historic events (the French Revolution) in his poem to show how the development of self and of self-consciousness deepen appreciation for, and enable him to withstand the difficult business of, living. Telling the story, his autobiography, to himself as he writes it for a public audience is the act of self-consciousness that defines the Romantic critical project and makes the Preface to *Lyrical Ballads,* which equally self-consciously explores the na-ture of the poet and of poetry, a watershed in the history of liter-ary criticism.

Woolf was clearly mindful of Wordsworth's exploration of the resources of the creative mind and of the creative act itself while writing her novel. However, Pamela Caughie's assertion that *The Waves* is a playing with textuality without reference to the real world—represented only by the assortment of linguistic phenom-ena that comprise the text—is a misreading. She maintains: "The six speakers do not represent the surface manifestations of some deep consciousness because the relation of surface to depth no longer pertains either. For Woolf's concern is not the relation of art to life but the relation of art to audience."[9] Life is not like the stories we tell, as Bernard says so elegantly when he comments on the limited ability of storytelling to order or detach experiences or "give the effect of the whole" (TW, 354).

"Whatever sentence I extract whole and entire from this cauldron is only a string of six little fish that let themselves be caught while a million others leap and sizzle making the cauldron bubble like boiling silver, and slip through my fingers." (TW, 354)

But even more obviously, as Bernard and the others know, without life there are no stories at all; Woolf does not deny the bubbling cauldron. Nor did she see the audience as the "final cause" of creation. However, it may be useful in reading this book to understand audience not merely as receptive, passive readers of books but rather the totality of human responsiveness to the stimuli of the many spaces and times we inhabit, as determined by the genetic code that wires our brains. Bernard, as his own audience, describes the way in which imagination functions in a nonliterary context. His "story" of leaving school is the kind we tell over to ourselves as we get on from one part of an ordinary day to another; indeed, the act of telling, itself, may help us to make the transitions. To understand that art is a particular, heightened form of this generalized experience of storytelling is an important point in our "reading" or understanding of the novel. But to assert that the book is concerned only with the nature of aesthetic intellection is to aestheticize or trivialize it.

Woolf begins with the characters' childhood because it is the foundation of memories and thus central to our character formation and the concomitantly unique nature of all our subsequent experience. As she had written in the introduction to the first American edition of *Mrs. Dalloway* in 1925:

> For nothing is more fascinating than to be shown the truth which lies behind the immense facades of fiction. . . . Books are the flowers or fruits stuck here and there on a tree which has its roots deep down in the earth of our earliest life, of our first experience.[10]

This description metaphorically suggests that all the experiences of a writer, but particularly the profound, because the first, experiences of childhood are likely to find their way into books. Usually these experiences are disguised before they issue, transformed, as parts of a fiction. However, in some cases, as is true of Woolf's novels, because of her diaries and memoirs that enable us to see their generative parts, we find a fairly accurate transcription of the "truth," the unadorned memories of her past. In *The Waves,* the "story" of the story of the lives of these six characters, Woolf starts at the beginning of consciousness, in childhood, and, specifically, of her own consciousness. This is so not only for the history of the six friends but also for the metastructure of the novel, the communications of the nameless narrator that frame or situate the sections of the friends' words through the device of comparing their lives to the hours between the rising and setting of the sun. The seminal importance of the first period of life as the grounding, not only of books but of all later experience, is described by Woolf even more articulately at the beginning of "A Sketch of the Past," written eight years after completing *The Waves*. The chapter prologues read like a record of her remembered childhood perception of summers in St. Ives, the waves, the light, and Talland House.

> If life has a base that it stands upon, if it is a bowl that one fills and fills and fills—then my bowl without a doubt stands upon this memory. It is of lying half asleep, half awake, in bed in the nursery at St Ives. It is of hearing the waves breaking, one, two, one, two, and sending a splash of water over the beach; and then breaking, one, two, one, two, behind a yellow blind. It is of hearing the blind draw its little acorn across the floor as the wind blew the blind out. (MoB, 64–65)

James Holt McGavran, writing in 1981, after Jeanne Schulkind had published *Moments of Being,* suggests that there is another level of significance to the house on the shore of the prologues and, we imagine, the childhood home of Bernard, Louis, Neville, Rhoda, Susan, and Jinny. In his essay linking the Wordsworths, Woolf, and *The Waves,* he begins:

> Critics from W. H. Auden to Harold Bloom have demonstrated the prominence of the seashore as a topos in English and American poetry of the last two centuries. . . . By building a house on the shore, writing a poem, one can "occupy spaces". . . .
> This poetic territory was first explored by Wordsworth . . . the blueprint of his house by the sea, is to be found in the "Ode: Intimations of Immortality from Recollections of Early Childhood," especially in the conclusion to the ninth stanza. . . .[11]

McGavran argues that Woolf's transformation of her own experience of Cornwall summers in a house that overlooked the sea "may be read as a feminist's highly conscious commentaries upon, or revisions of, the seminal Wordsworth text."[12] Thus, although recognizing the autobiographical origins of Woolf's house in *The Waves,* McGavran insists that the house, as metonymic poetic space, has been inherited from Wordsworth and the Romantics.

McGavran's argument, especially as he supports it with parallels between the novel and other Wordsworthian texts, particularly *The Prelude,* is convincing. However, I would argue further that the meaning we derive from reading the novel is inextricably tied not only to Wordsworth's and other writers' influences but to the act of discovery itself. Our reading, both in the literal sense of passing our eyes over the words, and in the more metaphorical sense of interpreting their collective significance, in partnership with authorial design, creates an inter- and intratextual web of references and cross-references that is the meaning, or, more accurately, the "experience," of the novel. The activity of reading, itself a repetition or reenactment of the author's activity of writing, is an instance of the personal and cultural referencing and cross-referencing constitutive of individual consciousness.[13]

The creation of patterns of consciousness starts for the six friends and for the reader in the first section of the novel where, in a stylized dialogue, Woolf establishes the children's self-consciousness about sensory perception. Their words of one syllable are a linguistic encoding of the fundamental patterns of intellection.

The reader's and the characters' experience of the process of individuation, dependent on the kinds of stimuli noted by each of the children, is almost simultaneous.

> "I see a ring," said Bernard, "hanging above me. It quivers and hangs in a loop of light."
>
> "I see a slab of pale yellow," said Susan, "spreading away until it meets a purple stripe."
>
> "I hear a sound," said Rhoda, "cheep, chirp; cheep, chirp; going up and down."
>
> "I see a globe," said Neville," hanging down in a drop against the enormous flanks of some hill."
>
> "I see a crimson tassel," said Jinny, "twisted with gold threads."
>
> "I hear something stamping," said Louis. "A great beast's foot is chained. It stamps, and stamps, and stamps." (TW, 180)

These very different observations, which read like the text of a primer, are meant to suggest the differences in personality or character of the children. However, as has been noted by others (Hermione Lee, Pamela Transue, Avrom Fleishman, and S. P. Rosenbaum, for example),[14] the statements are invariant stylistically. As Lee says: "*The Waves* is not difficult to read as poetry; its rhythm is agreeable and insidious. But it is difficult to read as a novel, in that its emphasis on rhythm overwhelms distinctions of character. Only the content enables us to distinguish between the voices."[15] And content, too, is so frequently similar that we must go back and look carefully to see which character "said" the speech we have been reading. To suggest that this uniformity of style re-flects Woolf's plan that the book "was to be an abstract mystical eyeless book: a playpoem" is to give too much importance to au-thorial intention, especially when she continues: "And there may be affectation in being too mystical; too abstract" (Diary III, 203).

However, more importantly, the uniformity may itself be Woolf's experiment in making the novel reveal the mind in relation to a "general idea"—in this case that the personality of each individual is a function of the "collective personality" of our common culture and history. As Bernard says, "'But when we sit together, close, . . . we melt into each other with phrases. We are edged with mist. We make an unsubstantial territory'" (TW, 185). We use the lan-guage of our friends, of our speech community, and of the larger society to which we belong. We discover, as does Lily Briscoe in *To the Lighthouse,* that our personalities are altered by our linguistic choices.

There are, then, two aspects to the characters' personalities and ours: the uniqueness of each consciousness, dependent on personal experience and the particular historic moment, and its collective aspect, the result of the common and, thus, historic experiences of our culture. In January 1929 Woolf mused in her diary, in a speculative mood raised by thoughts of the immortality of Orlando:

> Now is life very solid, or very shifting? I am haunted by the two contradictions. This has gone on for ever: will last for ever; goes down to the bottom of the world—this moment I stand on. Also it is transi-tory, flying, diaphanous. I shall pass like a cloud on the waves. Perhaps it may be that though we change; one flying after another, so quick so quick, yet we are somehow successive, & continuous—we human be-ings; & show the light through. (Diary III, 218)

As we read further in *The Waves,* we inscribe our own uniqueness and collective experience, doubling the developing process of indi-viduation and collectivization that the characters at various times both suffer and rejoice in.

The process of discovering one's uniqueness and the concomi-tant alterity of everyone else is shared by all the characters in the first chapter. Louis, suffering his isolation, hides behind a hedge. Jinny, sensing Louis's pain, follows him, thinking to ease it by kissing his neck. Susan, witnessing the kiss as she walks by, feels the pain of being excluded from this private moment. Bernard, seeing Susan in agony, goes to comfort her, leaving Neville in the toolhouse. Neville feels abandoned by Bernard who "'leaves [him] in the lurch; he follows Susan'" (TW, 187). And Rhoda, the isolate,

rocking her basin of white petals, knows that "'Neville has gone
and Susan has gone; Jinny is in the kitchen garden picking currants
with Louis perhaps'" (TW, 187). The middle-aged Bernard names
the experience of recognizing one's uniqueness as he recapitulates
those first conscious moments of his childhood: "'It was Susan
who cried, that day when I was in the tool-house with Neville; and
I felt my indifference melt. Neville did not melt. "Therefore," I
said, "I am myself, not Neville," a wonderful discovery'" (TW,
343). Yet we are also reminded of a "moment of being" in western
culture as we read these words because they play on Descartes'
ontological definition of being: "Cogito ergo sum." Through such
"collective" intertextual referencing, we understand that history
repeats itself but always with a difference. We recognize the forward thrust of civilization.

Woolf's use of archetypal figures, the translation or reuse of
myth, and our recognition of these are a parallel case of cultural
intertextuality. So the celebratory supper on the eve of Percival's
leaving for India is a variant of the last supper of Christ and the
Apostles. The woman writing in the garden in Elvedon (perhaps
Woolf's wink at her own practice) is also Clotho, spinner of the
web of personal history. But Woolf is implicitly saying that the
communal eating preceding Percival's departure is the expression
of a cultural universal; perhaps it is even genetically encoded behavior.[16] The woman writing is a reenactment of the need to make
a life story, to shape it as art—the very act arming us against death.

Woolf, through a particularly potent archetype, the loss of paradise or the expulsion from the garden, makes concrete the discovery of one's separateness and the otherness of the world. Perhaps
"Genesis" is itself the mythic retelling of the "'severance from the
body of our mother'" (TW, 261). The story of Eden, since the
Counter-Reformation, links original sin to sexuality. Thus, Woolf
connects the epistemological discovery of self to Jinny's kiss, Susan's sexual jealousy and Cainlike anger, and Bernard's discovery
that he is in love with Susan, revealed later as an enrichment of
the pattern when, retelling the story, he says, "'And being in love
for the first time, I made a phrase'" (TW, 343). Thus, Woolf in the
story of the story of the beginnings of these six children links
sexuality to a symbolic ejection from the garden. Bernard names
the garden "Elvedon," a childish expansion of Eden as perceived
by small people. He invites Susan to visit it with him to distract her
from the pain of having witnessed Jinny's kiss. But these children,
having experienced the fall into self-knowledge, are already intruders. Bernard says to Susan:

"Put your foot on this brick. Look over the wall. That is Elvedon. The lady sits between the two long windows, writing. . . . We are the discoverers of an unknown land. Do not stir; if the gardeners saw us they would shoot us. . . ."

. . . "Run!" said Bernard. "Run! . . . We are in a hostile country. We must escape to the beech wood." (TW, 186)

The repetition of the cultural topos of Eden, from the stores of our "racial memory," if we "read" it into the text of *The Waves,* becomes a part of the extra-character communication between author and reader for whom the Christian myth is an essential element of the western experience.[17] Such archetypes remind us of the convergences of our human needs to name our experiences and communicate them to others. As he retrieves it from his memory bank, Bernard's adult retelling of this "spot of time" is his own "recognition-reading" of the publicly shared myth and his particular experience. In recounting it he creates his own "history," modeled on "Genesis" and the Judeo-Christian story of creation, ex nihilo. In the beginning there was "'the loop of light,'" (TW, 180) or, as Bernard in his redaction says:

"In the beginning, there was the nursery, with windows opening on to a garden, and beyond that the sea. I saw something brighten—no doubt the brass handle of a cupboard. Then Mrs. Constable raised the sponge above her head, squeezed it, and out shot, right, left, all down the spine, arrows of sensation." (TW, 342)

Mrs. Constable's water-soaked sponge is, thus, the river of life transformed into the stream of conscious sensation and thought that marks each of us, making us unique. Indeed, our reading of this narrative is a parallel but unique re-creation of Bernard's story of his friends' lives. We may go farther and say that reader and author, creating and recognizing these repetitions, thus collude in the making of patterns that structure the book and contextualize it in our common experience. That we are, as we read, conscious of such participation makes us aware of language as the currency of exchange of ideas. Therefore, Woolf shows these very young children, as they first learn to communicate, becoming aware of language as itself a cultural artifact, based, as are the characters of the six friends, on patterns of similarity and difference. Ontology, as W. V. O. Quine has pointed out, recapitulates philology.[18] Awareness of language, especially its dual aspects of difference and similarity, is shared by a number of the children.

"Those are white words," said Susan, "like stones one picks up by the seashore."

"They flick their tails right and left as I speak them," said Bernard. "They wag their tails; they flick their tails; they move through the air in flocks, now this way, now that way, moving all together, now dividing, now coming together."

"Those are yellow words, those are fiery words," said Jinny. "I should like a fiery dress, a yellow dress, a fulvous dress to wear in the evening."

"Each tense," said Neville, "means differently. There is an order in this world; there are distinctions, there are differences in this world, upon whose verge I step. For this is only a beginning." (TW, 188)

Distinctions and differences can exist in language only because there are classes of words, samenesses, which make differences between classes possible. Without classes there is no "order in this world" but only randomness or chaos because difference among unique entities does not produce a usable and, therefore, useful system. And without differences there cannot be metaphors that point back to similarities.

Language, then, a subject of scrutiny by the characters, becomes one for us as well. We are subtly coerced into awareness of the medium of Woolf's art and of its power to alter us. From yellow words, fiery words, Jinny moves to a desire to possess a fiery dress, a yellow dress. Our memories and future desires, retrieved through images and expressed to others through words, create emotion and thought in the present.

"'Now you trail away,' said Susan, 'making phrases. . . . Now you tug at my skirts, looking back, making phrases. You have escaped me'" (TW, 186). All the others express their awareness of language, at the least, through such references to Bernard's phrases and storytelling. But Louis and Neville are poets as well. Louis says he "'shall assemble a few words and forge round us a hammered ring of beaten steel'" (TW, 292). Even Susan and Jinny, neither of whom lays claim to poetic expression, are part of the community of eloquence, inhabited by the others. Susan says:

"Sleep, sleep, I croon, whether it is summer or winter, May or November. Sleep I sing—I, who am unmelodious and hear no music save rustic music when a dog barks, a bell tinkles, or wheels crunch upon the gravel. I sing my song by the fire like an old shell murmuring on the beach."[19] (TW, 294)

The undifferentiated poetic voice of the six friends recalls for us the tradition of western culture to which these characters, Woolf,

and we belong and of which she reminds us when Louis recites
the austerely simple but beautiful

> O western wind, when wilt thou blow,
> That the small rain down can rain?
> Christ! that my love were in my arms,
> And I in my bed again!
>
> (TW, 317)

Thus, the part each of us inherits in the historic pageant becomes
clear as we read ourselves into the text through our own awareness
of language. Aided by memory and thought, we engage in pattern-
making that makes a structure for the novel and inserts it into
the cultural tradition of which it, too, is a part. We realize that
"civilization" is itself intertextual, revealing to those who study it,
repetition, contrast, and, above all, pattern. Our memories are
proof of this intertextuality—both as we note the actual repetition
of events and as we select those which, in turn, we record and
which thus become a part of "history." This statement is true in a
broad sense and specifically for the history or story of the characters in this book. To be alive and conscious, to remember, is to be
part of culture and history. Woolf's language and our own memories are the gage that this is so.

Authorial intentionality, no more than reading, is a function of
the mind that remembers patterns and memorializes them as story.
The many allusions to the words of other authors in *The Waves*
are the most direct and simplest example of pattern-making and
the collective tradition. The instances I cite depend on my own
idiosyncratic insertion into cultural history and may well be different from those of another reader who comes to the text with his
or her own experiences and a different set of expectations.[20] For
example, there is the "metonymic" relationship between the
Houghton Mifflin edition of Wordsworth, with its logo of the boy
riding the dolphin—an iconic reminder of our beginnings—and
Wordsworth's own embroidering of the Greek myth in "Ode: Intimations of Immortality" in which he describes the arrival of souls
into this world as a sea crossing.

> Hence in a season of calm weather
> Though inland far we be,
> Our Souls have sight of that immortal sea
> Which brought us hither,

> Can in a moment travel thither,
> And see the Children sport upon the shore,
> And hear the mighty waters rolling ever more.
>
> (Wordsworth, 190)[21]

There are, I believe, more intertexual connections in *The Waves* to Wordsworth than to any other writer. Two of the allusions are to *The Prelude,* but others, also setting off that "shock of recognition," are from the sonnets. Jinny, for example, describes dancing with a partner:

> "[the figure of the dance] holds us together; and then lengthening out, in smooth, in sinuous folds, rolls us between it, on and on. Suddenly the music breaks. My blood runs on but my body stands still. The room reels past my eyes. It stops." (TW, 246)

Wordsworth, in *The Prelude,* writes of ice skating:

> . . . and oftentimes,
> When we had given our bodies to the wind,
> And all the shadowy banks on either side
> Came sweeping through the darkness, spinning still
> The rapid line of motion, then at once
> Have I, reclining back upon my heels,
> Stopped short; yet still the solitary cliffs
> Wheeled by me—even as if the earth had rolled
> With visible motion her diurnal round!
>
> (Wordsworth, 203, I, ll. 452–60)

The similarity of these impressions of the effect of sudden deceleration might have flagged a memory but done little to promote pattern-making were it not for other instances of intertextuality. Less than one page after, Jinny, whom readers describe as living entirely in the body, says: "'We are together, high up, on some Alpine pass. He stands melancholy on the crest of the road. I stoop. I pick a blue flower and fix it, standing on tiptoe to reach him, in his coat. There! That is my moment of ecstasy. Now it is over'" (TW, 247). Jinny's words, in form, recall Wordsworth's subject and place in *The Prelude:*

> Loth to believe what we so grieved to hear,
> For still we had hopes that pointed to the clouds,
> We questioned him again, and yet again;

> But every word that from the peasant's lips
> Came in reply, translated by our feelings,
> Ended in this,—*that we had crossed the Alps.*
>> (Wordsworth, 268, VI, ll. 586–91)

The full force of Wordsworth's experience, his self-consciousness of imaginative expectation, loss, and recovery, is not present in Jinny's description. Although there are other places in *The Waves* in which Woolf, in her own terms, makes the workings of the Romantic imagination transparent, an allusion to the famous Alps passage serves to remind the reader of the web of connections and dependencies created through memory and thought in this culture.

Another example in Woolf's text, with the fillip of sharp aural recall but also more substantial connection to Wordsworth, is Louis's description of the children's communal awareness of each other and of the beauty of the natural world:

> "Now grass and trees, the travelling air blowing spaces in the blue which they then recover, shaking the leaves which then replace themselves, and our ring here, sitting, with our arms binding our knees, hint at some other order, and better, which makes a reason everlastingly."
> (TW, 201)

Thus Woolf translates "It Is a Beauteous Evening, Calm and Free" into her modern idiom.

> It is a beauteous evening, calm and free,
> The holy time is quiet as a Nun
> Breathless with adoration; the broad sun
> Is sinking down in its tranquility;
> The gentleness of heaven broods o'er the Sea;
> Listen! the mighty Being is awake,
> And doth with his eternal motion make
> A sound like thunder—everlastingly.
>> (Wordsworth, 170)

Bernard thinks: "'How fair, how strange . . . glittering, many pointed and many-domed London lies before me under the mist. Guarded by gasometers, by factory chimneys, she lies sleeping as we approach. She folds the ant-heap to her breast. All cries, all clamour are softly enveloped in silence. Not Rome herself looks more majestic'" (TW, 252). His praise is a self-conscious appreciation of Wordsworth's sonnet and of the beauty of London mixed with the modern, even Eliotesque sense of the unpoetic quality of gasometers in the fallen world of the present.

> Earth has not anything to show more fair:
> Dull would he be of soul who could pass by
> A sight so touching in its majesty:
> This City now doth, like a garment, wear
> The beauty of the morning; silent, bare,
> Ships, towers, domes, theatres, and temples lie
> Open unto the fields, and to the sky;
> All bright and glittering in the smokeless air.
> Never did sun more beautifully steep
> In his first splendour, valley, rock, or hill;
> Ne'er saw I, never felt, a calm so deep!
> The river glideth at his own sweet will:
> Dear God! the very houses seem asleep;
> And all that mighty heart is lying still!
>
> (Wordsworth, 170)

Woolf's allusion to "Composed Upon Westminster Bridge, September 3, 1802" is an instance of the collective consciousness of a particular social class in western culture. Wordsworth has entered our language and our memories so that we can share a moment of recognition of our common experience when we read Woolf's words. This collective experience through art is obliquely compared with Bernard's sense of collective consciousness on the train trip into London.

> "Meanwhile as I stand looking from the train window, I feel strangely, persuasively, that . . . I am become part of this speed, this missile, hurled at the city. . . . Over us all broods a splendid unanimity. We are enlarged and solemnised and brushed into uniformity as with the grey wing of some enormous goose (it is a fine, but colourless morning) because we have only one desire—to arrive at the station. I do not want the train to stop with a thud. I do not want the connection which has bound us together sitting opposite each other all night long to be broken." (TW, 252)

Cultural continuities represent collectivization through time; shared events are collective experience in space, as well. The sonnet and the train trip are concrete examples of each.

Louis's "'I am half in love with the typewriter and telephone'" (TW, 91), recalling Keats's "I have been half in love with easeful Death,"[22] shares, with Bernard's perception of London, a wry ambivalence about the nature, or even possibility, of poetic currency in the wasteland of the industrial present. But this verbal play, which pointedly reduces the poetic and emotional scope, and thus the "truth" of Keats's words, is not merely amusing wordplay. It illustrates Bernard's question of whether it is possible to get to "truth," to the *ding an sich* of experience, or to record it in a "true" story:

> "Let a man get up and say, 'Behold, this is the truth,' and instantly I perceive a sandy cat filching a piece of fish in the background. Look, you have forgotten the cat, I say. So Neville, at school, in the dim chapel, raged at the sight of the doctor's crucifix. I, who am always distracted, whether by a cat or by a bee . . . have made up thousands of stories; I have filled innumerable notebooks with phrases to be used when I have found the true story, the one to which all these phrases refer. But I have never yet found that story. And I begin to ask, Are there stories?" (TW, 305–6)

Thus, we make a pattern of this instance of intertextuality and an abiding question of Bernard's—whether there is an underlying "reality" of existence. So that we are fully convinced that collective consciousness exists, Woolf explores the same idea that "tease(s) out of thought"[23] through Rhoda who says:

> "'Like' and 'like' and 'like'—but what is the thing that
> lies beneath the semblance of the thing?" (TW, 288)

Thus, Woolf remarks on the limits of a language system to describe that which lies beneath the secondary characteristics of an object or experience.

When Rhoda says "'Oh, this is pain, this is anguish! I faint, I fail'" (TW, 213–14), a repetition of her earlier utterance "'Oh, but I sink, I fall!'" (TW, 193), she connects us to her opposite, Jinny, who says "'I tremble, I quiver, like the leaf in the hedge'" (TW, 212), which, in turn, reminds us of when she kissed Louis, crouching behind the hedge, in childhood. She, too, memorializes this event at Percival's dinner: "'The leaf danced in the hedge without anyone to blow it,' said Jinny" (TW, 261). Their words, when linked with the emotion of the kiss, form a web of connection with Shelley's "Epipsychidion":

> The wingèd words on which my soul would pierce
> Into the height of Love's rare Universe,
> Are chains of lead around its flight of fire—
> I pant, I sink, I tremble, I expire![24]

Two instances of intertextual connection are especially indicative of Woolf's method and our ability to see pattern in the novel.[25] The fourth section of *The Waves,* commemorating the reactions of the friends at the "last supper" before Percival's departure, ends with a sense of loss and finality. The last words are Neville's: "'How signal to all time to come that we, who stand in the street, in the lamplight, loved Percival? Now Percival is gone'" (TW, 277). In fact, Percival has been gone or, more accurately, never present for us since the beginning of the narrative because he is the only character of consequence who never speaks. However, in his non-presence he has organized experience; he "'inspires poetry'" (TW, 202).

But now we suspend disbelief and agree that Percival, in India, must be more absent. No longer in England, he is not accessible in the flesh to his friends. Yet, paradoxically, by having accepted the fiction of his leave-taking, we are now more firmly committed to his fictive "reality" than we were before. Thus, with a start, we read the first words of the fifth section.

> "He is dead," said Neville. "He fell. His horse tripped. He was thrown. The sails of the world have swung round and caught me on the head. All is over. The lights of the world have gone out. There stands the tree which I cannot pass." (TW, 280)

As we read these words, we are shocked by this second, even more final, loss. And we experience another jolt if we remember that we have read the words before. Both in meter and in sense, they recall the first line of Shelley's "Adonais": "I weep for Adonais—he is dead!" (Shelley, 291). The three equally stressed syllables, in Shelley's poem commemorating Keats—"He," "is," "dead"—preceded by the caesura, break the predictability and lulling regularity of the iambic meter and suggest the intrusive, undeniable, and irrevocable nature of death. Thus Neville, as in childhood, relying on words of one syllable to articulate the ineluctable, contextualizes the inexplicable fact of death within the pastoral elegiac tradition. The tradition is a cultural strategy for accepting death—the making of a commemorative poem.

Shelley's poem, in turn, refers to the most important example of the pastoral elegy in English, Milton's "Lycidas," which also states baldly the irrefutable "fact": "For Lycidas is dead."[26] In "Lycidas," as in "Adonais," the machinery, made conventional through successive instances of the pastoral elegy,[27] softens the blow of death through the recitation of the participatory grief of nature and the account, in the later Christian examples, of the ultimate redemption of the dead.

Yet in a second way the conventions of pastoral elegy soften the blow because they "regularize" through a cultural continuity, creating a repetitive pattern and, therefore, nullifying the pain of loss. These conventions are present in Woolf as well as in Shelley and Milton. Of the common rural experience of youth, the poet, speaking of himself and Lycidas says:

> For we were nurst upon the self-same hill,
> Fed the same flock, by fountain, shade, and rill.
> Together both, ere the high Lawns appear'd
> Under the opening eye-lids of the morn,
> We drove a field. . . .[28]

Similarly, Neville, after seizing with words what he imagines to have been the horrific death of Percival, looks back to his and Percival's common rustic beginnings:

> "Barns and summer days in the country, rooms where we sat—all now lies in the unreal world which is gone. My past is cut from me. They came running. They carried him to some pavilion, men in riding-boots, men in sun helmets; among unknown men he died." (TW, 280)

Woolf represents the traditional procession of mourners passing the bier of the dead in *The Waves* through the voices of Neville, Bernard, and Rhoda. She psychologically translates the tribute of flowers and the grieving of the natural world through the imagination of a character. Thus, Rhoda, walking through the commercial district of London, the fallen, modern world, robbed, for her, of its beauty and order because of Percival's death, says to herself:

> "Now I will walk down Oxford Street envisaging a world rent by lightning; I will look at oaks cracked asunder and red where the flowering branch has fallen. I will go to Oxford Street and buy stockings for a party. . . . On the bare ground I will pick violets and bind them together and offer them to Percival, something given him by me. Look now at what Percival has given me. Look at the street now that Percival is dead. . . . I like factory chimneys and cranes and lorries. . . . I am sick of prettiness; I am sick of privacy. I ride rough waters and shall sink with no one to save me." (TW, 286)

The rents in sympathetic nature and the floral tribute are figments of Rhoda's imagination. Rhoda's sense of the ugliness of London is the chaos in nature after the death of its favorite. For the final fillip, Rhoda, and not Percival, proleptically suffers the fate of Edward King, the subject of Milton's elegy, riding rough waters and sinking with no one to save her.

But none of these mourners, Neville, Bernard, nor Rhoda, is

the last to remind us of the inscription of Percival's death, or, by extension, of Woolf's inscription and our own, into the cultural context of the pastoral elegiac tradition. Bernard thinks, years later, of his visit to Jinny after Percival's death:

> "And then sitting side by side on the sofa we remembered inevitably what had been said by others; 'the lily of the day is fairer far in May'; we compared Percival to a lily. . . . So the sincerity of the moment passed; so it became symbolical; and that I could not stand. Let us commit any blasphemy of laughter and criticism rather than exude this lily-sweet glue; and cover him with phrases, I cried. Therefore I broke off, and Jinny, who . . . respected the moment with complete integrity, gave her body a flick with the whip, powdered her face (for which I loved her), and waved to me as she stood on the doorstep, pressing her hand to her hair so that the wind might not disorder it, a gesture for which I honoured her, as if it confirmed our determination—not to let lilies grow." (TW, 360–61)

The lily is the festering cliché that robs the moment of its fresh and natural grief. Jinny paradoxically saves freshness of feeling by memorializing Percival through her banal yet time-defying gestures.

Jinny, through her poetic language, most reminds us of Milton's "Lycidas." She says: "'My imagination is the body's . . . I do not like your lean cats and your blistered chimney-pots. The scrannel beauties of your roof-tops repel me'" (TW, 329). The first recorded use of the word "scrannel," according to the *OED*, is in "Lycidas":

> Blind mouthes! that scarce themselves know how to hold
> A Sheep-hook, or have learn'd ought els the least
> That to the faithfull Herdmans art belongs!
> What recks it them? What need they? They are sped;
> And when they list, their lean and flashy songs
> Grate on their scrannel Pipes of wretched straw.[29]

The *OED* defines scrannel as "Thin, meagre" and adds "Now chiefly as a reminiscence of Milton's use, usually with the sense: Harsh, unmelodious."[30] Woolf's use of the word, together with the adjective "lean," unmistakably recalls Milton and his poem. Our recognition of its origin reminds us of our collective intellectual experience and the continuity of our culture.

The death of Percival, which leads the friends to consider the history of their friendship, thus becomes a point of intersection for the characters as well as for Milton, Shelley, Woolf, and the reader.

It also excites memory traces apart from those connected to the pastoral elegiac tradition. Like the stone dropped into the pool around which minnows congregate, Percival is a locus of intertextuality, organizing and patterning the narrative. Summing up his relationship with Percival and the latter's beauty and importance, Neville translates his feelings into language that mirrors the wonder and admiration Percival inspires. "'Loneliness and silence often surrounded him. He often left me. And then, returning, "See where he comes!" I said'" (TW, 280). The strength of Neville's feeling, created by the return of Percival, is re-created in us as "'with a certainty of recognition and a shock of knowledge'" (TW, 366), we hear the echo of the words of Philo in the first scene of Shakespeare's *Antony and Cleopatra*.[31]

> *Philo.* . . .
> [*Flourish. Enter Antony, Cleopatra, her Ladies, the*
> *Train, with Eunuchs fanning her.*]
> Look where they come.[32]

While Philo demeans Antony, angry that he has become "The triple pillar of the world transformed / Into a strumpet's fool,"[33] his grudging admiration for the regal bearing and beauty of this extraordinary pair of lovers is conveyed by the utter simplicity of the announcement. It prepares us for Antony's own regal praise of love:

> *Antony.* Let Rome in Tiber melt, and the wide arch
> Of the ranged empire fall! Here is my space,
> Kingdoms are clay: our dungy earth alike
> Feeds beast as man. The nobleness of life
> Is to do thus; when such a mutual pair [*Embracing.*]
> And such a twain can do't, in which I bind,
> On pain of punishment, the world to weet
> We stand up peerless.[34]

We read of Neville's love for Percival as if it were the topmost layer of a cultural palimpsest made complex and rich through the story of Antony and Cleopatra, told by Plutarch, translated by Shakespeare, and borrowed by Woolf.

However, this example of intertextuality is important not only for its revelation of our insertion into western culture but for the way it reveals Woolf's method of plaiting together various strands of narrative as she follows the "wandering thread" to its end. For although there is no direct communication between the characters,

Bernard, as well as Neville, alludes to the Shakespearean text in thinking about his reaction to Percival's death.

> "Here are pictures. Here are cold madonnas among their pillars. Let them lay to rest the incessant activity of the mind's eye, the bandaged head, the men with ropes, so that I may find something unvisual beneath. . . . Mercifully these pictures make no reference . . . they do not point. Thus they expand my consciousness of him and bring him back to me differently. I remember his beauty. 'Look, where he comes,' I said." (TW, 283)

Bernard's expression of his appreciation of Percival's beauty is deepened and generalized when later he describes a moment of being during his Roman sojourn.

> "Leaning over this parapet I see far out a waste of water. A fin turns. This bare visual impression is unattached to any line of reason, it springs up as one might see the fin of a porpoise on the horizon. Visual impressions often communicate thus briefly statements that we shall in time to come uncover and coax into words. I note under F., therefore, 'Fin in a waste of waters.' I, who am perpetually making notes in the margin of my mind for some final statement, make this mark, waiting for some winter's evening.
>
> "Now I shall go and lunch somewhere . . . I shall observe with more than my usual detachment, and when a pretty woman enters the restaurant and comes down the room between the tables I shall say to myself, Look where she comes against a waste of waters. A meaningless observation, but to me, solemn, slate-coloured, with a fatal sound of ruining worlds and waters falling to destruction." (TW, 307)

First, we may note that Bernard's filing system is like his creator's. Of her moment of being in childhood, during which she stood before the flower bed at St. Ives, she wrote: "It was a thought I put away as being likely to be very useful to me later" (MoB, 71). We are, therefore, reminded through Bernard, of Woolf's still unwritten memoir as we are, too, of her diary in which she recorded, after finishing *To the Lighthouse:*

Thursday 30 September [1926]
    I wished to add some remarks to this, on the mystical side of this solitude; how it is not oneself but something in the universe that one's left with. It is this that is frightening & exciting in the midst of my profound gloom, depression, boredom, whatever it is: One sees a fin passing far out. What image can I reach to convey what I mean? Really there is none I think. . . . Life is, soberly & accurately, the oddest

affair . . . I used to feel this as a child—couldn't step across a puddle once I remember, for thinking, how strange—what am I? &c. By writing I dont reach anything. All I mean to make is a note of a curious state of mind. I hazard the guess that it may be the impulse behind another book. (Diary III, 113)

The fin far out is the spark of interest cutting into the boredom and gloom and connecting her to the universe. It ends the solipsistic depression Woolf had been suffering.[35] For Bernard, who repeats the image of the prologue to this chapter—"the same wave of light passed in a sudden flaunt and flash as if a fin cut the green glass of a lake" (TW, 302)—the fin is transformed into a beautiful woman who captures his interest in the midst of his solipsistic skin-shedding experience in Rome. The wonder of her beauty is realized through the Shakespearean cadence, "Look where she comes," which links this experience of Bernard's to his feelings about Percival's beauty and, in turn, to Neville's admiration for their friend.

However, Bernard's "naming" of the wonder of his experience is not the end of this particular concatenation of inter- and intratextual references. Just five pages later, Neville more explicitly reveals the source of Woolf's allusions.

"After all, we are not responsible. We are not judges. We are not called upon to torture our fellows with thumbscrews and irons. . . . It is better to look at a rose,[36] or to read Shakespeare as I read him here in Shaftesbury Avenue. Here's the fool, here's the villain, here in a car comes Cleopatra, burning on her barge. . . . This is poetry if we do not write it. They act their parts infallibly. . . ." (TW, 312)

"'Here in a car comes Cleopatra,'" Neville's translation of present reality, brings us back to Philo's words and to Woolf's own interest in Shakespeare.

We know from Woolf's diary that she had, in fact, been reading Shakespeare while writing *The Waves*. On Sunday, 13 April 1930, she wrote: "I read Shakespeare *directly* I have finished writing, when my mind is agape & red & hot. I never yet knew how amazing his stretch & speed & word coining power is, until I felt it utterly outpace & outrace my own, seeming to start equal & then I see him draw ahead & do things I could not in my wildest tumult & utmost press of mind imagine" (Diary III, 300–301). Her reading of Shakespeare was, in fact, part of her plan for writing this novel, even in its earliest days. She wrote in her diary: "The poets succeed by simplifying: practically everything is left out. I want to put practically everything in; yet to saturate. That is what I want to do in The Moths. It must include nonsense, fact, sordidity: but made transparent. I think I must read Ibsen & Shakespeare & Racine" (Diary III, 210). And there is more evidence of Woolf's special fascination with *Antony and Cleopatra* during her writing of *The Waves*. In "On Being Ill," speaking of the actual physical, rather than intellectual, grasp of meaning during an illness, she writes that "meaning . . . is all the richer for having come to us sensually first, by way of the palate and the nostrils, like some queer odour. Foreigners, to whom the tongue is strange, have us at a disadvantage. The Chinese must know the sound of *Antony and Cleopatra* better than we do" (CE 4, 200).

Brenda Silver's transcription of Woolf's reading notebooks also makes clear Woolf's interest in the figure of Cleopatra, as far back as 1923 or 1924. In volume XLVII of the notes in which, interestingly, Woolf had also copied lines 458–65 of Book VII of *The Prelude*—the section on the world of memory and thought—with the comment "Good quotation for one of my books,"[37] Woolf had written two notes on Cleopatra: "There are obviously people like Cleopatra who/stand for something in human nature, & so/get built up by general consent" and "Of course, the first thing is the immensely greater richness & subtlety of Cleo. in particular."[38] We know that her interest in the figure of Cleopatra lasted until the end of her life. In *Between the Acts,* Lucy Swithin presents Miss La Trobe with a heartfelt tribute: "She gazed at Miss La Trobe with a cloudless old-aged stare. . . . 'What a small part I've had to play! But you've made me feel I could have played . . . Cleopatra!' . . . 'I might have been—Cleopatra,' Miss La Trobe repeated. 'You've stirred in me my unacted part' she meant" (BtA, 152–53).

To look for confirmation of the importance in *The Waves* of Shakespeare, in general, or of *Antony and Cleopatra,* in particular, represents a very specialized sort of reading, not engaged in, certainly, by "common readers" who are more likely to be satisfied with a small reverberation of words dimly remembered, if they hear anything at all. Yet all these extratextual connections are present to the extent that one has prior knowledge and the desire to exercise one's memory and thought. However, intratextual connections are more accessible for most readers who, if they read carefully, will remember that neither Bernard nor Neville begins this complicated association of Percival, the beautiful woman, Cleopatra, and the fin, but Louis who, much earlier in the book, says: "'I, who would wish to feel close over me the protective waves of the ordinary, catch with the tail of my eye some far horizon" (TW, 240). Furthermore, these associations do not end with Neville's translation of a contemporary woman in a car on Shaftesbury Avenue into Cleopatra burning on her barge.

Bernard repeats the cadence in his final monologue when he describes the intensity of an early love: "'Look at a room before she comes and after'" (TW, 350) and, in recalling his friendship with Neville, makes a connection between the fin and Shakespeare.

> "Now and then I break off a lump, Shakespeare it may be, it may be some old woman called Peck; and say to myself . . . 'That's Shakespeare. That's Peck'—with a certainty of recognition and a shock of knowledge which is endlessly delightful, though not to be imparted. So we shared our Pecks, our Shakespeare's; compared each other's versions; allowed each other's insight to set our own Peck or Shakespeare in a better light; and then sank into one of those silences which are now and again broken by a few words, as if a fin rose in the wastes of silence; and then the fin, the thought, sinks back into the depths spreading round it a little ripple of satisfaction, content." (TW, 366)[39]

The sharing of their Pecks and Shakespeares—something that old schoolmates well might do and one of the very few allusions to this sort of communication in the novel—may explain Neville and Bernard's turning to similar account Philo's imperative announcing the entrance of Antony and Cleopatra. When Bernard, in old age, describes the horror of depression, he records the feeling that his self has deserted him: "'Nothing came, nothing. I cried then with a sudden conviction of complete desertion. . . . No fin breaks the waste of this immeasurable sea. Life has destroyed me. No echo comes when I speak, no varied words'" (TW, 374).

Precisely the echo of varied words, our memory of the many themes and variations in this novel, constitutes Woolf's method of patterning and our rich experience as we read. Three separate groups of words and images, which are themselves interwoven and contextualized, demonstrate Woolf's self-conscious reliance on the world of memory and thought in creating the structure of *The Waves*. These plaited strands center on history as consciousness, the imagination, and the transparency of the mind.

Of all the friends, Louis, as a child and an adult, has the keenest sense of the relationship of consciousness or, in particular, of memory and history, both in the sense of the actual events and of our collective remembrance of them. In a passage from the very beginning of the novel that might well have originated in Woolf's memory of her own moment of being in front of the flower bed at St. Ives (MoB, 71), Louis describes his state of mind:

"The flowers swim like fish made of light upon the dark, green waters. I hold a stalk in my hand. I am the stalk. My roots go down to the depths of the world, through earth dry with brick, and damp earth, through veins of lead and silver. I am all fibre. . . . Up here my eyes are green leaves, unseeing. I am a boy in grey flannels with a belt fastened by a brass snake up here. Down there my eyes are the lidless eyes of a stone figure in a desert by the Nile. I see women passing with red pitchers to the river. . . ." (TW, 182)

Through consciousness and the exercise of his imagination, Louis feels connected to the world, his imagination coextensive with that which it apprehends, not merely spatially, but through time as well. Aware of himself, of the small boy in grey flannels with a belt fastened by a brass snake, he is yet aware, in a primitive way, of the progression of civilization, of history, from the women with their red pitchers in ancient Egypt, to himself, standing among the flowers at his first school.

The importance of consciousness, of the exercise of memory and thought, and of the movement of civilization of which we are a part, is made a structural feature of the book through repetition of the image of women carrying pitchers to the Nile. Louis comes back to this figure repeatedly.

"I force myself to state, if only in one line of unwritten poetry, this moment; to mark this inch in the long, long history that began in Egypt, in the time of the Pharaohs, when women carried red pitchers to the Nile. . . . But if I now shut my eyes, if I fail to realise the meeting-place of past and present, that I sit in a third-class railway carriage full of boys going home for the holidays, human history is defrauded of a moment's vision. Its eye, that would see through me, shuts—if I sleep now. . . ." (TW, 220)

As we read, with our own eyes open and full attention paid to the text, we are aware, through memory, that we have already encountered these phrases, these "structuring" repetitions, or "ties / That bind the perishable hours of life / Each to the other," just as Louis, repeating them, is remembering his own past and his insertion into western civilization, making through them sense of himself and of the present moment that is defined by the "Louisness" of his particular perceptions.

"My roots go down through veins of lead and silver, through damp, marshy places. . . . I have yet heard rumors of wars; and the nightin-gale; have felt the hurrying of many troops of men . . . in quest of civilisation like flocks of birds migrating seeking the summer; I have seen women carrying red pitchers to the banks of the Nile. I woke in a garden, with a blow on the nape of my neck, a hot kiss, Jinny's. . . ." (TW, 241)

"Every day I unbury—I dig up. I find relics of myself in the sand that women made thousands of years ago, when I heard songs by the Nile. . . ." (TW, 263)

" . . . the eternal procession, women going with attaché cases down the Strand as they went once with pitchers to the Nile. . . ." (TW, 291)

"As a boy I dreamt of the Nile." (TW, 315)

"What has my destiny been. . . . That I remember the Nile and the women carrying pitchers on their heads; . . . I am not a single and passing being. My life is not a moment's bright spark like that on the surface of a diamond. . . . My destiny has been that I remember and must weave together, must plait into one cable the many threads, the thin, the thick, the broken, the enduring of our long history, of our tumultuous and varied day. There is always more to be understood. . . ." (TW, 316)

"But listen," said Louis, "to the world moving through abysses of infinite space. It roars; the lighted strip of history is past . . . we are gone; our civilisation; the Nile; and all life." (TW, 332)

The difference between the first five instances and the last is a matter of the relation of consciousness to the world. Individual consciousness—memory and thought, and imagination—accounts for Louis's ability to recall, to understand, his own past and that of civilization and to explain them to another. However, a species of nihilism predominates in the last example as Louis imagines a world no longer populated by sentient beings responsible both for creating and interpreting history—a world, in Bernard's words, "seen without a self" (TW, 376). Finally, Bernard reiterates Louis's sense of nihilism when he borrows Louis's images to suggest the difficulty of remaining highly conscious through the hard business of living:

"I said life had been imperfect, an unfinished phrase. It had been impossible for me . . . to keep coherency—that sense of the generations, of women carrying red pitchers to the Nile, of the nightingale who sings among conquests and migrations.[40] . . . and how can I go on lifting my foot perpetually to climb the stair?"[41] (TW, 373)

Woolf examines shaping consciousness, the equivalent of experience, through the "shaping" patterns of images conveying the transparency or coextension of the mind. Bernard explains the nature of the mind-world connection, borrowing, in advance of its composition, what would be Woolf's description from "A Sketch of the Past." She wrote there: "The quality of the air above Talland House seemed to suspend sound, to let it sink down slowly, as if it were caught in a blue gummy veil" (MoB, 66). Bernard says: "'Moving oneself in this radiant yet gummy atmosphere, how conscious one is of every movement—something adheres, something sticks to one's hands, taking up a newspaper even'" (TW, 350). Through our perception we are enlarged by the things of the world that are absorbed by, or become one with, our imaginations. This gummy substance, causing the things of the world to adhere to our consciousnesses, also binds moment to moment and, thus, is the basis of narrative. Bernard's explanation of our connection to life, amplified by the many instances of images suggesting transparency and globes, is illuminated by another description from "A Sketch . . . ," also from the same paragraph describing the gummy atmosphere above Talland House. The similarities with the descriptions of the prologues should also be noted. Woolf begins: "If I were a painter I should paint these first impressions. . . . There was the pale yellow blind; the green sea; and the silver of the passion flowers. I should make a picture that was globular; semi-transparent" (MoB, 66).

There are many instances in *The Waves* in which globular images serve as representations of the imagination's apprehension of the wholeness of reality. They remind us of their appearance, to the same purpose, in "The Journal of Mistress Joan Martyn" and their source in Wordsworth's *Guide to the Lakes*. The imagination projects itself into the world through these images, suggesting its substantiality, its solidity, the sense that it has "made" something for us and for others to share. Woolf repeats here the notion that the dinner party in *To the Lighthouse* is, for a moment, a solid creation of Mrs. Ramsay's, before it dissolves as the family and guests go their separate ways. At the dinner before Percival's departure for India, Louis begins, and Jinny contributes, to the same theme:

"Now once more," said Louis, "as we are about to part. . . . Something is made. Yes, as we rise and fidget, a little nervously, we pray, holding in our hands this common feeling, 'Do not move, do not let the swing-door cut to pieces the thing that we have made, that globes itself here, among these lights, these peelings, this litter of bread crumbs, and people passing. . . . '"

"Let us hold it for one moment," said Jinny; "love, hatred . . . this globe whose walls are made of Percival, of youth and beauty, and something so deep sunk within us that we shall perhaps never make this moment out of one man again." (TW, 275–76)

Percival, unlike his namesake in Arthurian legend, does not quest in search of the holy grail—metaphorically the meaning of life in Christian myth. He is himself the grail or platter from the Last Supper, later used to catch the blood of the crucified Christ. For he is the locus of "meaning" for the other characters: "'like a stone fallen into a pond round which minnows swarm'" (TW, 269–70). But we are also aware of a second level of significance suggested by this dinner scene. It is about the "fact," the apparently universal need, to create myth and to reuse it, comparable to a child's need to hear the same story over and over again. In this case, the "retold" myth is the story of the last Passover dinner as celebrated by Christ and the Apostles. Perhaps this particular story reveals another instance of genetically encoded behavior: the universal desire to share our most important moments, our triumphs and defeats, while satisfying the primary drive to nourish ourselves. Through the adaptation of such myths, we contextualize our experience and convey its shared meaning to others. Percival's strong impact on the friends' imaginations derives from memory of their common experience "so deep sunk within" them; childhood memories are peculiar to their shared experience. However, communal eating, embedded in the history of civilization, is part of our common cultural history.[42] A succession of these globe images suggests the ordering of chaos through the offices of the imagination. There is Bernard's

"Something lies deeply buried. For one moment I thought to grasp it. . . . After a long lifetime, loosely, in a moment of revelation, I may lay hands on it, but now the idea breaks in my hand. Ideas break a thousand times for once that they globe themselves entire." (TW, 284–85)

He repeats this image as he makes his final summation:

"Now to sum up. . . . The illusion is upon me that something adheres for a moment, has roundness, weight, depth, is completed. This, for the moment, seems to be my life. If it were possible, I would hand it to you entire. . . .

"But unfortunately, what I see (this globe, full of figures) you do not see." (TW, 341)

"But to return. Let us pretend again that life is a solid substance, shaped like a globe, which we turn about in our fingers." (TW, 350)

"The crystal, the globe of life . . . has walls of thinnest air. If I press them all will be burst. Whatever sentence I extract whole and entire from this cauldron is only a string of six little fish that let themselves be caught while a million others leap and sizzle, making the cauldron bubble like boiling silver, and slip through my fingers. Faces recur, faces and faces—they press their beauty to the walls of my bubble—Neville, Susan, Louis, Jinny, Rhoda and a thousand others. How impossible to order them rightly; to detach one separately, or to give the effect of the whole—again like music." (TW, 354)

In this last citation, the figure of the crystal globe becomes a cauldron, becomes a bubble rising from the cauldron, proving Bernard's point that it is impossible to order or detach these images. Indeed, the structural meaning of *The Waves* is that such ordering and detaching are impossible. The metaphorical slides create the complex and rich net of intratextual connections that bind character to character and make narrative sequence: "'the string of six little fish that let themselves be caught.'"

Thus, crystal globes and bubbles connect with images of the transparency of the walls of the mind. Jinny, as a child, first remarks the bubbles rising in a saucepan, her contribution to the litany of the children as they describe the activities of the school servants. "'Bubbles form on the floor of the saucepan,' said Jinny. 'Then they rise, quicker and quicker in a silver chain to the top'" (TW, 181). Neville transforms her image into a trope for narrative connection. He says of Bernard:

"But Bernard goes on talking. Up they bubble—images. 'Like a camel,' . . . 'a vulture.' The camel is a vulture; the vulture a camel; for Bernard is a dangling wire, loose, but seductive. Yes, for when he talks . . . a lightness comes over one. One floats, too, as if one were that bubble; one is freed; I have escaped, one feels." (TW, 200)

Bernard continues Neville's association:

"The bubbles are rising like the silver bubbles from the floor of a saucepan; image on top of image. . . . I must open the little trap-door and let out these linked phrases in which I run together whatever happens so that instead of incoherence there is perceived a wandering thread, lightly joining one thing to another." (TW, 208)

Just as we perceive connection in Woolf's narrative through such repetitions, Bernard understands that images and their repetition create narrative connection or sequence—because of common personal and cultural experience—for his friends. Bernard resorts to the equation between bubbles and narrative sequence two other times as well (TW, 233, 255).

Rhoda extends the metaphor of the bubbles to encompass the imagination, the organ responsible for producing narrative sequence. Through the trope she reveals her appreciation for the complex process by which mind is "fitted" or linked to the world it perceives—her version of Romantic coextension.

"Yet there are moments when the walls of the mind grow thin; when nothing is unabsorbed, and I could fancy that we might blow so vast a bubble that the sun might set and rise in it. . . ." (TW, 331)

Neville, too, repeats this image of coextension.

"But to myself I am immeasurable; a net whose fibres pass imperceptibly beneath the world. My net is almost indistinguishable from that which it surrounds. It lifts whales—huge leviathans and white jellies . . . I detect, I perceive." (TW, 324)

Almost reiterating Wordsworth's "of all the mighty world / Of eye and ear,—both what they half create, / And what perceive," Neville is saying only more self-consciously what Susan has already said:

"At . . . this still early hour, I think I am the field, I am the barn, I am the trees; . . . Mine is the heron that stretches its vast wings lazily. . . ." (TW, 242)

"I think sometimes . . . I am not a woman, but the light that falls on this gate, on this ground." (TW, 242–43)

Bernard, the storyteller, the artist, relies on the image of the transparent mind to suggest the heightened awareness produced by the extraordinary emotions of death and love. In old age, remembering his response to Percival's death, he recalls:

"To see things without attachment, from the outside, and to realise their beauty in itself—how strange! . . . and lightness has come with a

kind of transparency, making oneself invisible and things seen through
as one walks—how strange." (TW, 359)

And of his still earlier memory of that day in childhood when he
brought the weeping Susan to Elvedon, he says:

> "Then a wood-pigeon flew out of the trees. And being in love for the
> first time, I made a phrase—a poem about a wood-pigeon . . . for a
> hole had been knocked in my mind, one of those sudden transparences
> through which one sees everything." (TW, 343)

His impulse to make a poem about the wood-pigeon is an iteration
of G. M. Trevelyan's explanation in *History of England* of the etiology of the aesthetic impulse. The hunters of the primeval English
forest, hearing the birds singing in the canopy of the trees, were
moved to imitate them and make their own song. His description,
we remember, provided Woolf with a beginning for "Anon" in
which she, too, would explore the "expressive" theory of art. But
Woolf had read Trevelyan's book, published in 1926, which she
and Leonard owned, at least by 1928, because she quotes it in *A
Room of One's Own* for quite another reason.[43] She might well
have had it in mind as she wrote about Bernard's poem and his
many invitations, or memories of those invitations, to his friends:
"'Let us now crawl,' said Bernard, 'under the canopy of the currant
leaves, and tell stories'" (TW, 189).

Our consciousness of Woolf's dependence on expressive or Romantic aesthetic theory, seen here as the need to tell stories, to
make art, especially when, as Rhoda says, "'the walls of the mind
become transparent'" (TW, 335), brings us back to Wordsworth
and the subtext of *The Waves*. Bernard, in the same passage in
which he recalls his adventure to Elvedon, is keenly aware that he
cannot change the memory.

> "Down below, through the depths of the leaves, the gardeners swept
> the lawns with great brooms. The lady sat writing. Transfixed, stopped
> dead, I thought, 'I cannot interfere with a single stroke of those
> brooms. . . . Nor with the fixity of that woman writing.' . . . There
> they have remained all my life." (TW, 343)

But such unmodified memories serve an important function in all
human beings. As for Wordsworth and us, memory enables Bernard to experience the growth or continuity of his own personality
through time and to create, as well, his story based on it.

We might trace many more patterns or memory trails through

their windings.[44] Among the important ones are Louis's chained beast stamping on the shore and the metaphorical horse Bernard rides against Death. Both suggest that the creative impulse is an affirmation of life and resistance to death. Neither is an idealist's evasion. However, the metarepresentation of the aesthetic project in the text of the novel, the narrative voice, has the last words. In defiance of Bernard's heroic "'Against you I will fling myself, unvanquished and unyielding, O Death'" (383), the italicized "voice" flatly asserts the simple truth of the world—that nature endures while individuals perish: "The waves broke on the shore" (383).

Our conscious recognition of these rich braids of images is merely further proof of the action of "the world of memory and thought," both the subject of *The Prelude* and, as well, Wordsworth's explanation in this poem and in the Preface to *Lyrical Ballads* of the basis of creation: the spontaneous overflow of emotion recollected in tranquility which issues in art. The relationship that Wordsworth proposes, also in the Preface, between the poet and all other human beings—that the poet is endowed with a heightened version of the consciousness and imagination that mark us as human—is revived by Woolf in *The Waves* through the word-patterns of Bernard and his remarkable friends. It is made even more palpable to us through our own collaborative efforts at pattern-making, the result of our memory and thought. The very success of Woolf's pattern-making, not only in *The Waves* but in all her novels and in her last historical criticism, necessarily put her in touch with the flow of time. With increasing pressures on the empirical self—the fear of war and then of invasion, and the sense that art in such times does not have the attention of the public—Woolf seems to have suffered a loss, an end to that willing suspension of disbelief that marks the poetic self that feels rapture in creation, in discovering what belongs to what. Such a loss could explain Virginia Woolf's attitudes and actions in her last years. As if in repetition of the final "dialogue" between Bernard and the italicized voice in *The Waves,* she looked more and more to the Romantic poets who saw the truth that art may give us room for reflection, which leads us inescapably to face, but not to efface, our temporal condition.

7

Life as Text: Woolf and the Poetry of the "Unconscious"

It was a miserable machine, an inefficient machine, she thought, the human apparatus for painting or for feeling; it always broke down at the critical moment; heroically, one must force it on. She stared, frowning. There was the hedge, sure enough. But one got nothing by soliciting urgently. One got only a glare in the eye from looking at the line of the wall, or from thinking— she wore a grey hat. She was astonishingly beautiful. Let it come, she thought, if it will come. For there are moments when one can neither think nor feel. And if one can neither think nor feel, she thought, where is one?

—*To the Lighthouse*

Consciousness, Wordsworth's world of memory and thought, is central to our understanding of *The Waves* as we "prove" or experience the Wordsworthian hypothesis through our own memory and thought, exercised in our collusive reading of Woolf's text. Discovery of important patterns in our reading doubles the creativity of writing. Of the dynamics of reading in "Craftsmanship" (1937), Woolf asserted: "Thus one sentence of the simplest kind rouses the imagination, the memory, the eye and the ear—all combine in reading it" (CE 2, 247). She continues:

But they combine—they combine unconsciously together. The moment we single out and emphasize the suggestions as we have done here they become unreal; and we, too, become unreal—specialists, word mongers, phrase finders, not readers. In reading we have to allow the sunken meanings to remain sunken, suggested, not stated; lapsing and flowing into each other like reeds on the bed of a river. (CE 2, 248)

Thus, Woolf describes the other, less sung (until recently) term of the collaboration between the writer and the reader of novels. The "suggestions" of the writer are joined, through the reading process, with the unconscious mind of the reader who apprehends the "sunken, suggested, not stated" meanings through some other than the rational faculty. The operative word in this description of reading is "unconsciously"—a word and its synonyms that Woolf equally applies, over and over again, to the creative act. Although as professional readers we may then set our rational faculties working to prove, in the more common meaning of the word, what we have felt to be true (an activity that Woolf devalues in this particular statement), this subsequent conscious "discovery" of pattern is not to be confused with those first unconscious operations of mind on which it depends. We find, as does Lily Briscoe facing her blank canvas, that pattern emerges only if we "let it come."

As with *The Waves,* a rereading of Woolf's lectures, essays, and diaries, written during the last decade of her life, yields awareness of another important pattern of consanguinity, emotional and political, with the Romantic poets. This period of Virginia Woolf's teemingly creative life was marked both by new experiments and returns. Everything Woolf ever wrote reveals her appreciation for the paradoxical, the complex, the multifarious nature of existence. These words apply equally to the variety and interrelation of her work in her last ten years, particularly to the political and polemical essays of the close of her life, which were intimately connected to her father and to the poets whom he had introduced to her.

In January 1929, writing to Vita Sackville-West, Woolf said of a conversation between a Labour Party M.P. and Leonard: "[the Labour M.P.] abused the Duchess of Atholl: theres the dear old Labour party atmosphere all over again I thought; and rejoiced that I was not labour and not anything: this is what makes one serene—these secret thoughts" (Letters IV, 11). World events, the rise of fascism in Germany and Italy, the Spanish Civil War—the testing ground for the new rightist governments—and the response of the British left, which, among other outcomes, claimed the life of Woolf's own nephew, Julian Bell, compelled her to enter the political arena in ways she never had before. Nevertheless, she continued to distrust partisan politics (politics meaning to produce a definite effect in the world) in relation to the artist in the act of creation.

Woolf would never have quarreled with the premise that all literature is political, as we have come to define the word in its broadest sense. Insofar as literature expresses the attitudes of a writer to the world about her, no writing can escape the definition. However, this is to say nothing at the same time that it is to say everything, for, surely, it is so true as to be discounted in any argument one may advance about the nature of art. The sticking point for Woolf is whether great art can proceed from a teleologically "inspired" artist.

The inverted commas draw attention to the constitutional impossibility, from Woolf's point of view, of such an individual. The oxymoronic "teleologically inspired" defies her most firmly held ideas about the nature of art and the impulse that produces it. Her profoundest reflections on the aesthetic project, based on her wide reading and on her own experience, convinced her that all great art is unconsciously produced whereas, by contrast, art serving the ends of partisan politics is vitiated because it is consciously made. Her most important proof of this idea was the poetry of the Romantics, which her diary and letters show she was rereading with enthusiasm in her last years.

Woolf agreed that the artist was stirred by the political events of the day. In "The Artist and Politics," she says: "still it is a fact that the practice of art, far from making the artist out of touch with his kind, rather increases his sensibility. It breeds in him a feeling for the passions and needs of mankind in the mass" so that although he may "be ineffective, he is by no means apathetic" (CE 2, 231–32). However, sensitivity to the needs of mankind that might, in fact, cause the artist to leave his studio and "take part in politics" (CE 2, 232) is not equivalent to art that is politically inspired.

> Thus, it would be impossible, when we read Keats, or look at the pictures of Titian and Velasquez, or listen to the music of Mozart or Bach, to say what was the political condition of the age or the country in which these works were created. And if it were otherwise—if the *Ode to a Nightingale* were inspired by hatred of Germany; if *Bacchus and Ariadne* symbolized the conquest of Abyssinia; if *Figaro* expounded the doctrines of Hitler, we should feel cheated and imposed upon, as if, instead of bread made with flour, we were given bread made with plaster. (CE 2, 231)

Undeniably, then, and in spite of Woolf's political espousal of pacifism in the polemical *Three Guineas,* her position with regard to the production of art remained that the imagination of the artist was actively hurt by being forced to take up cudgels in the very space occupied by the art. She adopted, that is, a "politics of the unconscious" in relation to the artist while engaged in his craft.

To understand Woolf's position, we must return to *The Common Reader* and the first essays on Chaucer and the Greeks. In "The Pastons and Chaucer," Woolf uses the term "self-conscious" and, in this context, its opposite, "conviction." She contrasts "natural story-tellers like Mr Garnett" with "self-conscious story-tellers like Mr Masefield" (CR, 12). Woolf extends the contrast between natural or unconscious poetry—a poetry of conviction—and self-conscious poetry as written by the Romantics.

> For among writers there are two kinds: there are the priests who take you by the hand and lead you straight up to the mystery; there are the laymen who imbed their doctrines in flesh and blood and make a complete model of the world. . . . Wordsworth, Coleridge and Shelley are among the priests; they give us text after text to be hung upon the wall, saying after saying to be laid upon the heart like an amulet against disaster —
>
> Farewell, farewell, the heart that lives alone . . .
>
> — such lines of exhortation and command spring to memory instantly. But Chaucer lets us go our ways doing the ordinary things with the ordinary people. (CR, 17–18)

We can say, then, with corroborative evidence from other essays, that Woolf believed Chaucer's poetry to have been written by a poet who was in such complete accord, politically and socially, with the world he inhabited that he was utterly unconscious of the defining qualities of that society. Also and perhaps more important, Woolf used the term "unconscious," as it is meant in the market-place and not in the psychoanalytic sense, to apply to the conditions of production as well as to the values expressed in the product, as this citation from her lecture "The Leaning Tower" suggests.

> By analysing themselves honestly, with help from Dr. Freud, these writers have done a great deal to free us from nineteenth-century suppressions. The writers of the next generation may inherit from them . . . a mind no longer crippled, evasive, divided. They may inherit that unconsciousness which, as we guessed . . . is necessary if writers are to get beneath the surface, and to write something that people remember when they are alone. For that great gift of unconsciousness the next generation will have to thank the creative and honest egotism of the leaning-tower group. (CE 2, 178)

The term unconsciousness glares, used in this sense by Woolf, in opposition to the meaning we would expect in connection with Freud's name and the psychoanalytic project she describes. Once writers have undergone analysis and have been "cured," Woolf argues, they are able to write without the impediments created by awareness of self. Unconsciousness, thus, simply implies a negative that for Woolf is a positive: freedom from consciousness and, particularly, self-consciousness, both of which are lets to the automatic, semicomatose state described by Woolf elsewhere as necessary for successful creation. Her use of the term at the beginning of "The Leaning Tower" is an indication of how strongly Woolf associated this sort of unconsciousness with the Romantic poets. For in the opening of her talk to the Workers' Education Association, the basis for her essay, she read Wordsworth, not only as an example of a writer operating out of this valuable and necessary state but also as a theorist who, like her, grounded the possibility for real creativity in it. Defining unconsciousness from the point of view of the artist engaged in creation, Woolf says:

> Unconsciousness, which means presumably that the under-mind works at top speed while the upper-mind drowses, is a state we all know. . . . So it is with the writer. After a hard day's work, trudging round, seeing all he can, feeling all he can, taking in the book of his mind innumerable notes, the writer becomes—if he can—unconscious. . . . Then, after a pause the veil lifts; and there is the thing— the thing he wants to write about—simplified, composed. Do we strain Wordsworth's famous saying about emotion recollected in tranquility when we infer that by tranquility he meant that the writer needs to become unconscious before he can create? (CE 2, 166)

This statement is all the more provocative if we remember that Woolf implies in "The Pastons and Chaucer" that Wordsworth did not write from the undermind. Yet there Woolf also makes clear that natural storytellers, like Chaucer, who in creating become "unconscious," are still very much sophisticated artists in control of their materials: "For the story-teller, besides his indescribable zest for facts, must tell his story craftily, without undue stress or excitement, or we shall swallow it whole and jumble the parts together" (CR, 12). Craft, in other words, is equivalent to no "undue stress or excitement."

Do we strain Woolf's logic when we infer that "without undue stress or excitement" also applies to the tranquility described by Wordsworth and reinterpreted by Woolf as the precondition necessary to the attainment of unconsciousness in the moments of creation? If not, we can backtrack to Woolf's "political" conditions necessary to the fostering of successful aesthetic production. Such tranquility was achieved by Wordsworth because of the relative political stability in England in the late 1790s, permitting Wordsworth to live and write, unmolested, in the Lake Country. We can then understand the apparent reversal of Woolf's attitude toward the Romantics, from the first essay in *The Common Reader*, "The Pastons and Chaucer," to the last, "How It Strikes a Contemporary."

As we have seen in "The Pastons and Chaucer," Chaucer is Woolf's example of the unconscious poet, and Wordsworth, Coleridge, and Shelley are "among the priests" of nature (CR, 17). However, the Romantics' poetry, although self-conscious about its subject and about the implied relationship of self to world, also reveals the motive force behind it—its priestly power of belief. Thus, we understand Woolf's apparent shift in "How It Strikes a Contemporary": she now admires Wordsworth, Scott, and Austen for "the power of their belief—their conviction" (CR, 238). But Wordsworth's "conviction" is not, like Chaucer's, a matter of unconscious convergence with the values of the society in which he lived. Rather, his is an adherence to a personal and unique perspective on the world made possible precisely by the stable political conditions in England. In other words, in this last essay, Woolf has modified the meaning of "conviction," which largely explains why she sees in Wordsworth's writing proof of the paradox she explores in "On Not Knowing Greek": great literature "attain[s] that unconsciousness which means that consciousness is stimulated to the highest extent."[1]

This view of Wordsworth prevails in "The Leaning Tower" written seventeen years after "How It Strikes a Contemporary." Woolf's equation of "emotion recollected in tranquility" and unconsciousness is central to her criticism of the "leaning-tower" poets who spoil their poetry by writing, not in this state of healthful drowse but from the tops of their minds. Not surprisingly, Woolf offers Wordsworth's poetry, once again, as her working definition of the poetry of the unconscious. Comparing his poetry with Stephen Spender's "How it was that works, money, interest, building could ever / Hide the palpable and obvious love of man for man," Woolf says: "We listen to oratory, not poetry. It is necessary, in order to feel the emotion of those lines, that other people should be listening too. We are in a group, in a class-room as we listen" (CE 2, 175).

She then cites Wordsworth's poetry to which we listen "when we are alone. We remember that in solitude." And then she adds: "Is that the difference between politician's poetry and poet's poetry?" (CE 2, 176). There can be no doubt of Woolf's preference for poet's poetry and her belief that it rouses more emotion and makes a more lasting impress on the memory. Her diary notes concerning this lecture are perhaps even more revealing of her criticism of the leaning-tower poets, who mix politics with poetry, certainly to the diminishment of the latter. In February 1940, Woolf wrote:

> So, walking this mildish day, up to Telscombe, I invented pages & pages of my lecture: which is to be full & fertile. The idea struck me that the Leaning Tower school is the school of auto-analysis after the suppression of the 19th Century. Quote Stevenson. This explains Stephen's [Spender's] auto[biograph]y; Louis MacNeice &c. . . . Also I get the idea of cerebration; poetry that is not unconscious, but stirred by surface irritation, to which the alien matter of politics, that cant be fused, contributes. Hence the lack of suggestive power. (Diary V, 266–67)

Woolf believes that partisan politics is a base metal, threatening alloy to poetry. On the contrary, poetic touchstones—the best that has been thought, felt, and written—generate private, as opposed to group, emotion and consciousness. Suspect collective consciousness, described by Wilfred V. Trotter as responsible for the destructive actions of the herd, is also discussed by Freud, who refers to Trotter, and who describes the negative characteristics of a group, thus:

> A group is extraordinarily credulous and open to influence, it has no critical faculty, and the improbable does not exist for it. It thinks in images, which call one another up by association . . . and whose agreement with reality is never checked by any reasonable agency. . . .
>
> It goes directly to extremes; if a suspicion is expressed, it is instantly changed into an incontrovertible certainty; a trace of antipathy is changed into furious hatred. . . .
>
> Inclined as it itself is to all extremes, a group can only be excited by an excessive stimulus. Anyone who wishes to produce an effect upon it needs no logical adjustment in his arguments; he must paint in the most forcible colours, he must exaggerate, and he must repeat the same thing again and again.
>
> Since a group is in no doubt as to what constitutes truth or error, and is conscious, moreover, of its own great strength, it is as intolerant as it is obedient to authority. It respects force and can only be slightly influenced by kindness, which it regards merely as a form of weakness. What it demands of its heroes is strength, or even violence. It wants to be ruled and oppressed and to fear its masters. Fundamentally it is entirely conservative, and it has a deep aversion to all innovations and advances and an unbounded respect for tradition. . . .[2]

Such groups are "neoauthoritarian" in character, according to Leonard Woolf, writing in *After the Deluge* on the psychology of democracy. They appear, he argues, both on the right and the left of the political spectrum and have in common the subjugation of the individual to the group. When we add together Woolf's global terrors, inspired by the growing strength of Nazism and fascism in the 1930s, and her particular psychology, her need for privacy and dislike of invasion of her personal world, we can understand better her rejection, registered in aesthetic terms, of the public emotion of the leaning-tower poets.

Woolf's analysis in "The Leaning Tower" primarily concerns the effects on the reading public of the leaning-tower school in contrast with Romantic private or "unconscious" poetry. However, Woolf also describes the social and psychological causes and effects of writing unconscious poetry from the point of view of the writer. In the first place, writing private, unconscious poetry is not entirely a matter of choice but, as in the case of Wordsworth, rather, to a large extent, a question of historically determined forces that create a happy or hostile environment for poets and other writers. Thus, English male novelists of the nineteenth century, she argues, secure from a firsthand knowledge of the wars wracking Europe, wrote in and of a world unmarred by disruption and chaos. In "The Leaning Tower," Woolf explores the happy consequences of social equilibrium for the writer. Beginning with the statement that only Byron and Shelley, of the poets, experienced directly the wars of the period, she asserts that the nineteenth-century English writers' "vision of human life" was not affected by the continental conflicts.

> To the nineteenth-century writer human life must have looked like a landscape cut up into separate fields. In each field was gathered a different group of people. . . . But owing to that peace, to that prosperity, each group was tethered, stationary—a herd grazing within its own hedges. And the nineteenth-century writer did not seek to change those divisions. . . . He accepted them so completely that he became unconscious of them. . . . To us now the hedges are visible. We can see now that each of those writers only dealt with a very small section of human life—all Thackeray's characters are upper middle-class; all Dickens's characters come from the lower middle class. . . . but the writer himself seems unconscious that he is only dealing with . . . the type formed by the class into which the writer was born himself. . . . And that unconsciousness was an immense advantage to him. (CE 2, 165–66)[3]

Such writers lived, she argues, in a peace that passes conscious understanding and creates an environment that, not mysteriously, fosters genius. For similar political reasons, Chaucer and the writers of the Elizabethan age were equally blessed by living at a time in which a fortuitous confluence of social forces prevailed and promoted that unconscious state and conviction necessary to the production of great writing. She analyzed the reasons for the characteristic qualities of Elizabethan drama in "The Narrow Bridge of Art" as she would again in "Anon":

> One is rather trying to analyse a quality which is present in most of the great ages of literature and is most marked in the work of Elizabethan dramatists. They seem to have an attitude toward life, a position which allows them to move their limbs freely; a view which, though made up of all sorts of different things, falls into the right perspective for their purposes.
> . . . The public appetite, not for books, but for the drama, the smallness of the towns, the distance which separated people, the ignorance in which even the educated then lived, all made it natural for the Elizabethan imagination to fill itself with lions and unicorns, dukes and duchesses, violence and mystery. This was reinforced by something which we cannot explain so simply, but which we can certainly feel. They had an attitude toward life which made them able to express themselves freely and fully. Shakespeare's plays are not the work of a baffled and frustrated mind; they are the perfectly elastic envelope of his thought. . . . And it is true of all the Elizabethan dramatists that . . . they never make us feel that they are afraid or self-conscious, or that there is anything hindering, hampering, inhibiting the full current of their minds. (CE 2, 220–21)

While Woolf describes the phenomenon of unself-consciousness as difficult to explain, we feel behind her commentary Leslie Stephen's analysis of the social forces defining the period—a period of high nationalism in which the lower classes felt their interests to be in synchrony with those of the ruling class. These circumstances produced no leaning tower atop which playwrights sat, distorting their view of the ground.

Further, we read a possible political and psychological subtext. Woolf was made uncomfortably self-conscious by public occasions, particularly by those that roused the emotions of the group. And she had, as well, from Freud and her husband, psychological, political, and historical analysis that argued the reactionary nature of contemporary communal psychology.[4] Thus, it is no wonder that she should have regarded literature meant to arouse collective or public emotion with suspicion.[5]

Although Woolf was uncomfortable with, and disapproved of, communal emotion, she had undeniable pleasure in the act of private creation.⁶ Something of this pleasure is communicated in her essay "Professions for Women," in which Woolf enjoins her audience to picture her as a young writer of novels and to share her state of pleasurable drowse and its opposite, the sudden pain of wakening. Woolf eloquently describes through fishing metaphors an extraordinary delight, reminiscent of the preoedipal underwater world of "The Mark on the Wall."

> a novelist's chief desire is to be as unconscious as possible. . . . I want you to imagine me writing a novel in a state of trance. . . . The image that comes to mind . . . is the image of a fisherman lying sunk in dreams on the verge of a deep lake with a rod held out over the water. She was letting her imagination sweep unchecked round every rock and cranny of the world that lies submerged in the depths of our unconscious being. Now came the experience that I believe to be far commoner with women writers than with men. The line raced though the girl's fingers. Her imagination had rushed away. It had sought the pools, the depths, the dark places where the largest fish slumber. And then there was a smash. There was an explosion. There was foam and confusion. The imagination had dashed itself against something hard. The girl was roused from her dream. She was indeed in a state of the most acute distress. . . . she had thought of something, something about the body, about the passions which it was unfitting for her as a woman to say. Men, her reason told her, would be shocked. The consciousness of what men will say of a woman who speaks the truth about her passions had roused her from her artist's state of unconsciousness. (CE 2, 287–88)

Woolf's delineation of the pleasurable experience of creation and the distress of interruption caused by "invisible censors" and the subsequent return to self-consciousness emphasizes the consequences, both psychic and creative, to the author.⁷ Again employing the fishing metaphor, Woolf mourns the loss of that *dolce far niente,* the downtime when the imagination rambles, which is half the pleasure and reward for the angler of real fish and for authors alike. Major Hills, the M.P. who, in his spare time, wrote a book on fishing that Woolf reviewed, had written that when a fish jammed his reel, he looked up to find himself and the world changed. Woolf quotes him: "'I felt receptive to every sight, every colour and every sound, as though I walked through a world from which a veil had been withdrawn'" (CE 2, 302). And then she comments:

> Is it possible that to remove veils from trees it is necessary to fish?— our conscious mind must be all body, and then the unconscious mind

leaps to the top and strips off veils? Is it possible that, if to bare reality is to be a poet, we have, as Mr. Yeats said the other day, no great poet because since the war farmers preserve or net their waters, and vermin get up? . . . And the novelists—if we have no novelist in England today whose stature is higher than the third button on Sir Walter's waistcoat, or reaches to the watchchain of Charles Dickens, or the ring on the little finger of George Eliot, is it not that the Cumberland poachers are dying out? (CE 2, 302)

The creative failures that result from restrictions, from fetters, rocks, and shoals, are disruptions elsewhere described by Woolf, particularly in the *Granite and Rainbow* essay titled "Women and Fiction." There she argues the case against self-consciousness in a way that parallels her criticism of the leaning-tower poets.

> But the novels of women were not affected only by the necessarily narrow range of the writer's experience. They showed, at least in the nineteenth century, another characteristic which may be traced to the writer's sex. In *Middlemarch* and in *Jane Eyre* we are conscious not merely of the writer's character, as we are conscious of the character of Charles Dickens, but we are conscious of a woman's presence—of someone resenting the treatment of her sex and pleading for its rights. . . . It introduces a distortion and is frequently the cause of weakness. The desire to plead some personal cause or to make a character the mouthpiece of some . . . grievance always has a distressing effect, as if the spot at which the reader's attention is directed were suddenly twofold instead of single. (CE 2, 144)

Thus, the female writer is hampered by self-consciousness produced through knowledge of political or social victimization of women, as well as by the need to write, necessarily self-consciously, about an outcome of such victimization—archaic attitudes towards sexuality and other bodily functions. This latter self-consciousness is clearly another result of the social and cultural inequities of patriarchal society. The woman writer's nineteenth-century male counterpart, we remember, was not, according to Woolf, similarly plagued, and is, in fact, held up by her as particularly blessed by unconsciousness of the hedges that walled off one social class from another.[8]

Thus, the freeing of the writer's unconscious through the removal of both undue stress or excitement and restrictions permits the flourishing of his or her craft. But now we come to the paradox that explains so much of Woolf's polemical writing, particularly in the late 1930s when she argued, not a general case, for example, an alteration of the social position of women, as in *A Room of*

One's Own, but specific measures to achieve desired political ends. Such writing was a daunting task and one, we have reason to believe, she thought was doomed from the start. At the point in her career when the pressures of the world were forcing her to become political in the partisan sense and even to inform her fiction with historical and political issues, she looked more and more to the Romantic poets, her avatars of privacy, unconsciousness, and lack of preaching. They were, in the last years of her life, those whom she increasingly read, cited, and wrote about at length. These poets were, as Leonard Woolf argues in *After the Deluge,* the first great exponents of the new individualism, exploring the dim regions of their minds and personalities. Their subject and methods thus point to a tremendous historical shift, specifically in the development of literature and, more generally, in the character of society. As for the Romantics, the idiosyncracies of the ordinary person, the imagination of the poet himself, and nature are the subjects that Woolf found congenial and described as poet's poetry.[9]

Aside from her profound interest in and commitment to the subject matter of the Romantics, a comment in her diary for 22 June 1940 reveals another aspect of Woolf's appreciation of them—their technique, or the manner in which their style makes the real accessible.

> My book is Coleridge; Rose Macauley; the Bessborough letters. . . . I would like to find one book & stick to it. But cant. I feel, if this is my last lap, oughtn't I to read Shakespeare? But cant. . . . And I read my Shelley at night. How delicate & pure & musical & uncorrupt he & Coleridge read, after the left wing group. How lightly & firmly they put down their feet; & how they sing; & how they compact; & fuse, & deepen. I wish I cd invent a new critical method—something swifter & lighter & more colloquial & yet intense . . . more fluid & following the flight [of the mind], than my C.R. essays. The old problem: how to keep the flight of the mind, yet be exact. All the difference between the sketch and the finished work. (Diary V, 298)

The number of times she comments on, or aptly quotes, Shelley, Coleridge, and Wordsworth to describe her feelings in her diaries of this period is itself proof of her intellectual and emotional dependence on them; their creative involvement and technique serve as models for her as, say, Chaucer's could not do. These poets are her double-runners in this period of her life which she proleptically described as her "last lap."

But the Romantics were not merely for study and admiration of technique. In understanding their place in her emotional life at this time, we begin to appreciate the convergence of Woolf's intellectual argument about conviction—"that unconsciousness which means that consciousness is stimulated to the highest extent"—and her own imperious need for consolation: the necessary rapture that she could achieve either through reading or writing. From this perspective the Romantic poets were sometimes sheer solace, able to subdue the empirical self, as when she writes: "Indeed, after we'd heard Haw-Haw, objectively announcing defeat—victory on his side of the line that is—again & again, left us about as down as we've yet been. We sat silent in the 9 o'clock dusk; & L. could only with difficulty read Austen Chamberlain. I found the Wordsworth letters my only drug" (Diary V, 295). That sentiment, in part, is a desire that Woolf also attributed to her character Isa, both "book-shy" and "gun-shy," as in June 1940, she wrote "Pointz Hall," her working title for *Between the Acts:* "Yet as a person with a raging tooth runs her eye in a chemist shop over green bottles . . . lest one of them may contain a cure, she considered: Keats and Shelley; Yeats and Donne" (BtA, 19).[10]

Woolf, of course, would never have described herself as book-shy. The drug that freed her from the pain of political consciousness on this particular occasion was the literary antidote to Woolf's "gun-shy" miseries during the 1930s, especially at the very end, after war broke out. She hated "any of the feelings war breeds: patriotism; communal &c, all sentimental & emotional parodies of our real feelings" (Diary V, 302). Yet she also believed that it was impossible for her as a writer to make any change in the political landscape. When Benedict Nicolson charged Woolf and all of Old Bloomsbury with fiddling while Europe was moving towards the flashpoint, Woolf, according to Quentin Bell, defended her friends and herself through a comparison to the Romantic poets.

> She rested her case on the view that artists are unable, substantially, to influence society and that this was true even of the greatest writers: Keats, Shelley, Wordsworth or Coleridge. And this was the defence most applicable to her. . . . she had attempted to be politically active; it was the ability, not the inclination, that was lacking. Only in *A Room of One's Own* does she exhibit any great persuasive power and, politically, she was a much less influential writer than Harriet Beecher Stowe.[11]

Where, then, are we in understanding the writer of *The Years, Roger Fry, A Biography, Three Guineas,* and "Thoughts on Peace in an Air Raid"? These titles, in particular, represent all the genres in which Woolf made honest efforts to merge political involvement and writing. In 1939 when writing Roger Fry's biography, she began her own autobiography in which she recurs to her pleasure in the actual writing process. In the passage from "A Sketch . . . ," cited in chapter III, we see her ardent belief in the existence of pattern and unity in the universe.

> It [a moment of being] is or will become a revelation of some order; it is a token of some real thing behind appearances. . . . It is only by putting it into words that I make it whole; this wholeness means that it has lost its power to hurt me; it gives me, perhaps because by doing so I take away the pain, a great delight to put the severed parts together. Perhaps this is the strongest pleasure known to me. It is the rapture I get when in writing I seem to be discovering what belongs to what; making a scene come right; making a character come together. From this I reach what I might call a philosophy . . . that behind the cotton wool is hidden a pattern; that we—I mean all human beings—are connected with this; that the whole world is a work of art; that we are parts of the work of art. . . . we are the words; we are the music; we are the thing itself. (MoB, 72).

This statement, revealing her Romantic effort to record and create unity rather than to privilege chaos and interruption, is a precursor of Woolf's last two projects, both, ironically, but revealingly, unfinished before her death: *Between the Acts* and her literary history beginning with the essays "Anon" and "The Reader." The similarity between these works, the reproduction of the literary-historical pageant in *Between the Acts* and the unwinding of the ball of string to find the beginnings of culture in England, has been noted by others. But the impulse to find the pattern and see it whole, despite the aeroplanes overhead, the snippets of inconsequential conversation, and calves lowing in the fields—Woolf's novelistic rendering of the cotton wool of existence—has not been traced to the passage cited from "A Sketch . . ." or, more crucially, to the "communal psychology"—in Leonard Woolf's sense of the term—of the Romantic poets.

Woolf describes the rapture of unity achieved through the private act of reading in *A Room of One's Own* (75) and elsewhere. The enabling pleasure of wholeness achieved through writing is clearly linked by Woolf in "A Sketch . . ." to the preoedipal pleasure of her first memories of life, sitting on her mother's lap in the train and lying in the nursery at St. Ives and getting "the intensity of this first impression: the impression of the waves and the acorn on the blind; the feeling, as I describe it sometimes to myself, of lying in a grape and seeing through a film of semi-transparent yellow" (MoB, 65). "A Sketch . . ." provides the connection between Woolf's life and her other writing. The *"floating* incidents" (MoB, 77; my emphasis) that make up "A Sketch . . ." sometimes reappear in Woolf's fiction; we are excited when we discover their sources in her life.

The special importance of the second of her two "first" memories, that of hearing the waves from the nursery, is apparent when we consider the innumerable instances of wave and water imagery in Woolf's novels. It is as if that first deeply felt pleasure had colored her imagination, had run through it like wine through water, so that beauty and importance would, for ever after, in her adult life, be transcribed by her onto the written page in these terms.

Fiction tells us something about the imagination and preoccupations of a writer. However, arguing back to a life from the page of a novel or even an essay is a dubious proposition and one that must be done, if done at all, with extreme tact. On the other hand, I exempt from this caveat evidence supplied by a private diary communication which, in Woolf's case, reveals many of the same patterns and preoccupations that we find in her fiction. Both the diary and the memoir are curious borderlands of expression in which the "poetic" self may transcend the "empirical" but never leaves off contemplating, most forcibly and directly, the empirical self, "the self that loves a woman, or that hates a tyrant" (CE 2, 189) or that does any other of the thousand things necessary to the business of living. To depend, then, on the evidence of her language in these sources to explain Woolf's actions seems justified, particularly during a period in which political circumstances forced her to contemplate the empirical so directly and persistently and when she had seriously begun to doubt the ability of the poetic self to free her from worldly contingencies. Because Woolf believed that she might be in her "last lap," a sports metaphor she could well have taken from swimming, her diary entry of Sunday, 28 July 1940, exactly eight months to the day before she committed suicide by drowning in the tidal river Ouse, is particularly striking. In a paragraph that brings together a complex assortment of ideas and feelings, she wrote:

> Why do I mind being beaten at bowls? I think I connect it with Hitler. Yet I played very well. And, in an hours time, shall be repeating the other phrase wh. I made during the first game: a Season of calm weather. Such a curious peace; a satisfactory quiet. I shall see no one

in London Yes for a moment I believe that I can compass a season of calm weather. Yet 'they' say the invasion is fixed for Aug. 16th. A season of calm weather is the crown for which I'm always pushing & shoving, swimming like the hedgehog who cuts his throat with his paws Nessa said yesterday at C[harlesto]n, if he swims. . . . Judith and L. came on Monday. Thus our island will be invaded—my season of calm weather. Many <an island> a green isle—why cant I remember poetry? (Diary V, 307)

First, she alludes to two Romantic poems in one paragraph to transcribe her feelings precisely. The more significant of the allusions is to "Intimations of Immortality" because "a season of calm weather" for Wordsworth represents the adult's continued ability to reconnect with the uncomplicated satisfactions of childhood. In the ninth stanza, he writes:

> Hence in a season of calm weather
> Though inland far we be,
> Our souls have sight of that immortal sea
> Which brought us hither,
> Can in a moment travel thither,
> And see the Children sport upon the shore,
> And hear the mighty waters rolling evermore.
>
> (Wordsworth, 190)

The preoedipal wholeness of early childhood, preceding the necessarily conflictual development of self-consciousness, is mythically depicted by Wordsworth in this poem as a transoceanic voyage "remembered" by the adult, who images the children playing on the shore in close proximity to the waters of that first journey. James Holt McGavran, we recall, sees the "Intimations" ode as a precursor poem for much of Woolf's work and draws particular attention to the early portion of "A Sketch . . ."[12] In her diary Woolf uses the image of a season of calm weather, which transforms into a place of safety, the green isle of Shelley's poem, "Lines Written Among the Euganean Hills."

> Many a green isle needs must be
> In the deep wide sea of Misery,
>
> (Shelley, 376)

Registering her frustration, she claims not to remember Shelley's poem precisely, but we may note with interest that she had unconsciously recalled a poem in which the sea has quite an opposite association to the one it has in "Intimations."

Woolf feels the need for safety, for achieving her season of calm weather as she fears a German military invasion and more personal and certain intrusion, in the form of possible encroachments from her London life, that is, her unwanted or half-wanted relatives. All would destroy the peace and wholeness of her secluded life in the country. She fiercely expresses her fight to preserve this calm or green isle, "the crown for which I'm always pushing and shoving, swimming like the hedgehog."

In this last simile, through which she compares herself with an animal that struggles for safety and destroys itself in the process, Woolf reveals the great psychological paradox of these last years of her life. Her sister's depiction of the hedgehog that cuts its own throat was clearly resonant for Woolf. It suggests how complicated the connection between the life and death instincts was in this woman. We can imagine that the desire for wholeness, for the pleasure in recognizing that we are the words, the music, for merging with the world in the blissfully unconscious way of very young children, transformed into the desire to submerge herself in deep waters to achieve an unconsciousness that would end her mental pain. She anticipated her suicide with a number of imaginary scenarios, including one in her letter to Ethel Smyth about her literary history project.

> Did I tell you I'm reading the whole of English literature through? By the time I've reached Shakespeare the bombs will be falling. So I've arranged a very nice last scene: reading Shakespeare, having forgotten my gas mask, I shall fade far away, and quite forget. . . . (Letters VI, 466)

Here is an ironically humorous description of an ideal death, a Keatsian ceasing with no pain. The loss of consciousness, the fading far away, is pleasurable, with the beauty of Shakespeare's poetry the last stimulus the brain might recognize. We can compare this exit from the world with two others. In her last diary, for 2 October 1940, she reports that as the bombs were dropping the night before, she had said to Leonard: "I dont want to die yet." And then follows this description of a physically painful end.

> Oh I try to imagine how one's killed by a bomb. I've got it fairly vivid— the sensation: but cant see anything but suffocating nonentity following after. I shall think—oh I wanted another 10 years—not this—& shant, for once, be able to describe it. It—I mean death; no, the scrunching

& scrambling, the crushing of my bone shade in on my very active eye
& brain: the process of putting out the light,—painful? Yes. Terrifying.
I suppose so—Then a swoon; a drum; two or three gulps attempting
consciousness—& then, dot dot dot (Diary V, 326–27)

The desire to live, as Woolf feels the threat from the skies, is powerful. The pain she imagines, as she envisions this bone-scrunching
end, is as much a matter of contemplating the loss of self-consciousness—"of putting out the light" and not being "able to describe it"—as of thinking about skeletal destruction. However,
these two imagined ends, one "good," the other horrific, are different from her suicide in a number of important and related ways.
First and most significant is that the invented deaths are the result
of circumstances beyond Woolf's control; they were planned or
"made up" by her only in the telling. On the other hand, her suicide
was a seizing of the reins, a self-determining act of courage of the
sort that Clarissa Dalloway applauds in Septimus Warren Smith's
escape from Sir William Bradshaw, one of the "obscurely evil"
forces of life.

> She had once thrown a shilling into the Serpentine, never anything
> more. But he had flung it away. . . . A thing there was that mattered;
> a thing, wreathed about with chatter, defaced, obscured in her own life,
> let drop every day in corruption, lies, chatter. This he had preserved.
> Death was defiance. Death was an attempt to communicate; people
> feeling the impossibility of reaching the centre which, mystically,
> evaded them; closeness drew apart; rapture faded, one was alone.
> There was an embrace in death.
> But this young man who had killed himself—had he plunged holding
> his treasure? "If it were now to die, 'twere now to be most happy," she
> had said to herself once, coming down in white. (MD, 280–81)

Like Septimus, Virginia Woolf plunged. Perhaps Clarissa's sentiments explain Woolf's action; perhaps the narrator's words from
"The Mark on the Wall":

> Yes, one could imagine a very pleasant world. A quiet spacious world,
> with the flowers so red and blue in the open fields. A world without
> professors or specialists or house-keepers with the profiles of police-
> men, a world which one could slice with one's thought as a fish slices
> the water with his fin, grazing the stems of the water-lilies, hanging
> suspended over nests of white sea eggs. . . . How peaceful it is down
> here, rooted in the centre of the world and gazing up through the grey
> waters, with their sudden gleams of light, and their reflections. . . .
> (CSF, 81–82).

Although I do not romanticize a frigidly cold river in early spring, or underestimate the strength of her mental disorder, we can believe that, with an imagination like hers, there must have been real solace in submerging herself in the waters. Yes, one could imagine that she was drawn to the preoedipal pleasure she imagined in this underwater world, simultaneously populated, in the way of dreams, by red and blue flowers, like the flowers of her mother's dress. It is a world devoid of "specialists" like Sir William Bradshaw and Ellie Rendel, Woolf's own doctor, the compartmentalizing, hedge-growing, controlling forces of society. Woolf understood "Nature['s] . . . old game of self-preservation," her avoidance of "mere waste of energy, even some collision with reality" (CSF, 82). Certainly ending a life is such a waste. But Woolf also knew another truth about natural law: "I understand Nature's game—her prompting to take action as a way of ending any thought that threatens to excite or to pain" (CSF, 82). When we consider Woolf's deliberate equation of excitement and pain, and her equally considered one of emotion recollected in tranquility and unconsciousness, we are struck by the congruity, for her, of the most pleasurable of occupations, creation, and her final, concerted and very private act of uncreation, her death. The writer, as she had explained, must avoid all excitement. The woman, as those left behind had to understand, must avoid unbearable pain.

To suggest that a suicide—a reminder of inexplicable chaos in the universe—is part of a pattern may be an act of literary reconstruction, an expression of our need to create narrative closure. However, that Woolf's own words and phrases so aptly describe her last act may well be the most convincing proof of a pattern that governed her expression both in the word and in the deed.

Certainly and emphatically, pattern-making of this sort is not the same as the truth about a life. Nor is the need for literary closure equivalent to Woolf's drive to destroy herself. But Virginia Woolf had an imagination of such economy that to view her end in this way does not seem an outrage. By going willfully to her death, she took from life its power to hurt her. One must hope that in her final moments of physical discomfort, she experienced, as well, a rapture comparable to that which she had when, in writing, she put the severed parts together. From her point of view, as she submerged herself in the swirling waters, she made her final scene come right. With the dramatic facts of her death before us, the sunken and unstated meanings of her life and writing combine unconsciously, lapsing and flowing into each other like reeds on the bed of a river. Thus, we view her as the creator of her own life's pattern as she inalterably closed the gap between herself and the vast mass she called the world. As a writer she had, with preeminence, been the words. In her death, she became the thing itself.

Notes

INTRODUCTION

1. Virginia Woolf, "'Romance,'" in *The Essays of Virginia Woolf* II, ed. Andrew McNeillie (San Diego: Harcourt Brace Jovanovich, 1987), 74. All further references to the volumes of this collection of her essays will be cited parenthetically as Essays.

2. See Marshall Brown, "Romanticism and Enlightenment," in *The Cambridge Companion to British Romanticism,* ed. Stuart Curran (Cambridge: Cambridge University Press, 1993), 25. Brown says:

> The readers of this volume will find Lovejoy's famous essay "On the Discrimination of Romanticisms" amply confirmed: Romanticism cannot be defined. . . . Properly speaking, this chapter should be entitled "Romanticisms and Enlightenments," a multiplicity that leaves the student no hook except the little word "and" to hang a hat on.

3. Jerome McGann, *The Romantic Ideology: A Critical Investigation* (Chicago: University of Chicago Press, 1983), 20.

4. M. H. Abrams, "English Romanticism: The Spirit of the Age" in *Romanticism: Points of View,* ed. Robert F. Gleckner and Gerald E. Enscoe (Englewood Cliffs, N.J.: Prentice-Hall, Inc., 1970), 315–16.

5. McGann *Romantic Ideology,* 109–10. McGann argues:

> In studying English Romanticism, then, we must be prepared to distinguish three different phases, as it were, of "primary" (visionary) and "secondary" (or revisionist) relationships. In Blake, *The Marriage of Heaven and Hell* is "primary" in relation to works like *Milton* and *Jerusalem,* which are "secondary" and revisionist in this structure of relations. . . . In Wordsworth and Coleridge, on the other hand, we can observe a second phase of Romantic relationships. Here the initial works date from the Reign of Terror and they first appear in *Lyrical Ballads.* These works differ from Blake's in that they are already laden with self-critical and revisionist elements. Wordsworth's purely "secondary" phase is brief to the point of non-existence, for his greatest works—which are rightly judged the touchstone of first generation English Romantic poetry—incorporate vision and its critique from the start. . . .
> [The] third phase of Romantic relationships appears most typically in the period stretching from approximately 1808 to 1824—the literary years of a Romanticism in England which is initiated, dominated, and closed by Byron. In its primary phase Byron's work is already so deeply self-critical and revisionist that its ideology—in contrast to Blake, Wordsworth, and the early Coleridge—has to be defined in negative terms: nihilism, cynicism, anarchism.

6. Ibid., 82. Even McGann is unable to avoid the term "Movement," which implies something unified and definable.

7. Virginia Woolf, *The Waves* in *Jacob's Room and The Waves: Two Complete Novels* (New York: Harcourt, Brace & World, Inc., 1959), 306. All further refer-

ences, both to *Jacob's Room* and *The Waves,* will be to this edition and cited parenthetically as JR and TW.

8. M. H. Abrams, *Natural Supernaturalism: Tradition and Revolution in Romantic Literature* (New York: W. W. Norton & Co., Inc., 1971), 28.

9. For example, see Brown, "Romanticism and Enlightenment," 26–28, on the continuities between the Enlightenment and the Romantic period. Indeed, Woolf argued the same point:

> As for there being one period that is exclusively romantic, and another that is without romance, wherever we look in English literature we shall find Romance in the upper or in the under world. Further, even the age which we associate particularly with the revival of Romance contains Wordsworth, who 'drew straight from life' and 'shunned what is derived from other books'. . . . ("'Romance,'" *The Essays of Virginia Woolf* II, 74).

10. McGann in *The Romantic Ideology* says of the Romantic period: "Historians of ideas commonly argue that the age's political and social turmoil was matched by an 'epistemological crisis'; the coincidence of these disruptive forces represented themselves, at the cultural level, in a variety of so-called 'Romantic' forms" (40–41).

I would argue that the period of the two World Wars duplicated, in the early twentieth century, the social and political turmoil of the early nineteenth and was matched by a comparable epistemological crisis in the creative arts.

11. Woolf's own criticism of Richardson's *The Tunnel* (Virginia Woolf, "Dorothy Richardson" in *Virginia Woolf: Women and Writing,* ed. Michèle Barrett [San Diego: Harcourt Brace Jovanovich, 1979], 190) best explains why Richardson fails to communicate a Romantic intensity of vision:

> Here we are, thinking, word by word, as Miriam thinks. The method, if triumphant, should make us feel ourselves seated at the centre of another mind . . . we should perceive in the helter-skelter of flying fragments some unity, significance, or design. . . . But, then, which reality is it, the superficial or the profound? We have to consider the quality of Miriam Henderson's consciousness, and the extent to which Miss Richardson is able to reveal it. . . . Having sacrificed not merely 'hims and hers', but so many seductive graces of wit and style for the prospect of some new revelation or greater intensity, we still find ourselves distressingly near the surface. Things look much the same as ever.

12. The following descriptions and comparisons are not meant to devalue the Modernist writers but are merely an attempt to establish, by way of a necessarily crude shorthand, some of the qualities of Woolf's prose that warrant a study of her Romanticism.

13. Abrams, *Natural Supernaturalism,* 418–19.

14. Joseph Conrad, *Lord Jim* (New York: Bantam Books, 1981), 91. Marlow's description of his extraordinary moment of perception is preceded by two instances of heightened acuity. He says:

> "It gave me the opportunity to 'note' a starred scar on the back of his hand—effect of a gunshot clearly; and, as if my sight had been made more acute by this discovery, I perceived also the seam of an old wound. . . ." (90)

> "Indeed his torpid demeanor concealed nothing: it had that mysterious, almost miraculous, power of producing striking effects by means impossible of detection which is the last word of the highest art." (91)

He then adds:

"He pronounced, '*Mon Dieu!* how the time passes!' Nothing could have been more commonplace than this remark; but its utterance coincided for me with a moment of vision. It's extraordinary how we go through life with eyes half shut, with dull ears, with dormant thoughts. . . . Nevertheless, there can be but few of us who had never known one of these rare moments of awakening when we see, hear, understand ever so much—everything—in a flash—before we fall back again into our agreeable somnolence. I raised my eyes when he spoke, and I saw him as though I had never seen him before." (91–92)

15. E. M. Forster, *Howards End* (New York: Bantam Books, 1985), title page.
16. Another point of comparison between Joyce and Woolf is that Joyce delights in drawing attention to language, to words as the medium of his art, and so to the textual surface, while Woolf, with some notable exceptions, prefers to see through it to the created image and, thus, to the world. Stephen Dedalus, in *A Portrait of the Artist as a Young Man* (New York: The Viking Press, 1962), as a very young boy at Clongowes, thinks:

> Suck was a queer word. The fellow called Simon Moonan that name because Simon Moonan used to tie the prefect's false sleeves behind his back. . . . But the sound was ugly. Once he had washed his hands in the lavatory of the Wicklow Hotel and his father pulled the stopper up by the chain after and the dirty water went down through the hole in the basin. And when it had all gone down slowly the hole in the basin had made a sound like that: suck. Only louder. (11)

Abrams points out that Joyce "in a précis of English literary history which he composed in the spring of 1905, . . . gave 'the highest palms' to Wordsworth, together with Shakespeare and Shelley; and a few months later he wrote to Stanislaus Joyce, 'I think Wordsworth of all English men of letters best deserves your word "genius."'" This is the very time when Joyce was working on *Stephen Hero*, wherein he identified and analyzed 'moments' of epiphany" (*Natural Supernaturalism*, 421). Nevertheless, Abrams concludes that Joyce systematically translated "religious formulas into a comprehensive aesthetic theory, in which the artist, or artificer, undertakes to redeem both life and the world by recreating them into a new world. Joyce's new world, however, is radically opposed to Wordsworth's, for it is no other than the work of art itself" (422).
17. Vincent Arthur De Luca, "Blake's Concept of the Sublime" in *Romanticism: A Critical Reader* ed. Duncan Wu (Oxford: Blackwell, 1995), 18. De Luca defines the moment according to Thomas Weiskel's synthesis of the ideas of Burke, Kant, and Wordsworth (*The Romantic Sublime: Studies in the Structure and Psychology of Transcendence* [Baltimore: Johns Hopkins University Press, 1976], 11, 23–24).
18. Joyce, *Portrait of the Artist*, 172.
19. Ibid., 174.
20. William Wordsworth, *The Prelude* in *Selected Poems and Prefaces: William Wordsworth*, ed. Jack Stillinger (Cambridge: Riverside Press, 1965), 358. All further references to Wordsworth's poetry, unless otherwise noted, will be to this edition and cited parenthetically as Wordsworth.
21. Virginia Woolf, "A Sketch of the Past," in *Moments of Being*, ed. and intro. Jeanne Schulkind (San Diego: Harcourt Brace Jovanovich, 1985). All further references to Woolf's memoirs will be to this edition and cited parenthetically as MoB.
22. Lucio Ruotolo's study, *The Interrupted Moment: A View of Virginia Woolf's Novels* (Stanford: Stanford University Press, 1986), approaches the question of learning about the world and the self and their representation in Woolf's

art from another perspective. He argues that real achievement occurs for her characters because of actual moments of interruption that derail the mind from its smooth course and make it see something it had previously ignored. The difference between my reading and his is a matter of the weight assigned to the interruption and the subsequent pattern-making. Although Ruotolo privileges the interruption, I focus more on the behavior that follows from the experience—the repetition, generalization, and assimilation of the new material.

23. This word has for its root the Latin verb *reperīre,* suggesting that the material included in this group is returned to and reexplored.

24. Virginia Woolf, *Mrs. Dalloway* (New York: Harcourt, Brace & World, 1953). All further references will be to this edition and cited parenthetically as MD.

25. Virginia Woolf, "The Leaning Tower," in *Virginia Woolf: Collected Essays* 2 (New York: Harcourt, Brace & World, 1967), 180. All further references to the collected essays, unless otherwise noted, will be to the four volumes of this edition and cited parenthetically as CE.

26. Virginia Woolf, "Anon," in "'Anon' and 'The Reader': Virginia Woolf's Last Essays," ed. Brenda Silver, *Twentieth Century Literature* 25, nos. 3/4 (Fall/Winter 1979), 398.

27. Virginia Woolf, *To the Lighthouse* (New York: Harcourt, Brace & World, 1955), 52–53. All further references to the novel will be to this edition and cited parenthetically as TTL.

28. Virginia Woolf, "Kew Gardens," in *The Complete Shorter Fiction of Virginia Woolf,* ed. Susan Dick (San Diego: Harcourt Brace Jovanovich, 1985), 88. All further references to the short stories will be to this edition and cited parenthetically as CSF.

29. Perry Meisel also cites this description of Mrs. Ramsay's method of reading—by indirection finding direction out—in his introduction to *The Absent Father: Virginia Woolf and Walter Pater* (New Haven: Yale University Press, 1980), xviii.

30. Virginia Woolf, *The Letters of Virginia Woolf* VI, ed. Nigel Nicolson and Joanne Trautmann (New York: Harcourt Brace Jovanovich, 1980), 475. All further references to the letters will be to the six volumes of this edition (1975–80) and cited parenthetically as Letters.

31. Michael Ragussis, *The Subterfuge of Art: Language and the Romantic Tradition* (Baltimore: Johns Hopkins University Press, 1978), 13.

32. I believe that Donald Marshall has this reading of Romanticism in mind when he comments in the foreword to Geoffrey Hartman's *The Unremarkable Wordsworth* (Minneapolis: University of Minnesota Press, 1987): "Hartman wants not to decide on all those separations—spoken/written; inside/outside; metaphorical/literal; and so on—which must be asserted to give deconstructive analysis its purchase. Hartman thinks about this issue not only in terms of consciousness and self-consciousness: for him the quest to limit self-consciousness has always been definitive of romanticism" (x).

33. Leonard Woolf, *After the Deluge: A Study of Communal Psychology,* vol. I (London: The Hogarth Press, 1931).

34. Ibid., 243–44.

35. Virginia Woolf, "The Pastons and Chaucer," in *The Common Reader: First Series,* ed. Andrew McNeillie (San Diego: Harcourt Brace Jovanovich, 1984), 13. All further references to this volume and *The Second Common Reader,* ed. Andrew McNeillie (San Diego: Harcourt Brace Jovanovich, 1986) will be cited parenthetically as CR and SCR.

36. Meisel cites Woolf's belief, expressed in *A Room of One's Own,* in "the common life which is the real life and not of the little separate lives which we live as individuals" (161) as doubling the sense of Walter Pater in his *Apprecia-tions* essay on Wordsworth—"'the network of man and nature . . . pervaded by a common, universal life,' (A, 56)" (Meisel, 141). However, he does not go the further step of drawing a parallel between Woolf's notion of the common life and Wordsworth's democratic vision of the invisible forces that bind man to man and man to the world.

37. Alice Fox, *Virginia Woolf and the Literature of the English Renaissance* (Oxford: Clarendon Press, 1990). Although writing about the influence and pres-ence of Renaissance writers in Woolf's work, Fox mentions in her introduction: "At one time or another she [Woolf] has been likened—in style, method, or ideas—to Hazlitt, Lamb, Pater, Samuel Butler, T. S. Eliot, Henry James, Leslie Stephen, and Lytton Strachey" (15). Fox does not mention Wordsworth in this regard.

38. Edwin Muir, "Virginia Woolf," in *Virginia Woolf: The Critical Heritage,* ed. Robin Majumdar and Allen McLaurin (London: Routledge & Kegan Paul, 1975), 184.

39. An exception is Suzanne Scarfone's unpublished dissertation: "The Archi-tectonics of Fate: Equilibrium and the Process of Creation in the Work of William Wordsworth and Virginia Woolf" (Ph.D. diss., Wayne State University, 1985). Scarfone argues that "In order for Wordsworth to create and also to achieve mental equilibrium . . . the sympathetic heart of the self that feels must be de-tached from the creative mind so that he can initiate the poetic vigilance that allows him to control and master perception and to usurp the rival power of nature" (Vol. I, 6). Using Woolf's diaries, letters, and memoirs, Scarfone, like-wise, shows how Woolf develops strategies in her novels to "counteract [her] susceptibility to the emotional impact of sensation" (Vol. I, iv). Her psychological study has for underlying assumption the idea that Woolf's art (she reads *Mrs. Dalloway, To the Lighthouse,* and *The Waves*) is her effort to record, shape, and keep at bay her impressions of the external world—the "rival," as she calls it—that threatens to engulf her and to which she is simultaneously attracted. She reads Woolf's moments of being as a pathological state that, in order to preserve her mental equilibrium, she had to turn to creative use.

The following is a list of essays and books that explore Woolf's connections with Romanticism. It is, by no means, exhaustive.

Frank D. McConnell, "'Death Among the Apple Trees': *The Waves* and the World of Things," *Bucknell Review* XVI (December 1968): 23–39, reprinted in *Modern Critical Views: Virginia Woolf,* ed. Harold Bloom (New York: Chelsea House Publishers, 1986), 53–65; Avrom Fleishman, *Virginia Woolf: A Critical Study* (Baltimore: Johns Hopkins University Press, 1975), 226–27; Beverly Ann Schlack, *Continuing Presences: Virginia Woolf's Use of Literary Allusion* (Uni-versity Park, Penn.: Pennsylvania State University Press, 1979); Charles Schug, *The Romantic Genesis of the Modern Novel* (Pittsburgh: University of Pittsburgh Press, 1979), 189–225; James Holt McGavran, Jr., "'Alone Seeking the Visible World': The Wordsworths, Virginia Woolf, and The Waves," *Modern Language Quarterly* 42, no. 3 (September 1981): 265–91; Mark Hennely, "Romantic Symbol and Psyche in *To the Lighthouse,*" *Journal of Evolutionary Psychology* 4, nos. 3/4 (August 1983): 145–62; Nathaniel Brown, "The 'Double Soul': Virginia Woolf, Shelley, and Androgyny," *Keats-Shelley Journal* 33 (1984): 182–204; William J. Burling, "Virginia Woolf's 'Lighthouse': An Allusion to Shelley's *Queen Mab?*"

English Language Notes 22, no. 2 (December 1984), 62–65; Hermione Lee, "A Burning Glass: Reflection in Virginia Woolf," in *Virginia Woolf, A Centenary Perspective,* ed. Eric Warner (New York: St. Martin's Press, 1984), 12–27; Anca Vlasopolos, "Shelley's Triumph of Death in Virginia Woolf's *Voyage Out,*" *Modern Language Quarterly* 47, no. 2 (June 1986): 130–53; John Ferguson, "A Sea Change: Thomas De Quincey and Mr. Carmichael in *To the Lighthouse,*" *Journal of Modern Literature* XIV, no. 1 (Summer 1987): 45–63.

40. For the asymmetry of the father/son/mother and father/daughter/mother constellations, see Nancy Chodorow, *The Reproduction of Mothering: Psychoanalysis and the Sociology of Gender* (Berkeley: University of California Press, 1978), 192–99.

41. Virginia Woolf, *Contemporary Writers,* preface by Jean Guiguet (London: The Hogarth Press, 1965), 124.

42. I will discuss Woolf's second and third mentions, in 1924 and 1931, of *The Prelude* in chapter VI.

43. Virginia Woolf, *A Room of One's Own* (San Diego: Harcourt Brace Jovanovich, 1929), 107. All further references will be to this edition and cited parenthetically as ROO. Three Romantic writers—Coleridge, Keats, and Lamb—come in for Woolf's highest praise as having "androgynous" minds, with Shelley's right after them as "sexless."

44. Erich Auerbach, "The Brown Stocking," reprinted in *Modern Critical Views: Virginia Woolf,* ed. Harold Bloom (New York: Chelsea House Publishers, 1986), 19–40. I must note that Geoffrey Hartman uses these directional indicators in a similar way: "The horizontal extension of the scope of the poet's subject matter is only an aspect of something more important: its vertical extension, its inward resonance" (*The Unremarkable Wordsworth,* 9).

45. Woolf is quoting Wordsworth, "Elegiac Stanzas" (Wordsworth, 374). The full stanza is:

> Farewell, farewell the heart that lives alone,
> Housed in a dream, at distance from the Kind!
> Such happiness, wherever it be known,
> Is to be pitied; for 'tis surely blind.

46. M. H. Abrams took the title for his book from Yeats's epigraph to the *Oxford Book of Modern Verse* which Yeats edited in 1936.

47. Paul de Man, "Allegory and Irony in Baudelaire" in *Romanticism and Contemporary Criticism: The Gauss Seminar and Other Papers,* ed. E. S. Burt, Kevin Newmark, and Andrzej Warminski (Baltimore: Johns Hopkins University Press, 1993), 101–19.

48. Ibid., 102.

49. Ibid., 102–3.

50. Mark Salzman, "A Nice Guy Who Beats the Odds," *New York Times* (11 September 1994): Section 2, 43.

51. Ragussis, *The Subterfuge of Art,* 14.

CHAPTER 1. PROLOGUE

1. Virginia Woolf wrote in "Leslie Stephen" (1932): "Even today there may be parents who would doubt the wisdom of allowing a girl of fifteen the free run

of a large and quite unexpurgated library. But my father allowed it. There were certain facts—very briefly, very shyly he referred to them. Yet 'Read what you like,' he said, and all his books . . . were to be had without asking" (CE 4, 79–80).

2. Katherine C. Hill, "Virginia Woolf and Leslie Stephen: History and Literary Revolution," *PMLA* 96, no. 3 (1981): 352.

3. Leslie Stephen, "Wordsworth's Ethics," *Hours in a Library* in *Leslie Stephen: Selected Writings in British Intellectual History,* ed. Noël Annan (Chicago: University of Chicago Press, 1979), 202. The similarity between father's and daughter's words is probably not coincidental. Woolf wrote in "A Sketch of the Past": "When I read his [Stephen's] books I get a critical grasp on him; I always read *Hours in a Library* by way of filling out my ideas, say of Coleridge, if I'm reading Coleridge; and always find something to fill out; to correct; to stiffen my fluid vision" (MoB, 115).

4. William Hazlitt, "Mr. Wordsworth," in *The Spirit of the Age,* vol. 11, *The Complete Works of William Hazlitt,* ed. P. P. Howe (London: Macmillan, 1932), 86–87.

5. Describing her father in "A Sketch of the Past," written thirty-three years later, Virginia Woolf wrote: "Indeed I was on his side, even when he was exploding" (MoB, 112). The narrator's assertion that Rosamond and Phyllis took their father's side seems, then, to have had an autobiographical basis.

6. Virginia Hyman, "Reflections in the Looking-Glass: Leslie Stephen and Virginia Woolf," *Journal of Modern Literature* 10, no. 2 (June 1983): 197–216.

7. Virginia Woolf, *A Passionate Apprentice: The Early Journals: 1897–1909,* ed. Mitchell Leaska (New York: Harcourt Brace Jovanovich, 1990), 309. Hereafter cited parenthetically as APA.

8. Article, *Encyclopedia Britannica,* vol. 8 (Chicago: Britannica Inc., 1964): 478–79.

9. M. H. Abrams, *The Mirror and the Lamp: Romantic Theory and the Critical Tradition* (New York: W. W. Norton & Co., 1958), 169.

10. Indeed, later in the narrative, she has Joan say: "But figures are slippery things!" (CSF, 57) and "In sober truth, and without metaphor" (CSF, 58).

11. William Wordsworth, *Wordsworth's Guide to the Lakes,* intro. and notes E. de Selincourt (London: Humphrey Milord, 1926), 29. A reprint of the 1906 edition Virginia reviewed. Hereafter cited parenthetically as Wordsworth's Guide.

12. Hermione Lee, "A Burning Glass: Reflection in Virginia Woolf." Lee considers Woolf's metaphors but not her subjects, political views, or other aspects of Woolf's craft as evidence of her relationship to Romanticism.

13. In a note to the story, Susan Dick says: "As Susan M. Squier and Louise A. DeSalvo point out, VW is probably referring here to John Lydgate's *Temple of Glas,* which she seems to have confused with his *Troy-book*" (CSF, 290).

14. Walter Pater in *The Renaissance: Studies in Art and Poetry,* first published in 1873, devotes a chapter to the German archaeologist Heinrich Schliemann, who in 1871 discovered the site of ancient Troy.

15. Illuminations, the term for the handpainted illustrations in mediaeval and renaissance manuscripts, although only implied here, would be a significant example of the metaphors dependent on light and fire that Lee has isolated as characteristic Romantic metaphors for the imagination.

16. See *The Mirror and the Lamp* for a full account of the difference between mimetic and Romantic expressive theories of art.

17. Drew Gilpin Faust, review of "How Master Lost His Concubine," by Melton A. McLaurin, *New York Times Book Review* (17 November 1991): 30–31.

18. Louise DeSalvo, in "Shakespeare's *Other* Sister," *New Feminist Essays on Virginia Woolf,* ed. Jane Marcus (Lincoln: University of Nebraska Press, 1981), 61–81, says:

> Soon Joan's father finds out about her Journal. He is envious and realises that he is too lazy for such a task. He encourages her to continue keeping it; she has learned to read and write from him. (76)

There is nothing in Joan's reporting of her father's reaction to her and her journal keeping to indicate anything but his pride in her abilities. His emotional outburst, such as it is, concerns his regret over his own father's inability to write and so leave an historical record of his fathers before him as Joan is doing for the present moment. The issue of the sex of the historian does not appear as relevant to Giles Martyn as it does to DeSalvo. Perhaps DeSalvo has distorted her reporting of the interaction between daughter and father to bolster her thesis that this is a story about women's need to empower themselves by becoming historians who write women into the historical record. Correlatively, DeSalvo sees the male characters as the cause of the women's compromised power and skill—an idea that is borne out neither by the strong figure of Joan's mother nor her father's pride in her writing ability. Leslie Stephen was as proud and encouraging of his daughter's efforts as Joan's father was of hers.

19. Virginia Woolf, *The Diary of Virginia Woolf* V, ed. Anne Olivier Bell and Andrew McNeillie (San Diego: Harcourt Brace Jovanovich, 1984), 327. All other references to the diaries will be to the five volumes of this edition (1977–84) and cited parenthetically as Diary.

20. DeSalvo, "Shakespeare's *Other* Sister," 66.

21. Leigh Hunt, *The Autobiography of Leigh Hunt,* vol. 2, chapter XVI, 1850: 223.

22. Woolf in "A Sketch of the Past," commenting on when she was brought by George Duckworth to see her dead mother, says: "a desire to laugh came over me, and I said to myself as I have often done at moments of crisis since, 'I feel nothing whatever.'" (MoB, 92).

23. Joan's heightened imagination causes her to see ordinary life in a way that is comparable to Wordsworth's account of the aim of the poems in *Lyrical Ballads.*

> The principle object, then, proposed in these Poems was to choose incidents and situations from common life, and to relate or describe them, throughout, as far as was possible in a selection of language really used by men, and, at the same time, to throw over them a certain colouring of imagination, whereby ordinary things should be presented to the mind in an unusual aspect; and further, and above all, to make these incidents and situations interesting by tracing in them, truly though not ostentatiously, the primary laws of our nature: chiefly, as regards the manner in which we associate ideas in a state of excitement. (Wordsworth, 446–47)

24. Giles Martyn's decision to see that his father's tomb is carved seems a deliberate imaginative rewriting of history by Virginia Stephen since John Paston, also of Norfolk, "delayed to make his father's tombstone" (CR, 8).

CHAPTER 2. EPILOGUE

1. Woolf, "'Anon' and 'The Reader': Virginia Woolf's Last Essays," 356–441. All further references to these essays, Woolf's notes for them, and Silver's own

notes and commentary will be to Silver's compilation and cited parenthetically as A & R.

Silver's notational system has been preserved as have Woolf's anomalies of spelling and punctuation. Original spelling and punctuation in Woolf's diaries and letters are also intact.

2. Abrams, *The Mirror and the Lamp*, 22. Abrams cites the *Letters of William and Dorothy Wordsworth* as the source of the Wordsworth quotation.

3. Abrams, *The Mirror and the Lamp*, 78.

4. A distinction must be drawn between, on the one hand, "communal psychology," that vague network of cultural, social, and political forces called by Woolf in her notes "Crot, Ninn, & Pulley" (A & R, 374) and defined by Leonard Woolf in *After the Deluge: A Study of Communal Psychology* (vol. I), and, on the other, "group consciousness" or "group psychology," as Freud, building on others, had defined it in *Group Psychology and the Analysis of the Ego* (1922) and by which he meant, more specifically, the forces that clearly move a more limited and united portion of a population to certain beliefs and actions. The difference between the two concepts, further explored in the last chapter of this book, is not always noted by Woolf who, like some of her readers, often used them interchangeably.

5. William Wordsworth, "A Letter to the Bishop of Llandaff," in *The Prose Works of William Wordsworth* I, ed. W. J. B. Owen and J. W. Smyser (Oxford: Clarendon Press, 1974), 31–49.

6. In August 1909 Virginia had attended the Wagner Festival at Bayreuth with her brother Adrian and Saxon Sydney-Turner (Diary II, 221).

7. Allen McLaurin, "Consciousness and Group Consciousness in Virginia Woolf," in *Virginia Woolf: A Centenary Perspective*, ed. Eric Warner (New York: St. Martin's Press, 1984), 34.

8. Ibid., 36. Trotter's book was known to Freud who commented on it in his own treatise on group psychology, *Group Psychology and the Analysis of the Ego* (New York: Liveright Publishing Corp., 1967).

9. Leslie Stephen, *English Literature and Society in the Eighteenth Century* (London: Gerald Duckworth & Co., 1965).

10. Noël Annan, Preface, *Leslie Stephen: Selected Writings in British Intellectual History* (Chicago: University Chicago Press, 1979), xx, xxiv–xxv.

11. John W. Bicknell, "Leslie Stephen's 'English Thought in the Eighteenth Century': A Tract for the Times," *Victorian Studies* 6, no. 2 (December 1962): 114–15.

12. Stephen, *English Literature and Society in the Eighteenth Century*, 6.

13. Ibid., 6–7.

14. Silver, ed. "'Anon' and 'The Reader,'" 369. Silver says: "What is unclear, however, is whether in the end the book as a whole would have become, as her references to the work later in 1941 imply, a third *Common Reader*.

15. Silver uses the notation { } for representing a marginal insertion of a word or a phrase by Woolf.

16. Wordsworth, on the other hand, writing from within the tradition of authored and printed books, comfortably draws on metaphors of orality, describing the poet as "a man speaking to men," "modifying only the language which is thus suggested to him by a consideration that he describes for a particular purpose, that of giving pleasure. Here, then, he will apply the principle of selection. . . . [and] consider himself as in the situation of a translator" (Wordsworth, 453–54). The operative words are "speaking" and "selection." Spenser's poetry created a

further disunion between writer and audience, turning that audience into readers rather than auditors. Although Wordsworth's audience was, similarly, readers, Wordsworth metaphorically insists on "speaking" to his audience, on maintaining orality as the basis of his poetry. Although he grants that his words are not an unmediated response to passion and only a selection of the real language used by men, purged of its ability to give pain or to disgust, he self-consciously attends to the collective need to give and to respond to pleasure created through words conveying "the image of man and nature" (Wordsworth, 454). His description represents the level of self-consciousness achieved by that modern phenomenon, the critic, and shared by Woolf.

17. Woolf more closely analyzed "conviction" and "self-consciousness" in *The Common Reader* essay, "The Pastons and Chaucer."

18. Virginia Woolf, *Between the Acts* (New York: Harcourt Brace Jovanovich, 1969), 19–20. Hereafter cited parenthetically as BtA.

CHAPTER 3. ROMANTIC TRANSFORMATIONS

1. Tony Davenport, "The Life of *Monday or Tuesday*," in *Virginia Woolf: New Critical Essays*, ed. Patricia Clements and Isobel Grundy (London: Vision, 1983): 157–75.

2. Anca Vlasopolos in "Shelley's Triumph of Death in Virginia Woolf's *Voyage Out*" argues that in this novel the episode of the Dalloways "encapsulates the antagonism of two modes of being—the introspective, creative one and the worldly" (133). The Dalloways obviously represent the worldly while Shelley, introduced into the discussion by Clarissa Dalloway, invokes the creative. The choice of Shelley as the subject of Mr. Hilbery's research, but more importantly as Richard Allardyce's implied double, seems to confirm Woolf's comparable use of the poet to suggest the value of the creative and introspective life of Katharine, his "descendant," in *Night and Day*.

3. Virginia Woolf, *Night and Day* (New York: Harcourt Brace Jovanovich, 1948), 39. Hereafter cited parenthetically as NaD.

4. Citing an instance similar to Mary's in the case of Jacob Flanders, T. E. Apter says:

Fleeing the 'shock, horror, and discomfort' of a professor's luncheon, Jacob finds immediate relief in a solitary walk by the river:

for he draws into him at every step . . . such steady certainty, such reassurance from all sides, the trees bowing, the grey spires soft in the blue, voices blowing and seeming suspended in the air, the springy air of May, the elastic air with . . . whatever it is that gives the May air its potency, blurring the trees, gumming the buds, daubing the green. And the river too runs past, not at flood, nor swiftly, but cloying the oar that dips in it and drops white drops from the blade, swimming green and deep over the bowed rushes, as if lavishly caressing them. (JR, 36)

We can see here precisely what solitude offers, and why it is important. The trees are bowing; the spires are soft, all colours are blurred or muted so that there is a lessening of focus and clarity; yet this softening is seen to be part of the air's potency: as ordinary boundaries are diminished, thought grows more powerful. The movement of the river— 'not at a flood or swiftly'—mirrors the individual consciousness finding its own pace, whereby images and impressions no longer paralyse the perceiver, but generate further movement of the imagination and therefore provide the opportunity of self-realisation. This luxurious privacy is seen to be a necessity to sanity; it is the safety valve of the creative self, which is so often set upon by shifts, contradictions, falsehoods and injustice.

It is the assurance that consciousness remains inviolable, so it occurs not simply when one is alone, but when one is released from others' views.

(T. E. Apter, "Self-Defence and Self-Knowledge: the Function of Vanity and Friendship in Virginia Woolf," in *Virginia Woolf, A Centenary Perspective,* ed. Eric Warner [New York: St. Martin's Press, 1984], 86–87.)

    5. Gillian Beer, "Virginia Woolf and Pre-History," in *Virginia Woolf, A Centenary Perspective,* ed. Eric Warner (New York: St. Martin's Press, 1984), 106. Beer further points out that Woolf both read and was influenced by Freud in the 1930s. I would agree that in her later works her model for the mind seems influenced by Freudian metaphors. However, in the early 1920s, Romantic metaphors dominated, perhaps because she feared that Freudian explanations of character turned an imaginative work into a case study. In a review of *An Imperfect Mother* by J. D. Beresford (25 March 1920), she says as much.

> There remains the question whether we are not pandering to some obsolete superstition when we thus decree that certain revelations are of medical significance, others of human; that some are only fit for the columns of the *Lancet,* others for the pages of fiction. If it is true that our conduct in crucial moments is immensely influenced, if not decided, by some forgotten incident in childhood, then surely it is cowardice on the part of the novelist to persist in ascribing our behaviour to untrue causes. We must protest that we do not wish to debar Mr Beresford from making use of any key that seems to him to fit the human mind. Our complaint is rather that in *An Imperfect Mother* the new key is a patent key that opens every door. It simplifies rather than complicates, detracts rather than enriches. The door swings open briskly enough, but the apartment to which we are admitted is a bare little room with no outlook whatever. Partly, no doubt, this is to be attributed to the difficulty of adapting ourselves to any new interpretation of human character; but partly, we think, to the fact that, in the ardours of discovery, Mr Beresford has unduly stinted his people of flesh and blood. In becoming cases they have ceased to be individuals.

(Reprinted in *Contemporary Writers,* [London: The Hogarth Press, 1965], 153–54.)

    6. William Shakespeare, *Shakespeare: The Complete Works,* ed. G. B. Harrison (New York: Harcourt, Brace & World, 1952), 535, V, i, ll. 4–8. All other references to Shakespeare's plays will be to this edition and cited as Shakespeare.

    7. A significant difference between Mary's moment with the papers and Lily's with the salt cellar in "The Window" is that the former metonymically expresses the political project while the latter abstractly symbolizes, at a number of removes, Lily's decision not to marry: salt cellar = tree = painting = alternative to marriage. The difference points, as well, to the development of Woolf's craft.

    8. See Nathaniel Brown, "The 'Double Soul': Virginia Woolf, Shelley, and Androgyny," for a detailed account of Woolf's regard for Shelley's "sexless" mind (ROO, 107)—"Asexual or unisexual, the poet had transcended within himself all sense of gender distinction" (195–96)—as a model for the creative artist's. In *Night and Day,* Shelley hovers on unfurled wings above Woolf's visions of "sexless" or unisexual imagination in Katharine, Ralph, and Mary.

    9. Janet Lumpkin, "Woolf's 'Mark on the Wall' as a Voice in Transition," *Conference of College Teachers of English* 54 (September 1989): 28–33.

    10. Samuel Taylor Coleridge, *Biographia Literaria,* ed. J. Shawcross, vol. I (London: Oxford University Press, 1962), 107. Coleridge writes:

> *"Esemplastic. The word is not in Johnson, nor have I met with it elsewhere."*

> Neither have I. I constructed it myself from the Greek words, to shape into one; because having to convey a new sense, I thought that a new term would both aid the recollection of my meaning, and prevent its being confounded with the usual import of the word, imagination.

11. Woolf, herself, mentions for this date that Emma Vaughan had actually sent "Masses of book binding equipment" (Diary I, 56) for use by The Hogarth Press. This present arrived after "The Mark on the Wall" had been written and printed, but the recollection of their project is still a possible source for the mention of the canisters.

12. Edward L. Bishop, "Pursuing 'It' Through 'Kew Gardens,'" *Studies in Short Fiction* 19, no. 3 (Summer 1982): 272.

13. The significance of the illocutionary "appeared" followed by an anthropomorphic description will be discussed more fully in chapter 5 when I note such locutions in the "Time Passes" section of *To the Lighthouse*.

14. Susan Dick, in a note to the text, gives the following passage, which is uncanceled in the typescript and may have been inadvertently omitted from the printed text. It precedes the stylized conversation of the two women.

> They made a mosaic round them in the hot still air of these people and these commodities each woman firmly pressing her own contribution into the pattern, never taking her eyes off it, never glancing at the differently coloured fragments so urgently wedged into its place by her friend. But in this competition, the small woman either from majority of relatives or superior fluency of speech conquered, and the ponderous one fell silent perforce.
> She continued: — Nell, Bert, Lot, Cess, Phil, Pa. He says, I says, She says, I says I says I says — (CSF, 291)

This paragraph further confirms Woolf's sense of the solidity of words and their reality as being of equal strength with the objects in one's field of vision.

15. In a diary entry of July 1926, Woolf speculated:

> *Rodmell. 1926*
> As I am not going to milk my brains for a week, I shall here write the first pages of the greatest book in the world. This is what the book would be that was made entirely solely & with integrity of one's thoughts. Catch them hot and sudden as they rise in the mind— walking up Asheham hill for instance. Of course one cannot; for the process of language is slow & deluding. One must stop to find a word; then, there is the form of the sentence, soliciting one to fill it. (Diary III, 102)

This entry suggests the connection to a preverbal reality that Woolf attempted to represent through her written art.

16. Furthermore, the ironic or mock heroic tone of the questions suggests, at once, both the fusion with, and separation of, the narrative voice from the minds of the young man and woman. This tone, implying the seriousness with which the young people take themselves, a seriousness perhaps not shared by the rest of the world, indicates their romantic intensity and the narrator's appreciation of, yet distance from, it.

17. She wrote to Vanessa: "I'm getting doubtful whether I shall have the time to write the story called Monday or Tuesday—if not I don't know what to call the book" (Letters II, 445).

18. "Humble" would not, of course, have the same meaning for Woolf and Wordsworth. For her it would suggest the "cotton wool" thoughts of the day as they pass through the minds of educated, upper middle-class people.

CHAPTER 4. "SELF-CONSCIOUSNESS" AND "CONVICTION"

1. See Barbara Herrnstein Smith, *Contingencies of Value: Alternative Perspectives for Critical Theory* (Cambridge: Harvard University Press, 1988), par-

ticularly chapter 3, "Contingencies of Value," for a more self-conscious analysis than Woolf's of the relationship between aesthetic value and the hegemony of a particular social class.

2. This essay was first published in *TLS*, 24 April 1919 (CR, 250).

3. See chapter 7 for an analysis of Leonard Woolf's discussion of self-consciousness as a psychological, aesthetic, and political phenomenon in *After the Deluge: A Study of Communal Psychology*.

4. Thomas McLaughlin, "Virginia Woolf's Criticism: Interpretation as Theory and as Discourse," *Southern Humanities Review* 17, no. 3 (Summer 1983): 241–53. Citing the first of these sentences from *A Room of One's Own* as central to Woolf's aesthetic theory, McLaughlin argues that, for Woolf, "The mind is the passive object of both Nature and the artist. Meaning and shape exist in Nature and are imposed on the human mind, then brought into consciousness by the artist" (242). Yet it is difficult, if not impossible, to believe that meaning and shape exist in nature for Woolf after one has read the "Time Passes" section of *To the Lighthouse* in which she suggests that any meaning found is imposed by the volitional consciousness of human beings through their language, the narrator's included. Secondly, "Nature" with a capital "N" is here Woolf's shorthand for whatever forces compel both consciousness and external nature—"The mystery of life," as she called it in "The Mark on the Wall," "life," in "The Sentimental Journey" in *The Second Common Reader* or, simply, "it," in "Kew Gardens." Thus for Woolf, the split McLaughlin proposes between the artist and his/her mind is physically and philosophically meaningless. And further, if McLaughlin reads the artist as the agent responsible for making the invisible writing visible, is he not ascribing a purely active capacity to the artist's mind? To do so makes for a philosophical difficulty that Wordsworth's definition of the poet—different in degree but not in kind from other human beings—avoids.

5. Virginia Woolf, *Orlando* (New York: Harcourt Brace Jovanovich, Inc., 1956), 322–23. Hereafter cited parenthetically as O.

6. See George Johnson, "Evolution Between the Ears," review of *Bright Air, Brilliant Fire* by Gerald Edelman, *New York Times* "Book Review" (19 April 1992): 2; and Oliver Sacks, "Making Up the Mind," review of *Bright Air, Brilliant Fire* by Gerald Edelman, *The New York Review of Books* (8 April 1993): 42–49. For criticism of Edelman's theories, see John Horgan, "Can Science Explain Consciousness?" *Scientific American* 271, no. 1 (July 1994): 88–94 (review article). The *New Yorker* profile on Edelman (Steven Levy "Annals of Science: Dr. Edelman's Brain" [2 May 1994]: 62–73) illuminates the literary establishment's interest in his research and suggests the compelling nature of his metaphors for mind.

7. Mrs. Paston's desire for a new dress may well have been Virginia Stephen's inspiration for Dame Elizabeth Partridge's desire for new stockings in ". . . Joan Martyn," especially because Rosamond Merridew speaks of "draw[ing] . . . inspiration from the *Paston Letters*" (CSF, 35). Rosamond Merridew was excited by the ability to move up from Dame Elizabeth's legs to the reality of mediaeval brains and so to the king upon his throne. Woolf moves here from Mrs. Paston's dress to her sense of self and so to the nature of the mediaeval world.

8. The Greeks are the precursors of Woolf's novelistic method—leaving out more and more a description of reality from their stories.

9. Richard Payne Knight, *An Analytic Inquiry into The Principles of Taste* (1808), 401. Quoted in Vincent Arthur De Luca, 53.

10. Edmund Burke, *Philosophical Enquiry into . . . the Sublime and Beautiful*

(1958), 61, 63, quoted in Vincent Arthur De Luca, 35. Blake and his contemporaries' disagreement with Burke regarding the issue of whether the sublime is to be reached through the indeterminate and unbounded experience (Burke) or "Minute Discrimination," particularity, and distinctness (Blake) can be resolved if we instruct Burke, from beyond the grave, on the difference between an object seen distinctly and the multiple (theoretically, infinite) or unbounded ideas it may produce in one's mind. A correlate would be the existence of a finite word or signifier that yet may be multivalent in meaning. De Luca says: "The particularity, determinacy, and singularity of language are to be found in its signifers [*sic*], not in the indefinite plurality and ambiguity of its signifieds. The signifier is finite and, at the same time 'polyvalent,' or endowed with a surplus of signifying potential in relation to any given signified" (39). Another way to express this apparent contradiction is to say that Burke's "properly expressed" may well signal his agreement that forms or words may be distinct in character and yet may produce multiple simultaneous responses in the observer, such that no clear idea can be formed. Ambiguities in Blake's own theories of the sublime suggest that he was influenced by Burke despite his criticisms of the latter's positions.

11. McLaughlin, " Virginia Woolf's Criticism," 241.

12. René Wellek, "Virginia Woolf as Critic," *The Southern Review* 13, no. 3 (July 1977): 427.

13. Barbara Currier Bell and Carol Ohmann, "Virginia Woolf's Criticism: A Polemical Preface," *Critical Inquiry* (December 1974): 365.

14. The essay on Montaigne first appeared in *TLS* on 31 January 1924 (CR, 247), shortly before Woolf began writing *To the Lighthouse*. The assertions about the novel will be discussed in chapter 5.

15. Leonard Woolf said so, as well, seven years later in *After the Deluge*.

16. Vincent Arthur De Luca, "Blake's Concept of the Sublime," 18. See my introduction.

17. For a full discussion of the substitution of the poetic for the natural sublime, see De Luca's "Blake's Concept of the Sublime."

18. Jane Austen, as Woolf has described her in this essay, is a forerunner not just of women writers but, as she says, the moderns, Henry James and Proust. For F. R. Leavis, a critic much disliked by Woolf, Austen is also the beginning of the great tradition of the English novel.

19. See, for example, Nelson Hilton's "Blakean Zen," in *Romanticism: A Critical Reader*, ed. Duncan Wu (Oxford: Blackwell, 1995), 1–16; and Vincent Arthur De Luca's "Blake's Concept of the Sublime." Wu glosses Hilton's argument: "In effect, the poem [*Urizen*] is a catalyst for change within the reader—not so much a stable, defined artifact as 'a process that labors to bring forth processing'" (x). Hilton asserts that the unreadability or indeterminacy of the poem is, precisely, what Blake wants us to "understand" about poetry. Of De Luca's position Wu says: "Blake's understanding of the reading experience" is that "After a moment of indeterminacy when the reader's confrontation with the text precipitates a state of disengagement, the corporeal understanding is alternately frustrated while the intellect is released to find satisfaction in the 'wall of words'" (x) of the poem.

20. Conrad died 3 August 1924. Woolf's article appeared 14 August (CR, 260).

21. Mark Goldman, *The Reader's Art: Virginia Woolf as Literary Critic* (The Hague: Mouton, 1976), 3.

CHAPTER 5. "DEATH AND THE MAIDEN"

1. Paul de Man, "Time and History in Wordsworth," in *Romanticism and Contemporary Criticism*, 82.

2. Paul de Man, "Rousseau and the Transcendence of Self," in *Romanticism and Contemporary Criticism*, 34.

3. Ibid., 49.

4. de Man, "Time and History in Wordsworth," 93.

5. Ibid., 82.

6. Woolf more explicitly dramatizes this truth about distant views in *To the Lighthouse*. She compares Mrs. Ramsay's glancing away from the truth of mortality and Lily Briscoe's courageous facing of our common end. Mrs. Ramsay recollects her talk with the Swiss servant girl as she measures the brown stocking against James's leg:

> She would go into the maids' bedrooms at night and find them sealed like ovens, except for Marie's, the Swiss girl, who would rather go without a bath than without fresh air, but then at home, she had said, "the mountains are so beautiful." She had said that last night looking out of the window with tears in her eyes. "The mountains are so beautiful." Her father was dying there, Mrs. Ramsay knew. He was leaving them fatherless. . . . She had stood there silent for there was nothing to be said. He had cancer of the throat. At the recollection—how she had stood there, how the girl had said, "At home the mountains are so beautiful," and there was no hope, no hope whatever, she had a spasm of irritation, and speaking sharply, said to James:
> "Stand still. Don't be so tiresome," so that he knew instantly that her severity was real. . . . (TTL, 45)

Mrs. Ramsay's "spasm" is an instance of the visceral acknowledgment of death and her helplessness before it. But her command to James: "'Stand still,'" a third repetition of these words to her son (TTL, 42, 43), takes on more cosmic meaning as it enters into her dialogue with death. Her words are an expression of her devout wish that she might hold time still: "Oh, but she never wanted James to grow a day older! or Cam either. These two she would have liked to keep for ever just as they were, demons of wickedness, angels of delight, never to see them grow up into long-legged monsters" (TTL, 89). With no unintended irony Woolf fulfills Mrs. Ramsay's wish, never to see them grow up into long-legged monsters—not by the impossible holding still of time—but through Mrs. Ramsay's own death which deprives her of the seeing eye of consciousness.

Lily, more than Mrs. Ramsay, reveals willingness to confront this difficulty. Woolf addresses the question of Lily's struggle to create directly by dramatizing Lily's unflinching gaze—"'But this is what I see'"—and indirectly as she walks to the edge of the lawn with William Bankes.

> They both smiled, standing there. They both felt a common hilarity, excited by the moving waves; and then by the swift cutting race of a sailing boat, which, having sliced a curve in the bay, stopped; shivered; let its sails drop down; and then, with a natural instinct to complete the picture, after this swift movement, both of them looked at the dunes far away, and instead of merriment felt come over them some sadness—because the thing was completed partly, and partly because distant views seem to outlast by a million years (Lily thought) the gazer and to be communicating already with a sky which beholds an earth entirely at rest. (TTL, 34)

Lily registers a characteristic Romantic joy in movement and sadness in satiety and completion. Paradoxically, the artist "with a natural instinct to complete the picture," suffers when activity ceases. To be "entirely at rest" prefigures death. Like Wordsworth when he discovered he had already crossed the Alps, Lily experiences an emotional deflation. The psychological operation of the "distant views," which make both the Swiss girl and Mrs. Ramsay sad, are understood by Lily—"(Lily thought)." Woolf makes the same point in *Between the Acts* through Mrs. Swithin's observation: "'That's what makes a view so sad,' said Mrs. Swithin, lowering herself into the deck chair which Giles had brought her. 'And so beautiful. It'll be there,' she nodded at the strip of gauze laid upon the distant fields, 'when we're not'" (53). Both Lily and Mrs. Swithin are hearing the song of the female vagrant, singing of real time and the end of human consciousness in *Mrs. Dalloway.*

7. An exception would be Carolyn Heilbrun who, in *Toward a Recognition of Androgyny,* remarks: "To be sure, the effect of biographical criticism has encouraged readers to see the portrait of Mr. Ramsay as venial, that of Mrs. Ramsay as adoring, although Leonard Woolf and Quentin Bell, Virginia Woolf's biographer, thought Mr. Leaska's study more central to the author's vision than any other which had yet been made." From "Woolf and Androgyny," *Toward a Recognition of Androgyny* (New York: Alfred A. Knopf, 1973), 151–67. Reprinted in *Critical Essays on Virginia Woolf,* ed. Morris Beja (Boston: G. K. Hall, 1985), 75.

8. Recent readings of *To the Lighthouse,* as well as focusing on these figures, are impressive for their extraordinary heterogeneity. It is, perhaps, most true to say that Woolf, in her rich and Cleopatran variety, invites "a high degree of projection from the reader," which "dynamic is responsible for the unusual diversity of critical response to [her]" as Joan Lidoff maintains. (Lidoff, "Virginia Woolf's Feminine Sentence: The Mother-Daughter World of *To the Lighthouse,*" *Literature and Psychology* 32, no. 3 [Fall 1986]: 57.) For a summary of critical perspectives, see my article: "In Her Father's House: *To the Lighthouse* as a Record of Virginia Woolf's Literary Patrimony," *Texas Studies in Literature and Language* 34, no. 1 (Spring 1992): 34–35.

9. See Hermione Lee, *The Novels of Virginia Woolf* (New York: Holmes and Meiers, 1977), 136–37.

10. The following readings are all ultimately based on Nancy Chodorow, *The Reproduction of Mothering: Psychoanalysis and the Sociology of Gender* (Berkeley: University of California Press, 1978) or Jacques Lacan, *Écrits: A Selection,* trans. Alan Sheridan (New York: Norton, 1977); *Feminine Sexuality: Jacques Lacan and the école freudienne,* ed. Juliet Mitchell and Jacqueline Rose, trans. Jacqueline Rose (London: Macmillan, 1982).

Joan Lidoff, "Virginia Woolf's Feminine Sentence: The Mother-Daughter World of *To the Lighthouse*" *Literature and Psychology* 32, no. 3 (Fall 1986): 43–59. This reading all but annihilates the presence of Mr. Ramsay who is barely mentioned by Lidoff in her essay. Furthermore, by concentrating on Lily's efforts to fuse with the absent mother, Lidoff fails to take account of the rich treatment of Mrs. Ramsay, not as an object, but as a subject, both self-searching and self-critical, from whose perspective much of "The Window" is realized.

Ellen Rosenman, "The 'Invisible Presence': Virginia Woolf and the Creative Process," *American Imago* 43, no. 2 (Summer 1986): 133–50.

Margaret Homans, *Bearing the Word: Language and Female Experience in Nineteenth-Century Women's Writing* (Chicago: University of Chicago Press, 1986), 1–2, 277–88. Homans's premise is: "Western metaphysics, in Woolf's perceptive and mocking portrayal, requires that the mother remain perpetually out of reach in order for Mr. Ramsay and his kind to speculate forever on how to reach her, or to replace her with their own abstractions" (2). Homans finds the absent mother in the kitchen table offered to Lily by Andrew Ramsay as an explanation of his father's philosophical project. But it is Lily who imagines it as "one of those scrubbed board tables, grained and knotted, whose virtue seems to have been laid bare by years of muscular integrity" (38). The "mother," inferred by Homans from the "muscular integrity" as a final and female cause, is, thus, Lily's own creation, itself an extension of her figurative elaboration and not the invention of either man. This sleight-of-hand operation, to my mind, calls Homans's premise, at least as applied to her reading of this novel, into question.

11. Elizabeth Abel, "'Cam the Wicked': Virginia Woolf's Portrait of the Artist as Her Father's Daughter" in *Virginia Woolf and Bloomsbury: A Centenary Celebration,* ed. Jane Marcus (Bloomington: Indiana University Press, 1987), 170–94.

12. Woolf is using the word "mothers" metaphorically in this passage from *A Room of One's Own* in which she talks of a tradition of female writers. To think of Mrs. Ramsay, so unequivocally *not* a paradigm of the woman-artist, as functioning for Lily in this way, is, in fact, a very literal and reductive reading of Woolf's metaphor.

13. Notably Mitchell Leaska's *Virginia Woolf's 'Lighthouse': A Study in Critical Method* (New York: Columbia University Press, 1970).

14. Quoted by Woolf in her diary entry of 8 November 1930 (Diary III, 330). She continued: "but how crude & jaunty my own theories were beside his: indeed I got a tremendous sense of the intricacy of the art; also of its meanings, its seriousness, its importance, which wholly engrosses this large active minded immensely vitalised man" (330).

15. Woolf has been accused of subjectivism, of failing to acknowledge the world beyond the mind. However, Frank D. McConnell in "'Death Among the Apple Trees': 'The Waves' and the World of Things" argues compellingly that *The Waves* "becomes a radical criticism of 'mysticism' and of the subjective eye itself in the face of sheer phenomenalism" (65). Similarly, Alan Wilde in "Touching Earth: Virginia Woolf and the Prose of the World" (*Philosophical Approaches to Literature: New Essays on Nineteenth- and Twentieth-Century Texts,* ed. William E. Cain [Lewisburg: Bucknell University Press, 1984], 140–64) claims that Woolf moved from subjectivity in the story "A Summing Up" at the end of *A Haunted House* to objectivism in *Between the Acts.* The novels between these two texts, he maintains, are a record of Woolf's growing "recognition of the phenomenal, whatever its gaps and fissures, as the locus and source of experience" (160). Although Wilde cites *The Years* as the first of Woolf's novels clearly to represent the world of things, I see *To the Lighthouse,* in which Woolf, through Lily, explores the necessity of assimilating the point of view of Mr. Ramsay (associated with objectivism and empiricism) into her aesthetic vision, as the beginning of this shift. Even the fantasy *Orlando* conveys the strength of the phenomenal world in transforming the personality and desires of the individual.

16. Reuben Brower in "Something Central Which Permeated: 'Mrs. Dalloway,'" first published in *Fields of Light: An Experiment in Critical Reading* (New York: Oxford University Press, 1951) and reprinted in *Modern Critical Views: Virginia Woolf,* ed. Harold Bloom (New York: Chelsea House Publishers, 1986), 7–18, was the first to elucidate her technique.

17. For a full discussion of the relationship of narrative voice to the mind of the characters, see James Naremore's *The World Without a Self: Virginia Woolf and the Novel* (New Haven: Yale University Press, 1973).

18. This, the actual quotation from Yeats's preface to *The Oxford Book of Modern Poetry* published in 1936, reflects Yeats's position in the Romantic tradition which preserves the binary oppositions self/world, subject/object, and ideal/phenomenal.

19. Nautical metaphors form a subset of heroic images, particularly used by both Mr. and Mrs. Ramsay. Strangely, we learn of their possible origin in Woolf's life by extrapolating from Mrs. Dalloway's thoughts when she thinks: "As we are a doomed race, chained to a sinking ship (her favourite reading as a girl was Huxley and Tyndall, and they were fond of these nautical metaphors)" (MD, 117).

20. My colleague Roni Natov has helpfully pointed out the existence of a number of Norwegian folktales in which Boots, the youngest son, figures as the unpromising hero who becomes the successful quester. In "The Princess on the Glass Hill," the first mention of the hero is "the youngest was nicknamed Boots, of course" (*One Hundred Favorite Folktales,* ed. Stith Thompson [Bloomington: Indiana University Press, 1968], 206). A strikingly, although, no doubt, coincidentally, appropriate story for comparison with *To the Lighthouse* is "Boots and the Troll" in which Boots, after sailing to an island to accomplish his mission for the king, his symbolic father, is praised by the latter in exactly the words Mr. Ramsay gives to James after his successful sail—"Well done!" (63).

21. Although there is critical debate concerning the nature of Woolf's androgynous vision of the mature intellect, I find Toril Moi's account most persuasive. She argues in *Sexual/Textual Politics: Feminist Theory* (London: Routledge, 1989) that Woolf attempted to deconstruct the male-female opposition and so arrive at an inclusive androgynous self in *To the Lighthouse.* On this basis she claims that Woolf was a feminist—as defined by Julia Kristeva—of the type who rejects the masculine-feminine dichotomy "as metaphysical" (12). Mark Hennely in "Romantic Symbol and Psyche in *To the Lighthouse*" seems to support Moi's position, seeing gender crossings in sexual symbols (like "the vaginal protection of foot-coverings and the phallic vulnerability of exposed limbs" [159]) as Woolf's expression of the possibility of the androgynous nature of the minds of men and women.

22. Michael C. J. Putnam, *Virgil's Pastoral Art: Studies in the 'Eclogues'* (Princeton, N.J.: Princeton University Press, 1970). Of the corpus of Virgil's poetry, Putnam says:

> The *Georgics* discuss the obstructions nature puts in the path of man, forcing upon him the necessity of trial and hardship to make life viable. . . . Human emotion again destroys the ideal. It kills love and the poet, and ruins the possibility of poetry. . . . The *Aeneid* is the culmination of the sequence. . . . It, too, starts, as the *Eclogues* at first seem to do, as poetry of uninvolvement. . . . Allegiance to fate's progress precludes immediate submission to suffering or emotion, but gradually Aeneas is forced to confront the humanity which is at first easier to ignore. The supposedly simple heroism of establishing an allegorical model for the greatness of a future empire becomes a much more real struggle entailing carnage and violence which the hero must take part in as well as cause. Finally the power struggle centers on a defeated opponent who should be spared but is not, and emotion once more triumphs over reason. (17)

The analogy with Wordsworth's moral aesthetic and Lily's growth should be noted. Maria DiBattista has also observed the connection between Carmichael and Virgil, calling Carmichael, "the stern classicist who invokes a Virgilian vision of history and nature in the novel" (*Virginia Woolf's Major Novels: The Fables of Anon* [New Haven: Yale University Press, 1980], 76), but she does not go beyond this assertion. For the record, Woolf knew Virgil well. In "A Sketch" she mentions in passing: "my father jumped at a false quantity when we read Virgil with him" (MoB, 86).

23. J. Hillis Miller, "Mr. Carmichael and Lily Briscoe: The Rhythm of Creativity in *To the Lighthouse,*" in *Modernism Reconsidered,* ed. Robert Kiely and John Hildebidle (Cambridge: Harvard University Press, 1983), 167–89.

24. Ibid., 183.

25. Ibid., 188.

26. John Ferguson, in "A Sea Change: Thomas De Quincey and Mr. Carmichael in *To the Lighthouse*," identifies Carmichael with the Romantic man of letters, Thomas De Quincey, on the basis of some similarities between the Carmichael of the holograph manuscript (purged from the final version) and details of De Quincey's life. He points out as well that Woolf was also simultaneously working on a critical evaluation of De Quincey for *TLS,* some lines of which were found in the middle of the holograph. However, I suggest that Woolf recognized the value for her work of presenting Carmichael as *the* poet (a symbolic, rather than a particularized individual—hence, the purged details) whose classical imagination functions as the analogue of her own objectivist view of history and nature based on her assimilation of her father's philosophical position. Cam's remembrance of going to her father, sitting in his study with Mr. Carmichael or Mr. Bankes, with a question about Napoleon or Christ or a mammoth dug up in a London street (TTL, 281), points to the poet and her father's common perspective on history and nature, which hypothesis is confirmed by the conclusion of the novel.

27. Gayatri C. Spivak, in "Unmaking and Making in *To the Lighthouse*," in *Women and Language in Literature and Society,* ed. Sally McConnell-Ginet, Ruth Borker, and Nelly Furman (New York: Praeger, 1983), 310–27, maintains that in "Time Passes" "the search for a language seems strangely unattached to a character or characters" (311). By comparison, J. Hillis Miller, in "Mr Carmichael and Lily Briscoe . . ." although agreeing that Woolf presents this section of the novel "without any human consciousness as stay against entropy other than the intermittent and ineffectual presence of . . . Mrs. McNab" (180), refines on this position, arguing, as we have seen, that the trope of prosopopoeia in the representation of the elements introduces the human into this section. However, neither of these readings sees "Time Passes" as importantly peopled by the beach walkers who, in collusion with the narrator, deploy the prosopopoeias in their always timely questions which symbolically anticipate Lily's own and serve as the locus of Woolf's about the nature of the imagination and the function of art.

28. "Yet at that season earth too and the plains of sea, and unclean dogs and ominous birds gave presage. How often did we see Etna flooding the Cyclopean fields with the torrent bursting from her furnaces, and rolling forth balls of flame and molten rocks! Germany heard the clash of armour fill the sky; the Alps quaked with unwonted shocks. Moreover a voice was heard of many among silent groves, crying aloud, and phantoms pallid in wonderful wise were seen when night was dim. . . . Neither at that time did boding filaments ever cease to show themselves in disastrous victims, or blood to ooze from wells. . . ." This passage from the first book of *The Georgics* (in *Virgil's Works,* trans. J. W. Mackail [New York: Random House, 1950], 307 [ll. 466–80]) reads, in translation, like a continuation of Woolf's prose, both in sound and sense. Carmichael surely does not read Virgil because, as Peter Knox-Shaw asserts ("*To the Lighthouse:* The Novel as Elegy," *English Studies in Africa* 29 [1986]: 31–57), these "candlelight readings of Virgil delimit a Dark Ages" (41) but because his poetry provides a model for the middle section of the novel. It is of further interest that Woolf used J. W. Mackail's translation of Simonides in "On Not Knowing Greek" in *The Common Reader: First Series* (CR, 245). She also refers to his translations in the same essay.

29. The force of the optative mood and its unsaying is present in Wordsworth's "Tintern Abbey" in which the poet recognizes the possibility that "the power of

harmony" is "a vain belief" and in which, more compellingly, his praise of the River Wye ends with "many recognitions dim and faint" and "a sad perplexity":

> . . . I may have owed another gift
> Of aspect more sublime; that blessed mood,
> In which the burthen of the mystery,
> In which the heavy and the weary weight
> Of all this unintelligible world,
> Is lightened . . .
> While with an eye made quiet by the power
> Of harmony, and the deep power of joy,
> We see into the life of things.
> If this
> Be but a vain belief, yet, oh! how oft—
> . . . have I turned to thee,
> Oh sylvan Wye! . . .
>
> And now, with gleams of half-extinguished thought,
> With many recognitions dim and faint
> And somewhat of a sad perplexity,
> The picture of the mind revives again . . .
>
> (Wordsworth, 108–9)

30. In "The Lighthouse," Woolf, through a locution that is Wordsworthian both in form and content, seems again to deny that "the mirror was broken." For the narrator says: "And as happens sometimes when the weather is very fine, the cliffs looked as if they were conscious of the ships, and the ships looked as if they were conscious of the cliffs, as if they signalled to each other a message of their own" (TTL, 271). However, Woolf draws attention to the phrase through three repetitions, thus importantly qualifying the comparisons it introduces by intimating that the optative human impressions have no basis in reality. The question of the Great War as a destroyer of human faith in the correspondence between man and the natural world is again raised by Woolf in *A Room of One's Own* in 1928. There she writes: "Shall we lay the blame on the war? When the guns fired in August 1914, did the faces of men and women show so plain in each other's eyes that romance was killed? But why say 'blame'? Why, if it was an illusion, not praise the catastrophe, whatever it was, that destroyed illusion and put truth in its place? For truth . . . those dots mark the spot where, in search of truth, I missed the turning up to Fernham. Yes indeed, which was truth and which was illusion, I asked myself" (ROO, 15). Here, then, the Romantic resonance is not so surely rejected.

31. "'Like' and 'like' and 'like'—but what is the thing that lies beneath the semblance of the thing?" (TW, 288) asks Rhoda in *The Waves,* similarly frustrated by the same difficulties of language.

32. de Man, "Time and History in Wordsworth," 93.

33. Peter Knox-Shaw, "'To the Lighthouse': The Novel as Elegy," 43.

34. Although Lily fears scrutiny of her art by another, her dread is multiplied when the other is male. However, she feels safe with the asexual Mr. Bankes, who describes himself in a simile suggesting the dissonance between his attitudes and the masculine heroic tradition. Unable to respond to Mrs. Ramsay, he thinks: "He felt rigid and barren, like a pair of boots that have been soaked and gone dry so you can hardly force your feet into them" (TTL, 135).

35. The mock heroic tone of the narrative voice, although a criticism of Leslie

Stephen/Mr. Ramsay's self-conscious and self-pitying pose, does not represent Woolf's assessment of the real worth of his intellect and angle of vision.

36. Jane Marcus asserts that we should not put faith in the narrator's claim that Mr. Ramsay "forgot himself completely." She argues that his "reflections about morality and French novels and English novels" (TTL, 180) prove his egotistical need to believe in the endurance of his own books. However, I think she makes an unwarranted leap from Ramsay's "reflections"—surely one of the pleasures reading affords—to the unfounded intuition that they concern himself and the standing of his own work, not only because of the textual counterclaim but also because of Lily's later response to him. ("Still Practice, A/Wrested Alphabet: Toward a Feminist Aesthetic," in *Art and Anger: Reading Like a Woman* [Columbus, Ohio: Ohio State University Press, 1988], 243.)

37. The autobiographical connection between Woolf and Cam is apparent from this thought of Cam's that adumbrates Woolf's words at the beginning of "A Sketch of the Past," an evocation of one of her first memories of St. Ives: "It is of lying and hearing this splash and seeing this light, and feeling, it is almost impossible that I should be here; of feeling the purest ecstasy I can conceive" (MoB, 65).

38. Putnam, *Virgil's Pastoral Art,* 17.

39. This is John Stuart Mill's view of his marriage as described by Phyllis Rose in *Parallel Lives: Five Victorian Marriages* (New York: Vintage Books, 1984), 99–140.

40. Abel, "'Cam the Wicked,'" 188.

41. Elizabeth Abel argues in "'Cam the Wicked'": "Through Cam as well as Lily, then, Woolf adumbrates the claim from which much of her current preeminence in feminist literary history derives: 'we think back through our mothers if we are women.'" A reconciliation of this statement with Woolf's counterclaim that it is necessary to slay the Angel in the House, is, I think, achieved if we agree that she gained by thinking back through both her parents, once their presence was no longer a threat or impediment. Woolf's diary entry for 28 November 1928, which would have been Leslie Stephen's ninety-sixth birthday, supports my assertion: "Father's birthday. . . . I used to think of him & mother daily; but writing The Lighthouse, laid them in my mind. And now he comes back sometimes, but differently. (I believe this to be true—that I was obsessed by them both, unhealthily; & writing of them was a necessary act.) He comes back more as a contemporary. I must read him some day. . . ." (Diary III, 208).

42. Abel, "'Cam the Wicked,'" 171.

43. William Butler Yeats, *The Collected Poems of W. B. Yeats* (New York: The Macmillan Company, 1965), 292.

44. Ibid., 293.

CHAPTER 6. *THE WAVES*

1. Woolf attempted to communicate the various essences of Jacob through the various voices of both characters and narrator in *Jacob's Room* (1922). Through the narrative voice, she explores the Paterian conviction of human isolation—that we are all ringed round by a wall of personality beyond which we cannot pass and through which nothing can penetrate.

And everywhere we go wires and tubes surround us to carry the voices that try to penetrate before the last card is dealt and the days are over. "Try to penetrate," for as we lift the cup, shake the hand, express the hope, something whispers, Is this all? Can I never know, share, be certain? (JR, 93)

Thus, from a philosophical standpoint, her project to reveal Jacob's character is defeated before it begins. Yet our sense that Jacob moves on a stage behind a curtain of scrim is less a matter of philosophical solipsism than of Woolf's technical inability to balance the narrating consciousnesses with the coextensive "life" perceived by them. The reader, used to the conventions of the nineteenth-century novel, that serve to differentiate thought processes from world, is at sea, overwhelmed by the fluidity and superabundance of what seems pure consciousness. Moreover, the narrative voice does not change sufficiently as it merges first with the consciousness of one character and then another to allow the reader to follow its shifts. However, her difficulties in this novel constitute her last failure. But even this assertion must be qualified because towards the close of the book, Woolf begins to use the technique of smoothly shifting our gaze from one narrating consciousness to another, as she would in *Mrs. Dalloway* with the motor car and aeroplane, by using, say, the striking of Big Ben, heard in different parts of London by different characters, or a runaway horse observed first by Clara Durrant and then by Julia Eliot, or a sunset observed by Jacob in London and then by his mother in Scarborough, to change perspectives.

2. This diary entry represents the second time Woolf recorded this passage from *The Prelude*. She had written the same eight lines into her reading notebook in 1924. See note 34.

3. One may speculate that without the stated premises of these writers, the creation of the social science of psychology might have been set back many years.

4. Jean-Jacques Rousseau, *The Confessions* I (London: Dent, 1971), 1.

5. See Tzvetan Todorov, "Reading as Construction," in *The Reader in the Text,* ed. Susan R. Suleiman and Inge Crosman (Princeton, N.J.: Princeton University Press, 1980), 67–82.

6. As well as the pronoun "we," I have used "I" in this chapter, in defiance of the convention of anonymity I was taught to follow, because I want to reinforce in a formal way my point that reading is both a personal and collective project.

7. Virginia Woolf, *The Years* (New York: Harcourt, Brace & World, Inc., 1965), 369.

8. John Keats's description in "Ode to Psyche," *John Keats: Selected Poems and Letters,* ed. Douglas Bush (Boston: Houghton Mifflin Co., 1959), 205.

9. Pamela L. Caughie, *Virginia Woolf & Postmodernism: Literature in Quest and Question of Itself* (Urbana: University of Illinois Press, 1991), 50.

10. From the first American edition of *Mrs. Dalloway,* quoted by John Ferguson in "A Sea Change: Thomas De Quincey and Mr. Carmichael in *To the Lighthouse,*" *Journal of Modern Literature* 14, no. 1 (Summer 1987): 45–63.

11. McGavran, "'Alone Seeking the Visible World': The Wordsworths, Virginia Woolf, and *The Waves,*" 265–66.

12. Ibid., 266.

13. *The Waves* is not, however, the first novel in which Woolf relied on this premise. As Avrom Fleishman has noted of *Mrs. Dalloway:* "Not only are the characters' imaginations stocked with collective images, drawn from a larger community of mind, but the narrative employs these images to further characterize them." (*Virginia Woolf: A Critical Reading,* 84). Fleishman particularly mentions "Another collective phenomenon that figures strongly in *Mrs. Dalloway* is the

image of Shakespeare" (86). However, just as these images are, in the main, the "property" of the unseen narrator of that novel, rather than a consciously owned, self-actualizing language as of, say, Lily Briscoe in *To the Lighthouse,* so there is a more primitive use of collectivity in *Mrs. Dalloway* than there is in *The Waves.* The characters of the earlier novel do not aid in the explication of the premise of the collective imagination as they do in *The Waves* because they are not self-conscious about consciousness and its roots in a collective tradition.

14. See Hermione Lee, *The Novels of Virginia Woolf* (New York: Holmes and Meiers, 1977), 164; Pamela J. Transue, *Virginia Woolf and the Politics of Style* (Albany: State University of New York Press, 1986), 135; Fleishman, *Virginia Woolf: A Critical Reading,* 170; S. P. Rosenbaum, "The Philosophical Realism of Virginia Woolf," in *English Literature and British Philosophy,* ed. S. P. Rosenbaum (Chicago: University of Chicago Press, 1971), 350.

15. Lee, *The Novels of Virginia Woolf,* 164.

16. Freud, *Group Psychology and the Analysis of the Ego,* trans. and ed. James Strachey (New York: Liveright Publishing Corp., 1967). Freud remarks in a footnote:

> The study of such identifications, like those, for instance, which lie at the root of clan feeling, led Robertson Smith (*Kinship and Marriage,* 1885) to the surprising discovery that they rest upon the acknowledgment of the possession of a common substance [by the members of the clan], and may even therefore be created by a meal eaten in common. This feature makes it possible to connect this kind of identification with the early history of the human family which I constructed in *Totem and Taboo.* (42)

17. Woolf's inclusion of this myth and our reading of it do not point to a belief in the story beyond its being an underpinning of cultural assumptions of the majority in the western tradition.

18. Willard Van Orman Quine, *Word and Object* (Cambridge: M.I.T. Press, 1960). The epigraph to the book is a quotation from James Grier Miller.

19. Susan's perception that she sings her song or lullaby "by the fire like an old shell murmuring on the beach" is comparable to the more conscious maternal musings of Mrs. Ramsay: "so that the monotonous fall of the waves on the beach, which . . . seemed consolingly to repeat over and over again as she sat with the children the words of some old cradle song, murmured by nature, 'I am guarding you—I am your support,' but at other times . . . had no such kindly meaning, but like a ghostly roll of drums remorselessly beat the measure of life" (TTL, 27–28).

20. Beverly Ann Schlack in *Continuing Presences: Virginia Woolf's Use of Literary Allusion* notes allusions I have missed and omits others I cite.

21. McGavran, as another example of idiosyncratic cultural insertion, reads himself into the text of *The Waves* through the topos of the ocean and shore in British and American poetry.

22. Keats, "Ode to a Nightingale," *Selected Poems and Letters,* 206.

23. Ibid., "Ode on a Grecian Urn," 208.

24. Percy Bysshe Shelley, "Epipsychidion," *The Selected Poetry and Prose of Percy Bysshe Shelley,* ed. Carlos Baker (New York: The Modern Library, 1951), 288.

25. I have not included in the body of this chapter all the allusions I have found to the work of other writers or to other works of Woolf. I append those I have omitted here, conscious that this must be only a partial list, dependent on my personal reading history.

a. Neville's description of hearing about the dead man and being unable to pass the apple tree (TW, 191, 280, 281) and "the apple tree . . . connected with the horror of Mr Valpy's suicide" ("A Sketch of the Past," MoB, 71).

b. Susan's "I am not afraid of heat, nor of the frozen winter" (TW, 192) and *Mrs. Dalloway:* "Fear no more the heat o' the sun / Nor the furious winter's rages" (MD, 13) the source of which is Shakespeare, *Cymbeline,* IV, ii, ll. 258–59 in Shakespeare, 1414.

c. Rhoda's hatred of looking glasses (TW, 204) and "A Sketch . . ." (MoB, 67–69).

d. Bernard's "I shall pass from the service for the man who was drowned" (TW, 229) and "the drowned Phoenician sailor" (l. 47), "Mr. Eugenides, the Smyrna merchant" (l. 209), and "Phlebas the Phoenician, a fortnight dead" (l. 312) from T. S. Eliot's "The Waste Land" in *The Norton Anthology of Literature* II, ed. M. H. Abrams (New York: W. W. Norton and Co., Inc., 1968), 1781–97.

e. Neville's "my book, laid like a block of marble" (TW, 234) and "Now to recollect by the fireside on the white square of marble. From ivory depths words rising shed their blackness, blossom and penetrate. Fallen the book. . . ." ("Monday or Tuesday," CSF, 131).

f. Susan's "Mine is the heron that stretches its vast wings lazily. . . ." (TW, 242) and "Lazy and indifferent, shaking space easily from its wings, knowing his way, the heron passes over the church beneath the sky" ("Monday or Tuesday," CSF, 131).

g. Susan's "now swerving to avoid a puddle" (TW, 243) and Rhoda's "There is the puddle . . . and I cannot cross it" (TW, 285) and "There was the moment of the puddle in the path. . . . I could not step across the puddle" ("A Sketch . . . ," MoB, 78).

h. Bernard's "Fin in a waste of waters" (TW, 307ff.) and "[A] world which one could slice with one's thought as a fish slices the water with his fin" ("The Mark on the Wall," CSF, 81). It is noteworthy that the appearance of this image in the short story precedes, as well, that in the diary entry by ten years and does not at all suggest a negative experience.

i. Bernard's description of Susan: "She was born to be the adored of poets, since poets require safety; someone who sits sewing, who says, 'I hate, I love'" (TW, 348) and Rhoda's "I fear, I hate, I love, I envy and despise you" (TW, 330) and Woolf's description of Charlotte Brontë: "all her force, and it is the more tremendous for being constricted, goes into the assertion, 'I love', 'I hate', 'I suffer'" ("'Jane Eyre' and 'Wuthering Heights,'" CR, 157) and Isa's observation in *Between the Acts:* "The plot was there only to beget emotion. There were only two emotions: love; and hate" (90) and Catullus's "*odi et amo.*"

j. Bernard's "And I am so made, that, while I hear one or two distinct melodies, such as Louis sings, or Neville, I am also drawn irresistibly to the sound of the chorus chanting its old, chanting its almost wordless, almost senseless song that comes across courts at night; which we hear now booming around us as cars and omnibuses take people to theatres" (TW, 347) and "The audience was the singer; 'Terly, terlow' they sang; and 'By, by lullay' filling in the pauses, helping out with the chorus. Every body shared in the emotion of Anons song, and supplied the story. . . . Anon is sometimes man; sometimes woman. He is the . . . common voice singing out of doors, He has no house. He lives a roaming life crossing the fields" (A & R, 382).

k. Bernard's "The willow as she saw it grew on the verge of a grey desert where no bird sang" (TW, 351) and John Keats's "La Belle Dame sans Merci": "The sedge is wither'd from the lake / And no birds sing" (201).

l. Bernard's "But can anything be as clear as all that, I would say, following his gaze, through the branches, to a punt on the river, and a young man eating bananas from a paper bag?" (TW, 351) and "'Jacob's off,' thought Durrant, looking up from his novel. . . . each time he looked up he took a few cherries out of the bag and ate them abstractedly. Other boats passed them" (JR, 37).

26. John Milton, "Lycidas," *Milton's 'Lycidas': The Tradition and the Poem,* ed. C. A. Patrides (New York: Holt, Rinehart and Winston, 1961), 2, l. 8.

27. James H. Hanford, "The Pastoral Elegy and Milton's 'Lycidas,'" in *Milton's 'Lycidas': The Tradition and the Poem,* ed. C. A. Patrides, 27ff.

28. Milton, "Lycidas," 2, ll. 23–27.

29. Ibid., 6, ll. 119–24.

30. *The Oxford English Dictionary* vol. S, 262.

31. Neville's words seem to have struck Marguerite Yourcenar, who translated *The Waves* into French (*Les Vagues,* 1937). Woolf reports in her diary for Tuesday, 23 February 1937, that she and "the translator . . . went through *The Waves.* What does 'See here he comes?' mean & so on" (Diary V, 61).

32. Shakespeare, 1223, I, i, l. 10.

33. Ibid., 1223, I, i, ll. 12–13.

34. Ibid., 1224, I, i, ll. 33–40.

35. Although Leonard Woolf had half jokingly suggested to his wife that he would not be able to read her crabbed diary hand, were he to survive her (Thursday 3 February [1927]: "L. taking up a volume [of her diary] the other day said Lord save him if I died first & he had to read through these. My handwriting deteriorates" [Diary III, 125]), Woolf could not really have anticipated that readers would one day have access to her diary or that she would write, twelve years later, "A Sketch of the Past." Nevertheless, we cannot now exclude, from the patterning and contextualizing activities that we go through in reading her novels, the revelations of these autobiographical texts, even when they were written after the novels.

36. John Keats, "Then glut thy sorrow on a morning rose," "Ode on Melancholy," (209).

37. Brenda R. Silver, *Virginia Woolf's Reading Notebooks* (Princeton, N.J.: Princeton University Press, 1983), 228.

38. Ibid., 224–25.

39. Woolf's very clear equation of the fin with an idea suggests that Quentin Bell misreads her original diary entry. He says: "In September she had moments of deep depression in which she described herself in her diary as an 'elderly dowdy fussy ugly incompetent woman; vain, chattering and futile' and then she had her vision of a fin rising on a wide blank sea, and she woke in the early mornings with feelings of complete and utter despair." (Quentin Bell, *Virginia Woolf: A Biography* [New York: Harcourt Brace Jovanovich, 1972], II, 123.) Bell makes no distinction between the despair and the invigoration she likens to the fin.

40. John Keats, "Ode to a Nightingale," (207).

VII.
Thou wast not born for death, immortal Bird!
No hungry generations tread thee down;
The voice I hear this passing night was heard
In ancient days by emperor and clown;
Perhaps the self-same song that found a path
Through the sad heart of Ruth, when, sick for home,
She stood in tears amid the alien corn;

41. T. S. Eliot, "The Love Song of J. Alfred Prufrock," *The Norton Anthology of English Literature* II, ed. M. H. Abrams et al (New York: W. W. Norton & Co., 1968), 1774.

> And indeed there will be time
> To wonder, "Do I dare?" and "Do I dare?"
> Time to turn back and descend the stair . . .

42. Freud, in *Moses and Monotheism,* trans. Katherine Jones (New York: Vintage Books, 1967), continues the discussion of the significance of communal eating, arguing that the consumption of the totemic animal by the clan is a reenactment of the slaughter of the father of the primitive horde.

> Instead of the father a certain animal was declared the totem; it stood for their ancestor and protecting spirit, and no one was allowed to hurt or kill it. Once a year, however, the whole clan assembled for a feast at which the otherwise revered totem was torn to pieces and eaten. No one was permitted to abstain from this feast; it was the solemn repetition of the father-murder, in which social order, moral laws, and religion had had their beginnings. The correspondence of the totem feast (according to Robertson Smith's description) with the Christian Communion has struck many authors before me. (168–69)

43. I am indebted to Leila Luedeking, curator of the Modern Literary Collections at Washington State University, Pullman, who was able to set the date of ownership and reading of G. M. Trevelyan's *History of England* (1926), which Virginia Woolf used for the beginning of "Anon." She pointed out that Woolf refers to it and quotes it on p. 72 of *A Room of One's Own* (1928). I suggest that Bernard's invitation to the others to sit under the canopy of currant leaves and listen to his invented stories bears a resemblance, the source being Trevelyan's description, to Woolf's notion that the desire of the primeval English hunters to make their own song originated in listening to the birds singing under the forest canopy. Her description in *The Waves* might well have been taken from Trevelyan because she had read his book before she began her novel.

44. The intratextual patterns, more than suggesting some sort of communication between the characters which goes otherwise unreported in the novel, reveal, in a nonmystical way, and, despite their differences, the common life experiences and similar insertion into western culture of the friends. As other readers have, I must make special mention of the repetition by the characters of some of the language of the undifferentiated voice of the prologues, particularly by Bernard who, in the last chapter, seems to pull together phrases and images from a number of the previous prologues. He says:

> "Day rises; the girl lifts the watery fire-hearted jewels to her brow; the sun levels his beam straight at the sleeping house; the waves deepen their bars; they fling themselves on shore; back blows the spray; sweeping their waters they surround the boat and the sea-holly. The birds sing in chorus; deep tunnels run between the stalks of the flowers; the house is whitened; the sleeper stretches; gradually all is astir. Light floods the room and drives shadow beyond shadow to where they hang in folds inscrutable." (TW, 379)

This description repeats ideas and phrases from the prologues: "The grey cloth [of the sea] became barred with thick strokes moving, one after another" (TW, 179); "Blue waves, green waves swept a quick fan over the beach, circling the spike of sea-holly" (TW, 194); "The girl who had shaken her head and made all the jewels, the topaz, the aquamarine, the water-coloured jewels with sparks of fire in them dance" (TW, 225); "In the garden the birds . . . now sang together in chorus" (TW, 225); "Or perhaps they saw the splendour of the flowers making a light of flowing purple over the beds, through which dark tunnels of purple shade were driven between the stalks" (TW, 226); "And as the light increased, flocks of shadow were driven before it and conglomerated and hung in many-pleated folds in the background" (TW, 251); "The sun struck straight upon the house, making the white walls glare between the dark windows" (TW, 279); "The waves broke and spread their waters swiftly over the shore. One after another they massed themselves and fell; the spray tossed itself back with the energy of their fall" (TW, 279–80).

However, we do not have to wait for Bernard's "summing up" to see the relationship of the prologue voice to those of the characters. The first prologue includes the description: "The sun sharpened the walls of the house, and rested like the tip of a fan upon a white blind and made a blue fingerprint of shadow under the leaf by the bedroom window" (TW, 179–80). On the next page, among the early observations of the children, we read: "'Look at the house,' said Jinny, 'with all its windows white with blinds'" (TW, 181) and "'The walls are cracked with gold cracks,' said Bernard, 'and there are blue, finger-shaped shadows of leaves beneath the windows'" (TW, 181). But "influence" or repetition works both ways. Louis, for example, on the same page, describes the pounding of the waves, thus: "'The beast stamps; the elephant with its foot chained; the great brute on the beach stamps,' said Louis" (TW, 181). One hundred pages later, the voice of the prologue offers: "The waves fell; withdrew and fell again, like the thud of a great beast stamping" (TW, 280). That readers have wanted to make assertions about the prologue voice, unidentified and set in italic typeface, seeing it as more inclusive, general, and, somehow, above the voices of the characters, says as much about our assessment of narrative convention, that is, our expectations based on our past experience with western literature, and even typeface, as it does about the content of these introductory passages. The instances in which the prologue repeats words, phrases, or ideas that are first said by a character suggest, to the contrary, that Woolf conceived of the voice of the introductory sections as representing only one other voice in the polyphony of voices, different in kind but not in degree. The unidentified voice is, as much as any of the others, defined by the culture and history of western tradition.

CHAPTER 7. LIFE AS TEXT

1. Woolf thus suggests that the enraptured reader duplicates the writer's state of drowse. Further, her assertion in "On Not Knowing Greek" may be based on Joseph Conrad's *Lord Jim,* which she also cites in *The Common Reader* to explicate the Conradian "moment of vision." Marlow says of the Frenchman, the subject of his moment of being: "'Indeed his torpid demeanor concealed nothing: it had that mysterious, almost miraculous power of producing striking effects by means impossible of detection which is the last word of the highest art'" (*Lord Jim,* 91). The artist's mysterious power of producing striking effects by means impossible of detection is equivalent to his craft through which our consciousness is stimulated to the highest extent.

2. Freud, *Group Psychology and the Analysis of the Ego,* 10–11. Freud's book, originally published in 1922, following the arguments of Le Bon (*Psychologie des foules* [Paris, 1895]) and Trotter, develops a psychological explanation

of group behavior that clearly anticipates, by a number of years, the development of Nazism and fascism in Germany and Italy, respectively.

3. Although Woolf temporizes with the disclaimer "speaking roughly" (CE 2, 164), it is hard to understand how she could have omitted Wordsworth from the group of poets who had "felt the influence of the nineteenth-century wars profoundly" (CE 2, 164) unless she was being a strict constructionist, consigning the French Revolution and its aftermath entirely to the eighteenth century. However, in support of her position, one would have to agree that by the time Wordsworth had published *Lyrical Ballads* (1798) and written *The Prelude* (1805), the tumultuous emotions generated by the revolution were recollected by him in tranquility.

4. Leonard Woolf's *After the Deluge: A Study of Communal Psychology* (vol. I, 1931) supports the view, as does Freud's *Group Psychology* (which Woolf reported reading in December 1939 [Diary V, 252]), that the contemporary communal psychological impulse was authoritarian and antirational in origin and effect. By "communal psychology" Woolf, in his Preface to Volume I, says: "I mean the psychology of man as a social animal." He then gives an example:

> History seems to show that mass misery, if it exceeds a certain duration in time or intensity of suffering, has an effect on men's minds. The thought of men, when under the impulse of mass misery, issues in social and political action. The years 1922 to 1924 furnish a good example of this law of communal psychology. (22–23)

By "group psychology" Freud means something far less nebulous than the intricate web of associations and influences that form the basis of communal psychology. He differentiates the two when he says in chapter XI:

> Each individual is a component part of numerous groups, he is bound by ties of identification in many directions, and he has built up his ego ideal upon the most various models. Each individual therefore has a share in various group minds—those of his race, of his class, of his creed, of his nationality, etc.—and he can also raise himself above them to the extent of having a scrap of independence and originality. Such stable and lasting group formations, with their uniform and constant effects, are less striking to an observer than the rapidly formed and transient groups from which Le Bon has made his brilliant psychological character sketch of the group mind. And it is just in these noisy ephemeral groups, which are as it were superimposed upon the others, that we are met by the prodigy of the complete, even though only temporary, disappearance of exactly what we have recognized as individual acquirements. (61)

5. An apparent exception to this assertion would be Shakespeare's history plays, which, one could certainly say, were meant to inspire nationalist and imperialist sentiments in the public. However, Woolf would probably have argued that the impulse to create them was not self-conscious but issued from the perfect synchrony between Shakespeare and the political environment in which he wrote. Woolf, on the subject of collective feeling, writes in her diary for Sunday, 1 October 1939: "But peace—my private peace—restored. London tomorrow. Sunday clearing up. Oh how torturing life in common is! like trying to drink a cup of tea & always its dashed from one" (Diary V, 239). And on Friday, 26 July 1940, she recorded her response to planes passing overhead the day before: "When the 12 planes went over, out to sea, to fight, last evening, I had I think an individual, not communal BBC dictated feeling. I almost instinctively wished them luck" (Diary V, 306). Woolf, by way of comically understating the case, certainly raised herself above the group with her "scrap of independence and originality." But

more to the point, we can analyze her position in Freud's terms by saying that her antipathy toward the communal mind is the function of her very powerful "ego ideal" or superego. Freud argues that in these ephemeral groups "the individual gives up his ego ideal and substitutes for it the group ideal as embodied in the leader" and adds:

> In many individuals the separation between the ego and ego ideal is not very far advanced; the two still coincide readily; the ego has often preserved its earlier narcissistic self-complacency. The selection of the leader is very much facilitated by this circumstance. He need . . . only give an impression of greater force and of more freedom of libido [than do members of the group.] (61)

Woolf's extreme self-consciousness, self-control, and independence of mind were antithetical to the identification with the leader that Freud asserts is essential to absorption into the group mind.

6. Her diary account of reading Wordsworth's "Ruth" suggests both her admiration for, and pleasure in, the sort of concentrated, uninterrupted creative mood she imagines fostered this poem.

> All books now seem to me surrounded by a circle of invisible censors. Hence their self-consciousness, their restlessness. It wd. be worthwhile trying to discover what they are at the moment. Did Wordsworth have them? I doubt it. I read Ruth before breakfast. Its stillness, its unconsciousness, its lack of distraction, its concentration & the resulting "beauty" struck me. As if the mind must be allowed to settle undisturbed over the object in order to secrete the pearl. (Diary V, 229)

7. Similarly, Nathaniel Brown, in "The 'Double Soul': Virginia Woolf, Shelley, and Androgyny," says: "What Woolf was defending in herself was plainly that same 'visionary' imagination she ascribed to Shelley or Keats or Coleridge, which in the male was evidence of the androgynous mind, wherein the engine of the brain is shut off and the mind glides serene but unconscious, or rather is lifted to a different plane of consciousness" (193).

8. The hedge metaphor, analogous to the rocks, shoals, and crannies of the female writer's mind, is nevertheless used by Woolf to suggest positive results for the male writers in question.

9. Her thoughts on "invisible censors" in the diary entry of 7 August 1939, cited above, make clear the difference for her between the manacling self-consciousness of modern writers and, on the other hand, the uncomplicated directness and concentration on the individual by the Romantic poets.

10. But Isa's "book" is, finally, the newspaper. Indeed, Woolf was beginning to feel that a writer whose audience had given up books for the newspaper could "write no more."

11. Bell, *Virginia Woolf: A Biography,* vol. II, 221. Bell's source is Letters VI, no. 3634, to Benedict Nicolson (24 August 1940):

> But aren't you taking what you call 'Bloomsbury' much too seriously? I don't think that those people whom I suppose you to mean had the very great gifts that are needed to alter society. What puzzles me is that the people who had infinitely greater gifts than any of us had—I mean Keats, Shelley, Wordsworth, Coleridge and so on—were unable to influence society. They didn't have anything like the influence they should have had

upon 19th century politics. And so we drifted into imperialism and all the other horrors that led to 1914. Would they have had more influence if they had taken an active part in politics? Or would they only have written worse poetry? (421)

12. McGavran, "'Alone Seeking the Visible World,'" 266.

Bibliography

Abel, Elizabeth. "'Cam the Wicked': Virginia Woolf's Portrait of the Artist as Her Father's Daughter." In *Virginia Woolf and Bloomsbury: A Centenary Celebration.* Edited by Jane Marcus. Bloomington: Indiana University Press, 1987.

Abrams, M. H. *Doing Things with Texts: Essays in Criticism and Critical Theory.* New York: W. W. Norton and Co., Inc., 1991.

———. *The Mirror and the Lamp: Romantic Theory and the Critical Tradition.* New York: W. W. Norton and Co., Inc., 1958.

———. *Natural Supernaturalism: Tradition and Revolution in Romantic Literature.* New York: W. W. Norton and Co., Inc., 1971.

Ames, Christopher. "Modernism and Tradition: The Legacies of Belatedness." In *Studies in the Literary Imagination: Defining Modernism.* Edited by Randy Malamud. 25, no. 2 (Fall 1992): 39–61.

Annan, Noël. *Leslie Stephen: His Thought and Character in Relation to His Time.* Cambridge, Mass.: Harvard University Press, 1952.

Apter, T. E. "Self-Defence and Self-Knowledge: the Function of Vanity and Friendship in Virginia Woolf." In *Virginia Woolf: A Centenary Perspective.* Edited by Eric Warner. New York: St. Martin's Press, 1984.

Auerbach, Erich. "The Brown Stocking." In *Modern Critical Views: Virginia Woolf.* Edited by Harold Bloom. New York: Chelsea House Publishers, 1986. Originally published in *Mimesis: The Representation of Reality in Western Literature.* Translated by Willard R. Trask. Garden City, N.Y.: Doubleday, 1957.

Barzilai, Shuli. "Virginia Woolf's Pursuit of Truth: 'Monday or Tuesday,' 'Moments of Being' and 'The Lady in the Looking-Glass.'" *The Journal of Narrative Technique* 18, no. 3 (Fall 1988): 199–210.

Bazin, Nancy Topping. *Virginia Woolf and the Androgynous Vision.* Binghamton, N.Y.: Rutgers University Press, 1973.

Beer, Gillian. "Virginia Woolf and Pre-History." In *Virginia Woolf: A Centenary Perspective.* Edited by Eric Warner. New York: St. Martin's Press, 1984.

Beja, Morris, ed. *Critical Essays on Virginia Woolf.* Boston: G. K. Hall & Co., 1985.

Bell, Barbara Currier and Carol Ohmann. "Virginia Woolf's Criticism: A Polemical Preface." *Critical Inquiry* 1 (December 1974): 361–71.

Bell, Quentin. *Virginia Woolf: A Biography.* New York: Harcourt Brace Jovanovich, 1972.

———. "Who's Afraid for Virginia Woolf?" *New York Review of Books* 37, no. 4 (15 March 1990): 3–6.

Bell, Vanessa. *Notes on Virginia's Childhood: A Memoir.* Edited by Richard Schaubeck, Jr. New York: Frank Hallman, 1974.

Bicknell, John W. "Leslie Stephen's 'English Thought in the Eighteenth Century': A Tract for the Times." *Victorian Studies* 6, no. 2 (December 1962): 103–20.

Bishop, Edward L. "Pursuing 'It' Through 'Kew Gardens.'" *Studies in Short Fiction* 19, no. 3 (Summer 1982): 269–75.

Bloom, Harold. *The Anxiety of Influence: A Theory of Poetry.* New York: Oxford University Press, 1973.

———. "Feminism as the Love of Reading." *Raritan* XIV, no. 2 (Fall 1994): 29–42.

———. ed. and introduction. *Modern Critical Views: Virginia Woolf.* New York: Chelsea House Publishers, 1986.

Boyd, Elizabeth French. *Bloomsbury Heritage: Their Mothers and Their Aunts.* New York: Taplinger Publishing Company, 1976.

Brower, Reuben. "Something Central Which Permeated: 'Mrs. Dalloway.'" In *Modern Critical Views: Virginia Woolf.* Edited by Harold Bloom. New York: Chelsea House Publishers, 1986. Originally published in *The Fields of Light: An Experiment in Critical Reading.* New York: Oxford University Press, 1951.

Brown, Marshall. "Romanticism and Enlightenment." In *The Cambridge Companion to British Romanticism.* Edited by Stuart Curran. Cambridge: Cambridge University Press, 1993.

Brown, Nathaniel. "The 'Double Soul': Virginia Woolf, Shelley, and Androgyny." *Keats-Shelley Journal* 33 (1984): 182–204.

Burling, William J. "Virginia Woolf's 'Lighthouse': An Allusion to Shelley's *Queen Mab?*" *English Language Notes* 22, no. 2 (December 1984): 62–65.

Caughie, Pamela L. *Virginia Woolf and Postmodernism: Literature in Quest and Question of Itself.* Urbana: University of Illinois Press, 1991.

Coleridge, Samuel Taylor. *Biographia Literaria.* 2 vols. Edited by J. Shawcross. London: Oxford University Press, 1962.

———. *Selected Poetry and Prose.* Edited by Elisabeth Schneider. New York: Rinehart & Co., 1959.

Conrad, Joseph. *Lord Jim.* New York: Bantam Books, 1981.

Culler, Jonathan D. *On Deconstruction: Theory and Criticism After Structuralism.* Ithaca: Cornell University Press, 1982.

———. "Prolegomena to a Theory of Reading." In *The Reader in the Text.* Edited by Susan R. Suleiman and Inge Crosman. Princeton, N.J.: Princeton University Press, 1980.

Curran, Stuart, ed. *The Cambridge Companion to British Romanticism.* Cambridge: Cambridge University Press, 1993.

Davenport, Tony. "The Life of *Monday or Tuesday.*" In *Virginia Woolf: New Critical Essays.* Edited by Patricia Clements and Isobel Grundy. London: Vision, 1983.

Deleuze, Gilles. *The Deleuze Reader.* Edited and translated by Constantin V. Boundas. New York: Columbia University Press, 1993.

De Luca, Vincent Arthur. "Blake's Concept of the Sublime." In *Romanticism: A Critical Reader.* Edited by Duncan Wu. Oxford: Blackwell, 1995.

de Man, Paul. *Romanticism and Contemporary Criticism: The Gauss Seminar and Other Papers.* Edited by E. S. Burt, Kevin Newmark, and Andrezj Warminski. Baltimore, Md.: Johns Hopkins University Press, 1993.

DeSalvo, Louise A. "Shakespeare's *Other* Sister." In *New Feminist Essays on Virginia Woolf.* Edited by Jane Marcus. Lincoln: University of Nebraska Press, 1981.

———. *Virginia Woolf: The Impact of Childhood Sexual Abuse on Her Life and Work.* New York: Beacon, 1989.

DiBattista, Maria. *Virginia Woolf's Major Novels: The Fables of Anon.* New Haven: Yale University Press, 1980.

Diderot. "Lettre sur les aveugles." *Premières oeuvres* Vol. 2. Edited and introduction by Norman Rudich and Jean Varloot. Paris: Editions Sociales, 1972.

Dunn, Jane. *A Very Close Conspiracy: Vanessa Bell and Virginia Woolf.* Boston: Little, Brown and Co., 1990.

Eisenberg, Nora. "Virginia Woolf's Last Word on Words: *Between the Acts* and 'Anon.'" In *New Feminist Essays on Virginia Woolf.* Edited by Jane Marcus. Lincoln: University of Nebraska Press, 1981.

Faust, Drew Gilpin. "How Master Lost His Concubine." Rev. of *Celia: A Slave,* by Melton A. McLaurin. *New York Times Book Review* 17 November 1991: 1+.

Ferguson, John. "A Sea Change: Thomas De Quincey and Mr. Carmichael in *To the Lighthouse.*" *Journal of Modern Literature* 14, no. 1 (Summer 1987): 45–63.

Fleishman, Avrom. *Virginia Woolf: A Critical Reading.* Baltimore, Md.: Johns Hopkins University Press, 1975.

Forster, E. M. *Howards End.* New York: Bantam Books, 1985.

Fox, Alice. *Virginia Woolf and the Literature of the English Renaissance.* Oxford: Clarendon Press, 1990.

———. "Virginia Woolf at Work: The Elizabethan Voyage Out." *Bulletin of Research in the Humanities* 84, no. 1 (Spring 1981): 65–84.

Freud, Sigmund. *Group Psychology and the Analysis of the Ego.* Edited and translated by James Strachey. New York: Liveright Publishing Corp., 1967.

———. *Moses and Monotheism.* Translated by Katherine Jones. New York: Vintage Books, 1967.

Frye, Northrop. "The Drunken Boat: The Revolutionary Element in Romanticism." In *Romanticism Reconsidered.* Edited by Northrop Frye. New York: Columbia University Press, 1963.

Gleckner, Robert F. and Gerald E. Enscoe. *Romanticism: Points of View.* Englewood Cliffs, N.J.: Prentice-Hall, Inc., 1970.

Goldman, Mark. *The Reader's Art: Virginia Woolf as Literary Critic.* The Hague: Mouton, 1976.

Greenwald, Elissa. "Casting Off From 'The Castaway': *To the Lighthouse* as Prose Elegy." *Genre* 19 (Spring 1986): 37–57.

Gregor, Ian. "Virginia Woolf and Her Reader." In *Virginia Woolf: A Centenary Perspective.* Edited by Eric Warner. New York: St. Martin's Press, 1984.

Guth, Deborah. "Virginia Woolf: Myth and *To the Lighthouse.*" *College Literature* 11, no. 3 (Fall 1984): 233–49.

Hanford, James H. "The Pastoral Elegy and Milton's *Lycidas.*" In *Milton's Lycidas: The Tradition and the Poem.* Edited by C. A. Patrides. New York: Holt, Rinehart and Winston, 1961.

Hartman, Geoffrey. *The Unremarkable Wordsworth.* Minneapolis: University of Minnesota Press, 1987.

————. "Virginia's Web." In *Modern Critical Views: Virginia Woolf.* Edited by Harold Bloom. New York: Chelsea House Publishers, 1986. Originally published in *Chicago Review* 14 (Spring 1961).

Hazlitt, William. "Mr. Wordsworth." In *The Spirit of the Age: or, Contemporary Portraits. The Complete Works of William Hazlitt.* Vol. 11. Edited by P. P. Howe, 86–95. London: J. M. Dent, 1932.

Heilbrun, "Woolf and Androgyny." In *Critical Essays on Virginia Woolf.* Edited by Morris Beja. Boston: G. K. Hall & Co., 1985. Originally published in *Toward an Androgynous Vision.* New York: Alfred A. Knopf, 1973.

Hennely, Mark. "Romantic Symbol and Psyche in *To the Lighthouse.*" *Journal of Evolutionary Psychology* 4, no. 3/4 (August 1983): 145–62.

Hill, Katherine C. "Virginia Woolf and Leslie Stephen: History and Literary Revolution." *PMLA* 96, no. 3 (May 1981): 351–62.

Hilton, Nelson. "Blakean Zen." In *Romanticism: A Critical Reader.* Edited by Duncan Wu. Oxford: Blackwell, 1995.

Homans, Margaret. *Bearing the Word: Language and Female Experience in Nineteenth-Century Women's Writing.* Chicago: University of Chicago Press, 1986.

Horgan, John. "Can Science Explain Consciousness?" *Scientific American* 271, no. 1 (July 1994): 88–94.

Hussey, Mark, ed. *Virginia Woolf and War: Fiction, Reality, and Myth.* Syracuse: Syracuse University Press, 1991.

Hyman, Virginia. "Reflections in the Looking-Glass: Leslie Stephen and Virginia Woolf." *Journal of Modern Literature* 10, no. 2 (June 1983): 197–216.

Johnson, George. "Evolution Between the Ears." Review of *Bright Air, Brilliant Fire* by Gerald Edelman. *New York Times* "Book Review" (19 April 1992): 2.

Joyce, James. *A Portrait of the Artist as a Young Man.* New York: The Viking Press, 1962.

Keach, William. "Romanticism and Language." In *The Cambridge Companion to British Romanticism.* Edited by Stuart Curran. Cambridge: Cambridge University Press, 1993.

Kiely, Robert. "*Jacob's Room* and *Roger Fry:* Two Studies in Still Life." In *Modernism Reconsidered.* Edited by Robert Kiely and John Hildebidle. Cambridge: Harvard University Press, 1983.

Kirkpatrick, B. J. *A Bibliography of Virginia Woolf.* London: Rupert Hart-Davis, 1957.

Knox-Shaw, Peter. "'To the Lighthouse': The Novel as Elegy." *English Studies in Africa* 29, no. 1 (1986): 31–57.

Laurence, Patricia. "The Facts and Fugue of War: From *Three Guineas* to *Between the Acts.*" In *Virginia Woolf and War: Fiction, Reality and Myth.* Edited by Mark Hussey. Syracuse: Syracuse University Press, 1991.

————. *The Reading of Silence: Virginia Woolf in the English Tradition.* Stanford, California: Stanford University Press, 1991.

Lawrence, D. H. *The Rainbow.* New York: The Viking Press, 1971.

Leaska, Mitchell. *The Novels of Virginia Woolf from Beginning to End.* New York: John Jay Press, 1977.

————. *Virginia Woolf's 'Lighthouse': A Study in Critical Method.* New York: Columbia University Press, 1970.

Lee, Hermione. "A Burning Glass: Reflection in Virginia Woolf." In *Virginia Woolf: A Centenary Perspective*. Edited by Eric Warner. New York: St. Martin's Press, 1984.

———. *The Novels of Virginia Woolf.* New York: Holmes and Meiers, 1977.

Levenback, Karen. "Virginia Woolf's 'War in the Village' and 'The War from the Street': An Illusion of Immunity." In *Virginia Woolf and War: Fiction, Reality and Myth*. Edited by Mark Hussey. Syracuse: Syracuse University Press, 1991.

Levy, Stephen. "Annals of Science: Dr. Edelman's Brain." *New Yorker* (2 May 1994): 62–73.

Lidoff, Joan. "Virginia Woolf's Feminine Sentence: The Mother-Daughter World of *To the Lighthouse*." *Literature and Psychology* 32, no. 3 (Fall 1986): 43–57.

Lilienfeld, Jane. "'The Deceptiveness of Beauty': Mother Love and Mother Hate in 'To the Lighthouse.'" *Twentieth Century Literature* 23, no. 3 (October 1977): 345–76.

Love, Jean O. *Virginia Woolf: Sources of Madness and Art.* Berkeley and Los Angeles: University of California Press, 1977.

Lovejoy, Arthur O. "On the Discrimination of Romanticisms." In *Romanticism: Points of View*. Edited by Robert F. Gleckner and Gerald E. Enscoe. Englewood Cliffs, N.J.: Prentice-Hall, Inc., 1970.

Lumpkin, Janet. "Woolf's 'Mark on the Wall' as a Voice in Transition." *Conference of College Teachers of English* 54, no. 19 (September 1989): 28–33.

Majumdar, Robin and Allen McLaurin, eds. *Virginia Woolf: The Critical Heritage.* London: Routledge & Kegan Paul, 1975.

Malamud, Randy. *The Language of Modernism.* Ann Arbor, Mich.: UMI Research Press, 1989.

———, ed. *Studies in the Literary Imagination: Defining Modernism* 25, no. 2 (Fall 1992).

Marcus, Jane. *Art and Anger: Reading Like a Woman.* Columbus: Ohio State University Press, 1988.

———. "'No More Horses': Virginia Woolf on Art and Propaganda." In *Critical Essays on Virginia Woolf*. Edited by Morris Beja. Boston: G. K. Hall & Co., 1985.

———. *Virginia Woolf and the Languages of Patriarchy.* Bloomington: Indiana University Press, 1987.

———, ed. *New Feminist Essays on Virginia Woolf.* Lincoln: University of Nebraska Press, 1981.

———, ed. *Virginia Woolf: A Feminist Slant.* Lincoln: University of Nebraska Press, 1983.

McConnell, Frank D. "'Death Among the Apple Trees': *The Waves* and the World of Things." In *Modern Critical Views: Virginia Woolf*. Edited by Harold Bloom. New York: Chelsea House Publishers, 1986. Originally published in *Bucknell Review* 16 (1968).

McGann, Jerome J. *The Romantic Ideology: A Critical Investigation.* Chicago: University Chicago Press, 1983.

McGavran, James Holt. "'Alone Seeking the Visible World': The Wordsworths, Virginia Woolf, and *The Waves*." *Modern Language Quarterly* 42, no. 3 (September 1981): 265–91.

McLaughlin, Thomas. "Virginia Woolf's Criticism: Interpretation as Theory and as Discourse." *Southern Humanities Review* 17, no. 3 (Summer 1983): 241–53.

McLaurin, Allen. "Consciousness and Group Consciousness in Virginia Woolf." In *Virginia Woolf: A Centenary Perspective.* Edited by Eric Warner. New York: St. Martin's Press, 1984.

———. *Virginia Woolf: The Echoes Enslaved.* Cambridge: Cambridge University Press, 1973.

Meisel, Perry. *The Absent Father: Virginia Woolf and Walter Pater.* New Haven: Yale University Press, 1980.

Melia, Margaret E. "Portrait of an Artist as a Mature Woman: A Study of Virginia Woolf's Androgynous Aesthetics in *To the Lighthouse.*" *Emporia State Research Studies* 37, no. 1 (Summer 1988): 5–17.

Miller, J. Hillis. "Mr. Carmichael and Lily Briscoe: The Rhythm of Creativity in *To the Lighthouse.*" In *Modernism Reconsidered.* Edited by Robert Kiely and John Hildebidle. Cambridge: Harvard University Press, 1983.

Milton, John. "Lycidas." In *Milton's Lycidas: The Tradition and The Poem.* Edited by C. A. Patrides. New York: Holt, Rinehart and Winston, 1961.

Moi, Toril. *Sexual/Textual Politics: Feminist Literary Theory.* London: Routledge, 1989.

Moore, Madeline. *The Short Season Between Two Silences: The Mystical and the Political in the Novels of Virginia Woolf.* Boston: Allen and Unwin, 1984.

Naremore, James. *The World Without a Self: Virginia Woolf and the Novel.* New Haven: Yale University Press, 1973.

Novak, Jane. *The Razor Edge of Balance: A Study of Virginia Woolf.* Coral Gables, Fl.: University of Miami Press, 1975.

Putnam, Michael C. J. *Virgil's Pastoral Art: Studies in the 'Eclogues.'* Princeton, N.J.: Princeton University Press, 1970.

Quine, Willard Van Orman. *Word and Object.* Cambridge: MIT Press, 1960.

Ragussis, Michael. *The Subterfuge of Art: Language and the Romantic Tradition.* Baltimore, Md.: Johns Hopkins University Press, 1978.

Richardson, Dorothy M. *Pilgrimage* II. *The Tunnel* and *Interim.* New York: Alfred A. Knopf, n.d.

Richter, Harvena. *Virginia Woolf and the Inward Voyage.* Princeton, N.J.: Princeton University Press, 1970.

Rose, Phyllis. *Parallel Lives: Five Victorian Marriages.* New York: Vintage Books, 1984.

Rosenbaum, S. P. "The Philosophical Realism of Virginia Woolf." In *English Literature and British Philosophy.* Edited by S. P. Rosenbaum. Chicago: University of Chicago Press, 1971.

Rosenberg, Beth Carole. *Virginia Woolf and Samuel Johnson: Common Readers.* New York. St. Martin's Press, 1995.

Rosenberg, John. *Dorothy Richardson: A Critical Biography.* New York: Alfred A. Knopf, 1973.

Rosenman, Ellen. "The 'Invisible Presence': Virginia Woolf and the Creative Process." *American Imago* 43, no. 2 (Summer 1986): 133–50.

Rousseau, Jean-Jacques. *Confessions.* 2 vols. London: Dent, 1971.

Ruotolo, Lucio P. *The Interrupted Moment: A View of Virginia Woolf's Novels.* Stanford, Calif.: Stanford University Press, 1986.

Sacks, Oliver. "Making Up the Mind." Review of *Bright Air, Brilliant Fire* by Gerald Edelman, *New York Review of Books* (8 April 1993): 42–49.

Salzman, Mark. "A Nice Guy Who Beats the Odds." *New York Times* (11 September 1994): Section 2:43.

Scarfone, Suzanne. "The Architectonics of Fate: Equilibrium and the Process of Creation in the Work of William Wordsworth and Virginia Woolf." Ph.D. diss., Wayne State University, 1985.

Schlack, Beverly Ann. *Continuing Presences: Virginia Woolf's Use of Literary Allusion.* University Park, Penn.: Pennsylvania State University Press, 1979.

Schug, Charles. *The Romantic Genesis of the Modern Novel.* Pittsburgh, Penn.: University of Pittsburgh Press, 1979.

Schulze, Robin Gail. "Design in Motion: Words, Music, and the Search for Coherence in the Works of Virginia Woolf and Arnold Schoenberg." In *Studies in the Literary Imagination: Defining Modernism.* Edited by Randy Malamud. 25, no. 2 (Fall 1992): 5–22.

Shakespeare, William. *A Midsummer Night's Dream.* In *Shakespeare: The Complete Works.* Edited by G. B. Harrison. New York: Harcourt, Brace & World, Inc., 1952.

————. *The Tragedy of Antony and Cleopatra.* In *Shakespeare: The Complete Works.* Edited by G. B. Harrison. New York: Harcourt, Brace & World, Inc., 1952.

Shelley, Percy Bysshe. *The Selected Poetry and Prose of Percy Bysshe Shelley.* Edited by Carlos Baker. New York: The Modern Library, 1951.

Silver, Brenda R. *Virginia Woolf's Reading Notebooks.* Princeton, N.J.: Princeton University Press, 1983.

Simpson, David. "Romanticism, criticism and theory." In *The Cambridge Companion to British Romanticism.* Edited by Stuart Curran. Cambridge: Cambridge University Press, 1993.

Spivak, Gayatri C. "Unmaking and Making in 'To the Lighthouse.'" In *Women and Language in Literature and Society.* Edited by Sally McConnell-Ginet, Ruth Borker, and Nelly Furman. New York: Praeger Publishers, 1983.

Smith, Barbara Herrnstein. *Contingencies of Value: Alternative Perspectives for Critical Theory.* Cambridge: Harvard University Press, 1988.

Steele, Elizabeth. *Virginia Woolf's Literary Sources and Allusions: A Guide to the Essays.* New York: Garland Publishing, Inc., 1983.

Stephen, Leslie. *Leslie Stephen: Selected Writings in British Intellectual History.* Edited by Noël Annan. Chicago: University of Chicago Press, 1979.

Suleiman, Susan R. and Inge Crosman, eds. "Introduction: Varieties of Audience-Oriented Criticism." In *The Reader in the Text: Essays on Audience and Interpretation.* Princeton, N.J.: Princeton University Press, 1980.

Thompson, Stith, ed. *One Hundred Favorite Folktales.* Bloomington: Indiana University Press, 1968.

Todorov, Tzvetan. "Reading as Construction." In *The Reader in the Text.* Edited by Susan R. Suleiman and Inge Crosman. Princeton, N.J.: Princeton University Press, 1980.

Transue, Pamela J. *Virginia Woolf and the Politics of Style.* Albany: State University of New York Press, 1986.

Tremper, Ellen. "In Her Father's House: *To the Lighthouse* as a Record of Virginia Woolf's Literary Patrimony." *Texas Studies in Literature and Language* 34, no. 1 (Spring 1992): 1–40.

Virgil. *The Georgics* in *Virgil's Works.* Translated by J. W. Mackail. New York: Random House, 1950.

Vlasopolos, Anca. "Shelley's Triumph of Death in Virginia Woolf's *Voyage Out.*" *Modern Language Quarterly* 47, no. 2 (June 1986): 130–53.

Wellek, René. "The Concept of Romanticism in Literary History." In *Concepts of Criticism.* Edited by Stephen G. Nichols, Jr. New Haven: Yale University Press, 1969.

———. "Romanticism Re-examined." In *Concepts of Criticism.* Edited by Stephen G. Nichols, Jr. New Haven: Yale University Press, 1969.

———. "Virginia Woolf as Critic." *The Southern Humanities Review* 13 no. 3 (July 1977): 419–37.

Wilde, Alan. "Touching Earth: Virginia Woolf and the Prose of the World." In *Philosophical Approaches to Literature: New Essays on Nineteenth- and Twentieth-Century Texts.* Edited by William E. Cain. Lewisburg, Penn.: Bucknell University Press, 1984.

Woolf, Leonard. *After the Deluge: A Study of Communal Psychology.* Vol. I. London: Hogarth Press, 1931.

Woolf, Virginia. "'Anon' and 'The Reader': Virginia Woolf's Last Essays." In *Twentieth Century Literature.* Edited by Brenda R. Silver 25, no. 3/4 (Fall/ Winter 1979): 356–441.

———. *Between the Acts.* New York: Harcourt Brace Jovanovich, 1969.

———. *The Captain's Death Bed and Other Essays.* Edited by Leonard Woolf. New York: Harcourt, Brace & World, 1950.

———. *Collected Essays.* 4 vols. Edited by Leonard Woolf. New York: Harcourt, Brace & World, 1967.

———. *The Common Reader.* Edited by Andrew McNeillie. San Diego, Calif.: Harcourt Brace Jovanovich, 1984.

———. *The Common Reader.* Edited by Leonard Woolf. New York: Harcourt, Brace & World, 1953.

———. *The Complete Shorter Fiction of Virginia Woolf.* Edited by Susan Dick. San Diego, Calif.: Harcourt Brace Jovanovich, 1985.

———. *Contemporary Writers.* Edited by Jean Guiget. London: The Hogarth Press, 1965.

———. *The Diary of Virginia Woolf.* 5 vols. Edited by Anne Olivier Bell and Andrew McNeillie. San Diego, Calif.: Harcourt Brace Jovanovich, 1977–84.

———. *The Essays of Virginia Woolf.* Vols. I–III. Edited by Andrew McNeillie. San Diego, Calif.: Harcourt Brace Jovanovich, 1986–88.

———. *Granite and Rainbow.* Edited by Leonard Woolf. San Diego, Calif.: Harcourt Brace Jovanovich, 1986.

———. *Jacob's Room and The Waves.* New York: Harcourt, Brace & World, 1959.

———. *The Letters of Virginia Woolf.* 6 vols. Edited by Nigel Nicolson and Joanne Trautmann. New York: Harcourt Brace Jovanovich, 1975–80.

———. *The Moment and Other Essays.* Edited by Leonard Woolf. New York: Harcourt, Brace & World, 1947.

———. *Moments of Being.* Edited by Jeanne Schulkind. San Diego, Calif.: Harcourt Brace Jovanovich, 1985.

———. *Mrs. Dalloway.* New York: Harcourt, Brace & World, 1953.

———. *Night and Day.* New York: Harcourt Brace Jovanovich, 1948.

———. *Orlando.* New York: Harcourt Brace Jovanovich, 1956.

———. *A Passionate Apprentice: The Early Journals: 1897–1909.* Edited by Mitchell Leaska, San Diego, Calif.: Harcourt Brace Jovanovich, 1990.

———. *A Room of One's Own.* San Diego: Harcourt Brace Jovanovich, 1929.

———. *The Second Common Reader.* Edited by Andrew McNeillie. San Diego, Calif.: Harcourt Brace Jovanovich, 1986.

———. *Three Guineas.* San Diego, Calif.: Harcourt Brace Jovanovich, 1966.

———. *To the Lighthouse.* New York: Harcourt, Brace & World, 1955.

———. *Virginia Woolf: Books and Portraits.* Edited and preface by Mary Lyon. New York: Harcourt Brace Jovanovich, 1977.

———. *Virginia Woolf: Women and Writing.* Edited and introduction by Michèle Barrett. San Diego, Calif.: Harcourt Brace Jovanovich, 1979.

———. *The Voyage Out.* San Diego, Calif.: Harcourt Brace Jovanovich, 1948.

———. *A Writer's Diary.* Edited by Leonard Woolf. New York: Harcourt, Brace & World, 1954.

———. *The Years.* New York: Harcourt, Brace & World, 1965.

Wordsworth, William. *Guide to the Lakes.* Edited by Ernest de Selincourt. London: Humphrey Milord, 1926.

———. *The Letters of William and Dorothy Wordsworth: The Early Years: 1787–1805.* Edited by Ernest de Selincourt. Oxford: Clarendon Press, 1967.

———. *The Prose Works of William Wordsworth.* Vols. I and II. Edited by W. B. J. Owen and Jane W. Smyser. Oxford: Clarendon Press, 1974.

———. *Selected Poems and Prefaces.* Edited by Jack Stillinger. Boston: Riverside Editions, 1965.

Yeats, William Butler. *The Collected Poems of W. B. Yeats.* New York: Macmillan, 1964.

Yvard, Pierre. "Forme et significations dans 'Kew Gardens' de Virginia Woolf." *Les Cahiers de la Nouvelle: Journal of the Short Story in English* 1 (1983): 159–63.

Index